WHIGGERY AND REFORM, 1830–41

Whiggery and Reform, 1830–41

The Politics of Government

Ian Newbould

Stanford University Press
Stanford, California
1990

DA
539
.N48
1990

69924

Stanford University Press
Stanford, California
© 1990 Ian Newbould
Originating publisher: The Macmillan Press Ltd,
  London
First published in the U.S.A. by
  Stanford University Press, 1990
Printed in Great Britain
ISBN 0-8047-1759-1
LC 89–62180
∞ This book is printed on acid-free paper

To
Carla
Adrian, Sophia and Alexandra
and to
my Mother and Father

Contents

Acknowledgements

I wish to thank Her Majesty the Queen for her gracious permission to consult the Melbourne Papers and Queen Victoria's papers in the Royal Archives at Windsor Castle. I am particularly grateful to Miss Jane Langton, then with the Royal Archives, for her assistance. I am indebted as well to the late Earl Spencer for his permission to read the papers of the second and third Earls, to Lord Lambton for access to the papers of the first Earl, to Lord Blake who provided special hospitality while I consulted the papers of the 14th Earl of Derby which were then in his possession at Queens College, to the Trustees of the Broadlands Papers, which were held in the National Register of Archives, for permission to quote from Lord Palmerston's papers, and to the archivists of the several collections which were consulted at the British Library, the National Libraries of Scotland and Ireland, the Universities of London and Leeds, at the Devon County Record Office and at the Bodleian Library, Oxford.

A number of people have been of help in my work. In particular, I would like to thank Iorwerth Prothero of the University of Manchester who taught me how to think. I would also like to pay a debt of gratitude to the Fellows of Wolfson College, Oxford, who elected me to a Visiting Fellowship and thereby provided the time for writing most of this book. Anthony Brundage and Angus Hawkins have been kind enough to read and comment on all or parts of the manuscript. The editors of *Parliamentary History* and *Parliaments, Estates and Representation* have kindly allowed me to republish pieces which first appeared in those journals. Without the expert assistance of Marilyn Gibboney, who produced several versions of typescript from unsteady, inkstained pages, this book would not have been possible.

Finally, I owe humble thanks to my family who supported me in one form or other over several years: my mother and father, and especially my wife and children who endured absence in the pursuit of Whiggery. Without their support, the writing of history would be far less pleasurable. It is for this reason that the book is dedicated to them.

IAN NEWBOULD

List of Abbreviations

Abbreviation	Source
Abbreviation	*Source*

Add.MSS	British Library:
	    Broughton Papers
	    Holland House Papers
	    Macvey Napier Papers
	    Peel Papers
	    Place Papers
	    Ripon Papers
	    Russell Papers
	    Wellesley Papers

BP	Broadland Papers, Historical Manuscripts Commission
BrP	Brougham Papers, University College London
DP	Derby Papers, Lord Blake, Queen's College, Oxford
EP	Ellice Papers, National Library of Scotland
FP	Fortescue Papers, Devon County Record Office
GP	Grey Papers, University of Durham
GrP	Graham Papers, microfilm, Bodleian Library, Oxford
LP	Lambton Papers, Lambton Estate Office, Chester-le-Street, Co. Durham
MCA	Mulgrave Castle Archives, Mulgrave Castle, Whitby
MP	Monteagle Papers, National Library of Ireland, Dublin
OP	O'Connell Papers, National Library of Ireland, Dublin
PP	Parkes Papers, University College, London

PRO	Public Record Office, Kew:
	    Russell Papers,
	    Granville Papers

RA   Royal Archives, Windsor Castle:
                           Melbourne Papers,
                           Victorian Archives
SP   Spencer Papers, Althorp Park,
                           Northamptonshire
Drummond Papers   National Library of Ireland, Dublin
Letterbook of L. G. Jones Marylebone Public Library, London
O'Connell transcripts   Mr M. R. O'Connell, Dublin, transcripts
                           of the following collections:
                             Mrs M. Bennett, Kilkenny
                             Fitzsimon Papers
                             Harrington Papers
                             E. G. More O'Ferral Papers
                             Rathcon Papers
                             Mrs Anne Smithwick

1

'Colours and Cries, Buff and Blue'[1]

Whig and Tory, I am persuaded, are the only distinctions that Englishmen will accept because like a domino at a masquerade, they mean nothing and cover everything.

T. Sotheran Estcourt, 1856[2]

It seemed to me then [1819] as it does now that the Whig party had from the Revolution of 1688 endeavoured to accommodate itself to the wants of the time, without binding itself slavishly to precisely the same course.

Lord John Russell, 1874[3]

The Whig is an elusive character. The early nineteenth-century world was often unsure just who was and was not a Whig. Palmerston, with birth, property and party affiliation, was not. Labouchere, middle class, half-foreign, but half-Baring, was. Indeed, one modern historian of the *genus* has concluded that 'a man was a Whig if Whiggery accepted him as such, and there is no more to be said.'[4] But once categorised, there was less difficulty in understanding what the Whig stood for. Not all of the opinions were flattering, but few could doubt that Whiggery and Toryism signified *something*. Whig and Tory, if we disregard their suspected Celtic etymologies,[5] had no inherent meaning, but Russell, despite his accommodating Whig party that did not follow 'precisely the same course', would nevertheless have been surprised at the suggestion that 'Whig' lacked meaning. The strength, and perhaps weakness, of the term was surely the universality accorded it by those who called themselves Whig. Althorp, heir to the Spencer estates, could have been nothing other than a Whig. Even so, when he went up to Cambridge, his mother told him to 'beware of all Whigs', and his strongest prejudices were of the old Tory school. But there he found the

1

Whigs more to his taste than the Tories, and almost imperceptibly he began to espouse Whig opinion. A trip to Italy during the peace completed his education, and when he returned, it was as a determined supporter of Mr Fox.[6] Too much should not be made of this, for there is much force in the suggestion that Whigs were born and not made. On the other hand, there was a corpus of belief to which Whigs were attached, and as Stanley and Graham demonstrated in 1834, unacceptable views required a change in party. Grey's son Howick resigned in a huff in 1839, but his Whig principles remained strong, and he did not move across to Peel. Stanley and Graham's views, on the other hand, were not in accordance with those which dominated Whig thought; as a consequence, they became Conservatives.

The Whigs of the 1830s had a clear view of what they stood for, a view conditioned by history and the legacy of Fox. It was a view that looked back to the seventeenth century and the principles of the glorious revolution, to the Whigs' opposition to George III's absolutist assault on the constitutionalism which had developed in that earlier century, and to the advocacy of peace, retrenchment and reform as the antidote to the constitutional imbalance by which George III had managed to keep 'the people's ancient friends' out of office for fifty years.[7] It was a view which stressed the aristocracy's duty to curb a monarch's abuse of executive privilege which could threaten to provoke mob rule or democracy. 'Placed as they are between the Crown and the people' wrote the Foxite T. L. Erskine in 1819, the 'unquestionable' duty of the aristocracy was to 'exert the influences of rank and property' which, when 'wisely, honestly and seasonably exerted', would provide stability and harmony in society.[8] Additionally, it was a view which urged the claims of Whigs, not Tories, as the true inheritors of this aristocratic tradition and as guardians of reform movements; just as democrats threatened the balance of the constitution from below, the Tories' love of place and disregard for the people's just demands threatened it from above. In 1810, Francis Jeffrey of the *Edinburgh Review* described the two 'violent and pernicious factions – the courtiers, who are almost for arbitrary power – and the democrats, who are almost for revolution and republicanism'. Between these two stood the 'most respectable band – the friends of liberty and of order – the Old Constitutional Whigs'.[9] It was this attitude that sustained the Whigs during their fifty years in the wilderness of opposition and formed the backbone of every electoral address, journal leader and after dinner speech. In the autumn of 1830, as the Whigs prepared finally to take office, the *Edinburgh Review* compared the Whig party which, with due regard for its principles, 'willingly and habitually sacrifice place and power to maintain them', with the Tory party which *profess* principles, but from a 'rooted and habitual' love of place, quickly *abandon* them.[10] Writing nearly half a century later, Russell could still refer to the Whig aim as that described by Grey: to promote the cause of civil and religious liberty without endangering the prerogatives of the Crown, the privileges of parliament or the rights and liberties of the people. 'According to my view', he wrote, 'the Tory party cared little for the cause of civil and religious liberty, and the Radical party were not solicitous to preserve those parts of the Constitution which did not suit their speculation and theoretical opinions'. The Whig course, difficult, even perilous, was 'to hold a middle way, to observe the precept of Daedalus and to avoid the fate of Icarus'.[11]

There was as much fiction here as there was fact. The Whig party was far from a monolith during the fifty years before it came to power. Burke, the creator of much of the myth, had joined Portland by the end of the eighteenth century, and left the more liberal Whigs to Fox. The Foxite Whigs, numbering more than a hundred members after 1807 and two hundred by 1818,[12] formed the basis for the nineteenth-century Whig party, but it could scarcely have been said to have represented a single view. The Grenvillites among them tended to break away on the questions of war with France and parliamentary reform; of the Foxite Whigs, the Fitzwilliams were opposed to reform, Carlisle, Devonshire, Spencer and Lansdowne unsympathetic. Apart from an agreement on the desirability of Catholic emancipation, unity was not a distinguishing feature of pre-1830 Whiggery.[13] Nor, should it be said, were the Tories as insensitive to the need for reform as the Whig apologists would have their readers believe. Tories were not just the party of Eldon, Sidmouth and the Six Acts, and were responsible for a liberalism not unsympathetic to many of the Whigs' ideals. But all this mattered little. The importance of the mythology lay in the Whigs' acceptance of its main precepts as fact. Althorp's Cambridge education was devoid of the exactitude of the historical tripos, and his seat among the Foxites undoubtedly left him with a perverted view of the younger Pitt and George III. That view nevertheless sustained him for the rest of his career.

Similarly, Holland's reference in 1832 to members of the old opposition who had 'uniformly maintained the principles of peace and reform'[14] was mistaken, but it represented the driving force of his political convictions while in office. Wrong though their history was, the Whigs' interpretations enabled them to reconcile continuity with change, an ability that drew praise from even the major critic of that interpretation, Herbert Butterfield: 'Whatever it may have done to our history, it had a wonderful effect on English politics'.[15] The metaphor of Whiggery was not historically sound, but it was real and it did signify.

The difficulty of the Whig interpretation was that it developed as an ideology of opposition by the 'intellectual gladiators', as Macaulay called them,[16] who had to rely on their powers of advocacy rather than a personal 'interest' to promote their careers. If, as Samuel Johnson thought, 'the first Whig was the Devil', it was because, as Boswell opined, the Devil was impatient of subordination; 'he was the first who resisted power'.[17] But by 1830, the Whigs were reigning in Heaven and faced with the realities of power. As a consequence they found themselves, as all governments must, adopting measures which did not fit a tight ideological mould. The very composition of Grey's ministry suggested that accommodation to political necessity was as essential an ingredient to Whig as to Tory government. As a creed, 'Whiggism' did not lend itself to this change very well. The attack on the corrupt use of patronage, a hallmark of Whiggery in opposition, did not sit well with office, for it was soon clear that what the Whigs had been opposed to was *Royal* and *Tory* patronage. Writing in 1907, Lord John's nephew G. W. E. Russell contrasted the Tories' barren centres of learning with the educational opportunities offered Whig neophytes at Chatsworth, Bowood, Woburn and Holland House. The circle was an aristocratic family partly he agreed, but for the man of genius, Whiggery meant a *'carrière ouverte aux talents'*.[18] Leaving aside the place made in the Tory party for the Peels, Robinsons and Huskissons, Russell's statement is a revealing commentary on the Whig myth. Clever repartee was necessary for one to succeed at Holland House, as the London apothecaries' production of a particular draught for those frightened by the company will attest, but Macaulay's 'want of pedigree', for all his talents, did not go unnoticed. If it was true, as Macaulay told his sister in 1831, that Lady Holland had never heard of the parable of the talents, that fact says as much about the Whig view of office as it does about the atheism at Holland House.[19] When Sir Francis Baring discussed the promotion of Lord Seymour to the House of Lords in order to succeed to the Dukedom of Somerset as Master of the Mint, he told Melbourne that nobody would quarrel with such a move: 'a future Duke people will bear to have put over their heads. It is a reason which offends nobody – merit nobody likes to see promoted'.[20] Grey was not as absolute in opposition to merit, but scarcely less supportive; 'not that I wish to exclude merit if I should meet with it' he told Princess Lieven in stating his preference for aristocracy in his government, 'but, given an equal merit, I admit that I should select the aristocrat, for that class is a guarantee for the surety of the state and of the throne'.[21]

Patronage was only one area where the boundaries of 'legitimate' political conduct had to be redrawn. Where the Whigs had decreed a foreign policy of peace, they found themselves, while in office, at war in China, Afghanistan, and almost so in France. The Hanoverians' war against France could be regarded as an excuse for the abolition of civil liberties at home and as evidence of the monarch's desire to reverse the English constitutional gains of the seventeenth and eighteenth centuries,[22] but Palmerston's note to Melbourne concerning the display of troops in Canada and Afghanistan which would 'convince the world that we are able and as ready to defend our interests' was not the stuff of a higher morality.[23] Moreover, where Whiggery had stood for civil and religious liberties, Whigs in office found themselves forced, among other things, to transport prisoners abroad, to employ spies in the Home Office, to suspend habeas corpus and the constitution in Canada, and to coerce the Irish Catholic to pay tithes for an alien Church. And perhaps most ignominious of all, where Whiggery had opposed the Royal patronage behind which George III had entrenched himself and the Tories for half a century, Whigs climbed back into office following the bedchamber incident in 1839 on the strength of Royal favour.

There were sound reasons for all of this, of course. The aspirant will say much, and as Professor Gash concluded about Peel's principles in office being different from those in opposition, 'A Conservative Government had after all to govern.'[24] But no one likes a braggart, and despite their inevitable and oft-justified claims of persevering in lesser evils for the greater good, the Whigs were unusually vulnerable to the accusation of false piety.

Johnson himself had foreseen the difficulty in 1773. 'It is ridiculous for a Whig to pretend to be honest' he told Boswell. 'He cannot hold it out.'[25] When Lady Clarendon, the Tory-born wife of the Whig Privy Seal, saw her father's interest defeated in the 1841 St Alban's by-election due to the most gross and obvious bribery of the Whig Lord Listowel's supporters, her 'little sort of lurking idea that Whigs were purer' was shattered; 'this election' she confessed, 'has driven me back towards Toryism.'[26] It was perhaps naive of the Earl of Verulam's daughter to discover at that date that Whigs, like Tories, relied on influence, corrupt or otherwise, in the working of the system, but through her disillusion, it can be seen how the Whigs' fall from grace was inordinately steep as a result of the claims of propaganda. It was not long before opponents criticised them for what was regarded as hypocrisy and love of place. To the Radicals, who looked with increasing scepticism at the 'finality' of reform and the government's unwillingness to tackle the obstinacy and independence of the House of Lords, the Whigs were 'an unnatural party standing between the People and the Tory aristocracy chiefly for the pecuniary value of the offices and the vanity of power'.[27] To the Tories, they were men who, once in office 'seemed really to be like the Indians – they inherited all the qualities of those enemies they killed'.[28] This view of the Whigs' lack of principle has persisted. Not all accounts have gone as far as one recent essay which suggested that the Whigs purposely spurned conscience as a political device in favour of a Machiavellian ethic,[29] but with the Whigs themselves writing the first histories of the age of reform, there was ample fodder for a historical counterblast to the Whig view that Whig principles alone were responsible for the period of stability and harmony which followed their hold in office. Drawing heavily on the arguments of the Whigs' Radical and Tory opponents, a new generation of historians has described the Whigs as aimless wanderers composed of 'squeezable materials'[30] who, having reformed parliament, were prepared to sacrifice any principle for the sake of office. Divided and tottering, the 'post-1832 species' of Whig relied for support on the Queen, the Irish and Radicals.[31] Bankrupt of principle and policy, they increasingly drew their inspiration from Radical concepts for further reform, and by doing so threatened the institutions of the Crown, Church and Aristocracy. It was Peel, whose new Conservatism allowed a peaceful fusion of the old and new orders, of the aristocratic and middle classes, who created the conditions for what has come to be known as the Victorian compromise.

This view has been put most forcefully by Norman Gash, whose work on Peel has largely shaped both his and our view of Whig politics during the 1830s. The rudimentary philosophy of action and coherent organisation which characterised the nascent Conservative party are features of party which Gash has adopted to describe the new 'Liberal party'. Just as Peel constructed a large and unified Conservative party from the incoherent and disorganised supporters of Wellington, so too did Melbourne and Russell oversee the transformation of an inchoate collection of Grey's Reform bill supporters into a unified Liberal party. The non-party system of 1833 gave way to one in which two large parties divided parliament, if not the nation, by 1841. Unlike Peel, however, Melbourne and Russell are characterised as being led by, rather than leading, their party. Their reasons for allowing themselves to be so led provide the interpretative framework on which the Whigs have been subsequently viewed. In contrast to Grey, who gave his ministries strong leadership and a fundamentally conservative character,[32] Melbourne and Russell's political instincts and hunger for office allowed them to adopt the Radical programme of their English and Irish popular supporters. Discomfited and betrayed, respectable, old fashioned Whigs were swept aside by a newer breed of leaders whose weak attachment to historical Whig principles allowed them to be goaded into attacking the Church, threatening the Lords and flirting with dangerous constitutional innovation.[33]

The purpose of this study is to develop a comprehensive view of the Whigs during the age of reform far different from that of those, like Gash, Conacher or Blake, who have studied the Whigs through the eyes of Peelite or Conservative opponents. If we strip the hyperbole from the Whigs' own interpretation of their history and their record, it is possible to find some consistency in the pattern of Whig government in the 1830s, a pattern that was determined largely by the course of events but which did not contradict Baring's description of 'a body of men . . . who in bad times keep alive the sacred flames of freedom, and when the people are roused, stand between the constitution and revolution, and go with the people, but not to extremities.'[34] Such consistency was based on a basic understanding of the need to maintain traditional aristocratic authority against the democratic mob mentality. As might be expected of a body of substantial landowners, Whig reform was meant to strengthen, if not to sanctify, rank, property and authority. It was meant to reinforce the role of the owner of property. It was in a very real sense paternalistic. It could not abide zealots, whether Radical or ultra Tory, Catholic or Protestant, whose dogmatism could threaten the maintenance of existing order. This fear of what Francis Jeffrey termed 'opposite excesses which must always expose the peace and liberties of such a country as England'[35] was a more practical policy of governance than was Whig mythology. And this policy was based on a moderating, conservative principle, it will be argued in this study, which characterized Melbourne's governments as much as it did Grey's. The need to shore up 'traditional elites' and to emphasise the role of the 'natural leaders', postulated as the principle of the 1834 poor law,[36] was just as much a characteristic of the measures and strategies of the younger post-Grey Whigs as it was of the older generation who appeared to provide direction and meaning to the coalition which introduced Reform. Melbourne, it is true, was not blessed with the strong parliamentary majorities which Grey possessed, and in order to pursue what Professor Southgate has properly termed his 'Conservative Cause',[37] he and Russell had to ensure the support of an unsympathetic and often unruly parliamentary majority, and at the same time govern with Peel's support. Interparty co-operation, moreover, had actually begun under Grey's leadership; once Reform was passed, little carried without Peel's assistance. But far from earning support by a Radical philosophy of action, they did what they could to keep at bay Radicalism, and indeed Liberalism, if by that term is meant an adhesion to the politics of ballot and corn law abolition. By governing in an alliance with Peel, and yet supported by those pursuing dangerous innovation, aristocratic Whiggery was uncomfortable with the concept of a unified Liberal party. It will be argued as well, as a consequence, that the notion of a strong two-party parliamentary system is difficult to sustain by the fact of Whig-Peel co-operation and further, by the near absence of a unifying philosophy and coherent organisation on at least the Whig side of parliament.

The King's dismissal of Melbourne's government in 1834 and the subsequent Conservative electoral gains forced the Whigs into an alliance with the Radicals who kept them in office on questions of confidence. But though the appearance of a two-party system was created for the remainder of the decade as each side tested its strength in the House of Commons, an unofficial alliance with the more philosophically congenial Peel allowed the government to legislate in a moderate manner. Indeed the 'tacit understanding'[38] with Peel preserved the government when occasional Radical withdrawals of support threatened to put an end to the Whigs' parliamentary majority. Peel let it be known during the first reformed parliament that he would not join Radicals in partisan attacks, and he maintained that policy for most of the 1830s. This implicit alliance served the interests of both the Whigs and Peel. The Conservative leader was engaged in a struggle for authority with the ultra Tories in his own party, and had little interest in turning the government out while his party, and the electorate, were not yet prepared for return to office on his terms. The Whigs too were content with an arrangement that forced the Radicals to toe the line. Like most politicians, they were happier in office than out, but they believed enough of the Whig mythology to think that their being in office was necessary for the maintenance of order at a time when social discontent in England and Ireland, not to say in Europe, threatened the established order. This view had been profoundly enhanced by the struggles needed to carry Catholic emancipation and parliamentary reform, when delays had pro-voked popular discontent so dangerous that the ameliorative benefit of each reform was nearly obliterated. Believing as they did that moderate reform, timely conceded, was the only way to maintain the economic and social ascendency of the propertied interests, they were concerned lest the fact of Tory government provoke a radical cry for extreme reforms in Church and State which no government could safely resist. In January 1835 Russell spoke privately of the requirement for peace in England and Ireland necessitating the Whigs' return to office;[39] the following year Melbourne responded to a challenge by Lyndhurst in the Lords by stating that 'as to holding office . . . I conscientiously believe that the well-being of the country requires that I should hold it and hold it I will'.[40] It was this conviction that the existence of the Whigs 'prevents the extremes from rushing into immediate and fierce collision'[41] which sustained those who found it necess-ary to justify deviation from Whig principles. 'I am sure you will agree with me' wrote a cabinet minister to Holland, the keeper of the Whig conscience, 'that the lawful use of patronage is to keep the party together as long as we can by distributing favour, not to unworthy persons, but to those worthy persons who are politically serviceable'.[42] If the promotion of civil and religious liberties was a necessary precondition of a balanced constitution and social stability, so too were Whigs in office.

The view that Whiggery was more a large faction in government than a unified party controlling half of the political world is developed in the following chapter. It is shown how, despite the appearance of large parliamentary voting blocs, there seemed to be no community of purpose among the Whigs and their 'supporters', and less coherence than what is to be found for earlier parliaments. The Whigs, it is suggested, were as much unwilling as unable to organise within and without parliament, so concerned were they, throughout this period of reform, with the Radical propensities of those who would offer organisational support. Whigs might rely on their votes in parliament, but they generally discouraged the efforts of agents like Joseph Parkes, whose notion of popular politics did not quite square with aristocratic, albeit reformed, government. It was, in fact, the dangerous process ultimately required to bring about the reformed governing system which would influence Whig notions of governance. The Whigs' attachment and commitment to Reform is discussed in the next two chapters, where it is shown the Whigs had little idea of office early in 1830, and less expectation that Reform would or should be promoted. That they eventually took up the issue had more to do with circumstance, and with Whig fears that a myopic Wellington could not guarantee the safety of rank and property, than with any long held goal of taking office to reform the system. The Whigs' aristocratic and conservative attitudes to government and Reform were evident. The Bill was brought in to restore landed influence, and though further reaching than many had wished to see, necessary if the determination to safeguard property and influence were to succeed. The property-owning middle classes would, it was hoped, be moderate, but the means of achieving the measure, the threats to order aroused by dogmatic passions of the aristocracy and people, would have a profound impact on Whigs in office. Dogma and passion, hallmarks of both left and right, could not be countenanced if Whiggery was to survive.

Factionalism among the Whigs, which featured so prominently during Grey's post-Reform government of 1833–34, was not prompted by a debate between conservative or radical principles, but by a marked difference of opinion over strategic considerations. The extent to which one faction, headed by Grey and guided by Stanley, wished to effect a close if not open arrangement with Peel in order to pursue a moderate course, is discussed in Chapter 5. Stanley and Grey, of course, would lose to the faction led by Melbourne and Russell, and described recently as 'liberal Anglican Whigs'.[43] These 'younger' Whigs who feared that an open union with Peel would provoke dangerous popular outrage, were scarcely less moderate than Grey's supporters. The Gashite argument of a radical Whiggery triumphant over Grey's conservative party is dealt with in Chapters 7, 8 and 9, where, it is argued, Melbourne's governments were as single-minded in the pursuit of moderate reform and the resistance to Radical influences as Grey's governments had been. The parliamentary majority was based on tactics and strategy that had little to do with governance, which, it is argued, relied on the mutual need of Melbourne and Peel to deny influence to their respective dogmatic and ultra supporters. The suggestion that similar principles guided Greys' and Melbourne's governments is further elaborated in the discussion of Whig legislation in Chapters 6 and 11, where, it is postulated, the legislative programme for the whole of the 1830s was Grey's. Neither new measures nor new principles were added to Grey's programme of essential and moderate reforms of Church and State designed to safeguard the traditional institutions of the nation. The suggestion, therefore, that one government was 'old fashioned', conservative Whiggery, and the other Radically inspired, is without substance or meaning. If one was conservative or Radical, so too was the other. In both cases, Peel's support was understood to be critical for success; measures which did not have his support were known to have no chance of passing, and had tactical rather than legislative significance.

Finally, the circumstances which brought to an end the Whig-Peel understanding are dealt with in Chapters 10 and 12. Two conditions were responsible for the decline of the Whigs by 1841. In the first place, Peel's failure to control his party's ultras, who in turn forced him to substitute partisan attack for 'government in opposition', rendered Melbourne's Whigs more susceptible to a slender parliamentary majority. More ominously, the increasing attraction of the Whigs' parliamentary supporters to constitutional and corn law reforms did not coincide with the Whigs' own belief in moderation or with the political sympathies of the electorate. It is shown that the Conservative victory in the 1841 election had less to do with Peel's leadership or organisation than with the re-establishment of a traditionally conservative electorate almost from the moment Reform was enacted. The Whigs' 1841 'free trade' budget and electoral strategy were not in keeping with the principles which had sustained them throughout the decade of reform; they were introduced as a result of the loss of Peel's support, and as an election gamble. But they were out of character for Whigs who, since 1830, had observed principles of moderation and conservatism. Such deviation from Whig consistency was a mistake, albeit one brought on by circumstances generated to a large extent by Peel's ultra followers who dictated the course of events from 1839. The instincts of the electorate were to support the old causes of Church, land and aristocracy, the very institutions which, in this view, were 'threatened' by the Reform Act. The 1841 defeat of the Whigs, in other words, reflected a final revenge for 1832. Neither the Whigs nor Peel, who had come to terms with the Reform Act and who had collaborated with the governments of both Grey and Melbourne, could survive against the forces of reaction which triumphed in 1841. The conservative cause of moderate reform had little chance of success in a political world which had manifestly not been threatened by the events of 1830–32. Reform, not Peel, destroyed the Whigs.

2
Party and Management

Times have changed, and words with them. My grandfather in 1755 or 1756 was nearly impeached for saying he was to *manage* the House of Commons, and We are assailed with invective and menace because we do not *command* them.

Lord Holland, September, 1836[1]

Most of the apparent continuities, like the myth of a long-standing two-party system, have been invented in retrospect by politicians and publicists seeking the justification of a pedigree.[2]

Recent historical analysis has described the 1830s as a period when party developed into an all encompassing system with two great parties dividing the political spectrum. This view had not always held sway. Sir Lewis Namier, who stressed the primacy of individuals over groups, thought that political ties to the monarchy were stronger than party affiliation in the late eighteenth and early nineteenth centuries. The concept of party he attributed to a false reading of the division lists; 'in action there could be but two: the ayes and the noes, the Government party and the Opposition – which fact has reinforced the delusion of a two-party system'.[3] Namier was not without influence. One historian of party in this period described the early nineteenth century as 'an obvious export market for deep-frozen Namier concepts'.[4] Namierites aside, much the more dominant views are expressed by those like Derek Beales, who noticed the prevalence of bloc voting in this study of the division lists in the 1830s,[5] and Gash, whose study of Peel led to the conclusion that it would be a 'mistake' not to see in this period the emergence of a modern party system, 'that is to say, a body of politicians with coherent organization and a rudimentary philosophy of action'.[6] When looked at from the standpoint of the Whig grandees, the concept of two modern and nearly monolithic parties dominating the age of

13

reform cannot be sustained. The Whig leaders certainly never thought themselves to be heads of a unified party, they distrusted and neglected organisation, and they were unable to garner as much loyalty in parliament as is often suggested. Why the notion of two large parties is not entirely helpful as a description of the Whigs forms the subject of this chapter.

It is true that, during the 1830s, the concept of party underwent a great deal of change and began to acquire a more modern meaning. When Holland, keeper of the Whig conscience, said in February 1830 that 'party seems to be no more',[7] he was using the older, Whiggish concept of a political group acting in opposition to monarchical privilege, for he had been led to think that the Tories' acquiescence in Catholic emancipation might put an end to the old Whig–Tory dichotomy. In the sense that party implied partisanship, there was, in 1830, a desire to rid the system of its pejorative connotation; 'I admit', Henry Brougham wrote to Lord Stanley, 'one is naturally sick to death of the state of parties and wishes anything rather than a party campaign like the end of the last [session]'.[8] It was also presumed that the great families and the cabals, 'party, in the usual acceptation of that term' as the *Morning Chronicle* put it,[9] would disappear if tolerable judgement and responsive government continued. It was this older concept that *Tait's Edinburgh Magazine* used as well, when it rejoiced at the results of the first reformed elections which seemed to indicate that 'party of all kinds and denominations lies on its death-bed'.[10] There is no doubt that the Radical Tait was correct in his judgement that great families and cabals could never dominate as the eighteenth-century connections had, although it might be questioned whether this development was the result simply of the Reform Act. Conversely, there is also no doubt that on the great trials of strength in the House of Commons ('confidence' motions whether in name or substance), the division lists point unmistakably to the scarcity of the 'independent' member[11] and the solid allegiance of each parliamentary party to either government or opposition.

But just as the barons of Runneymede would have been surprised to hear of the crucial role ascribed to the Magna Carta by seventeenth century constitutional experts, the Whigs of the 1830s would have found the current arguments of party development strangely unfamiliar. However much their imprecise but interchangeable use of the terms Whig, government or Liberal party suggests an understanding or even acceptance of a more modern concept of party, the notion of a unified party governed by a common philosophy was not one that they could have countenanced. Whigs accepted the support of large numbers of parliamentarians whose views differed from their own, but did all they could to prevent those views from influencing their governance. Many members supported the government in the 'confidence' motions after 1835, not because they associated themselves with the Whigs' 'rudimentary philosophy', but because they preferred it to the Tory alternative, or what was widely feared by many, an irremoveable Whig–Tory coalition. This is not quite the same thing as giving up one's independence to become a party member. In 1833, Greville described a large portion of the Commons as composed of 'moderate men who belong to no party but support government'.[12] It was to this group that James Grant referred five years later in his pamphlet *The British Senate in 1838* when describing those members like Thomas Wyse who voted and acted with the Liberal party on most great questions but always did so from 'principle' and not because they were 'mixed up' with that party.[13] Brougham, in fact, thought that the Reform Act had weakened the influence of party. In his view, the government's majority was not made up of nominees and persons with few constituents, as formerly, who were attached to the ministry as members of a party. Except for the officeholders, government could count on few 'thick and thin men'. 'As long as men are men and this Government is to be carried on in Parliament and by the confidence of 2 or 300 people all independent of us' he told Grey, 'there is no such thing as getting a blind confidence – and keeping people from exercising a will of their own. They want and ought to think for themselves'.[14] Melbourne said as much in 1841 when the new parliament met to decide the fate of his government. 'No one knows beforehand what parliament or members of parliament will do or how they will vote' he told Russell. 'They are summoned and counsel together. They come for that purpose and must be permitted to decide according to the circumstances of the time and the arguments which they hear.'[15]

The ability of the Whigs to predict, before each new house met, the voting behaviour of all but a handful of members on the Speakership or Address contradicts Brougham and Melbourne's assessment as far as the general support or opposition to the government was concerned, but it says little about the coherent organisation and rudimentary philosophy of action that have been postulated as the bench marks of the new party system. It says only that slightly more than half the House of Commons preferred Whigs in office to Tories, and slightly less than half Tories to Whigs. In the sense that this division was a change from earlier times when government was His Majesty's and had the general support of all members, opposition only coming on specific measures, it could be said that party was developing. But if such a 'non-party' system ever did exist, the existence of two parties largely dividing parliament between them was the standard pattern well before 1830,[16] and it is arguable that the number of important divisions rather than the numbers on those divisions was of more significance after that date. Moreover, on all but the trials of strength, the government was never sure of its support until the questions were debated and amended, and a speech for or against a particular measure could spell the difference between success and failure. It was generally agreed, for instance, that a brilliant speech by Lord Stanley secured the passage of the Irish coercion bill in 1833,[17] and in 1835, a weak speech by Buxton followed by a strong one from Sir George Grey caused the suspension of compensation payments to the West Indian planters to be dropped.[18] It could be argued that any mention in accounts and diaries of the effect of good speaking is the exception proving a different rule, but the widely held view that Althorp's personal qualities had been necessary to guarantee even the Reform Bill a safe parliamentary passage[19] suggests that the pull of party was not all-pervasive.

To argue, as Gash has, that from 1832 the Whigs formed part of a unified party committed to an increasingly Radical policy[20] is to neglect the separate ideologies of the disparate groups that were coming to be known collectively as the Liberal party. It is to use a device, moreover, which was commonly used in the 1830s by Tories who were determined to taint the Whigs with Radicalism. The phenomenon was noted by the *Edinburgh Review*, which in 1835 criticised the Tory Sir John Walsh's recently published *Chapters of Contemporary History*. In his pamphlet Walsh described the whole nation as one split into two great opposing parties, Conservative and Radical. Unlike the period a decade earlier when public men, he argued, Whig or Tory, were agreed on the constitutional requirements, there was but one party committed to opposing democratic trends and to upholding the constitution in its three branches. The other, devoid of all traces of the once respectable Whig party, was led by the movement.[21]. The Tories were not the only group to describe the political world as one dominated by two ideological entities. Mrs Grote, who was dismayed that her husband George was one of the few Radicals who had not tamely submitted to the Whigs' anti-Radical posture by virtually dropping all demands for further reforms, described the Radical party as one reduced to a mere twenty members.[22] The more common Radical tendency was to describe the growth of a two-party structure, as the *Westminster Review* did in 1837, in which the one party was dominated by 'moderate' Radical views: ballot, shorter parliaments, new electoral boundaries, abolition of the corn laws and a radically reformed Irish Church.[23] But the goal of the *Westminster Review* and similar Radical journals was clear. Faced with a government adamantly opposed to these measures, the more devout Radicals' last hope was to convince the Whigs of the need to listen to a 'unified' party which would otherwise withdraw its lifegiving support. The transparency of their claim that the government and its supporters formed an ideological unity was evident from the title of the *Westminster*'s first article in 1837, which set out the terms under which the Radicals would continue their 'alliance' with the Whigs. The Whigs' persistent refusal to encounter any of these demands also makes it evident that any party of which they formed a part could not be described on that basis as 'moderately Radical'.

Looked at from the standpoint of the 1830s, then, the concept of two all-encompassing parties is one that was given great prominence by those groups whose partisan purposes were served by describing the system as such. To emphasise the use of the term 'party' in that sense is to encourage a view of Whiggery handed down by its opponents. As a description of the government, its policies or its supporters, the terms Liberal and Liberal party gained widespread, though far from universal, use during this period. Indeed they were often used by the Whigs themselves. But Whigs generally distinguished between the groups that made up that party, especially after the dismissal of 1834 which forced them to rely on Liberals and Radicals for parliamentary support. In 1835, Russell was determined 'to hold our own Whig course' and to construct a new ministry composed of the 'Whiggest part of the Whigs'. Later that same year, Holland spoke of the differences among the Whigs and Radicals in the Liberal party, and in 1837 he talked hopefully of the 'comparative strength in the Whiggish or aristocratical wing of the Reform party'. Again, in 1840, when Melbourne followed his normal practice of appointing Whigs to ecclesiastical office, he recommended one candidate to Russell as 'not only a Liberal, but a Whig . . . the only persons who can be relied upon in new questions'.[24] All were referring to those people who would not agree to exactly those demands listed by the *Westminster Review*, and it was in order to retard the progress of these measures that the Whigs had governed by a tacit understanding with Peel, whose support, to the disgust of many in his party, allowed most of the important legislation of the period to be carried. Describing the new system as one which saw the formation of two monolithic blocs is not helpful in understanding this interparty cooperation.

The bloc voting which has led Beales to conclude that between 1835 and 1845 'two "strongly organized, disciplined parliamentary parties" [Namier's phrase] all but divided the House of Commons between them' was based largely on a comparison of six important divisions showing a remarkable degree of consistency in party alignment.[25] Gash, D. H. Close and W. O. Ayedelotte have arrived at essentially the same conclusion following their own study of the division lists.[26] It is to be questioned, however, to what extent a study of non-policy divisions – Speakership elections, amendments to the Address, votes of non-confidence – can be regarded, as Beales did, as the 'touchstone' of party allegiance, or, as Close argued, evidence that the vigour of the two-party system was at this time exceptional and unequalled until after Palmerston's death in 1865.

To what extent can such analyses of a few divisions of a specific type clarify the question of party? From 1830 to 1841, for all but a few months of which, the Whigs, under first Grey and then Melbourne, governed, several hundred divisions were held in the House of Commons. A large proportion of the House took part in many of those divisions. More commonly, only a few hundred participated. Divisions were held on what could be classed as both policy and non-policy issues. And, of course, many motions and bills were carried without formal divisions. But with such a wide variety to choose from, selective use of a single type of division has obvious pitfalls, and, it will be argued here, raises the same problems of subjectivity and preconceived notions as has the study of the more traditional source materials. To begin with, the divisions which Beales suggested were the 'touchstone' of party – that is, the non-policy divisions – do not support, as well as they might at first glance appear to do, the conclusion that party was unusually well developed after 1835. From 1835 to 1841 there were 34 divisions which fall into the 'touchstone' category – 16 in the 1835 parliament, 18 in the 1837 parliament. All were, in essence, confidence questions.[27] In the 1835 parliament, 719 members voted in these divisions. 649 voted only for government or opposition with no cross-voting; 54 members switched their votes once, 16 further members more than once. Of the 746 members who voted in the 1837 parliament, 619 fall into the first category, 34 into the second and 21 the third.

These divisions undoubtedly indicate a high degree of allegiance to both front benches. It is interesting to compare this result with the division lists of the first two parliaments of the Whigs' tenure of office, those of 1830–31 and 1831–32. During the first, three 'touchstone' divisions took place.[28] Of the 650 members who voted, 280 did so only for the Whigs, 237 only for the Tories, 97 cross-voted once. In the second of these parliaments, 684 members took part in eleven major divisions associated with Reform.[29] Apart from one unusual division,[30] only ten members cross-voted at all, and most of these only once. Clearly, allegiance on this type of division was the same in 1830–32 as it was in 1835–41. Yet, despite Beale's judgement that 'political involvement [a large number of members voting] is more than half-way to political affiliation',[31] the earlier period has not been characterised as one with a strong party system. Melbourne, who succeeded Grey as Whig Prime Minister in 1834, admitted that the government had no substantial party of its own, and that it could not have stood without the Reform Bill, which 'gave us a transient, phrenetic and epileptic strength'.[32] The government's defeat on its first budget is ample testimony to this judgement. It is clear too that the opposition was equally fragmented. This being the verdict as well of the historians, what can we learn from the study of these divisions? If the results of the divisions of 1835–41 are evidence for the emergence of disciplined, organised parties, then surely similar results for 1830–32 would be evidence for the same conclusion? But the historians of party have not suggested this. The reverse would obtain as well: if parties are held to be weak in 1830–32, the evidence of the division lists provides little help in assessing the state of party in the later period. And what should be made of the absence of such 'touchstone' divisions in the parliament of 1833–34? It might be argued that their absence – likely the result of the government's unusually large majority in the Commons – is evidence of a degree of allegiance which made confidence motions unnecessary, and that the existence of such divisions before and after speaks to the weakness of party and the narrowness of majorities. The allegiance which might have obtained had a narrower majority prompted calls for 'touchstone' divisions is a question, albeit speculative, which cannot easily be swept aside. Had there been a narrower majority, and had 'touchstone' divisions produced a pattern similar to those of 1831–32 and 1835–41, could it then be argued that party was strong in 1833–34?

If, as we are told, party became more disciplined after 1835, it would be useful to know to what extent the members' allegiance, as determined by the 'touchstone' divisions, could be relied upon in other divisions, and to what extent their voting patterns correspond to the pre-1830 period. In the study which follows, a large number of divisions were analysed. Each member's allegiance, as established by his performance on the 'touchstone' divisions,[33] was tested on the other divisions. For the purpose of this analysis, a distinction is made between legislative questions of some significance, admittedly a loose term, and the large number of divisions which took place on less important questions which often had only the minority votes recorded.

In the first of these categories – the divisions of some importance[34] – there were not many members who could be relied upon by government on any regular basis. While it would be dangerous to suggest that adherence to a party line should be of a twentieth-century nature in order to satisfy the evidential requirements for a developing party structure during the 1830s, there is little evidence that members could be relied upon, or that allegiance was stronger after 1835 than before. The results are shown in Table 2.1.

The members classified as ministerial[35] are those who voted only for government, who never cross-voted. Ministerial fringe generally voted with government, but opposed the government in more than 10 per cent of the divisions, and range from a low of opposition on only 10 per cent of the votes, to almost total and constant opposition. Thus, for example, only 22 per cent of the ministers' supporters voted only for the government, if they voted at all, in the 1833–34 parliament, a proportion which dropped to 11 per cent in the 1837–41 parliament.

Table 2.1

	Ministerial	Ministerial fringe	Waverers	Total
1833–34	107 22%	126 25%	262 53%	495 100%
1835–37	79 20%	156 40%	156 40%	391 100%
1837–41	42 11%	149 38%	195 51%	386 100%

It should be pointed out that this type of analysis does not lend itself easily to a tabulation of opposition members. To treat the opposition members in a similar fashion for the non-'touchstone' divisions, would be to overlook the fact that the opposition leaders supported the government on a wide range of issues. As a result, the opposition members who voted with the government in more than 10% of the recorded votes would be classed as opposition 'waverers'. Large numbers, in fact, did so; during the 1833–34 parliament for example, 184 of the 211 opposition members would be considered waverers because they voted with the government in more than 10 per cent of the 24 recorded divisions.[36] It would be misleading to suggest that these members did not vote with or as a party; they were often, if not usually, voting with Peel and the opposition leaders in doing so.

When the results of all of the several hundred other divisions[37] are analysed, the results are shown in Table 2.2.

If compared to a similar study by Austin Mitchell of voting patterns in the parliaments from 1812 to 1826,[38] doubt is again cast upon the conclusion that the later 1830s was a period of unusual

Table 2.2

	Ministerial	Ministerial fringe	Waverers	Total
1831–32	97 23%	228 54%	97 23%	422 100%
1833–34	91 18%	267 54%	137 28%	495 100%
1835–37	36 9%	281 72%	74 19%	391 100%
1837–41	40 10.5%	291 75.5%	55 14%	386 100%

party growth. Mitchell's investigation revealed a degree of allegiance far greater than that of the 1830s.

Table 2.3

	Ministerial	Ministerial fringe	Waverers	Total
1812–18	253	78	102	433
	58%	18%	24%	100%
1818–20	261	80	48	389
	67%	21%	12%	100%
1820–26	250	99	114	463
	54%	21%	25%	100%

It will be noted that the government fringe group never made up more than a fifth of the total number of government supporters. This is a much smaller number of less reliable supporters than what has been found for the 1830s. And Mitchell, it should be pointed out, was much more stringent in his definition of a fringe member. If a member had voted against the government once on one of the 'touchstone' motions which determined his government or opposition status, he was not allowed a single cross-vote on any of the several hundred remaining divisions to be classified as fringe. If a member had not cross-voted at all on the 'touchstone' motions, he was allowed to cross-vote on up to 1 per cent of the other divisions. Anything more than this was enough to be classed, not as a fringe member, who was 'prepared, very occasionally, to desert', but as a waverer, 'whose voting record indicates no attachment to either party'.[39] Using the same criteria, rather than the more generous 10 per cent threshold allowed in my study, the pattern which emerges for the parliament of 1831–32 (which had the strongest record of allegiance of the 1830s) is strikingly loose and virtually without trace of party:

Table 2.4

	Ministerial	Ministerial fringe	Waverers	Total
1% criterion	97	61	264	422
	23%	14%	63%	100%
10% criterion	97	228	97	422
	23%	54%	23%	100%

It would appear that the 'touchstone' divisions, when looked at in a wider context, do not offer in themselves much convincing evidence that party was highly developed. These particular divisions say little about the cause of the members' voting behaviour other than that there was little change in the members' opinions as to which party they wanted in or out of office. They say little about the actual size of those parties, or of the members' views of their policies and programmes. They say little about discipline, and nothing of organisation. Concerning this latter question, the fact is that members were not dependent for their positions on parties, which had neither apparatus nor funds to influence the elections which were almost entirely locally controlled. Parliamentary members received letters and circulars from the whips – a system with partial success – but had no other visible proof of party membership. Support for a non-policy motion did not imply support for the party on policy. Peel's complaint during the 1841 elections that too many candidates spoke on the hustings for themselves rather than the party,[40] is not surprising. In 1840, when, as Beales cites Gash as evidence for the argument that party was essentially developed,[41] the Conservative whip tallied only eight doubtful Radicals on an approaching confidence motion, Peel was warned by his lieutenants that he would have to shift his attitudes on policy questions, or face the breaking up of his parliamentary support.[42] Support on a confidence motion was clearly a different matter from support on policy, suggesting that it would be misleading to read too much into a handful of 'touchstone' divisions. Close's view that the vigour of the two-party system was unequalled for a quarter century suggests perhaps that the divisions were evidence of a temporary phenomenon which had more to do with the political circumstances of the late 1830s than with the existence of highly organised parties. Yet he too emphasised the strength of the two-party system in describing the left and right wings of each party, as if there was no doubt that two organised parties shared the House. It is to be wondered if Namier's stricture against making too much of a system of ayes and noes has been left unheeded. To be sure, there was little switching of votes on these particular divisions in the late 1830s. But it is not immediately clear whether members acted independently or as a result of organisation and discipline; nor is it evident that their support was general. Those lists, it *is* clear, fail to speak to the question.

To the failure of the division lists to provide convincing evidence of a tightly-knit Whig party must be added the Whigs' own eschewal of effective organisational management. Their attitude towards the basic management of parliament, elections and the press, and the lacklustre attention given to these matters, leaves very much the impression that unlike the Conservatives, there was anything but the 'body of politicians with coherent organization'[43] which has been postulated as a necessary condition for party. A study of these matters provides further evidence that the Whigs mistrusted many of their more liberal supporters and regarded themselves as a distinct political group. Where it can be argued that a more modern party system was developing, Whiggism had little understanding and sympathy for such a system and consciously tried to avoid what Whigs regarded as its fatal attractions.

Management of parliament was a task which the Whigs took to with a good deal of difficulty, and it was quickly apparent that the job was much harder than the occasional rallying of the troops necessary in opposition. When Grey's government was formed in 1830, Edward Ellice, Secretary to the Treasury, was put in charge of managing the party. Assistance in the Lords was given by the Duke of Richmond, and in the Commons by Lord Althorp. Management of the Lords was comparatively simple. Pulled unwillingly away from their country pursuits by the less casual attendance required of government members, the Whig peers were comforted by the knowledge that their bodily presence was unlikely to make much difference in the counting of heads. Proxies notwithstanding, no government bill could pass the Lords without the support of the Tory majority, and the presence of an able Whig speaker or two was the important consideration. A party dinner for the leading peers took place on the eve of each session to find out how many were pledged to government. Attendance was considered the equivalent of a pledge, and because not all invitations were accepted, it was deemed prudent to sound out Whig peers beforehand to learn whether an invitation would be welcome. At the dinner, the peers were informed of the government's policies for the session; coming after the equivalent of a pledge had been given, this practice suggested that in the Lords at least, party allegiance was less dependent on government policy. The rank-and-file ministerial peers who were not given invitations to dinner were sent circulars at the start of each session; before important debates, speakers and proxies were arranged. These tasks Richmond carried out rather better than Lords Strafford and Falkland, his successors during Melbourne's administration.[44]

Edward Ellice, who owed his position as Secretary to the Treasury to his wife's brother, Lord Grey, was the most successful of the whips in the House of Commons. According to Charles Wood, who succeeded him, he had the ability to get on with most people and was the only one who could 'keep things together'.[45] His mercantile connections gave him influence with the MPs who represented the City and trading interests, his advanced views on certain issues influence with the Radicals, his Scots background influence with the Scots Members and his attitude towards Irish Church reform influence with the Irish liberals and O'Connellites.' The great problem for Ellice was that his role as Treasury Secretary and closeness to Grey, who took a great interest in electoral matters, took too much time for party electoral matters, and left too little for management of the Commons. To add to the difficulty, Althorp, officially in charge of leading the Commons, took the view that formal procedures for managing the House and whipping in Members were unnecessary. As a result, there was no clear system for ensuring Members' attendance. Althorp and Ellice *both* sent notes, when and if they saw fit, requesting Members to turn out for debates and divisions; this practice led to confusion and uncertainty. The extraordinary importance of the Reform Bill simplified their job somewhat, although the defeat of Althorp's first Budget within four months of taking office should have warned him of the dangers of continuing without a more ordered approach. And despite the comparatively easy task of keeping Members up to the mark during the Reform Bill period, Ellice was worn out by the Spring of 1832. In April he told Grey that no other Treasury Secretary had attempted to manage the House alone, at least not since 'modern' times when the business of the Commons had so much increased; no one since the war, he added, had been forced to go on without at least one, and usually more, assistants.[46] Althorp, however, rejected all requests for aid. Ellice had more than once asked for assistance and had been given vague and unfulfilled understandings that the request might be supplied, but there never was a deputy appointed with authority from Althorp to help manage the House; despite Ellice's threat to resign, nothing was done. When his wife died at the end of July, he took the opportunity to resign his position at the Treasury, although he did agree to manage the election expected at the end of the year.[47]

Wood, Grey's son-in-law, was recommended by Ellice to succeed at the Treasury. He came to the position fully realising the difficulties that lay ahead, and warned Grey that the inefficient management and communication with Members of the House led to difficulties on particular divisions and to ignorance in the cabinet of the feelings of its supporters. This was a complaint made by Ellice as well.[48] After diverse correspondence it seemed understood by September that Thomas Young, Melbourne's secretary, would be appointed to help with the whip, but Althorp, determined to try the experiment of going on without *any* whips at all, would not allow the appointment.[49] In February 1833, Ebrington, who was reckoned to control over 100 votes in the Commons,[50] discussed with Hobbhouse the need for Althorp to call together all the Members friendly to government to ascertain the extent of their general support; in March, Ellice suggested to Holland that a committee of Spring Rice, Poulett Thomson, Macaulay and Duncannon do the same.[51] None of this Althorp would accept. The results were predictable. Despite a nominal majority of over 200, the government was defeated on a Tory motion to reduce the malt duties in April when only 152 votes could be mustered against. Wood was partly to blame, for he had sent out nothing more than the ordinary circular instead of the three-line *'earnestly* and *particularly'* required for important occasions, but it was widely suspected that the inefficient state of Althorp's staff was the source of difficulty.[52] Like Ellice before him, Wood complained to Grey that the job could not be done without the old system of whippers-in or the stimulus of Reform which had 'kept people right'.[53] Althorp's reluctance to alter the system nevertheless carried the day. Grey and Althorp's lack of interest in day-to-day political concerns was at the root of the problem. Both had taken office in 1830 against their own personal wishes, and it was no secret that with Reform behind them, their interests lay in Northumberland and Northamptonshire. It was for this reason that Melbourne thought the estimates of Althorp's value in the House of Commons exaggerated; he told William IV so when the King made Althorp's removal to the Lords the pretext for dismissing the government in 1834.[54] But Althorp's tiredness does not explain his refusal to allow Wood assistance which would presumably have made his own job of leading the House of Commons much easier. On several occasions, Althorp felt the force of difficulties which could be traced to his own neglect of the whip. In February 1834, for example, he was forced to call a meeting of the government's supporters after two particularly embarrassing divisions on his budget. On the 18th, Tory support was all that stood between the government and defeat on a Radical motion to reduce the number of pensions. The three Lennoxes, whose brother the Duke of Richmond was in the cabinet and whose sisters were on the pension list, were among those who opposed the ministry.[55] Three days later, the government only narrowly defeated the Marquis of Chandos' motion to reduce the malt tax when 100 'supporters' voted for Chandos. It is unlikely that a stronger whip would have been able to convert opponents, but there was no excuse for the absence of the government's supporters. At the subsequent meeting, Althorp warned the MPs that unless they gave more regular and consistent support, the government could not be carried on.[56] This was too little too late. A year earlier Richmond and Greville had discussed the problem and realised that little could be done until Althorp retired, when a new leader should make better discipline a *sine qua non*.[57] Perhaps the government's unusually large majority at the elections of 1832 had drawn Althorp into a false sense of security, but whatever the cause of his *insouciance*, Richmond's assessment was a damaging indictment of Whig leadership. It is also a commentary on the weak state of party.

Before the session got under way in 1835, Wellesley told Melbourne that it was 'indispensibly necessary without delay to establish some authority for the management of the affairs of our party'. This use of the term 'party' points unmistakably to the notion of a body of supporters who did not agree with government on a wide range of issues and who could not be counted on without an unusually large dose of guidance, if not cajolement. Referring to Peel's encouragement of Bonham's activities at the Carlton Club, he regretted that while 'the enemy is fully organized . . . we are without rule or guide'.[58] Wellesley's note of alarm concerned electoral and parliamentary affairs, both of which had been run down badly since Ellice had been in charge. It was to set the base aright that a new Treasury Secretary was appointed – E. J. Stanley, the Member for North Cheshire. Little is known of Stanley's appointment,[59] but it is likely that Ellice, a good friend, was responsible. Stanley was on good terms with Joseph Parkes, the Radical liberal from Birmingham who was involved in registration and electoral activities; this connection would soon lose Stanley the trust of the Whig leaders. Parkes thought Stanley 'a good whipper in',[60] and the unusually high number of Members who voted in the trials of strength between 1835 and 1841 would support that view. On the other hand, he made no strong impression on Holland, who seems to have regarded Ellice as the chief whip as late as January 1836.[61] Russell, the leader of the Commons, had the good sense to appoint R. M. O'Ferrall as an assistant whip,[62] but like his predecessor Althorp, Russell also sent letters summoning Members to important debates and divisions; clearly, there were still no well defined procedural rules to prevent confusion. Stanley found it useful, as Althorp had toward the end of his tenure of office, to call all of the ministers' supporters to periodic meetings at the Foreign Office (the only space close to Parliament large enough) when the government's plans were announced or explained, but ministers rarely asked for advice from the Members at these meetings. During his first term as Treasury Secretary, Stanley had the double advantage of a majority sufficiently comfortable to prevent defeat, but small enough to keep Members who did not wish to give the King another excuse to call on Peel, up to the mark. After the election of 1837, when the majority on several questions was extremely narrow, whipping-in became much more crucial, and difficult. Russell's 'finality' declaration and the government's willing reliance on Peel's support did not help. At the end of the 1838 session, Ellice told Melbourne that Stanley had been unable to do a good job and 'prays for relief'. 'If you want to keep your party together in the House of Commons', he added, 'you must get a new Secretary.'[63] But Melbourne, whose main ambition by that time was to deny Radicals any influence, would not consider moving Stanley to the Colonial Office as had been suggested, for he was 'too much connected' with Durham and Parkes.[64] He would have done well to heed Ellice's advice, for on the fateful Jamaican division in May 1839 which was followed by the ministry's resignation, it seems clear that those Whigs whose absence reduced the government's majority to five had not been warned of the importance or closeness of the division.[65]

Whig management of the Commons leaves very much the impression that force of argument and details of legislation were preferred to organisational activity. The government expected votes from their supporters, and was happy when it got them, but was quite prepared to count on opposition support when the going got rough. More than once leading ministers would switch argument and rely on Tory support, causing great dismay to those who had whipped up support on the basis of a different argument; there was little thought given to the damage such action might have on the whips' ability to build a majority on other questions. In neither written accounts nor deeds can one find that attention to organisation that characterised the Conservatives' parliamentary behaviour. To be sure, Peel, unburdened with office, had considerably more time to spend on the mechanics of party. Even so, it is his recognition of the value of organisation that one sees in his discussions with Bonham, and which is missing from the Whigs' record. The omission is more striking yet in electoral activity.

Whiggery was faced with an uncomfortable dilemma once Reform was passed. Without proper electoral organisation, maintenance of office would become increasingly difficult. But on the liberal side, political activity attracted many people who actively promoted, or were at least not opposed to, further constitutional reform. There was a striking difference here from the situation confronting Peel, who was busy tempering reactionary ultra conservatism within his party. Promotion of electoral activity posed for him little ideological difficulty, for few of his supporters would challenge the nation's institutions. The difficulty of the Whigs lay not only in restraining more violent activists, but in discouraging those of their own connection who appeared eager to galvanise the wide support attracted during the Reform crisis. The tendency of the moderate Whig leaders therefore was to abstain from party organisation, because of the nature of those who promoted it. Their reluctance was noticeable in the preparations for the first reformed elections in 1832. From St Petersburg, 'Radical Jack' Durham pressed Ellice and Grey to avoid the 'suicidal act' of dissolving Parliament before a sufficient register of voters had been effected.[66] But little was done, for Durham, 'puffed up and inflated'[67] over his popular Reform role and his sympathies for more substantial Irish Church reform than the Whigs favoured, was a doubtful adviser. He had been sent to Russia in large part to be got rid of. Moreover, in many minds, Ellice was scarcely more trustworthy. Melbourne thought him a 'cunning, designing knave' who was too closely associated with 'Durham and the masses'.[68] This judgement of Ellice was somewhat harsh, but coming as it did from the man who was to lead the Whigs during much of their tenure in office, the attitude is of some importance in explaining Whig reluctance to organise electoral activity. What hurt Ellice's reputation among many Whigs was not so much his support of Durham as it was his readiness to leave a great number of organisational matters to Joseph Parkes, whose circle, he knew, went much further on reforming issues than did the Whigs.[69]

Yet alarm at the radical proclivities of many government supporters was not as dominant a feature as it would come to be. Whig activity in 1832 seems better characterised as lethargic. Charles Wood did a creditable job chairing the election committee by exchanging information with constituency agents, but he was unable to raise a subscription as Ellice had done in 1831,[70] when Reform had rendered electoral activity respectable. A central fund did not exist. Want of money in constituencies was common; in Dublin, where the Repealers could apparently have been beaten for £2,000, Grey asked Ellice disconsolately 'Where is that sum, or any part of it to be found?'[71] Ellice, for his part, spent most of his time in Scotland; his persuasion of James Fleming to give £20,000 worked to great effect.[72] Grey knew that his son-in-law Wood was ineffective in managing the elections or in raising a chest, but he was reluctant to persuade Ellice to take on the task because Ellice's wife (Grey's sister) had recently died.[73] Though many candidates looked to Ellice for advice and assistance, it was to little avail. 'They have the advantage of us in power', he told Holland.[74] Ellice's comment and Grey's reliance on family members to direct affairs suggests that Whig activity relied overly much on the methods of the eighteenth-century 'connections'. Reluctance to follow Durham's advice concerning registrations adds to the impression. Graham, who was responsible for the registration provisions in the Reform Bill, recognised both the need and advantage of proper attention, and saw to it that his paid agents in Cumberland were scrupulous in this regard.[75] Few others were as fastidious. With reports of apathy and slackness in registration common,[76] Althorp could think only of his earlier wish to have had the county overseers put the names on the list without claims being made.[77]

It could be argued that attention to central organisation was unimportant in 1832 when Reform was expected to provide Grey with a good majority, and when the Tories were not obviously gaining ground by superior activity.[78] But by December 1834, the perception that Bonham's superior organisation had given the Conservatives a probable advantage made the issue of organisation increasingly important. Whether superior organisation and attention to registration had any significant impact on an electoral system which was to a large extent local in nature rather than national – and there is as much evidence that the impact of organisation was slight as there is that it was important – it is clear that all parties *perceived* increased organisation as essential. Yet despite this perception, ideological disputes with those Whigs and liberals who wished most to organise prevented the leading Whigs from exercising organisational leadership. Because the election committee, organised by Ellice and headed by Thomson, Duncannon, Hobhouse and Mulgrave, based its electoral strategy on a 'union of all Reformers', Melbourne did what he could to stifle its efforts. 'For God's sake', he wrote to Mulgrave, 'get our people, if you can, not to pledge themselves about Ballot and the duration of parliaments.'[79] Mulgrave, however, was loth to discourage active participation by liberals and Radicals in the Whigs' cause. Instead, for example, he held out an olive branch to Durham, whose attempt to woo the Movement during a speaking tour in the North and Scotland had angered the Whig leadership by his promotion of further constitutional reform and his portrayal of the Whigs as anti-reforming in nature.[80] There seemed little doubt that the election committee's liberalism was far more advanced than that of the leadership. Mulgrave, Hobhouse and Duncannon, who carried on the bulk of the committee's work at Ellice's house at 3 Cleveland Square, worked with Parkes to discourage contests between Whigs and Radicals.[81] Yet the Whig leaders' hostility to Radicals was so obvious that E. L. Bulwer, brother of the Radical candidate for Marylebone, asked Mulgrave if the Whigs' playing of the 'old game of Ingratitude' was safe or prudent.[82] What most concerned Melbourne, Russell, Rice, Holland, Wellesley, Palmerston and the Greys, was the widespread call by many newspapers and liberals, of both Whig and Radical persuasion, for measures which would help to effect a 'union of Reformers'. The Whigs' strategy to counter this pressure was to prevent Radicalism from gaining ground as a result of the King's dismissal of Melbourne's ministry.[83] Russell and Howick both denounced Radical demands for parliamentary reform in several speeches.[84] Grey went so far as to refuse to allow a younger member of the family to oppose Ingham at South Shields on the grounds that no Grey should be patronised by Durham, who had first suggested a Grey candidacy.[85] Yet the activities of the election committee – Hobhouse's public association of the Whigs with ballot and triennial parliaments during his Nottingham campaign is an example[86] – caused Melbourne to dissociate himself from that group's work. Believing as he did that Durham's radicalism had much to answer for the King's dismissal of his ministry, Melbourne had no faith in those who would continue to associate with Durham and his principles. 'I have not taken much cognizance of what is going on at Cleveland Row', he wrote to Rice, 'despairing of being able to manage or control. The fact is that these [electoral] matters are in the hands of those who, from the commencement of the late administration, pursued the system which necessarily led to its downfall.'[87]

The subsequent elections, which brought the Conservatives to within a few dozen seats of the combined opposition, further alienated the Whig leaders from the liberal organisers. While the Whigs regarded the results as proof that a Radical programme would be suicidal in the face of an obviously conservative electorate, the Cleveland Square group became increasingly convinced that active organisation of the electorate was essential to the cause of reform. Ironically, at the very time that Peel and Bonham began to increase the efforts of the 'Carlton Street Gang', Whigs viewed central electoral activity as an insidious democratic inroad on the aristocratic preserve. Party organisation, in short, appeared to Whigs as a euphemism for Radicalism. And Radicalism, the elections had convinced them, was a quick road to political demise and the emasculation of the landed aristocracy. It is not surprising that the Whig mind had difficulty in dissociating electoral organisation from Radical politics, for in the fifteen months following the ministry's dismissal, the group which was most concerned with organisation was simultaneously trying to hold the Whigs, first in opposition, then in government, to a Radical programme. Joseph Parkes, the leading agent of the 1834 election committee, was behind the Radical drive. Neither Whig nor Radical, his sharp political instincts and wide circle of contacts in both camps gave him an unparalleled usefulness in organisational matters. William Thomas portrays him as a chameleon-like character who followed his Whig sympathies and demagogic reputation as the occasion required; by frequenting the worlds of the Whig aristocracy and the dissenting middle classes, he 'personified the nascent Liberal party'.[88] The dismissal and the subsequent elections convinced Parkes of the need both to 'work the Reform Act' and to keep the Whigs away from a coalition with the Conservatives. The Reform Association was born of this dual necessity. Although, as Parkes had recently told Durham, he could not 'brook the degradation of mind' of lending himself to a governing party, and thought the Whigs 'cold, selfish, factioning men',[89] he was instrumental in organising the Reform Association which was officially founded on 21 May 1835.

The Reform Association figures prominently in the growth of the party system which characterises the politics of the late 1830s. It began with the goal of pointing out to the country the facility and effect of organisation, fund-raising and the registration of voters; within a few months, several dozen local associations were formed. A notable feature of the Association, however, was the lack of participation by the Whig party leaders. Apart from Lord Ebrington, who formally moved to establish an association, most of the few hundred people who met at the British Coffee-House on Cockspur Street to found the organisation were Radicals and advanced Liberals. Parkes, along with the Radicals Hume and Warburton, provided the inspiration.[90] But the Whigs refused to join. Russell had spent most of that spring trying to hold the party to a Whig course; he could not be part of a group whose leading members he had tried to keep his distance from at the time of the Lichfield House meeing.[91] By October, none of the ministers had joined. Through Ellice and E. J. Stanley, the whip, communication of sorts was possible; Melbourne often talked with Parkes about the state of the registration. But there was no singleness of purpose as existed between Bonham and Peel at the Carlton Club, no *encouragement* of electoral organisation. The foundation of the Reform Club six months later did little to alter this situation. Whigs remained at Brooks's, Radicals at the Reform, proto-Liberals at either. What followed was continual concern by individual Whig magnates that the registration was not being properly attended to when election contests went badly, and equally continual concern from the Reform Association headquarters that the Whig leaders as a group would not support its activities. Whigs would grow increasingly conscious of the need to counter Peel's efforts by improving organisational activity, and would often rely on Parkes to moderate the demands of their more liberal supporters; but his close association with the Radicals and the movement for parliamentary reform, and eventually, Corn Law repeal, would not allow Whigs to commit themselves wholeheartedly to his course. In 1839, Coppock, who had served as secretary to the Reform Association since the autumn of 1835, was not to be considered for a minor government sinecure because of his role at the Association which would have brought embarrassment to the Whigs.[92] Parkes' suggestion that Coppock assume another name as secretary says much about the mutual lack of trust between the Whigs and electoral organisers. By 1841, Parkes could only conclude that 'unless some organisation is made by the Whigs', he would no longer 'waste' his time working on their behalf.[93] Six years earlier, Melbourne had expressed the wish that he never had.

The Whigs' management of the press, haphazard and not very well done, resembled the rest of their organisation. Weakness in maintaining good relations with the press was due, to some extent, to the lack of interest shown by both Grey and Melbourne in arranging sympathetic support in the newspapers. Grey thought that although it was desirable to have the government position outlined in at least one paper with a large circulation, control was impossible when public opinion was opposed to the ministry's.[94] Melbourne saw little value in a friendly press, and took little interest in what the papers said. 'If you can do anything with the press, well and good', he told Ellice in 1836. 'I do not care much about it myself . . . its articles have not the effect which is supposed.'[95] Both leaders reflected the notion, widespread at the time, that the press lacked any influence over the views of the public. It was generally assumed that proprietors pandered to the readers' tastes; profits depended on responding to public appetite, not on shaping it. What influence the press possessed was with the Members of Parliament, but here too, there was little to give the leading Whigs cause to consider the press important. The inability of *The Times* to generate opposition to the government's new Poor Law Bill in 1834 seemed to Holland 'signal proof' of the prediction that the Reform Act would strengthen parliament against the press.[96] Behind this belief was a notion that the

Members of Parliament held to their views as a result of deeper influences. Like Althorp, who thought that Reform made whips unnecessary, Holland's remark reflected a belief that Members took their own view of issues, or of constituents' wishes; the press could not convince them that their own sources of information were unsatisfactory or their views in need of change.

Apart from Palmerston, who showed a great interest in the papers by feeding them stories and articles concerning both foreign and domestic policy,[97] the group most involved with the editors were those same more liberal Members of the government who were most interested in party organisation generally. Their efforts were not always welcome. Grey, for example, was not at all happy with a scheme, devised by Ellice and Durham within a few months of the Whigs taking office, to have James Silk Buckingham paid £500 to write articles praising Grey and his government.[98] It was not simply because the plan proved unworkable that it was dropped within a few months. Grey was of the opinion that the press was too often influenced by no consideration except profits and circulation, which could increase only by losing 'no opportunity of shewing itself adverse to the influence of Property and Station'.[99] This view suited the Whig mind. It is not coincidence that during Grey's tenure in office, Brougham was the one Whig who worked hard at influencing the papers. Never trusted by his colleagues from the time of his victory over the Whig interest in the Yorkshire election of 1830,[100] Brougham had his secretary Le Marchant communicate with five London dailies – *The Times*, the *Morning Chronicle*, *Globe*, *Sun*, and *Courier*.[101] His productivity was prodigious. According to Le Marchant, he often sent 200 letters a morning to the London and provincial liberal papers; *The Times* was at one point so subservient that it was nicknamed 'Brougham's Gazette'.[102] Although *The Times* and the *Globe*, whose proprietor Col. Torrens had close connections with Melbourne's secretary Thomas Young, were considered as the accredited organs of the Grey government and certainly did receive the most ministerial information, there was clearly no government paper. Grey's explanation to Princess Lieven for such lack of control put very nicely the reason:[103]

We might purchase a paper that is not read, which would do us no good till it got into circulation; and then it would do just like the others. The truth is, that the profits of a paper extensively taken in are so great, that they are quite beyond any temptation that could be held out to them.

Thus, despite their reception of advanced notices, the editors and proprietors maintained an independence which often proved extremely embarrassing to the government. By the summer of 1834, neither the *Globe* nor *The Times* supported the Whigs. Le Marchant complained of the *Globe*'s 'pusillanimity' – Torrens had begun to reject his articles – and wondered if Stuart of the *Courier* might be a more 'efficient' ally.[104] The conduct of *The Times* seemed proof to the Whigs that attempts to curry favour with the press were fruitless. In 1833, Thomas Barnes, its editor, began to make demands in return for his support.[105] Believing that the middle classes were so opposed to the government that his circulation would drop unless he catered to their interests, he attacked the ministry for refusing to consider the state of the Corn Laws.[106] The thrust of his conduct was demagogic; the government, he told Hobhouse, had done nothing to realise the just expectations of 'the people'.[107] Barnes' concern for the populace was likely influenced by John Walter, proprietor of *The Times*, whose motive for opposing the Whigs had less to do with the rising middle classes than the lower orders. Walter, a Berkshire magistrate, was known as a poor man's J.P. who acted leniently towards paupers who appealed to his high-Tory paternalism. As such, he was opposed to the other magistrates who had persuaded the Whigs to reform the old poor laws, and, in doing so, to restore social 'discipline' and reduce the rates.[108] In 1834, when the government introduced the new poor law, *The Times* went into permanent opposition. Althorp enquired of Brougham, the object of Barnes' published fury, 'whether we should declare open war with *The Times* or attempt to make peace',[109] but the break was final. When Peel formed his government in December, the Conservative leaders had reached an agreement with Barnes over future policy, 'thus kissing the hands of King Press', quipped Holland, 'before . . . those of King William'.[110]

Dismissal of the Whigs from office convinced the coterie of liberal party organisers that a manageable press was of more importance than ever. Spurred on by Parkes, they convinced the former Whig Member for Banbury, Col. John Easthope, to buy up the ailing *Morning Chronicle* as a rival to the increasingly hostile

Times. Although Ellice had a stake in the paper, Easthope provided the bulk of the necessary £16,500.[111] The tone of the paper was soon more decidedly Radical than most Whigs hoped. This is not surprising, for with Grey's retirement in July, those who had the most influence with the *Chronicle*'s editor, John Black – Parkes, Brougham, Durham and Le Marchant – were the members of the party most anxious to push the Whigs more solidly in the direction of further constitutional reforms. In August, Grey complained of the daily tone of the ministerial press in holding out expectations of more effective reforms 'now that the chief obstacle to them [himself] was removed'.[112] Brougham, of course, was at that very moment trying to outflank Durham as the potential leader of the 'movement'. The 'union of reformers' which followed the 1835 elections produced a moderation of the *Chronicle*'s content, for with Brougham and Durham gone from the Whig ranks and the maintenance of the liberal union of utmost necessity, Parkes was able to convince Black that encouragement of the extreme radicals was not in the liberal interest. Parkes' position was, in essence, that of the moderate radicals; while wishing to drive the Whigs on, he did not want the hotter heads among their supporters to drive them into an alliance with Peel and the moderate Conservatives. Thus, although Ellice and Le Marchant acted as a conduit for the Whigs in opposition and, from May 1835, in government, to the point where the *Chronicle* became known as the government organ in the same way that *The Times* had earlier been known, the *Chronicle* was in reality Parkes' journal. The paper supported the Whigs because Parkes, at that stage, thought that Radicals and Liberals had no choice but to support them.[113] To this extent, the *Chronicle* was more the voice of the moderate Radicals and Liberals than of the Whigs, and would remain so only so long as the Radical sufferance of the Whigs was to last. This was, from the Whigs' point of view, unfortunately not long. Russell's finality speech late in 1837, which prompted a small but vociferous number of Radicals to hostility towards the government, prompted the *Chronicle* to take an increasingly critical posture. Le Marchant, who was praised by Ellice in 1835 as the one who did most 'in managing the press and Rads',[114] found himself unable to counter the newly won influence which the militant Radicals Wakely and Leader were exercising over Black. Easthope, he told Holland, had virtually dropped his connection with the government. There was no organ, he complained, through which the government could explain its policy to the 'Liberal Party'.[115] The final break came in the spring of 1839 with a series of attacks on the Whigs' continued opposition to constitutional reforms. Parkes had been hard at work for months in an attempt to moderate Radical discontent and had often written to Easthope to check the paper's 'rasping' of the ministry; in the end, he was forced to admit a loss of control over its conduct.[116] The *Chronicle*'s call on March 25 for ballot, household suffrage and shorter Parliaments prompted Russell to order all communication with the paper stopped;[117] its rejoicing at the government's resignation on May 7 – what Spring Rice noted as 'open war, much better than war in disguise'[118] – was evidence that it could no longer be considered the government print. A scheme to set up a new paper friendly to the government failed for lack of ministerial support. Poulett Thomson proposed a new organ, and was supported by Le Marchant and Stanley, but none of the Whig ministers approved of such an undertaking.[119] Fonblanque, described by Queen Victoria as 'the best' of the London editors, gave the Whigs some support by attacking the independence of the Radicals in his *Examiner*;[120] the *Globe* and *Courier* continued to take a Whiggish line, though without any direct connection with the government.

The Whigs, as always, were loth to become directly involved with any paper. Their reasons for not doing so illuminate the Whig attitude to organisation and party in general. Poulett Thomson was a free-trader who made no secret of his support for the Anti-Corn Law League. Despite his rise to the Presidency of the Board of Trade, his mercantile background and close connections to Warburton, Hume and other Radicals made him suspect in the eyes of his Whig associates. To have him in charge of trade and commercial policy was one thing; the times and the needs of government made that acceptable. To follow his lead in organising official propaganda was quite another. Thomson symbolised much of what Whiggery was fighting against; he personified the difficulty in what one historian has described as 'the alliance between the cultured and broad-acred Whig aristocrat and politically determined Liberal parvenu, fighting his way through a fiercely competitive industrial and commercial system [which] was uneasy long before late Victorian developments made it impossible'.[121] Moreover, as Thomas noted, the press had little comfort to offer the landed aristocracy, which resented 'its intrusion into their political interests' and its development in the growing towns. 'Journalists', he concluded, 'were looked on as interlopers'.[122] Poulett Thomson, like the Cleveland Square group with which he was associated, represented the new style of politician who would attempt to galvanise public opinion and rise to power on its strengths. This system the Whig mind could comprehend, but at the close of the 1830s, could in no way accept. It is not surprising that this should be the case; a half-century later, Gladstone's Midlothian campaign would evoke a similar response from the great aristocracies. Whigs had come into office to preserve aristocratic influence by legislating a reform of the parliamentary system; if the Bill was meant to be a check on the executive, it was also meant as a check on the unbridled demands of the populace. Aristocrats should perhaps have foreseen the extent to which the political world, and control, would pass from their country estates and London houses to a wider world. But they chose not to view Reform, and their own role in the political realm, in that way. If the press was an intrustion into their affairs, so too was electoral and party organisation, which, while becoming an increasingly necessary evil, was an evil to which they could give no wholehearted commitment. Peel could curry favour with Walter of *The Times*,[123] and draw on Carlton Club funds to secure press support when necessary,[124] but the Whigs could not. The Conservative leader might organise a party and electoral machine to work the Reform Act; the Whigs held to the older view that elections turned more on issues and policies. From the moment Reform was passed, organisation of the reform cause fell into the hands of those people whose visions were of middle class, urban influence. They looked forward to the altered social circumstances of the nineteenth century. Whiggism, on the contrary, was a creed whose Foxite cause of civil and religious liberty looked back to an earlier age. By inclination, its methods were those of the pre-Reform system.

3

A Ministry for Reform

Nought's permanent among the human race Except the Whigs
not getting into place.

Byron, *Don Juan*[1]

A very rainy day – as Lord North said 'not a day to turn a dog
out'.

Hobhouse diary, 16 November 1830[2]

The notion that Earl Grey would lead a mixed reform government
before the year was out was not obvious at the beginning of 1830.
There were few signs that an opposition sufficiently large to
topple the Tories could, or indeed would, be mounted. At sixty-
five, Grey was thinking more of capping his long career in
opposition by retirement from office. Althorp, heir to the Spencer
estates, seemed equally impervious to the lure of power; management of his horses at Althorp park was more to his taste. Most
curious of all, the issue that would dominate and permeate the
whole of society was scarcely alive. In February, Grey warned his
son not to be harnessed to parliamentary reform, 'which will
always be opposed by the Crown, and on which you cannot rely
on the support of the People'.[3] Nor was it obvious that Reform,
once it became inevitable, would be a Whig measure. Three weeks
before he joined an administration founded on that question,
Russell hoped that Wellington would bring in a successful plan.[4]
Though Wellington's government was considered to rest on a
narrower, more conservative base of support than its predecessors, the Duke and Peel had overcome a rather weak parliamentary position by granting Catholic emancipation when that
question could no longer be avoided. By the end of the 1829
session, ultra Tory discontent with the government's Catholic and
economic policies produced what Henry Brougham described as 'a
fixed opinion that the present Government cannot last long – that
is – in its present state', but the Tory leaders' willingness to do

what was right for Ireland convinced most of the opposition that they could be safely entrusted with office. There was 'an equally strong impression', continued Brougham, 'that one way or another the Duke of Wellington must be in office – which is a great part of his strength.'[5] It was not until Wellington would not undertake measures seen to be in the national interest that the opposition considered replacing him at the helm. By the late summer of 1830, Reform became the issue of the moment, but most politicians, apart from the most die-hard ultra Tories and Radicals, were willing to let the Tories see it through. Fifty years of Tory rule came to an end not because the Whigs led a successful assault on the Wellingtonian citadel, but because the Duke himself, by refusing to do what most observers and participants in the political process thought necessary, brought about the end of his government and the fall of the old parliamentary system. The Whigs came into office somewhat reluctantly in order to preserve property and aristocracy, the very institutions which Wellington's inactivity threatened to undermine. How they did so, and how they viewed Reform, shall first be addressed.

Although the ultra Tory country party attacked the government from the start of the year, it would be a mistake to suggest that the issue of agricultural distress or ultra Tory concepts of parliamentary reform rendered Wellington's downfall a matter of time. The Marquess of Blandford's motion to disfranchise decayed and close boroughs, aimed at those like Peel 'who have contrived to bring themselves and their independence into parliament', gathered the support in February of only 87 ultras, Whigs and Radicals.[6] Fragmentation on the opposition benches had much to do with Wellington's strength. At the opening of the session the *Morning Chronicle* listed six parties in the Commons: the regular supporters of the ministers; the old Whig opposition; the high Tory opposition; Lord Althorp's party, consisting of Liberals and Reformers and independent members; Huskisson's party; and a small number of members under no banner.[7] This number was not unusual, for the notion of a united opposition that might replace government had scarce meaning in pre-Reform parliaments. In 1818 it was said that an opposition numbering 173, if well-managed and supported by public opinion, was sufficient to defeat any government. A ministry could usually hold on to office as long as its members could agree to support the Prime Minister. Since the beginning of the century there had been ten administrations, only one of which, Addington's in 1804, had been forced out through forfeiture of the confidence of the House of Commons, and he, in fact, resigned when his majority shrank to thirty-seven.[8] The collapse of Liverpool's ministry in 1827 increased the trend of multiple parties and coalitions,[9] and the very existence of a new Tory administration that was dependent on a narrower base of support than its predecessors was Wellington's strength as well as his weakness.

The Whigs certainly posed little threat. Since Ponsonby's death in 1817, sporadic efforts to unify the Whigs in opposition had failed. The formation of Wellington's government and the emergence of the Catholic issue helped to heal the split that Canning's ministry had created in Whig ranks, but while some like Holland, Russell and Althorp were prepared to bring together as many of the opposition groups as possible to turn the government out for a good Catholic bill, others like Grey were reluctant to discourage the Duke by an organized opposition.[10] Whig disunity gave strength to the government, and the Tories' *volte face* on Ireland disarmed the Whig camp further. At the end of 1829, Russell could see no grounds for general opposition, an opinion shared by Brougham, who told Stanley that 'after the *dreadful sacrifices* Peel has made to the C. question, it would be extremely painful to oppose him with any factiousness'.[11] Brougham's questioning of 'party' was an attitude with wide currency after Emancipation. In February 1830, Russell told Grey that 'politics are in so strange and uncertain a state that one knows not how questions will be decided or how parties will ultimately form themselves'. Even that staunch Tory the Duke of Cumberland opined that 'with respect to Whigs and Tories now, it appears to me that that idea should be laid completely aside'.[12] This opinion presumably reflected the general satisfaction with the outcome of the Catholic crisis and the expectation that Wellington could be trusted with office. It was an opinion that would die hard, for as late as 12 July 1830 the *Morning Chronicle*, in no sense a government print, recorded its view that 'if those who conduct the Government of this country act with tolerable judgement, such a thing as party, in the usual acceptation of that term, will be no longer possible'. Wellington did not, in the end, act with such 'tolerable judgement', and when Reform emerged as the panacea to cure all ills, the metaphor of party resurfaced from its dormant state beneath a thin layer of intra-party 'co-operation'.

If the ultra Tories provided the only consistent opposition during the first weeks of 1830, the Whigs were not entirely uncritical. Though unsure of their tactics, there was a general Whig belief that only by pressing the government on individual matters could Wellington be kept up to the mark. 'I do not wish them out', Holland told Grey, 'for I know not what to wish *in*—but I do wish while they are in to compel them if possible to do what is right, which if *compelled* they will do—but which if left to themselves they certainly would not.'[13] This ambivalence, described by Grey as 'a friendly neutrality', was shared by most of the leading Whigs[14] and produced an inchoate if not non-existent opposition strategy. Though Russell had claimed in 1829 that 'measures not men is the maxim of a tailor and not of a man', he and Althorp, who were prepared in 1830 to find fault only with measures,[15] rendered any co-ordinated attack on Wellington's position impossible. Brougham, for example, found that when he and a number of Whigs supported the ultra Tory Knatchbull's amendment to the address, others of his party saved the government by opposing the motion.[16] At the end of February, on the other hand, Brougham and Althorp told several Whigs that because Graham had secured enough support from Whigs, ultra Tories and Canningites to jeopardise the ministry on a motion calling for retrenchment in the Navy, they would have no choice but to oppose Graham's motion, having 'no wish to upset the Government'.[17] Efforts to end this chaos on the Whig benches were taken early in March when three 'back bench' Members[18] asked Althorp to lead some semblance of a unified opposition. On the condition that forty-five Members should agree to meet at his rooms in the Albany, Althorp accepted the invitation. It is not clear who attended the meetings. Brougham, Howick, Russell and the leading Whigs certainly came, and the *Morning Chronicle* reported 'independent members of both Houses' met. The first gathering on 3 March had only twenty-seven participants, though upwards of forty usually attended thereafter.[19]

The purpose of Althorp's 'group of forty' was not to give a generally hostile opposition to Wellington, but to make the admittedly weak opposition more effective by being less frequent. Shortly after the first meeting, Althorp made it clear in the Commons that he would not support an unfriendly motion on the state of the nation, preferring an honest, discriminating support of the government and close supervision of its measures rather than

factious attacks and unruly opposition.[20] The principal interests of
the group were economic. In Althorp's view, the junction extended only to retrenchment and reduction of taxes, the measures
he thought essential for the relief of distress. On all other points,
members would continue 'as much disunited as ever'.[21] His
opinions were not shared by all, and the indiscipline nurtured by
years in opposition nearly scuttled the project at its launching.
Graham refused the invitation to the first meeting because of
Althorp and Brougham's opposition to his earlier Admiralty
motion, and though he was persuaded to attend the following
meetings, he taunted the Whigs throughout the spring for their
feeble hostility to Wellington.[22] Howick reported that 'several'
stayed away for fear of pledging themselves against a change in
the currency, and it was evident that there was little willingness to
sacrifice what Althorp hoped would be minor differences. Baring,
for example, agreed to support retrenchment, but like several
others, would not support a tax reduction. Some thought that the
government had reduced taxes as far as could be expected; others
like Baring, did not, but refused to press for reduction in order to
avoid the expected alternative of a property tax. The existence of
these differences of opinion was no secret. During a Commons
debate on government expenditure, Burdett, one of the forty,
spoke strongly against the group and actually advised an
increase.[23] It is small wonder that Althorp's group had little
influence on government or opposition. Common dissatisfaction
with government was not the stuff of party, and until July, when
the issue of Reform loomed larger in the nation, Althorp's group
had little meaning and few travellers.

If an issue was central to the creation of a party, so too was a
leader. On this point as well, Whiggery had some difficulty, for
Grey showed little inclination to lead. 'I have no longer the powers
of either body or mind that are required for such a task', he wrote
to his son from Northumberland, where he sat out the first few
months of the session.[24] But as reports of the government's
activities reached him at Howick, he grew increasingly circumspect of Wellington's own ability to lead. 'If I am to judge by the
King's speech', he wrote to Holland, 'the Government are not
sufficiently aware of the general condition of the country, or of the
feeling which is rising as distress increases.' Convinced, probably
correctly, that the distress which the Government recognised in
'some parts' was both general and intense, he doubted that

Wellington's personal power and influence was enough to weather the storm.[25] His policy of outward neutrality was based, therefore, on the premise that open opposition would weaken the Duke's standing at a time when growing discontent with government required strength at the top.

But how to limit distress? Grey was hopeful that the government would base its strength on more than the disunity of its opponents by taking measures that would earn his support,[26] but nowhere is there a trace of what he thought those measures might be. Presumably he would have liked posts offered to his Whig colleagues – he had complained to Brougham of 'the sort of recruits that are sought',[27] but what a strengthened government might have done was not part of his thinking. Perhaps he was piqued at not being offered a government post, even though he would most likely have rejected one, and those who regard Grey's conduct as guided by personal ambition surely find their case here. By failing to offer an alternative approach, his attitude could be seen to have smacked of partisanship. Was his advice to Howick – 'Let the Ministers find the remedy. Do not pledge yourself and propose nothing', guided by a desire to save Wellington from criticism or to have him suffer political humiliation?[28] This latter conclusion seems doubtful, but if Grey did mean to support Wellington, his correspondence to his colleagues provides little evidence that he knew what Wellington or anyone else could do to limit distress. He was critical of the government's giving in to demands for tax reduction, and took a disparaging view of Althorp's group for the same reason. 'I have not a head capable of understanding political economy and . . . I hate the subject' he told Holland; he warned Howick that 'banking is not exactly the best subject' for union.[29]

Grey's neutral position was particularly undermined by fear of social unrest and the bitterness engendered by the King's speech. 'The newspapers, in their attacks upon the landowners, have succeeded in destroying all respect for rank and station, and for the institutions of government' he wrote to Ellice. 'Another year like the past, and who can answer for the consequences?'[30] This fear of the threat to society and property, the basis of much of the Whig thinking in the 1830s, forced Grey to re-evaluate his own attitude to government. He had hoped that Wellington's 'effective leadership' would allow for a peaceful retirement, but when struck by the similarities in the country to pre-revolutionary France, he admitted privately that if his being at the head of government should be 'absolutely necessary', he could not refuse. In March he had suggested the 'formation of a party' to form a government if Wellington could not deal with the dangers and difficulties; by May, he reviewed with Althorp the possible members of a Whig administration.[31] His own involvement in these plans stemmed from a somewhat vain notion that no one else was qualified to lead the Whigs, although he was probably correct. 'There is nothing approaching this damned fellow in the kingdom when he mounts his best horse', Creevey had written ten years earlier.[32] The lack of unity in Althorp's opposition group seemed to Grey evidence that Althorp had insufficient influence and authority to control men and direct their affairs,[33] a view prophetically true; with no obvious alternative, he came down from Northumberland at Easter.

But the Humber was no Rubicon, for Grey still hoped that Wellington could prevent disorder. The Huskissonites made it known that if Wellington would offer the Foreign Office to Grey, they would end all hostility. Grey was tempted. If acceptance of office could provide the stability and strength which the government lacked, crisis might be averted.[34] The King's natural antipathy to Whigs made an immediate offer unlikely, but his death in June and William IV's less dogmatic approach left Wellington free to make Grey an offer. But would he? There had been no feelers. Grey became convinced that change was necessary in order to give the ministry strength in both Houses;[35] he decided to force the Duke's hand by attacking him openly. On 30 June he declared that the administration was incapable of advantageous conduct, and that its measures were not of a character 'by which the honour, the consequences or the power of the country would be forwarded'. Grey was now declared against the ministry. His object, he told Princess Lieven, was to make it impossible for Wellington to make less than a fair offer; anything 'of a contrary description' would be rejected.[36] Grey could not have failed to see the paradox in this course. He had been critical of previous hostility to Wellington. Such action might give the government an appearance of weakness that would by itself encourage disorder. If the Duke were to refuse to make an offer now, Grey's declaration of hostility could foster the weakened Wellingtonian image that he was trying to prevent. But through this gamble, he hoped, would come strength.

Grey's attack was the first of an orchestrated series. In the Commons, Russell announced his refusal to give confidence to a

government which 'from its vacillation, its incompetence, or its
hostility to popular rights' deserved none. Graham, Althorp and
Brougham added to the onslaught, prompting O'Connell to remark that the change of course was 'manifestly the first ebullition
of a settled party spirit'.[37] Hobhouse recorded the scene at Althorp's a few days later:

There were about 60 members there, . . . (many of) whom I had
not seen before. It seems they had been discussing about
forming a systematic opposition, and when I came in Coke and
others were congratulating the company upon the good old
times of Whiggism and party being likely to be restored under
the auspices of Lord Althorp.

More moderate heads than Coke were to prevail. The group agreed
that only if the administration met the new parliament without
additional strength would the Whigs engage in regular opposition.[38] But if Grey was now their declared leader, a unifying issue
had not yet emerged. Reform hovered in the background, but
there was little discussion of it, and certainly no pressing of the
point. Principles were nebulous. On 1 July, the day after Grey's
speech, *The Times* lamented the difficulty of designating principles
'by the names of those who pressed them. We cannot tell "who"
represents "what" '. Russell thought that Whigs would be 'firm
but moderate' when parliament met; if ministers behaved themselves, there would be 'no cause for regular opposition'. Grey left
town, but with no preconceived notions; he corresponded mainly
with his old ally Holland, heard nothing of what was going on,
and concluded there was little to know.[39]

Two months later, Grey prepared to return to London 'for good
or for bad'. 'It is a great sacrifice', he wrote, 'but I have no choice'.
It mattered little that Wellington had not offered him a post, for
events in the intervening weeks had rendered that superficial
alteration of the government meaningless. The issue on everyone's
lips was now Reform, and few doubted that the new parliament
could avoid some change in the system. The resurgence of this
question took place in July and August during the elections made
necessary by the accession of William IV. Although the ultra
Tories had flirted with Reform earlier in the year, there was far
from widespread acceptance by the governors that their house was
in need of re-ordering until the elections showed them otherwise.
The elections were not specifically contested on the question of

Reform, nor did anti-Reformers lose heavily to Reformers. The Reform question was not overwhelming and did not sweep the hustings. 'The most significant fact', wrote Professor Brock 'was less that so many people demanded Reform than that practically no one opposed it.'[40] In so far as Whigs went beyond traditional electoral influences to defeat Tories, they generally did so by campaigning against the government's incapacity and illiberality. Graham, for example, contrasted the Tory 'court' party which claimed Royal power and privilege with the Whig 'country' party which stood to uphold popular rights, feelings and happiness.[41] It would be wrong, too, to suggest that contests between Whigs and Tories were the dominant theme of these elections as they were in 1831. One of the most influential contests, in Yorkshire, was noteworthy as much for the pre-election dispute between Whig moderates and Brougham as it was for the polled results. This was by no means unusual. In the judgement of *The Times*, the main contest in the country was between the Tories and ultra Tories.[42]

Of far greater moment for the promotion of Reform among the traditional elite was the erosion of the aristocracy's deferential powers. The inability of the magnates to control elections in both borough and county seemed obvious to Brougham's secretary Le Marchant, who told Baring that the one great feature of the elections 'is that the small gentlemen and the independent farmers separate themselves from the aristocracy'.[43] Where there once had been no contests, there were now expensive struggles in which voters showed themselves less likely to follow their usual allegiances. Not only was bribery more difficult and expensive, but electors were urged by reformers to use their votes honestly rather than to give in to 'dishonest' influence. What Professor Perkin has described as the higher morality of the 'entrepreneurial ideal'[44] was clearly beginning to pay dividends for reformers, for through their attack on both patronage and corruption, and their unwillingness to distinguish between the two, the aristocracy began to doubt the value of a system that was giving way to uncontrollable anarchy.

Whig as well as Tory felt the protest. Not least affected were the Bedfords and Greys. At Bedford, where a member of the Russell family had been returned without contest for more than forty years, Lord John went down to what his father termed 'anti-aristocratical' feelings. Though it was reported before the poll that 'things look very promising',[45] his hastily organised political neophytes had little experience in predicting such a rude and sudden electoral awakening. Russell's defeat was an indication that aristocratic Whigs were no more immune from electoral protest than Tories. If any did not see that new truth in Bedford, they could not fail to do so in Yorkshire, where Brougham was put forward by Edward Baines of the *Leeds Mercury* in an attempt to show the landed aristocracy that squirarchical influence could no longer dominate the county. Brougham was an outsider; he was scarcely the sort to represent the Yorkshire landed interest. Charles Wood, Grey's son-in-law, opposed his candidacy at the adoption meeting, but the reluctance of the Whig magnates to oppose him with cash provided Brougham with an enormous victory. His election address was described as an 'ill conditioned fling at the Whigs', and he declared in an 'anonymous' pamphlet *The Result of the General Election* that 'the aristocracy has been taught a lesson.'[46] Grey could complain that the elections had turned Brougham's head, but the loss of prestige made Whigs realise that they could no longer straddle the Reform fence with impunity. Nor could they dally. Delays in settling the Catholic question, Grey knew, had given popular leaders an unnecessary power of mischief. The 'Bainesocracy of Leeds' had pointed out in a painful manner the urgency of regaining control of the system. If they wanted to recover popularity, the aristocracy could no longer delay reform by maintaining what Brock described as the 'ramshackle affair'.[47]

Most eyes were now on the Duke. Revolution in Paris and uprisings in Brussels made it important that the growing agitation for Reform be met with a positive response. Reports that the government had lost up to fifty seats in the elections[48] led most observers to doubt that Wellington's administration could stand without additional strength from among those who were now advocates of reform. Greville thought that if Wellington would open his doors, 'he might serve to himself a long and honourable possession of power'. The sentiment was shared by *The Times* and *Guardian*, both of which called for an accession of some individual Whigs.[49] Wellington seemed aware that some aid was necessary. He had asked Melbourne to join his government in July and hinted that a refusal might bring the ministry to an end. But he would not have the Whigs. The invitation to Melbourne was his response to the Whigs' declaration of hostility in parliament, but when Melbourne told him that he could not join without Grey, the offer was withdrawn. The Whig leader had been 'very hostile to him lately'.[50]

Wellington's offer to Melbourne was a shrewd attempt to save his administration by isolating the ultra Tories who had caused him the greatest embarrassment. Melbourne was no reformer and had served in a previous Tory ministry. If he could carry with him enough Canningites and Huskissonites, Wellington could continue without the ultras' support. The offer was also cynical, for Wellington had little liking for Melbourne or his supporters. When the invitation was rejected, the government carried out a vigorous electoral campaign against the Canningites and Huskissonites in order to have reliable supporters returned. The campaign was a failure, for most of these groups were returned to the Commons.[51] Nevertheless, Wellington was either bold or desperate enough to try his hand at union again. Huskisson's accidental death on 15 September made a renewed offer more attractive, for with this uncompromising government critic removed, his followers were thought more likely to support the administration. On 1 October, Wellington opened negotiations with Palmerston through Lord Clive. What the Duke did not know was that the Canningites and Huskissonites were now convinced, as were the Whig leaders, that the elections made reform an urgent necessity. Government influence turned loose against their interests during the elections made them favour a cleansing of the system that would put electoral arrangements out of ministerial reach. Melbourne and Palmerston were thus more naturally inclined towards the Whigs and had decided, before Wellington's overture to Palmerston, that a Tory offer would be rejected. Even if he gave them three or four positions, Melbourne told Brougham, the Duke would still be a 'dictator' who would follow his own notions.[52] When Wellington learned from Palmerston that neither he nor his colleagues would join an administration that did not include Whigs, negotiations were ended and Wellington was left to face the new parliament alone.[53]

By the end of October, the Whigs' position was settled. There had been some pressure from Brougham and Graham for a formal agreement with the Canningites, but public considerations, and a distrust of Brougham's taking Reform into his own hands, made this approach undesirable. Holland had learned from Melbourne and Palmerston that their group was disposed to co-operate 'without any positive engagement', and Althorp warned Brou-

gham that a premature agreement would give the public 'an
opportunity of saying that we were very moderate and mealy-
mouthed as long as there was a chance of the Duke taking us in
but that now we despair of this, we are becoming violent'.[54] It
seemed doubtful that Wellington would make such an offer,
although Russell had not yet given up on him,[55] and as the
meeting of parliament approached, the decision was made to give
Wellington the opportunity of bringing in his own plan of Reform.
If he would not, the Whigs were prepared to turn him out.[56]
Unlikely as the prospect of a Wellingtonian reform measure
appeared, it was not thought impossible. 'After all', Grey told
Holland, 'it would not be a more violent change than that which
we have witnessed on the Catholic question.' In September, the
Whigs learned from Wellesley, the Prime Minister's brother, that a
plan would in fact be introduced. Following the 'swing' riots in
the autumn, public speculation mounted; several rumours, 'much
believed' thought Holland, had it that Reform would be mentioned in the King's speech.[57]

But of course it was not. Grey's call on the Lords to avert the
'destruction of the Constitution' by reforming Parliament brought
Wellington's bold denial of all need for Reform. 'You have announced the fall of your government' Aberdeen told the Duke as
he took his seat.[58] Indeed he had. Although not more than twenty
members had come to Althorp's rooms in the Albany before
parliament assembled, more than two hundred were there on the
13th. It might be argued that much of the increased opposition
was a fact before parliament opened, but there were many whose
support of the Whigs was based on Wellington's statement.
Hobhouse declared that his opposition was determined by the
government's conduct, for he was no 'party politician'. The
Morning Chronicle reported other lesser known MPs who had come
to London planning to support Wellington and had changed their
minds after his declaration.[59] In September, Cleveland thought
there was 'no man so proper or desirable to be Premier' as
Wellington. Now, he was among a number of peers who went into
opposition, including Lord Bath who 'came to town intending to
leave his proxy with the Duke, and went away with it in his pocket
after hearing his famous speech'.[60] Aberdeen had been correct.
Wellington sealed the fate of his government. On the eve of the
statement, Graham told Brougham of the discussion, negotiation
and arrangement that would be necessary 'not only before we can

bring Palmerston and his friends into line in favour of Reform, but before you can meet the views and wishes of our own friends.' Within a few days, union of all in opposition was assured: on 6 November, the Canningites agreed to support a general reform motion; on the 15th, the ultra Tories joined.[61] The Duke's myopia was the source of the lime.

The one thing that can be said about the fall of the Tory government was that its wounds were self-inflicted. In the judgement of *The Times*, Wellington paid the consequences of not knowing the mood of the country when he made his reform statement: 'None but the willfully blind want, at this time of day, reasons for reform.' The *Manchester Guardian* concurred; the ministry's end came, it wrote, 'chiefly through the inability of its leader to comprehend, or his indisposition to follow, the signs of the times'.[62] An alternative view had the Whigs plotting an overthrow for their own political ends. Before the year was out, the radical tailor Francis Place wrote that the Whigs proposed reform because there was 'no other means' of gaining power, a view shared by Dr. Southgate, who noted the 'brute fact' that the Whigs obtained and retained power by reforming the House of Commons.[63] Professor Flick argued that Wellington's downfall was determined by July 1830, when a more forceful Grey was looking only for an issue. By October, the Whigs 'made it clear that they were more determined than ever to overthrow the Duke in November, and that they were definitely considering an advocacy of parliamentary reform as a principle means of accomplishing their goal'. More recently, Professor Clive described the Whigs as desperately hoping to get back into office by taking up the question of reform because of its popularity: 'The Whigs saw it as the master key to political power.'[64]

Such a view fails to take notice of two important considerations. In the first place, the Whigs took up Reform because their own view of the political system convinced them that it was necessary. Otherwise, Melbourne later told Russell, it would have been 'the *foolishest* thing ever done'. To have carried on with an unreformed parliament was to threaten the maintenance of the territorial magnates of all parties, and though the views of the new government were varied, the Whigs thought for the most part like Holland. 'I never was a keen *reformer*', he told his son, 'but I think reform now absolutely inevitable, and I am sure that if it be so, the sooner it is done, the better.'[65] Secondly, the Whigs were quite prepared to support a Wellingtonian measure. 'I certainly shall support a [Tory] proposal for Parliamentary Reform', Grey told Princess Lieven in October, and in this determination he was supported by most of his party.[66] Russell told Holland on 18 October that 'if members keep at peace, propose reform and reduce the civil list, I apprehend I shall give few votes in opposition before Xmas'. Two days later he asked Ebrington to consider moving an address to the King to strengthen the basis of Wellington's administration, which, if it were to admit Grey and Althorp, could hold on to office. And only a few hours before Wellington's statement, Althorp told the Commons what had been worked out at his home a few days earlier: if the government would bring forward measures 'such as I can conscientiously approve of, they shall have my best support . . . and I believe . . . of those who usually act with me'.[67]

Wellington had the ball in his court but could not take it, opposed as he was to even moderate reform. Perhaps he thought that a strong denial of any need for change would guarantee a parliamentary majority by regaining the support of the ultra Tories. He claimed later that he had reason to believe they were beginning to take alarm at Reform, and his Treasury estimates showed a Tory majority of between 72 and 114.[68] There is no reason to suppose that the Treasury list was incorrect as far as it went, for the government's later defeat was partly to blame on his speech of 2 November. His mistake was in thinking that the ultra Tories would not support Reform. Their leaders were convinced by the agricultural revolts that a measure was essential 'to win back the respect and confidence of the people'.[69] But his greatest mistake by far was in thinking that the demand for Reform was ephemeral and would pass away without his support.[70] By arguing for the *status quo*, the Duke created a self-fulfilling prophecy in reverse. His statement gave a spark to the cause of Reform that frightened the most determined defender of the old system into conceding reform. 'We did not cause the excitement', Grey wrote to the King's secretary in March 1831. 'We found it to be in full vigour when we came into office; and the King told me that everyone of the King's late Ministers, except the Duke of Wellington, when they took leave of him, acknowledge that some Reform was necessary.'[71] It was the speech in the Lords that brought the government down, not the Whigs. *The Times*, which on 4 November predicted that Wellington's declaration would probably attach to his administration some of the high Tories, admitted on the 22nd that he was defeated by a change in public opinion which was unprecedentedly absolute and sudden, and 'produced by his own words'.

Although the Duke's resignation was followed by rumours that both Richmond and Anglesey were called to the closet, it was obvious to all that, as Baring wrote to his wife, 'it signifies nothing whom they send for – they must come to Lord Grey'.[72] Forty years in opposition left the new Prime Minister with a great deal of reticence. He had wondered in August 'who would wish to take their [Tory] places'? Now, with office in hand, he confided to Princess Lieven more cause for 'doubt and apprehension than for triumph', feeling 'appalled at the difficulties' surrounding him.[73] The great difficulty was to pass a measure of reform through a lukewarm Commons and a hostile Lords. In order to accomplish this task, Grey chose an aristocratic body of men 'to show that in these days of democracy and Jacobinism that it is possible to find real capacity in the high aristocracy . . . that class is a guarantee for the security of the State and the Throne.'[74] His cabinet of thirteen included only two, Charles Grant and Brougham, who were not family of peers and baronets. Of the four not in the Lords, Althorp was heir to the earldom of Spencer, Palmerston was an Irish peer, Graham a baronet and Grant a great landowner. Two weeks after Hobhouse noted that 'the potentates begin to tremble for their acres', Grey was head of the most aristocratic cabinet of the century, one said to have 'represented a larger acreage than any of its predecessors.'[75] It was, as well, a cabinet of connections. Grey's family took seven places.[76] Lansdowne, Richmond and Holland were cousins. The Spencers were represented by Althorp, Carlisle and Devonshire, all three of whom were first cousins to Duncannon and his sister, Melbourne's wife. Palmerston was not yet married to his mistress, Melbourne's sister, and Duncannon, like Grey's wife, belonged to the Ponsonby family. Goderich was the outsider; he could claim only to have been in Althorp's form at Harrow.[77] The Whigs were indeed all cousins. In 1818, 51 of the 113 MPs who signed a requisition pressing Tierney to be Whig leader were related to each other; the list included three sets of father and sons and seven sets of brothers.[78] This state of affairs is scarcely surprising, for it would have taken a determined young man to have otherwise joined the Whigs in their perpetual condition of opposition. Still, it rankled. Hobhouse heard complaints at Brooks's of the family party in the administration, which perhaps explains the cabinet's reluctance to frequent the club; Macaulay confessed that it required 'not a little courage to represent the Whigs . . . as deaf to the claims of private interest and family connection'.[79] It was pedigree, of course, which would be counted on to provide safety through moderation.

Whig notions of parliamentary reform were diverse and, as was recently suggested, 'cannot be compressed into a single, internally consistent theory'.[80] Some, like Grey, Brougham, Althorp, Holland and Russell, had been reformers for a number of years, and although their advocacy of Reform had never been consistent, their views were in many ways dissimilar from those of Melbourne, Palmerston or Richmond, who had never much cared for the question. Needless to say, each had his own conception of what was necessary and of what to expect from a bill. On the other hand, any government brought to life on the issue of Reform that sat Brougham and Durham at the same table as Richmond and Lansdowne knew that it was not mixing water with fire. By its very nature, the old system produced parliamentarians who shared a similar general outlook. Reformers assumed that the system was in need of repair, but apart from the radical politicians whose influence the bill tried to minimise, none questioned the basic premise of a system of community representation based on deference. The terms of the bill were drafted and settled upon with little rancor. Indeed Durham, usually considered the most liberal reformer in the cabinet, had suggested that Richmond, among the most conservative, be a member of the committee that drew up the bill.[81] One finds fewer accounts of the drafting of the measure and the government's discussion of its features than of any other major topic of the period. The absence of such source material does not in itself, of course, make a case for harmony, but when the Whig propensity to snipe on almost every other issue is considered, the comparison is striking. Obstructionism in the Lords caused considerable debate and dissension over the tactics of passing the bill, but when the events from November 1830 to May 1832 are viewed as a whole, the impression left is of a government in essential agreement on what was to constitute reform of parliament.

There was much room for common ground among ministers. All could agree that Reform was not based on an abstract theory of political rights. Macaulay might argue in the Commons that the bill was part of an historical continuity that began with Magna

Carta, but hegelian descriptions of this sort meant little to ministers, if to him; it is not mere chance that this 'Whig interpretation' has been put by his biographer in a chapter titled 'Oratory'.[82]
The Whigs found themselves proposing Reform not because
speculative logic dictated a measure, but because circumstances
made it necessary. Holland, the most notable adherent to Whig
mythology, drew from his understanding of history the need to
limit Crown authority and executive interference in the affairs of
the Commons. But he had written in 1817 of 'This cursed business
of Reform', and his aside to Hobhouse, that 'the time was come
and it must be done' had a ring of resignation about it. So too has
Melbourne's confession to Queen Victoria that 'I wasn't much for
it, I saw it as unavoidable'.[83] Macaulay's threat to property played
as great a role in 1688 as the threat to liberty. In 1819 Russell
scorned the 'wild and visionary theorists' who called for annual
parliaments and universal suffrage. His language reflected the
general view that theory was best left to democrats and jacobins.
Melbourne's later remark that Grey thought the bill 'just a measure
to satisfy the people at the moment, and nothing more' belies
perhaps his own thoughts more than Grey's, but when Grey made
his first speech on the subject as Prime Minister, his reference to a
'happy medium' suggested a practical rather than philosophical
approach to the problem.[84] The closest that the Whigs came to
theory was their belief that power was the preserve of property
and intelligence, the basis of all representation. But their views of
this principle were shaped more by their own historical perceptions of what Russell termed 'good government' than by abstract
speculation.[85]

Public opinion had made reform necessary. Russell, whose
belief in the need for reform had little to do with the wider public
attitude, was nevertheless unwilling to push the question without
widespread support. In 1827 he opposed a measure because of 'a
great lukewarmness on that subject throughout the country'. Grey
had said as much to the Lords in 1810: 'Until this country shall
have expressed its opinion, the examples of the other nations of
Europe should deter us from any precipitate attempt to hurry . . .
a measure.'[86] Now, public demand allowed the committed reformers to put long-held views into practice. Latecomers to
reform, on the other hand, came to accept the notion not because
their views of the system led to no other conclusion; the force of
that public opinion alone persuaded them that change was necess-

ary. Melbourne, for example, was brought in for Peterborough in 1816 by Lord Fitzwilliam to oppose Reform, but he admitted at the time that though he thought it unnecessary, 'if the people should ever become seriously and perseveringly desirous of it, I should think it my duty to support it'.[87]

The Tory contention that the Whigs legislated out of fear does not stand up to scrutiny. The Tory view was supported by Professor Hamburger, who argued that the Whigs' desire to avoid revolution at any cost made them vulnerable to James Mill and the philosophic radicals' policy of threatening revolution in order to frighten them.[88] Melbourne's argument in the Lords, 'that there must come a time when both the legislative and executive powers must yield to the popular voice or be annihilated', could be used to give credence to this theory. So too could Macaulay's defence of an 'honourable' appeal to fear that recalled the French aristocracy's resistance to reform in 1783 which led to 1789: 'They would not endure Turgot; and they had to endure Robespierre.'[89] But it was one thing to use what the Tory Lord Sandon termed arguments '*ad terrorem*' against aristocrats with less sense than Melbourne, and quite another to be guided by it. Like all Whigs, Melbourne's use of the word 'people' meant, as he told Russell, 'the majority of all its inhabitants who form any opinion upon politics . . . one class of people excluding many other classes'. To put a finer point on it, he spoke somewhat disparagingly in 1836 of 'our boasted middle class', that part of the political nation whose influence had predominated in 1830.[90] It was not fear of revolt which activated the Whigs in 1830, for the middle classes were not revolutionary. Rather, it was the realisation that the middle class could, in the future, be called forth to revolt as they had done in France and Belgium. 'If the great mass of the middle class are bent upon that method of enforcing their views', Holland told Grey, 'there is not in the nature of society any real force that can prevent them.' Grey concurred. 'A great change has taken place' he told the Knight of Kerry[91]

in all parts of Europe since the end of the war in the distribution of property, and unless a corresponding change be made in the legal mode by which that property can act upon the governments, revolutions must necessarily follow. The change requires a greater influence to be yielded to the middle classes, who have made wonderful advances both in property and intelligence.

There is an awareness of the dynamics of social change and of the need for government to reflect shifts in the social structure in such statements, an awareness moreover that squares with the 'dysfunction' which the political sociologist regards as a pre-condition of revolution. The Whigs broached the question with calm, clear minds. The 'principle' of his bill, Grey told the Lords, was to 'prevent the necessity of revolution',[92] an entirely different matter from acting out of fear of imminent revolt.

It is difficult not to see in this attitude a concessionary impulse. Professor D. C. Moore has argued that Reform was not a concession as much as a cure. He is correct in seeing a curative element in the act insofar as there was concern about an increasing urban penetration of the county communities which threatened the local pre-eminence of the landed interest. Indeed, Althorp stated in the Commons that the purpose of the original clause 18, which took away the borough voter's right to a county franchise, was to ensure that 'the county constituency should not be overpowered by the inhabitants of the towns.'[93] But it cannot be held that this cure of the counties was the primary motive for the bill. As soon as he was faced with opposition to the clause, Althorp abandoned it. Enfranchising the middle classes, on the other hand, was a well thought-out concession to the new property-holders. Melbourne's observation – 'I don't like the middle classes . . . I like what is tranquil and stable',[94] doubtless expressed the innermost thoughts of the territorial magnates, but it thereby expresses as well the concessionary nature of the bill. It might be more to the point to argue that the middle class franchise was *the* curative element in the bill. Once settled with the franchise, men of substance would reduce the prospect of popular discontent and disorder by allying themselves with the aristocracy rather than the lower classes. 'Sufficient property', Durham said, would ensure their 'independence from the mob'. A modern critic has described this reasoning as a cynical attempt by the aristocratic order of 'old Corruption' to buttress itself against the people by keeping the gentry and industrial middle classes 'in good humour'.[95] But such was the nature of nineteenth century thought that what might today be thought of as social insularity was regarded in 1830 as the essence of good government. Francis Jeffrey, who drew up the bill for Scotland, was as forthright as unequivocal on the curative nature of the Whig concession: 'any plan must be objectionable', he wrote to Russell,[96] which, by keeping the Franchise very high and exclusive, fails to give satisfaction to the middle and respectable ranks of society, and drives them to a union founded on dissatisfaction with the lower orders. It is of the utmost importance to associate the middle with the higher orders of society in the love and support of the institutions and government of the country.

It is one thing to argue that middle class pressure brought about a middle class franchise, and quite another to conclude that the measure was designed 'to diminish the power of the gentry and to transfer the predominant authority to the middle classes'.[97] In 1898, when Dicey gave this opinion, and by which time the middle classes had assumed the authority that the 1832 Act apparently held out to them, it might have seemed logical to assume that the pressure which caused the Whigs to reform parliament prompted them 'to transfer predominant authority' to the class which produced the demand. The 'Whig interpretation' that Dicey's opinion gave rise to was a result of the logical error of confusing causality with aims. An overreliance on Macaulay's writing and speeches compounds the error. His basic notion, expressed in 1829 as 'our fervent wish . . . that we may see such a reform in the House of Commons as may render its votes the express opinion of the middle orders of Britain', was one that most Whigs could not accept. Althorp recalled in 1841 that he alone had wanted 'to throw more weight into the manufacturing and commercial scale', but his was a voice in the wilderness.[98] Possession of property led to the belief that the middle classes could be relied on to respect rank and property. 'Neither warped by interest nor obscured by passion',[99] they had a mark of respectability which Whiggery felt it could trust. The £10 franchise, Stanley explained, would be given to 'such persons as might safely exercise it with advantage to themselves and to the existing institutions of the country'; it would lend to the constitution what Melbourne described as 'authority, consent, reputation and opinion'.[100]

It was not the intention that the ten-pounder would inundate parliament with middle class ideology. Apart from the oft-forgotten consideration that the middle classes were too busy getting on with industry and commerce to take the step of getting a seat, it was not obvious that the bill would provide them with easier access. The *Edinburgh Review* expected the new Commons to be influenced by 'the middle classes as well as the upper'; the more utilitarian *Westminster Review* reasoned that the landed interest must always exercise the greater sway in public affiars, 'for that class alone have much leisure to meddle in them'.[10] Commercial centres like Liverpool, Newcastle or Hull, Grey reminded the Lords, had always returned persons 'connected with these places by great possessions in the neighbourhood'; a wider franchise would not necessarily alter that pattern. Thos. Attwood, in fact, noted that commercial men had usually been returned by close boroughs rather than industrial towns, and predicted in the Commons that the abolition of close boroughs would result in less representation of the commercial interests.[102] Support for his argument came from *A Letter to Lord John Russell on the Reform Bill*, published anonymously in 1831: of the 39 merchants sitting for boroughs, the bill would unseat 16; 4 of the 10 members of the West Indian interest would be displaced, as would 10 of the 20 connected with the East Indian and Asiatic empire, 14 of 31 city and country bankers, 2 shipowners and 2 manufacturers. Woolley's study of the first reformed parliament shows that Attwood's prediction was not far off. Less than half of the members returned for new boroughs were manufacturers, merchants or bankers, the total number of which ('somewhere in the region of seventy') was less than in 1831 and no more than of lawyers.[103] Attwood feared that the people were 'essentially aristocratic and imbued with respect for their superiors and hatred of their neighbours raised by accident above themselves.'[104] It was on this middle class deference that the Whigs, on the other hand, relied. Woolley's conclusion, that the middle classes when given the franchise 'preferred to remain faithful to the old aristocratic Connexions', was one that Whiggery would have expected.

In the sense that Reform was intended to restore to the landed interest that influence which Palmerston thought 'indispensible to the safety and prosperity of the country', the bill was, as Moore suggested, curative rather than concessionary. In February 1831, Melbourne complained of O'Connell's meddling in all elections and places 'where he has no property or natural connection'; it was this very interference that the Bill was meant to reduce.[105] The Whigs regarded their measure as 'conservative'[106] not because it fell short of radical principles, but because it was meant to strengthen aristocratic influence. Grey knew that if the terms of the bill were considered carefully by those magnates who recoiled at all thought of Reform, the less it would be found to prejudice the 'real interests' of the aristocracy. Grey referred, presumably, to the government's preference for the representation of interests over population which favoured country to town. Apart from the 65 extra seats given to the county constituency, 73 borough seats, each with a registration in 1833 of less than 500 electors, were little more than nomination boroughs. Several large towns were unrepresented, and as many smaller ones were left with one or two members.[107] 'We overdid it' remarked Russell in 1837 when he saw the overrepresented and less populous agricultural south turning against the Whigs. But it could not be said that he had done it blindly. When pressed during debate in 1831 to explain the disproportionate weighting of redistribution, he declared of ministers that 'anomalies they found . . . and anomalies they meant to leave'. Althorp, too, knew that the landed interest was the great gainer from the bill; measures like corn law repeal, he told Brougham later, would be delayed as a result.[108]

A bill that was to restore aristocratic power by taking from the landed interest its influence in a large number of close boroughs was a paradox that would cause considerable perplexity among its opponents. In order to make their point, the Whig leaders distinguished between due and undue influence. 'Wherever the aristocracy reside', Russell declared in his introductory speech,[109]

> receiving large incomes, performing important duties, relieving the poor by charity, and evincing private wealth and public virtue, it is not in human nature that they should not possess a great influence upon public opinion, and have an equal weight in electing persons to serve their country in Parliament . . . But if by aristocracy those persons are meant who do not live among the people, who know nothing of the people, and who care nothing for them – who seek honours without merit, places without duty, and pensions without service – for such an aristocracy I have no sympathy; and I think the sooner its influence is carried away with the corruption on which it has thriven, the better for the country, in which it has repressed so long every wholesome and invigorating influence.

Perhaps Lord John was thinking of the lord mentioned in his memoirs, who when asked to suggest a nominee for one of his boroughs, returned a waiter from White's Club.[110] But with fifty-six English boroughs alone having fewer than fifty electors apiece, none needed prodding by example. The moral benefit of cleansing the nomination boroughs of undeserved influence was obvious. Giving up their influence in sixty-five old boroughs would secure the aristocracy's legitimacy and property, Grey instructed his fellow peers – 'nothing is taken away but the odious power possessed by the few.'[111]

That aristocratic influence was not expected to disappear can be gauged from Althorp's reaction to the news that his Northampton-shire seat would be contested by an outsider at the first reformed election. Thinking that the Whig–Tory arrangement in the county had ensured a split return without a contest, he complained to his father that the entry of another candidate compelled him to go to 'an absurd expense because some wrong-headed people choose it and insist upon dragging me into it against all reason and common sense.'[112] Lord Euston, an interloper with no prospect of prevailing against the Spencer influence, soon retired from the field, but Althorp's irritation at the prospect of an unnecessary and expensive election is revealing. Trevelyan might uphold the Whig mythology of his forebear Macaulay by stating that only Grey's aristocratic party was capable of 'peacefully handing over the power of the aristocracy to the middle classes', but the more recent conclusion of another historian, that the bill 'did not hand over power to the middle classes because it was not intended to',[113] is a more satisfactory explanation of the magnates' attempt to main-tain the territorial aristocracy in greatness. The bill was thorough, far more so at least than many observers had expected, but it was not designed to relinquish aristocratic authority. Why it was so far reaching, and the effects on a surprisingly weak government of the resultant struggle to carry the measure, form the purpose of the next chapter.

4
Whiggery and the Bill

When our administration was formed in 1830, it was clear it could
not have stood without the reform bill, which gave us a transient,
phrenetic and epileptic strength.

Melbourne to Brougham, 1835[1]

the bill at last must be carried by force and fear, not from
conviction or affection.

Althorp, November 1831[2]

What had once been an intellectual exercise became the stuff of
political reality in the autumn of 1830. Whig notions of reform
could no longer be confined to the abstract. Government was now
at hand, brought to life in order to transform into legislation what
had hitherto been little more than speculation on how the system
might be improved. Surprisingly little time was required. It is
likely, in fact, that more experienced ministers might have foreseen the storm of criticism which attended the introduction of the
bill, and might have taken more time to prepare an issue of such
importance. Grey, however, in pressing for an extensive measure,
allowed his judgement to be influenced by both haste and
optimism. His policy would threaten both Reform and the political
future of Whiggery itself. Within a few months of taking office, it
became evident not only that the Whigs' parliamentary position
was terribly weak, but that Grey was able to control his government with only the greatest difficulty, that the King's support
which made office first possible was unlikely to continue, and
most ominously, that the juxtaposition of electoral forces which
created a Whig government was evidently temporary. Reform
might triumph, but it was far from clear that Whiggery could
survive the struggle necessary for that triumph, or that Toryism
could not.

There can be little doubt that the impetus for a thorough
measure of Reform came from Grey, who was convinced that delay

would be dangerous. Conditions out of doors required an extensive measure; a problem with a social origin could not be addressed by nibbling. The public outcry that followed Wellington's speech and the manifestation of anti-aristocratic activity at bye-elections held since November produced what Lansdowne termed 'a hot pit' on the subject of Reform and added to the government's view that without a substantial alteration of the system, social disintegration could not be far off.[3] Within a week of the Duke's statement, the Prime Minister was convinced that taking one seat from each rotten borough would not be enough; by the time that his government was formed and a committee set up to prepare a plan for the cabinet's consideration, he had put an outline together for the committee to consider.[4] Without the moderating constraints that politicians feel as they approach office, Grey was now able to give fresh airing to views that went back to the days of his Friends of the People. He put 'Radical Jack' Durham in charge of the committee that was to prepare a plan for the cabinet, and impressed on Russell, the author of most of that draft, his conviction that none but a large measure would do.[5] The Irish demagoguery that followed the delay in granting Catholic emancipation had impressed on the Whigs the need for haste if the Cobbetts and Hunts in England were not to be given the opportunity to make use of agitation for their democratic ends.[6]

A system that resisted change for four centuries was thus to be dismantled in the space of a few weeks. This urgency presented little problem for Durham, Russell, Graham and Duncannon, who like Lenin in exile had given the subject a great deal of thought. The committee began its work in December; by 15 January a plan 'large enough to satisfy public opinion . . . yet . . . to run no risk of overthrowing the form of government' was before the cabinet.[7] It was, Graham thought, 'on the whole' well received, 'Brougham alone dissentient and disposed to carp by raising little points when he could.'[8] Piqued by his failure to have the Mastership of the Rolls, the Lord Chancellor felt further slighted when left off Durham's committee. Cabinet discussion of the bill provided him the chance to vent his spleen. So strenuously did he maintain a ludicrous defence of the close boroughs – there would be no seat left for 'a clever young lawyer' – that Grey thought the King might be tempted to resist disfranchisement.[9] But apart from Lansdowne, who thought that the plan went 'rather beyond than short of what **is expected**',[10] reaction was generally favourable. Dur-

1am's radicalism did not cause the trouble with his more conservative colleagues that it might have done. His suggestion of quinquennial parliaments and ballot had been accepted by the committee on the condition that the borough qualification be raised to £20 from £10. None of these proposals found much favour in the cabinet and were quickly dropped. Durham, tempered by illness, was not up to a row. He told Grey to alter the bill as he pleased and admitted to Brougham that he preferred the lower qualification to ballot.[11] His absence from cabinet meetings due to ill health no doubt facilitated some calm as well. On 30 January, with the principles of the bill settled, Grey delivered the proposals to the King and was able to report 'his complete and cordial consent'.[12] The Prime Minister had much cause for satisfaction. The bold measure which he knew to be necessary had passed an important hurdle. Grey's fright at Brougham's obstreperous conduct pointed out his vulnerability to a cabinet split. The willingness of his colleagues to set aside individual preferences for the good of a commonly agreed plan augured well for its prospects.

Monarchical acceptance of the government plan was based on an assurance from Grey that the bill would pass through parliament if blessed with the King's consent. Early in February, Grey twice repeated to the King his opinion that there was not much to be feared.[13] It might be regarded as naiveté or wishful thinking on the part of Grey to suggest that a plan as extensive as his would pass unchallenged through an aristocratic parliament, but there is no doubt that he thought it would. The force of logic that led him to think that the bill would save the aristocracy would surely not fail to work on his fellow peers and their connections in the Commons. Although the radical leader Joseph Hume warned Althorp in January that a dissolution of parliament for what he assumed would be a moderate measure would at the very least be necessary,[14] Grey chose to rely on reports that trickled through of Tory support. Grey did not knowingly mislead the King. His insistence that the bill would pass, despite rumours that Tory support was premised on the expectation of a moderate plan,[15] suggests that he was given to self-deception. The Treasury whips might have given him unsubstantiated evidence that an extensive measure would succeed in order to prevent its substitution by a weaker measure before it was introduced. It is also conceivable that cabinet secrecy prevented whips from knowing the extent of the measure, and that they based their predicted majority of seventy on the expected reception of a moderate measure.[16] The most likely explanation of Grey's optimism was his knowledge that no government could replace his as long as Reform remained undecided. Although Princess Lieven warned him that his friends and adversaries both agreed that he had 'no party whatever' and was 'at the mercy of any temporary coalition' that could upset him 'any day',[17] it would not have been unreasonable to brush aside such comment and assume that the Whigs could not be replaced. Defeat on Reform could not fail to provoke a damaging crisis and a more democratic measure; on the good sense of his opponents would hinge the success of his measure.

It could not be doubted that until Reform was introduced, the Whigs had cut a sorry figure in the Commons and that Princess Lieven's view of the government's parliamentary strength was correct. On 11 February, two days after her letter to Grey, Althorp introduced his first budget, which according to Hobhouse, was so 'universally decried' that the government could not have stayed in office were it not for their anticipated reform of parliament.[18] The budget was a clear expression of Althorp's doctrinaire and somewhat Parnellite economic views. But by introducing changes in commercial policy which upset colonial interests, by proposing new taxes which alarmed holders of landed and funded property, and by failing to reduce the size of the increasingly unpopular civil list, the Ministry provided the opposition forces a ready issue with which to weaken their new government.[19] Radicals and ultra Tories who sympathised with Reform initiatives joined in the attack on the budget measures which were eventually amended and chopped beyond recognition. Inexperience as governors had led to what was in essence a coalition ministry, built on a single issue, to tempt its political fates by this uncautious introduction of economic theory for which there was neither known nor assumed widespread support. The cold reality of politics triumphed over the euphoria of newly-held office. This 'unfortunate' position was described by Baring:[20]

Scarcely a debate without a blunder, or rather some dissatisfaction. Our Civil List was not defended, though certainly defensible without difficulty. Our budget was knocked to pieces without a blow, and our new taxes changed and patched . . . Palmerston makes an unfortunate speech on going into army estimates . . . Peel laughs at him and is unpunished.

A sullied Althorp refused to resign as some suggested, thinking of the obvious dangers that such a course would unleash among those expecting a reform of parliament. Grey's lack of interest in financial affairs had not prepared him for the strength of feeling evoked by the budget; 'how much preferable is the life of a dog to that of a Minister', he wrote.[21] He remained nevertheless undaunted, knowing that the reception which Reform received would be the real test of his ministry.

The boldness of the measure caused a sensation when introduced on March 1. Russell's seemingly perverse disregard for opposition alarm – 'More yet' he smiled after Schedule A had been greeted with astonishment[22] – was obviously premised on the belief that the bill would pass. It was soon unfortunately clear that the Whigs were mistaken; a collision with the forces opposed to reform could not be avoided, an encounter that would strain government unity and weaken the Whigs' political standing with both King and country. It was not only Tories like Ellenborough, who wondered if ministers had not wanted 'to be beat upon Reform and so to go out', who saw little future for the bill. Hobhouse and Burdett, the Westminister radicals, thought that 'a Revolution would be the consequence' of the certain failure.[23] Le Marchant recorded 'the astonishment' which would likely have given Peel a large majority had he chosen to divide the house at that 'crucial moment'; several 'staunch Reformers' whom he spoke to were 'found to be wavering'.[24] Thus, despite the newly-won support from sceptics like Hobhouse,[25] Hume and O'Connell, and Greville's view that although 'the other day nobody would hear the possibility of it, now everybody is beginning to think it will be carried',[26] prospects were weak. Stanley doubted Ellice's reckoning of a majority of sixty-seven; 'entre nous', he wrote to Anglesey in Ireland, 'I must doubt its success in the house'.[27] When Althorp's budget proposal to alter the preferentially lower duty on colonial timber was defeated on 18 March, any confidence ministers had was shattered. Grey had twice declared in the House of Lords against modifications designed to encourage moderate Tory support; within a day of the timber defeat, he began to prepare the King for dissolution and an appeal to the country.[28]

At first glance, the elections of 1831 augured nothing but good for the future of Whiggery. Holland was jubilant on the eve of elections. 'Le vin est tiré', he wrote to Grey; 'il faut le boire'.[29] And indeed Reform did triumph. The bill, the Whigs knew, must now pass through the Commons with ease; the Lords could not fail to respect the wish of King and people. Timely and moderate reform of the system would re-establish popular support for property and the institutions of the country. But such, of course, was not to be an accurate description of what followed. Before Reform received Royal assent, turmoil both in and out of doors threatened the very peace and security which Reform was meant to restore. In many respects, the elections, and the political agitation which followed, could not be regarded as a Whig triumph. In several ways, the 1831 elections revealed the political problems facing Whiggery.

First, the very request that parliament be dissolved brought to an end the King's unconditional support for his Whig government. Unlike his brother George IV, William had more sympathy for Whigs than for ultra Tories; he had, as Duke of Clarence, sat among the Whig peers in the House of Lords. Grey's assurance that Reform would pass through parliament with little difficulty encouraged the King's belief that the measure was supported by the respectable landed classes, and that the Whigs were in touch with the feeling of the nation. He believed that Reform would be welcomed by responsible Whigs and Tories alike, and indeed, thought that the Tories might have introduced a measure in 1830 but for that 'cunning old rascal Elton . . . and that abominable fellow the Duke of Cumberland who . . . ought to be ashamed of himself.'[30] Suggestions of dissolution therefore came as a great surprise and a cause for alarm. Was the bill perhaps not widely supported as Grey suggested it was? The King's great worry was the risk of demagoguery and electoral disorder throughout the Kingdom. He explained this 'final and conclusive' objection to elections when Grey had Taylor sound him out in March, but consented in the end from the fear that refusal would provoke even more damaging agitation.[31] The elections, in William's view, served to confirm his suspicion that Reform was not the desire of respectable landed society. He told Princess Lieven that the judgement of the clerics of the universities should be considered 'as the touchstone of the saner portions of his subjects'; when they returned anti-Bill men, he became uneasy. It was his view that the popular feeling which produced intimidation and demagoguery was artificial, and to have bowed to this pressure he regarded as a mark of weakness. Rather than support the Whigs' bill, he turned his attention to arranging a narrower measure that would be acceptable to what he viewed as 'respectable' popular opinion.[32]

He stood by the government during the summer while the bill was debated in the Commons, but as bye-election losses mounted and the Lords argued the case against the need for this reform, his own belief in the necessity of a Whig government waned.

A second problem exhibited during the elections was the difficulty in persuading Whigs of the need to organise, a problem which was believed to cause substantial electoral damage in succeeding elections. Apart from the efforts of Treasury officials to raise what money it could for needy candidates, Whig central electoral organisation was almost non-existent. Ellice, the Treasury Secretary, subscribed from the wealthy at Brooks' and the Travellers and within a day of the dissolution had pledges nearing £15,000.[33] Of the total amount, which approached almost double the first day's figure, Cleveland was responsible for £12,500, Devonshire for £1,200, Melbourne and Strafford for £1,000 each. Duncannon manged to collect £1,275, but Durham, Russell and Lansdowne only £100 apiece and E. J. Stanley £50.[34] Reports that Northumberland would subscribe £100,000 for the Tories and Faversham his whole fortune[35] seemed exaggerated, but the general trend was clear enough. Unlike the Tories, whose Charles Street committee provided for a sizeable surplus after the elections were over,[36] the Whigs' central electoral officials were faced with a chronic shortage of money. In contrast to the following three general elections, it is doubtful that the lack of central organisation did the government much harm in 1831. Registration drives were yet to come, and Tory money proved in these exceptional elections unable to overcome the physical and political suasion of Reform. Northumberland's fortune was not enough to prevent his candidate from being forced to retire from the contest ; Gascoyne, who reputedly paid up to £100 per vote in Liverpool, was unable to overcome the Reformer's advantage.[37] It required not a little courage to oppose with one's fortune a measure that seemed all but through, particularly when the early returns suggested a clear victory for Reform.[38] Ellice was able to buy the four Holmes' boroughs on the Isle of Wight with a £4,000 contribution from Lord Yarborough. Le Marchant, Brougham's secretary, reported 'several' bought this way. In several cases, funds were used to pay anti-Reform candidates not to compete.[39] Yet reform was an issue that required comparatively little money. The new parliament would be little more than a constituent assembly which would dissolve itself once its task was complete. It was thus a wise magnate who left the running to the obvious winner and held his funds in preparation for the race that would come when traditional influences would not be so obviously set aside. 'None but a madman', predicted *The Times* on 2 March, would repurchase their seats. Only eleven county elections were contested, a gain of two from 1830,[40] and the general impression is one of Tory reluctance to enter the fray.

This retreat of the anti-Reform forces provided the Whigs with a victory more apparent than real. The elections were to a great extent an aberration. There was much to suggest that the government's victory was not, in fact, more than a temporary rejection of Toryism. Tories, like several lukewarm Whigs, were powerless to stop the swelling tide in favour of Reform, but there was little evidence that the anti-aristocratical mood would be permanent. 'The feeling of the country', wrote Sir Francis Baring from Hampshire,

> was wholesome, very loyal and very aristocratical, though they for that one time threw aside the Tory members. My personal impression is that the first, or perhaps the second, reformed House will be very country-gentleman.[41]

Baring's account was prophetic. Hampshire south was back in Tory hands in 1835; by 1847 the northern division was returned to the protectionists. Tories were not automatically the natural party of the landed magnates, but the Hampshire experience points out the advantage that fifty years of office had given the Tory party where the normally local influences prevailed. The Whigs, as a party, could take little succour at the results when viewed in this light. Local county influences were to be strengthened by Reform, and these were influences which were not necessarily Whig. Public enthusiasm for its authors was to provide an extraordinary victory in the first reformed elections, but by 1835 few were willing to vote Whig in gratitude for Reform. Local alliances which defeated the Tories in 1830 in many instances scarcely survived the fall of Wellington's government. Lost or uncontested seats were quickly re-established by local Tories who, for example, returned anti-Reformers in seven of the first nine bye-elections held after the 1831 elections.[42] Graham might despair that the Whigs' opponents would gather courage 'from a miscalculation of the real state of public feeling',[43] but in the eyes of both King and

Tory organisers, opportunities did exist to dish the Whigs. Accounts of a Tory demise were greatly exaggerated.

The agitation aroused during the elections, and continued throughout the succeeding parliamentary history of the Reform bill, shattered ministerial unity. Grey's leadership was in the process undeniably and irrevocably weakened, a problem which would test his own resolve to continue in office and impair the Whigs' authority until Melbourne would re-establish unity in 1835. The difficulty of maintaining the coalition of forces which constituted the government had been recognised from the beginning. Wellington's government had been turned out by a number of groups that could not on their own have commanded a majority in the Commons, and though there was a common conviction that the continuation of Wellington's government would be a danger, this conviction was not the stuff on which to build a party. Grey's choice of Althorp to lead the Commons was an important step in forging a consensus among the disjointed phalanx of members being asked to support the new ministry. Althorp's popularity had risen since his group was formed in the spring, and his personal integrity and knowledge of affairs stood him well with his colleagues. He spoke poorly – 'scarcely the ability to call a coach' thought one critic – but he was, in Russell's words, 'the honestest, most disinterested of statesmen'. Grey had doubted his ability to lead in April, but in November he made his own acceptance of office conditional on Althorp's. Although reluctant to shoulder the rigours of office, Althorp's resistance was overcome at the knowledge that Grey would otherwise be forced to have Brougham to lead the Commons.[44] Brougham had been a special problem, for if his eccentric genius made him a difficult ally, his spleen made no one wish him for an enemy. He tore up an offer of the Attorney-Generalship which he would 'most certainly not' accept and held out for the Mastership of the Rolls which was worth £7,000 p.a.. But Althorp refused to serve if Brougham were given that position, and told Grey that the Yorkshire victor's conduct was so unpopular with colleagues that his being in office would break up the ministry within three months if put in an irremovable post.[45] On the other hand, it was feared that if he were not in government, a public outcry at the exclusion of the *vox populi* would ensue. As a final irony, Brougham was put on the Woolsack; the Whigs' dilemma pointed out the dangers of steering a middle course.

The first great crisis of the Whig *via media* arrived in October 1831 with the Lords' rejection of Reform. Since the election, speculation on the Lords' reception of the bill had prompted two ministerial groups to emerge. The one, led by Palmerston, hoped to avoid a clash with the upper house by amending the bill if necessary. The other, led by Holland and Brougham, were prepared if required to create sufficient peers to see the whole bill through the Lords. Grey sympathised with this position until the peers defeated the bill by the unexpectedly large majority of 41,[46] by which time attitudes had hardened. Palmerston's group, which included Lansdowne, Goderich, Richmond, Stanley, Melbourne and Carlisle, hoped to negotiate an altered bill with the Tory 'waverers' Harrowby and Wharncliffe, who for their part were trying to get support for this course from the Bishops and the City.[47] Grey agreed to these negotiations in order to gain time, but he had little expectation that any altered bill could satisfy the competing demands of both groups in his government, of the Tory opposition, of the determined Reformers in the Commons, and most ominously, of the mobs that were rioting in Bristol, Derby and Nottingham. He told Wharncliffe that there was little hope of an agreement for the waverers' proposed elimination of Schedules A and D; to the King's secretary he admitted privately that the waverers wanted more concessions than would be consistent with his pledge in parliament.[48] The fact was that the changes agreeable to Grey were unacceptable to Palmerston and Melbourne, who in many ways were unwilling to leave as much in the Bill as were Harrowby and Wharncliffe.[49] Moreover, the government knew that Wharncliffe's 'memorandum of agreement' did not have the support of either Wellington or Peel, who were adamantly opposed to negotiations.[50] Nor did it have the support of a sizeable number of Ministers who were able to scuttle negotiations by forcing an early meeting of parliament. The timid Whigs welcomed rumours that the meeting of parliament, set for 22 November, might be delayed beyond Christmas to allow for a 'cooling off' period. Durham, Holland, Brougham, Ellice and Duncannon, on the other hand, argued that an early meeting of parliament was of the greatest importance if the people's confidence were to be maintained. Delay would only feed rumours that the government meant to weaken the bill, and make it difficult to keep the extremists – 'unions, affiliated societies, armed associations and what not' Holland described them – from bringing unbearable pressure on government. 'My firm opinion', Brougham told Althorp, who with Russell had not entirely wished for an early meeting, 'is that the unions etc. will get *too far ahead* if we delay'.[51] Melbourne, as Home Secretary responsible for public order, was particularly vulnerable to this argument, and when confronted with serious rioting, he decided that the bill as it was must pass. Despite his first impression that time was necessary for passions to cool, he threw his weight behind those who did not want to change the major provisions of the bill. 'It is a very dangerous way of dealing with a nation', he told Taylor 'to attempt to retract that which you have once offered to concede.'[52] Largely due to Melbourne's conversion, the cabinet decided on 19 November that parliament should meet earlier. Grey had argued successfully four days earlier that 'after all it is only a question of a fortnight', but he now found himself on the losing side of an 8 to 3 majority.[53] According to Palmerston, it was Melbourne who 'turned the scale' toward an early meeting, his reaction to the riots sufficient to convince Althorp and Russell.[54]

There was little doubt that Holland and Brougham had won a considerable victory over their more conservative colleagues. They regarded negotiations with the Tory waverers as 'treachery'[55] and had emphasised the dangers of the political unions with more force than conviction. Grey had suspected such a plan. He doubted that Radical pressure in the towns and parliament was backed by a genuine mood of public complaint;[56] he had asked Althorp to have Joseph Parkes persuade Thomas Attwood's Birmingham Political Union not to transgress the law in order that Holland and Brougham's argument might have less force.[57] The cabinet's decision, Grey was convinced, ruled out all possibility of a dispassionate discussion of the bill's merits, the only hope of its passing the Lords. 'I never felt so confident in my life' he wrote to Althorp, 'that our decision last night was wrong.'[58] For the first time as Prime Minister, he found himself unable to guide his colleagues, a disappointing state of affairs that did not sit well. He could not resign if a greater crisis were to be averted, but there were few moments from this point until he finally retired in 1834 during which he felt confident and in charge. His sense of duty and capacity to mediate disputes – Littleton thought him incomparable in this respect[59] – allowed him to continue, but as he complained to Holland during the discussion with the Tory waverers, continual dispute 'tries one's patience'.[60] It is difficult to avoid the conclusion that Grey's undoubted skill as a grand strategist, in evidence through his understanding the value of a conservative reform which would safeguard the aristocracy, was not matched by an equal adroitness as a political tactician. He was, as a consequence of important miscalculations, responsible in this sense for a good deal of his own misfortune. In July 1830, he pressed publicly for a cabinet post which he thought Wellington would offer. When no offer came, the very thing Grey had been trying to prevent – hostility to Wellington – increased. Again, early in 1831 he thought, incorrectly, that Reform would pass without dissolution. Most recently he was willing to trust the bill to the Lords on the strength of its merits, thinking that a second chance could be arranged without clamour or creation of peers. He was to complain in 1832 that had he known of the threat to the aristocracy that lay ahead he would never have proposed Reform,[61] but the wonder is that he had not foreseen the struggle. His misreading of Wellington's thinking in the summer of 1830 was evidence of a larger failure to understand the Tory mind with its sanctification of the constitutional *status quo*. By issuing a challenge to the House of Lords, Grey made conflict inevitable, for each step that created public support, first for 'a' bill and then for the 'whole' bill, produced at the same time an equal determination among the Tory peers not to allow any measure. Grey made the mistake of thinking that logic and self-interest would persuade. It was quite clear to Althorp, on the other hand, that the Tories could not be made to see the advantage of Reform. 'We must', he told Stanley, 'look more to keeping the support of our friends than to conciliating our enemies; the first is possible, the second is not, and the bill at last must be carried by force and fear, not from conviction or affection.'[62].

Russell's third and final bill contained a number of minor changes; conversations with the Tory waverers led the government to think that the peerage might allow the measure to pass.[63] The amendments were not what the conservative Whigs had hoped for,[64] but they did appear to find favour with the Tory waverers in the Commons. By balancing a reduction in the number of disfranchised agrarian boroughs against an addition to the newly franchised industrial boroughs, the government was able to increase its majority by 36 votes on second reading. But there seemed little reason for optimism. The refusal of Peel and the leading Tories to acknowledge any improvements in the bill gave little hope for anything more than a minority of 20 or 25 in the Lords.[65] Creation of peers, or possession of the power to do so, was quite obviously the only option open to ministers. On 2 January, the cabinet agreed to a demonstration of power: if the King would create 10 or 12 peers, the Tories might recognise the futility of further opposition. Such agreement was not easily reached; when the King responded that the government should not 'beat about the bush' with 8 or 10 when 20 were thought necessary, dissension in the sorely split ministry could scarcely be overcome. None believed that 20 would be enough to offset the desertions that a larger creation would likely provoke; the anti-creationists could not consent even to 20. The King came to Grey's rescue on 15 January by agreeing to create an indefinite number, if and when necessary, but it would not be long before the contentious issue re-emerged.[66] Despite the King's imploring,[67] renegotiations with the Tory waverers for a drastically amended bill were by now out of the question. Ministers had gone as far as they could, without splitting, to placate the peerage. There were signs that some peers would back down. Early in February, Richmond reported 14 likely converts for the second reading; by the end of the month Wood thought 25 ready to shift.[68] But predictions, Grey knew, could be vaporous. 'I wish I could know a little more distinctively,' he asked plaintively, 'who are the persons who compose "la longue queue" and what is the real length and substance of it'.[69] It was doubtful, too, that the committee stage would be successful. Thus, by the end of February, Althorp and Brougham renewed the pressure for a large creation. Amidst faction and bad feeling, openly reported to be running high,[70] Althorp threatened to resign if a large creation did not precede the second reading. Grey refused to bow to such 'an unqualified evil'. Until a crisis actually arrived, he told Althorp, 'I doubt anything could induce me to be a consenting party to a large creation of peers'.[71]

Grey's determination appeared to be vindicated when the bill passed second reading in the Lords on 14 April. Seventeen waverers changed their votes; 12 peers who had not voted in October now supported the measure.[72] Few, however, doubted the necessity of creation before the bill was safely through committee. Agreement on a good batch had in fact been reached earlier in April. Grey had reconciled himself to this fearful course by reasoning that public discontent at the loss of the bill would prompt irresistible demands for more democratic reforms such as universal suffrage and ballot. He told the King that if the bill were to fail, the creation of 50 or 60 peers would be necessary; only by resisting alterations could democracy be checked.[73] When Lyndhurst's amendment, in committee, to postpone Schedule A passed by 35 votes on 7 May, Grey steeled himself for the fight to save the system. He had warned the Lords that postponement would result in either a large creation or the resignation of his ministry; with Richmond alone dissenting, he informed the King that the decision was his. Grey preferred resignation, and was far from upset that the King chose this course. When Wellington's attempt to form a government faltered, he told Holland that 'I begin to be afraid that the attempt may fail: but I trust to the Duke's obstinacy and pride . . . I wish to God they were fairly in office'.[74]

Althorp shared Grey's sentiments, being equally tired of office, and far from opposed to the King's request that the Tories pass an 'extensive reform'. 'We must not let our anger get the better of our honesty', he told his father, 'and we must support the Bill in whosesoever hands it is'. He appealed to Ebrington to set aside a motion, announced in the Commons on 10 May, hostile to a possible Wellington administration; he did not want factious opposition.[75] It is not clear that all of the Whig leaders were as hopeful as Grey and Althorp that the Duke could pass a bill, but even those like Brougham and Durham, who thought he could not, considered a failed attempt likely to guarantee a Whig measure once returned to office.[76] At a large gathering of Reforming MPs at Brooks's on 13 May, the Whigs' position was hotly debated. Althorp and Stanley agreed that Ebrington's motion should be given up, and despite a strong declaration of hostility towards Wellington by the body of Brooks's members, the moderate course prevailed. Wellington would be given a chance. Graham explained to Palmerston, who had been absent, the Whigs' thinking.[77]

> By this course we avert the necessity of immediate dissolution, but impose the necessity of a larger measure of Reform; if it be refused, dissolution becomes inevitable, and we appeal to the country on the extent of that measure . . .; if it be granted, we shall have all the advantage of a more popular Right of Election; and the Ministers who have passed it, will suffer from the disgrace of filching our plans and of adopting our Bill . . . Had the motion of Ebrington's been **made,** it would have looked like

a scramble for place without regard to our measure; it would not have been high-minded conduct and we should have suffered.

Allowing Wellington the opportunity to govern was doubtless the right policy, but it was one that threatened the Whigs' standing with Reformers throughout the country. Campbell's quip at Brooks's – the Whig plan was to 'let the Duke carry the Bill in the Lords, and send it down to the Commons and then to accept it, and then to turn out the Duke' – reflected his unease at the prospect of Wellington earning the gratitude of the nation; so did Macaulay's trenchant comment in the Commons the next day: 'If others wish to have infamy and place, let the House of Commons at least have honour and Reform'.[78]

Wellington's failure to form an administration left the King no choice but to go back to the Whigs. The public outcry which followed their resignations carried them back in triumph. Holland and Althorp pressed now for a large addition to the peerage, and even Palmerston and Lansdowne were willing to create 10 or 15 as a demonstration of power;[79] the King's opposition to this step and the knowledge that Wellington would withdraw his opposition to the bill[80] decided the issue. A last minute hitch, brought about by the Tories' speaking out strongly against Reform in the Lords on 17 May, prompted the cabinet to force the King into a written declaration allowing an unlimited addition to the peerage should it be necessary, but it was not. Grey's announcement the following day that the government possessed full powers to pass the bill was met with loud cheers. Well it might have been. None had wanted to swamp the Lords, and knowledge of the power made its invocation, as hoped, unnecessary. Taylor wrote to several Tory peers to make the point clear, and in less than a week, the bill was disposed of before a half-empty chamber.[81]

'A session more successful for the Ministry than that of 1832 could not well have been', wrote Russell in 1874. A near half century of hindsight gave him good reason for self-congratulation, for the intervening years dispelled most of the doubts that persisted throughout the Reform period. King, Lords, Commons and Church survived the clamour, as did property and respect for rank. Further reform was carried out in near tranquility. Constitutional change, when it came, was well-considered and temperate. Almost alone in Europe, England escaped revolution in 1848. In 1874 there was little to suggest that she need fear one. Governed for the most part by the aristocracy, the middle classes had fulfilled the hopes of 1832. England's wealth had grown alongside its liberty. 'We had carried into effect', concluded Lord John, 'a change that has given prosperity for more than forty years, without convulsion, without infringing the prerogatives of the Crown, the privileges of the two Houses of Parliament, or the rights and liberties of the people.'[82] Reform had allowed the English industrial achievement to provide for prosperity untrammelled by the constitutional uncertainties of its continental counterparts. Most gratifying to the Whigs, this achievement was the product of their efforts only. Unlike the revolution of 1688, the other great entry on the Whig banner, Tories could not share in its triumph. Crown and Lords did not emerge unscathed as Russell had suggested, but Whig mythology did not rely overly on a strict adherence to all details. Reform sat proudly on a Whig plinth.

The oft-quoted aphorism that 'what the Tories said was true, but what the Whigs did was necessary' cannot be valid, for as John Cannon has pointed out, the remark contains an internal contradiction: the Tories had argued that Reform was *un*necessary.[83] And in doing what they thought was necessary, the Whigs relied on the moderate, conservative nature of the middle classes. Whereas Tories placed a greater confidence in the borough owner's ability to stem the tide of discontent, Whigs put their faith in the ten-pounder. Without his support, respect for property, rank and station would be a dead letter. To be sure, there were many doubts in Whig minds throughout the eighteen months of turmoil which accompanied the bill's progress. This is scarcely surprising, for by taking the course which they did, the Whigs were asking their fellow aristocrats to rely on an untested social class to strengthen the underpinnings of a society which, by common patrician consent, was in need of preservation. This was as much a leap in the dark as were the reforms of 1867 and 1884 and, as an act of innovation, a step of great political courage. For lurking in the shadows of every Whig mind was the thought that the comfortable Tory argument against Reform, that protest against the system was transient and of little moment, was one that would brand Whigs, if wrong, as traitors to their traditions. It was also an act of courage to reject the Tory contention that Reform, once offered, would be but the first of a series of demands that no government would be able to resist. But here as well, the Whigs put their faith in the conservative nature of the middle class and its readiness to accept the basic premises of both a propertied society and the remodelled constitutional framework. The Whigs did not mean that the bill would be final in any absolute sense, but that it would, as Grey argued in the Lords, 'restore satisfaction and confidence in the decisions of the legislature' at a time when that confidence was severely shaken.[84] They were not blind to the fact that social change might make further constitutional alteration necessary; Sidney Smith thought the bill should put Reform to rest for thirty or forty years, 'an eternity in politics'.[85] What they hoped would be laid to rest was the notion that the institutions of the country were unable to cope with change. Melbourne argued this case during the first great debate in the Lords in October 1831. The bill, he said,[86]

> will make other changes necessary to adapt it to the working of the Constitution, and to the circumstances of the country; but to effect these changes I rely on the elasticity of the Constitution, and on its adapting power, which has preserved and improved it in past times, and will not fail, I hope, to preserve it and improve it on future occasions.

Of most concern to the Whig mind was force needed to pass the bill. If the threat to create a large number of peers had not already reduced the authority of the landed classes, the fears of an uprising and a run on the banks in May 1832, as well as the fact of the Lords' abstentions, 'absolutely destroyed', Russell thought, 'their privileges as a House of Parliament, and reduced them to a cipher in the working of the constitution.' This occasion, he recalled, was the only time in his political life when he felt uneasy about the result.[87] There is good reason to doubt Russell's somewhat hyperbolic interpretation and to argue, on the contrary, that the decline of the aristocracy's power was as much cause as effect of the whole Reform process. But there can be little doubt that the stormy history of the bill gave reason for alarm. Melbourne told Russell in 1839 that he could not accede to any proposal to alter the corn laws, for even if popular, 'we shall still only carry it by the same means as we carried the Reform Bill, and I am not for being the instrument . . . of another similar performance'.[88] It was evident by that time, moreover, that the Whigs' own political prospects were weakened by the inexorable return to prominence of the forces of reaction opposed to Reform. But despite these doubts, the Whigs had been convinced that the disease was worth the remedy. Reform, said Grey, was 'to prevent the necessity of revolution'. Brougham's language had more edge. 'Good God', he warned the Lords, 'will men never learn wisdom, even from their own experience [Catholic Emancipation]? Will they never believe, till it be too late, that the surest way to prevent immodest desires being formed, aye, and unjust demands enforced, is to grant in due season the moderate requests of justice?'[89] The conservative results of the conservative bill bear out the accuracy of the Whig analysis. 'This will clip the aristocracy' wrote Lady Belgrave in 1831, 'but a good deal must be sacrificed to save the rest.'[90] Of immediate concern to the Whigs, however, was the first test of their new system. Could a moderate, safe reform return the kind of parliament it was designed to do? Would the ten pounder, grateful at being heard, pledge his newly-won franchise to the old order, or would he join with Radicals in pledging candidates to destructive reforms in Church and State? How the new electorate would act, and to what extent parliament and indeed the nation would be governable, were the issues facing Whiggery by Christmas 1832.

5

The Grey Ministry, 1833–34

There is no certainty in our councils, and I fear there will be no public confidence in them.

Le Marchant Diary, 23 June 1833[1]

the rock we shall split on will be Ireland.

Althorp, 2 January 1833[2]

The real test of the new bill was not only the nature of the new electorate, but equally the nature of government arising from this wider sovereign power. Once it was realised that Reform had not turned the system over to the rabble, Grey found himself heading a ministry whose aims were not at all as clear as when first formed in 1830. If there was a general Whig goal, it was to see that radicalism would be rejected as a serious political force, that the 'destructives', in Graham's words, would not 'overpower the conservatives'.[3] But how that aim was to be realised in other than the elections, in which the Whigs opposed movement candidates far more strenuously than in 1831, was not at all settled. The new government was to pursue a legislative course of moderate reform, but the extent to which it would rely on support from one or other parliamentary group was the subject of much internal debate and friction. Grey's difficulty in maintaining ministerial harmony was hereby aggravated, not reduced as he might have hoped by the passage of Reform. The most striking feature of his government, which had an overwhelming majority in the lower house, was the insecurity produced by division. Within seventeen months of achieving the greatest electoral victory of the century, Grey retired, unable to brook his loss of authority.

Russell had predicted the size of the majority long before the electorate went to the polls. 'We shall have about 400, the Tories

158, the Radicals 100', he told Lady Holland in September.[4] Following the elections, most observers had him remarkably close. Creevey set the figures at 149 Tories and 509 Whigs and Liberals, Walsh 'upwards' of 400 Whigs, 130 Conservatives and 100 movement, Buckingham 150 Conservatives, 408 Whigs, 96 Liberals and 4 independents, Durham 468 Reformers and 138 Tories, and Mahon 150 Conservatives, 320 Ministerialists and 190 Radicals and Repealers.[5] Taken at face value, these figures suggest an overwhelming government victory. Raw numbers, however, can be misleading, and the striking feature of the election results is the uncertainty with which the Whigs faced the new parliament. Despite a seemingly overwhelming victory in the elections, the Whigs lacked confidence to a greater degree than they did later in the decade when the number of government and opposition supporters was more evenly balanced. What was not clear to the Whigs was the allegiance of each group in the new House. Grey was extremely pleased with the results, which convinced him that the public had not adopted republican sympathies. He felt that Radicals were left hopelessly weak, an opinion formed by their failure to defeat 'constitutional Reformers', particularly in London. He assured Graham that there was little radical power to fear in the new parliament. O'Connell's amendment to the Address on 8 February, which mustered only 40 votes against 428 was 'undeniable proof' that the feeling of the House and public was 'strongly excited against the Radicals and Repealers'.[6] Few would argue with Grey's view that, without tumult or violence, the elections had satisfied the expectations of the Act and answered those critics who said Reform would bring destruction.[7] Nevertheless, the detailed assessment of the results which Wood provided from the Treasury warned that the Whig victory was less than overwhelming and that independent factions would be very strong. Based on past and expected performances of Members, rather than on election manifestoes, Wood's list predicted the following:[8]

137 Tories	– 'opposition'
22 Waverers	– 'Sandon, Geo. Bentinck, Bethel and the like who are not always to be depended upon although 3/4 will always vote with us.'

303 Steady Supporters	– 'including all those members of the Gov't., Ellice, & those whose opinions are perhaps more liberal than those of the compound cabinet.'
123 Supporters	– 'of different shades from Ebrington to Warburton – men agreeing mostly with Althorp in opinion, & who voted steadily with us under the bond of the Reform Bill – but upon whom we cannot depend now so entirely to sacrifice their own opinion.'

34 English and Scotch Radicals – 'Hume and Co.'

38 Irish Repealers

The government could not fail to see their vulnerability to a combination of Tories, Radicals, Repealers and 'supporters of different shades'. Before parliament had scarcely met, it was evident that on a number of issues, the government was not immune to the pressure of parliamentary numbers. This possibility was more likely on questions like slavery, where a number of interest groups not connected to the ministry found fault with government legislation. Althorp was worried that Stanley's slavery plan, which attempted to steer a path between the anti-slavery movement and the Whigs' own determination to protect the slave-owners, would be 'fatal' to the government. Indeed the anti-slavery party, with support from sympathetic Whigs, Tories and Radicals, came within seven votes of defeating the government, and the plan succeeded only by an alteration which suited the anti-slavery views.[9] A similar Whig reluctance to introduce factory legislation was undermined by a union of liberals, Radicals and Church and Tory paternalists. The strength of the factory reformers was so great, Wood concluded, that a government compromise measure was necessary if the 'much greater evil' of a more radical ten hours bill was to be avoided.[10] Budgeting matters too were susceptible to concerted pressure. In April 1833, Radical support for a motion to halve the malt tax caught the government out in a thin House, and it was only Peel's later support for the government that prevented a reduction which few Whigs wanted. Most notable of the budget measures that did not conform to Whig thinking was the reduction of assessed taxes in 1834. The previous year, ministers had refused to reduce these taxes; now they were forced to bow to wide pressure from radical and commercial interests in doing just that.[11]

Although ministerial legislation was vulnerable to a combination of pressure groups, the government's hold on office was not. The main cause of this stability was not so much the alteration of measures to weather parliamentary storms, as it was Peel's determination to take a neutral position whenever the Ministry was threatened. Peel's position of 'neutrality' was set out in a letter to Goulburn in January 1833, where he showed a distinct reluctance to co-operate with the ultras in his own party in bringing the government down with Radical aid.[12] His goal was not to deny the place of party in the immediate post-Reform period, but to lay the foundation of a future moderate Conservative party that would include many of the moderate Whigs and Liberals who now supported Grey. Factious opposition would be of no value to this cause, given the state of parties and the unlikelihood of winning immediate elections. An unsuccessful attempt to govern would strengthen radicalism in and out of parliament. To Croker, a staunch advocate of a union with Radicals in order to drive the Whigs from office, he asked 'what is to happen then? The question is not, Can you turn out a Government? but Can you keep in any Government, and stave off confusion?'[13] More than that, factionalism would give an importance to the ultra Tories that would stifle the opportunity for the gradual, dispassionate and deliberate reform that he believed institutions like the Church needed, and elevate the cause of agricultural protection and currency reform that his basic middle-class nature could not accept. For Peel, ultra Toryism, like ultra Liberalism, was an anathema to his determination to 'conciliate the goodwill of the sober-minded and well-disposed portion of the community'.[14] In May 1834, when the resignation of four cabinet members made the government's future uncertain, he continued to advise caution to Goulburn. 'My opinion', he wrote,[15]

is decidedly against all manoeuvring, all coquetting with the Radicals, for the mere purpose of a temporary triumph over the

Government . . . How can the Conservative party, if again called to the Government, hope to maintain itself, except by conciliating the goodwill, at least by mitigating the hostility, of many of the more moderate and respectable supporters of the present Government? The surest way to prevent this is by finese and party tactics.

For the duration of Grey's government, then, Peel did all he could to prevent the moderate Whigs from being driven into adhesion with their more radical and liberal supporters by the 'finesse and party tactics' of his own ultras. When, for example, these ultras, whom Gash termed 'the excitable Tory Bourbons, who had forgotten nothing and learned nothing from the events of 1832', threatened to oppose the Irish Church bill despite the Whigs' dropping of the controversial 147th or appropriation clause, Peel had Wellington temper their zeal. With the dissenting interest so strong, he feared that elections (which must follow a failed Conservative attempt to govern) would strengthen the democratic party and force more radical Church measures on a new Whig-liberal government.[16] Peel had good cause for concern. He supported the Whigs' Irish Church and tithe bills, and thought that the ultra Tory obstinacy was an attempt to force the party to join with the Radicals, who were opposed to the Irish policy for entirely different reasons.[17] Moreover, he had let the Whigs know, through Sir Herbert Taylor and Princess Lieven, that he would keep aloof from the Radicals on all questions, and would particularly welcome a moderate Irish bill.[18] In February 1833 he said as much in public during the debate on the Address, and pointedly complimented Stanley, who was known to be the defender of a moderate Irish policy in the government.[19] In April, he answered Althorp's appeal for support against the Tory Attwood's motion for currency reform by speaking in favour of the gold standard,[20] and a few days later, following a government defeat late on a Friday evening when a combination of Radicals and Tory agriculturalists supported the Whig Ingilby's motion to halve the malt tax, he actually instructed the Whigs not to resign.[21] For the remainder of Grey's government, Peel was to succeed in keeping the ultras relatively quiet and in allowing himself the freedom to support the principles of Whig moderation with which he could find little fault.[22]

Manifestation, if not offers, of support from moderate Tories was not entirely welcomed by all members of the government, and provided a constant source of friction in ministerial circles. As the results of the elections became known, a furious debate on parliamentary strategy took place. The division was between those like Stanley, who thought that the only way to restrain the rapid progress of the movement or Radical party was 'to give the *Centre droit* an opportunity of supporting us against the *Extreme gauche*', and those like Russell, who thought that the philosophical Radicals would be 'very numerous & very formidable if Gov't. does not conciliate them'.[23] More was involved here than the counting of heads and the strength or weakness of the Radicals, for defeat by this group was extremely unlikely. At one level, the debate concerned the malleability of the large group of 123 'Ebringtonians' on Wood's list, and the most likely method of keeping from its ranks the political principles and aims of the smaller but more extreme Radicals, both English and Irish. But deeper than this was the serious division in the government brought on by the question of Irish Church reform.[24] In pressing for a coercive and less reformist Irish approach, the Stanley faction used the argument that the Commons would support strong coercion and weak reform. If the Ebringtonians would not, Peel would. The anti-Stanley group, on the other hand, argued that reliance on Tory support, and the coercive attitude that this would imply, would play into the Radicals' hands and provoke further reaction and agitation in Ireland. 'I hear, & from good authority', Holland pressed Grey, 'that Tory & *Wellington* language is very much lowered. They talk of helping us to keep down Radicals, but we must for the very purpose of preventing the ultimate triumph of the latter carefully avoid encouragement of such language & desire of such assistance'.[25] Ellice argued that only by keeping the Tories in steady opposition could the government 'manage the Rads, Repealers, etc.', and that rumours of a Stanley 'clique' dominating the cabinet would endanger the support of the 'H. of C. friends'.[26] Holland, Ellice and the others who opposed Stanley therefore urged that unless the Ebringtonian party were satisfied with the government's measures, they would be drawn into the radical camp, with consequent danger to the government's majority. Wood made a point of Ebrington's importance at the conclusion of his estimates of party strength, and it was this group that Le Marchant also referred to when he noted that members were not in any way pledged by the vote on the Address to support the administration, and that it was by the measures on the Irish

Church that the government would 'stand or fall'.[27] Althorp was less circumspect, warning Grey directly that if the Commons should slip out of the ministry's hands and run wild, 'as it will do unless we get the command of it by taking the lead in popular measures', Reform would lead to revolution.[28]

Irish Church reform, then, was the occasion of a deeper struggle over the source of Commons support and the whole nature of post-Reform Whiggism. Grey was determined to stand by Stanley, and when Ellice again resorted to the argument that any movement in Stanley's favour would lose much of the government's support in the new House, the Prime Minister dug in his heels. If Stanley was too moderate for the 'impatience' of the government's friends, Grey answered, his only course would be to assist the King in forming a Tory government which he would himself support.[29] The forcefulness of Stanley's opponents in cabinet had some effect nevertheless, and for the first few months of 1833, before the harsh coercive laws for Ireland were secured, nothing was done to upset the Radicals or Ebringtonians. At Wood's instigation, Stanley in fact actively courted Ebrington's support for his Irish coercion and Church bills, and in May Ebrington's pressure on Ellice prompted the government to appoint a committee on army and navy appointments and sinecures.[30] Ebrington's support for the crucial division on the dropping of the 147th clause of the Irish Church bill did not prevent Grey, however, from having to canvass as many Tories as Whigs at the Queen's Ball,[31] and the ease with which the government accepted the Tory aid that was often necessary on difficult divisions, despite Ebrington's support, suggests that reports of his importance were overplayed. On a number of occasions upwards of 170 'ministerial' supporters, many of whom counted among Wood's 123 Ebringtonians, opposed the government and Ebrington on reforming motions. In four of these divisions, when the government whip was particularly weak, Tory support was all that stood between the ministers and embarrassing defeat.[32]

Within a few months of the opening of the 1833 session, it was obvious that the government was not much interested in courting the support of the group of more liberal supporters which favoured reforms of the constitution, reductions in the army, state pensions and sinecures, repeal of the corn laws and a much weakened Church. That ministers preferred Tory support was made strikingly clear on 15 July, on a motion by the liberal minded

Sir John Wrottesley for a call of the House three days hence. His object was to assure a full House to support the ministry in the event that the Lords should reject the Irish Church bill. The government could scarcely support the intent of the motion, for though the Tory dominated Lords had recently declared its hostility to the ministry by successfully censuring its Portuguese policy and by throwing out Brougham's local judicature bill, they had not yet dealt with the Irish bill. More importantly, Grey had assured the King that there would be no collision between the two Houses. Althorp followed Wrottesley by arguing, as Peel had already done, that this 'menace' to the other House could not be supported.[33] The government's managers were taken by surprise. The motion was the work of Duncannon, Ellice, Ebrington and Littleton, who, with Althorp's knowledge, if not concurrence, had canvassed all ministerial supporters in an attempt 'to over-awe the Lords'.[34] When Althorp was followed by Russell and Stanley, who ridiculed Wrottesley in a hard speech that took a swipe at O'Connell, the motion was as good as lost.[35] Barnes of *The Times* was justified in thinking the Ministry's actions 'cruel' to Wrottesley and 'our friends'.[36] Wrottesley had been asked by Duncannon and Littleton to make the motion as 'a man of standing and authority in the House',[37] and his supporters were those who had previously supported the government against the hostile Tory Portuguese motion in June and intended to do so again. 'What is the meaning of opposing Sir J. Wrottesley's motion?' Holland intoned to Grey, '& sneering at O'Connell who handsomely & at the expense of his own consistency supported it? Surely surely surely mortifying friends who mean to help you at a pinch, sneering at those who prefer you to your enemies . . . cannot be good policy.'[38] Holland was by now one of the few who argued that the views of the government's 'natural' supporters in the Commons should be heeded. In the spring of 1834, he told Grey that it would be dangerous to disregard Ebrington's advice to placate supporters disgruntled at the government's use of Tory support in opposition to a radical motion to reduce pensions,[39] but Ellice, who agreed, knew this tack to be hopeless. 'If you are to rely on the Tories for support', he asked Grey sarcastically, 'pray ask them for better means of resisting the feelings of the Country, in addition to an alliance with the Tories, than the assistance of the Duke of Richmond's members.'[40] Peel's own political position nevertheless made him less the 'enemy' than Holland's unpragmatic yet principled Whig view allowed. On any question that did not compromise government legislation, most of the Whigs preferred his support to that of the more extreme liberals and radicals.

The fact was that the Whigs were politicians. Accepting Radical support and radical proposals for reform violated not only the grain of Whig thinking, but the mood of the electorate. Public euphoria generated a great Reform electoral victory in 1832, but within a few months of those elections, a return to normalcy was evident. Hobhouse's defeat by the Radical Evans at the Westminster bye-election in May 1833 caused many observers to think otherwise, that the government was not moving fast enough in the direction of reform. Barnes told Hobhouse that the only vigour shown by the government was on Irish coercion, and that remedial measures were 'all but forgot'; his *Times* declared that 'the mind of the country is undergoing an anti-Ministerial change', . . . 'they must recall "the people" to their standard'.[41] But the Westminster defeat offers little proof for Halévy's contention that 'six months after the general election the electorate gave their representatives a serious warning.'[42] Although Evans polled higher than Hobhouse, it could just as well be argued that the 738 Tory votes, non-existent in 1832, cost Hobhouse his seat.[43] In March the Tories had already gained a seat in London at the government's expense, a process repeated at Sunderland in April. Reformers could argue that the government's pace of reform should quicken, but when to these losses were added seven others before the next election, the Whigs could scarcely be blamed for taking an opposite view from that expressed in *The Times*. Of the 42 bye-elections in 1833–34, the Tories gained ten seats, the Radicals only one.[44] There were already signs that Church and Irish questions could do the Whigs little electoral good, especially in the counties, and it was doubtful that more reforms, or collision with the Lords, would have strengthened the government's position in the country. The reality facing the Whigs was the return to traditional influences after 1832, influences which were more often than not Conservative. The abandonment of the more liberal parliamentary supporters was not 'pretty',[45] but the electorate that both Peel and the Whig leaders were courting was of a different temper.

If sheer numbers, and the reluctance of both Radicals and Tories to allow each other to gain too much influence over the government, provided the Whigs with just enough parliamentary security to make it through the 1833–34 sessions, the cabinet's propensity for internal disunity was cause for alarm. Too much can be made of cabinet disputes, for all governments are beset with problems that give rise to resignations and threats. What made Grey's management of a seemingly ungovernable administration particularly difficult was the combination of extreme political differences over Irish Church matters and personal feelings and rivalries that gave little room for compromise. At the centre of most of the friction was Stanley. Grey's promotion of Stanley to a cabinet post in 1831 was done in the expectation that he would 'very soon place himself virtually . . . in the decided lead of the House of Commons' and replace Althorp as the ostensible head of the Treasury bench.[46] His independence and arrogance soon lost him the confidence of his colleagues. Russell's jealousy did not help matters. He had threatened to resign until offered a cabinet seat also,[47] but the source of difficulty was far from simply personal. Stanley's brazen attempts to rule Ireland with a heavy hand found little sympathy among his Whig colleagues. Within a week of appointment to cabinet, his contempt for Whig feeling led him to anounce an altered and 'tyrannical' Irish arms bill that none of an astounded cabinet, including Grey, knew about. Before long, his opponents in cabinet realised that, as Littleton described him later, Stanley was 'the clog or dead-weight' to the movement of reform.[48] A number thought his bias against the Irish so considerable that he was 'hated by all parties in that country', and, as Holland recorded, 'no proposal coming from him is considered on its own merits [even] by the High Protestant faction'.[49] By August 1832, Holland led demands for his replacement as Irish Secretary;[50] by the end of the elections which had alone maintained a semblance of peace in the cabinet, Grey had a difficult time in preventing open rupture. In the autumn of 1832, there was much ill-feeling over the terms of the proposed Irish legislation, and Stanley's own threats to resign should his views not carry caused a great deal of resentment. Grey's support carried the cabinet, but Stanley's insistence on a pledge against further reforms was stoutly resisted by Althorp, Russell, Holland and Durham.[51] Not content with Durham's attitude, Stanley demanded Radical Jack's written assurance that he would abide by the decision. Grey persuaded an 'unreasonable' Stanley to back down, but wondered to Althorp 'what can he want more?'[52]

An answer was soon forthcoming. Anglesey, the Lord Lieutenant of Ireland who had carried on a running disagreement with

Stanley over Irish policy, made public not only the government plans for Ireland, but also the extent of the differences within the ministry and especially between him and his Irish Secretary.[53] Stanley was already upset that Anglesey was making him appear unpopular in Ireland; he made it clear that he would not stay on as Irish Secretary if the Lord Lieutenant were not removed.[54] With the cabinet in the 'very agony of dissolution' for three or four days, plans were hurriedly made to have a reluctant Melbourne go to Ireland in Anglesey's place.[55] But Stanley's opponents in the cabinet refused to allow him this 'victory'. This was the very moment when rumours of Tory support made them suspicious of Stanley's loyalties. They persuaded the cabinet that Anglesey's undoubted indiscretion should be overlooked, for his removal would have too great an effect on the Ministry's support in the Commons. When Ebrington told Stanley that he would support his Irish coercion and Church bills only if Anglesey stayed in Dublin, Stanley was forced to retreat, but not before leaving his colleagues with the impression that he was selfishly promoting private interests rather than those of the ministry or public. He 'extorted' the promise that both he and Anglesey should be moved by Easter.[56] But this last was a bluff. To Brougham, one of his most steadfast opponents, he wrote in March, 'I must on all accounts remain in my present place . . . for I like it, and feel that I am fit for it . . . it is quite for the advantage of the Government that I should not be moved.'[57] When Easter came, Grey found it impossible to persuade the cabinet to allow anyone less liberal than Anglesey to implement the new coercion law, and Stanley, the author of that measure, had little choice but to move alone.[58] Durham's resignation, expected and welcomed by all,[59] together with Goderich's reluctant acceptance of the Privy Seal, left the Colonial Office open for Stanley where his services for the abolition of slavery were to be more satisfactory to that portion of the government who succeeded in getting him out of an Irish office.[60]

Holland noted in his diary that in the face of the government's determination to stick by the Lord Lieutenant, Stanley 'had the good sense not to stickle for a triumph over Ld. Anglesey'.[61] What Holland could not have known was that as far as Irish affairs were concerned, Stanley had lost all faith in most of his cabinet colleagues and would presently embark on a course to break the government in two. Although Russell is usually credited with 'upsetting the coach' in May 1834, the evidence is clear that from the spring of 1833, Stanley had set himself on a collision course with his colleagues. When Stanley resigned in 1834, Holland noted that he had evidently for some time been planning to leave. In fact, Stanley had not planned to 'leave' so much as to form with the King's full concurrence and help, a centre or coalition party of moderate Whigs and Tories which would exclude Tory ultras and Whig appropriationists and would be relieved of looking to Wood's 'Ebringtonian' party for support. It was Stanley, not Russell, who split the Whigs, and his relationship with the King, moreover, played a major role in the latter's determination to dismiss Melbourne's government in November 1834.

The first outward sign that Stanley meant to pursue his own course came on 21 June 1833, when, to the surprise of most of the cabinet and all of the government's supporters, he announced that the contentious 147th clause would be dropped from the Irish Church bill. The cabinet had decided to amend rather than drop the clause in order to placate the House of Lords and the King, but on the morning of the announcement, which because of Althorp's absence from gout had been left in Stanley's hands, a hurried consultation with the King resulted in the unexpected deletion of the clause altogether. The affair had all the markings of a royal coup, engineered with Stanley's assistance. Stanley had known for three weeks that the King wanted the clause dropped,[62] but Littleton, the new Irish Secretary, was told that Sir George Grey had the day before suggested the idea and that after the meeting with the King, Graham, Grey and Stanley, who alone knew of the change, had 'no time' to consult their colleagues.[63] Why Stanley had not mentioned the King's request at the two cabinet meetings held to arrive at an amended clause[64] must be conjectured, but Grey's allowing the clause to be dropped without a full discussion can only be described as an indiscretion. The appropriation principle which formed the basis of the clause had been the most contentious issue in the cabinet since the creation of peers debate in 1831.

The King's reasons for meddling in the details of the government's bill had little to do with the subject of the Irish Church itself, for his understanding of the matter bordered on ignorance. As for his views on the religious controversies raging in Ireland, there is some evidence that he held a more liberal position than Stanley. During the late 1820s, he supported the cause of the Irish Catholics. 'I am for the Catholics' he declared in 1827, 'heart and soul to the very backbone'. The previous year he had said that they must be liberated, and when the emancipation bill came before the Lords in 1829, he supported it. Emancipation was not a concession, he argued in debate, but an 'act of justice' that was long due.[65] Taylor, his secretary, told Holland, moreover, that the King had little or no sympathy with the Irish Church, but that 'persons about the King (princesses and others)' had reminded him of George III's attachment to it 'and of the reproach to which he would expose himself by practically repudiating the conscientious maxims of his fathers life'.[66] This is not to argue that William welcomed Church reform. At most, Taylor told Stanley, he 'admits the importance and necessity of correcting abuses'.[67] But he had little of that high Tory trepidation of touching the Church. What made him unsympathetic to the Whigs' measure was the political consequence of its introduction. If the granting of one reform were to encourage further agitation by O'Connell, a man 'so totally lost to all sense of honour and integrity . . . the most bitter . . . enemy of *any* government',[68] property, society and its institutions would be in danger. 'The cry for abolition of tithes and of other rights', he had Taylor write to Wellesley's secretary,[69]

is raised by those who agitate, and seek to revolutionize and destroy, in order to raise themselves on the ruin of the existing fabric. One step produces another, and . . . the legal and rightful tenure of property will be the next question; nay, Law and Right will become dead letters in the attempt to raise the House of *want* against the House of *have*.

Despite these misgivings, the King was willing to sanction measures of reform if it was 'clearly understood' they had obtained the 'concurrence and approbation' of the Church. His principle, Stanley was instructed, was '*Conservative* . . . the Establishment must not be lowered nor shaken.'[70] What the King was saying was that there was to be no recurrence of the dangerous collision over the Reform bill, when assurances that that bill was acceptable to the House of Lords were found wanting. Just as the clerics of the universities had been the touchstone of respectable society's acceptance of parliamentary reform, the 'High Dignitaries' of the Church would be the litmus of Irish reform. Stanley could only assure the King that the bill was safe in the Commons, and when the Lords' hostility towards the government broke out on the Portuguese debate shortly before the

Church bill was to go into the Commons committee, William feared a renewed collision of the two Houses, a 'catastrophe . . . hazardous to all'.[71] From this point, until the final dismissal of the government in November 1834, the King's sole concern was to avert this collision; Irish Church reform was not really the issue.

The Portuguese motion in the House of Lords, taken on 3 June, was the turning point in the King's attitude to his government. Amid rumours that an ultra Tory ministry was being planned at Apsley House, [72] Grey told the King that should the Lords' hostility towards his government continue, the ministry with the support of the Commons and country, would resign.[73] The King's immediate reaction was to defuse the crisis. There was little doubt that the Portuguese debate was an ultra Tory show-piece for Irish Church purposes, and the King's immediate reaction, apart from a show of support for the government, was to criticise Wellington for his motion and to reprimand the Archbishop of Canterbury for the Bishops' conduct in the Lords.[74] But the manifestation of support for Grey was *pro forma*. On 6 June a motion had been carried in the Commons upholding the Government's Portuguese policy; this motion effectively denied the validity of the Lords' censure motion, and established for the first time the principle that a defeat in the Lords on a censure motion was insufficient to cause the downfall of a government. Although Grey did not state publicly the principle that a government with the support of the King and Commons could nullify the effect of a censure motion in the Lords, Melbourne was to do so in 1836,[75] and Grey himself believed that a certain result of the House of Commons motion was a 'further loss of influence and character by the House of Lords'.[76] This issue, together with the Reform bill crisis, had pointed out the limitations of the upper house.[77] The King had not failed to see a similarity to the earlier crisis of 1831–32; Brougham's call for a creation of Peers[78] added to his fears. He must forge a new ministry. In a lengthy letter to Stanley which began by expressing the King's opinion that Stanley and all acting with him would join any administration the King chose, Taylor explained the King's view of the relationship between the Commons and Lords and the importance of bringing about 'some *union* of the two *Conservative* parties' which was the 'anxious wish and object of the King'.[79]

It was against this background that Stanley made his announcement on the 147th clause in the Commons. He did not reply to the

King directly until reports circulated that Wellington was being pressed to oppose the bill even though the clause had been dropped. In a letter marked '*most strictly secret*' that should on no account, he urged, be made known to his colleagues, Stanley told Taylor that he should 'see with satisfaction any such infusion into the present government as should tend to draw the two houses more nearly together'. Adding that the line taken by Peel 'has been such as materially to facilitate any such future arrangements', Stanley warned the King that the Lords' rejection of his now moderate measure would make a union impossible.[80] The following day, Taylor was able to report that Wellington had been persuaded to shake himself loose from the 'violence' of the Duke of Cumberland and the 'stupidity' of the Duke of Gloucester. With the Irish bill thus as good as passed, the King, he concluded, was 'looking forward to an arrangement which might secure to him . . . yourself & Sir Robert Peel'.[81]

Stanley had had the eye of the King since December 1830, when, following his bye-election defeat to the radical Henry Hunt at Preston, the King brought him in for Windsor as a mark of favour to the new government.[82] Before long, his attitudes in general and on Ireland in particular found favour with the King, and official correspondence between the two shows an uncharacteristically warm familiarity. The King was obviously delighted with Stanley's inclination to distrust those of his colleagues who advocated a more liberal course. When Stanley told him later in 1833 that Littleton and Wellesley's new tithe plan was adopted on 'my *principles* so entirely', and was likely to displease the Radicals and many ultra supporters of government, Taylor answered that the King had often 'adverted with satisfaction' to his attitude towards those who, under the plea of reform, 'contemplate the destruction of the Church, as a step, & doubtless a material one, to general Revolution'.[83] The day before he first discussed with Stanley the prospect of a union, William had cause to rejoice that the new Colonial Secretary's first resolution had carried in the Commons and that 'a young member has come forward in so promising a manner'.[84] For Stanley, the King's suggestion of a union with Peel must have seemed a life-line. Unable to influence the government to the degree he would have liked, and out of favour with many of its supporters, a moderate Whig/Conservative coalition would find him in the midst of like-minded men and enable him to have the influence that his colleagues seemed keen to deny him. What contacts he had with Peel suggested mutual understanding and sympathies. Both had served on the Irish tithe committee appointed in 1831, and by the spring of 1832, Stanley was already working with the Conservatives behind his colleagues' backs. In April, he asked for and received Grey's consent to submit to Peel a memorandum on which was to be found the tithe committee's report, but a letter from William to Stanley two months earlier shows that the report had already been shown to the King, and that Peel had helped Stanley draught it.[85] The King had every reason, then, to believe that Stanley and Peel could work together. His letter of 14 July that specifically mentioned Peel's name as Stanley's future partner was answered in the intended manner. Stanley was worried that his position was too delicate even for this confidential correspondence, and wrote 'I can only say that in point of principle I see no dissimilarity between myself & the individual to whom you refer nor, on my part, is there any personal feeling, which should stand in the way'.[86] With the King's permission, Stanley brought Richmond into the discussions,[87] and before long, a sub-cabinet of Stanley, Richmond, Ripon and sometimes Grey was holding meetings to discuss what Stanley was terming 'Conservative' proceedings.[88]

During the spring of 1834, Stanley's position in the government weakened still further. Under renewed pressure from the Irish members, the reformers in the government found it increasingly difficult to stand by Stanley when their inclination was to support some reduction in the size of the Irish Church. Before the session had . begun, Althorp correctly forecast the dissolution of the cabinet on this question. 'It can be postponed but for a very short time', he told Littleton, '& whenever it is really forced on, we shall be obliged all of us to take our own line'.[89] The cabinet agreed to try an Irish tithe bill that was based on Stanley's 1832 bill, but when pressed in the Commons for changes which Stanley could not accept, the government was put in an embarrassing and awkward position. In an attempt to avoid confrontation, Duncannon had during the recess proposed a commission of enquiry into vacant Irish parishes, and had secured the agreement of all the Irish reformers in the cabinet and of Grey and Melbourne. It was hoped that Stanley, who had once declared that the Irish Church, 'to be loved . . . needed to be but known', would, by agreeing to an enquiry, allow the full cabinet to oppose Commons pressure for change by referring to the eventual report of such a commission.

But Stanley knew the likely results of any enquiry. He opposed the plan, and in order to avert an open break, the matter was dropped.[90]

Stanley's adamant opposition to any compromise on the question caused his opponents' frustrations to swell and made the final break inevitable. Russell's speech on 6 May which prompted Stanley to pass the note to Graham that 'Johnny has upset the coach', was but one example of a fettered cabinet's final inability to keep its silence. On 1 May, Althorp did not want to resist the principle of a motion by the Irish MP H. W. Barron for a select committee to study the question of Irish Catholic education, but Stanley's opposition to any discussion of this subject which was tied so closely to appropriation forced the cabinet to instruct Littleton to 'shuffle through it' as best he could.[91] Only the comparative quiescence of the Irish members, who were holding their wrath for the tithe debate that was set to begin the following day, put off an open clash. During the tithe debates, when O'Connell raised the question of Church revenues and Stanley answered by reaffirming his opinions on it, Russell could not longer be quieted. In February, when the cabinet compromise of a commission of enquiry was dropped, Russell had answered Holland's 'long lecture' on the need for solidarity by writing[92]

Why not preach to Stanley? Why abandon a measure which Lord Grey, Ld. Lansdowne, Althorp, yourself & others approved, and made me yield to an opinion which is not theirs or yours? I will tell you – Because Stanley is determined – because he says that if such a measure is pressed, the sooner the ministry breaks up the better – & none of you *dare* to urge him to change this opinion.

Behind this tirade lay a great deal of justice, and Stanley's unwillingness to bend towards the majority of the cabinet, all of the government placemen and the majority of the government's supporters in the Commons, was bound to lead to collision. When the tithe debates began, the first hurdle to be cleared was a motion by More O'Ferrall on 2 May to put off debate for a week in order that the government would have time to reconsider the bill and offer some concessions to the Irish. Russell was asked by Grey not to make his opinions known on the question, and after a stormy cabinet session, agreement was reached to oppose the motion.[93] In these circumstances there is little wonder that Russell reacted to Stanley's pledge to maintain Church revenues undiminished. Russell's impetuosity led him to read more into Stanley's speech than what was actually said, but the fact that Stanley answered O'Connell at all was highly impolitic. He knew, after two cabinet meetings that week, that the majority of his colleagues had, with difficulty to their consciences, agreed to abstain from speaking out in deference to his wishes, and he would have more properly left Littleton, whose bill it was, or Althorp, leader of the Commons, to answer to O'Connell. Russell's declaration, 'that the revenues of the Church of Ireland were larger than necessary for the religious and moral instruction of the people and for the stability of the Church itself'[94] should not be seen as an attempt to drive his rival for leadership from the party, for had he wanted to persevere in this course, there had been several opportunities that week alone to do so. A few weeks later, he was to tell Stanley that 'I feel quite sure that if this vexatious question should be once settled, it will be the anxious desire of our party that you should be in a position to take the lead when it shall fall vacant.'[95] His actions, moreover, do not appear to have been premeditated. He had agreed on the 2nd that the government should not quarrel openly, and would not likely have spoken out on the 6th had Stanley not stood up as government spokesman.[96]

Certainly Stanley did not see the question in terms of leadership, and when he resigned three weeks later, it was not because of Russell's speech. His first inclination was to resign immediately, but when the cabinet agreed to continue with Littleton's bill as it was, a truce was arranged.[97] Although Littleton suspected that Stanley meant to prevent accommodation on the issue in order to join 'another' government, the matter would probably have rested where it was if H. G. Ward had not given notice of a motion, set for 27 May, to reduce the revenues of the Church. The government, as Holland explained to Grey, was once again in a dilemma, for the only way to avoid a certain defeat on the motion, which most of the cabinet in fact approved, was by a compromise that Stanley was not likely to accept.[98] In an effort to prevent Stanley's resignation, likely to follow an almost certain majority for Ward's motion, Brougham tabled two motions to remedy the abuses of pluralism and non-residence in Ireland.[99] A few days later, Ellice showed Stanley and Graham a plan to save on tithes by the leaving of certain benefices vacant on the death of the incumbent.[100]

Though only by such compromise could appropriation be avoided, Stanley would have none of it. The tithe bill, he had told the King, was adopted on 'my *principles* . . . entirely', and he could not, he told a correspondent the following month, disregard the 'importance of maintaining steadily the principles of *Conservative* as opposed to *destructive* reform.'[101] He accused his colleagues, ironically, of discussing the measure out of his presence, and was certain that Ellice's plan was prepared by Abercromby and O'Connell. 'I was asked to give my assent', he told Spring Rice later. 'You may guess the nature of my answer. Four days afterwards I resigned.'[102]

Graham, who according to Littleton was known to have 'long been engaged' in quiet intercourse with the Tories,[103] resigned for reasons similar to Stanley. He had for some time believed that Grey had not been able to withstand radical pressures for unnecessary changes in Irish policy, and in January had nearly left over what he regarded as O'Connell's undue influence.[104] In many respects, Graham still warranted a liberal reputation, for in that same week, his liberality persuaded him to tell Palmerston that if the House of Lords would not support the government's Portuguese policy, which had the approval of the King, government and 'the representatives of the people', the 'refractory body must be changed, and the majority must be converted by the use of the Prerogative into a decided minority'.[105] But on Irish affairs his earlier support for reforms had given way to the view that only by coercion could disturbances be ended. After Russell's speech on 6 May, Graham took more persuading to stay in than Stanley,[106] and he followed Stanley quite willingly at the end of the month. Richmond and Ripon, the other members of the 'mezzo termine'[107] party who had been holding sub-cabinets, went as well. Richmond, described by Brougham as a 'hot Orangeman and ultra Protestant'[108] had been given a place in the government in 1830 as an ultra Tory parliamentary reformer and had wanted to leave once that measure had passed.[109] He nevertheless stood by Stanley against his opponents, and was to follow him again in 1846 as a protectionist. Ripon's departure owed as much to dissatisfaction with his own position as with the Irish issue. He had been moved from the Colonial Office to Privy Seal in 1833 very much against his own wishes and had complained bitterly at the lack of work. Given the Earldom of Ripon as a sop, Goderich wanted both the Home Office and a Garter. Grey persuaded him not to resign in

1834 when his request for the Presidency of the Board of Trade was turned down, but he refused to attend Cabinet meetings after-wards, and welcomed the excuse to leave in May.[110]

The immediate casualty of the broken government was the Prime Minister, whose four years at the helm had seemed an endless struggle to prevent what was now taking place. Grey's reluctance for office was well known, and only the preservation of the Whig cause had prompted him to continue beyond 1832. Each new crisis weakened an already slender resolve. During the struggle to get Stanley's Church bill through the Lords in July 1833, his last great act of perseverance, Grey suggested to Holland that Althorp should succeed him.[111] In August, he spoke again of the plan, and at a cabinet meeting during the final week of the session had to be prevailed upon, chiefly by Brougham and Lansdowne, not to retire on the spot; such a retreat, they argued, would be 'unreasonable and dangerous'. If Richmond, who was known to be on close terms with the King, left with him as suspected, the King might replace the ministry with the Tories or a coalition.[112] Grey was nevertheless determined to retire in No-vember when the cabinet planned to reassemble, and it was only the urging of his colleagues that persuaded him to remain.[113] What made his resolve give out in 1834 was a growing inability to influence cabinet decisions as strongly as he would have liked. In January, when a minority of Richmond, Melbourne, Stanley, Althorp and Grant opposed his support for Palmerston's policy of establishing Donna Maria's liberal government in Portugal, he offered his resignation to the King and withdrew it only at William's entreaty.[114] It had taken him six hours to persuade Graham not to resign in January, and in February he told Ellice that he was having increasing difficulties seeing his way through all the problems surrounding him, 'for I am completely worn out'. At Easter, he told his son that he would retire in time for new writs to be issued before the session was out, and thought Althorp should succeed with Stanley leader in the Commons.[115]

There was an uncharacteristic bluff and bravado to Grey's performance that might have accounted for his lack of control. When he did retire in July, he was hurt at the ease with which his colleagues, and the King, acquiesced in the decision. What Hol-land termed 'the frequent & somewhat imprudent declarations' of the previous year had led everyone to think that the decision to retire had been made, and lacked only an opportunity.[116] The resignations in May made it clear that Grey could no longer prevent a split, and when Althorp resigned in July, as he had threatened to do in May, [117] a rather shell-shocked Grey found himself unpleasantly pushed aside. The issue in July was the public meetings clause in the renewal of the 1833 Irish Coercion Act. The Irish administration and the majority of the new cabinet agreed with Melbourne's opinion that public sentiment in England did not support the prohibition of free discussion at public meetings. But Grey was insistent that the clause should remain in the bill, and at a cabinet meeting of 29 June, prevailed against Wellesley's advice and Althorp's strong protestations. [118] Two days after Grey introduced the renewal of the bill in the House of Lords, O'Connell, who had earlier been told by an indiscreet Littleton that the meetings clause would be given up and had discontinued agitation against the measure on that account, complained that he had been exceedingly deceived; he told the Commons of the Irish Secretary's 'promise'. [119] With yet another cabinet division made public, O'Connell and Peel led a savage attack and produced, in Howick's account, 'a most wretched evening . . . I never saw a party so completely destroyed except on the famous night in May 1832 when the embryo Tory Gov't was demolished.' [120] This was too much for Althorp, who had protested against the cabinet decision to Grey privately and had been told in return that the Prime Minister would resign if the bill as it stood was not stoutly maintained. Explaining to Grey that he could not longer abide the 'loss of face' by supporting a government that was being forced against its will, he resigned. [121] The Prime Minister, 'tired of these power-play situations which have occurred about once a month', saw little choice but to leave at the same time. Two years earlier, when faced with internal revolt against his support for Stanley, he had stood by his principle that no government could go on which was not master of its actions. 'You must take me as I am', he had told Althorp. Now, without Stanley's support, Grey's position in the face of those 'who never would permit me to pursue my own measures, in my own way', was found to be untenable. 'My political life is at an end.' [122]

6

Reform Government, 1833–34

> we must endeavour to correct these abuses which affect the Constitution, and the various institutions of this country . . . we have endeavoured to bring forward those measures of Reform which have been submitted to your Lordships, and to the other House of Parliament, strictly, I repeat, upon Conservative principles – wishing to cover the weak parts of the Government, and strengthen it against the attacks of its enemies, and to secure the confidence of its friends.
>
> Grey, House of Lords, 1833[1]

Although it is common to refer to the eighteen thirties as a 'decade of reform', it was the two year period of Grey's first reformed government that saw most of the initiative in this respect. Parliamentary committees and Royal Commissions were struck, plans for legislation laid, action taken. In his speech opening the parliament of 1834, the King recalled that more numerous and more important questions had been considered by parliament during the previous year than during any other.[2] The 1834 session was to be scarcely different. At first glance, this state of affairs could be seen to follow a Whiggish pattern: having fought for reform of parliament, reformers had won in the first reformed elections an overwhelming victory which allowed them to continue a reforming path. This thesis, however, is not very useful in explaining the Whigs' role, or their conception of it, in the formulation of the several reforming measures. Professor Hamburger has examined the view of the Whigs as 'somewhat left-wing and as liberal' in an illuminating essay on the Whig conscience. His conclusion, that the Whig intelligentsia like Macaulay reflected a general Machiavellian rejection of moral or conscientious considerations, might appear to be overly stated;

but his depiction of the Whig, who in Acton's words 'acquiesced in the existing order', as one whose reform impulse was 'to reduce discontent, to undermine the extremes, to solidify the centre, and thus to promote stability', is an apt description of an aristocractic party whose goals reflected paternalistic patrician values.[3] The Whigs, said Grey, would reform by removing what even their friends deplored, and by opposing those 'wild and extravagant projects' which 'promised peace and freedom but would end in despotism and anarchy'.[4]

At the end of the first session of the reformed parliament, the government published a lengthy pamphlet, *The Reform Ministry and The Reformed Parliament*, in which several ministers and advisers wrote a defence of their measures. In the conclusion to the piece, the view was put forward that the old partisan system of parliamentary politics had been superseded by a reformed House of Commons where the majority were partisans only of 'good government'.[5] To emphasise the point still further, Le Marchant, Brougham's secretary and editor of the pamphlet, drew from Grey's speech in the Lords on the occasion of the Irish Church bill quoted above. Behind the self-serving tributes lay a certain degree of reality. It would be wrong to underestimate the Whigs as party politicians, but there was a strong belief common to most of them that only the most generally accepted dogmas of religious and civil liberty should influence legislation. There was no agenda of Whig reforms which awaited only the passage of parliamentary reform for long sought implementation. The major legislative acts of these two years came after conditions and movements in the country made legislation necessary. Grey's government did not set out to right wrongs and reform abuses. Rather, it tried to shape legislation to treat the problem at hand in a manner that reflected its members' own aristocratic precepts of the *via media*. His speech on the Irish Church bill was a restatement of Whig thinking on the reform of parliament, and by following that same principle after 1832, the Whigs' main concern was to safeguard the rights of property, maintain the primacy of the landed classes, and to provide whatever change was necessary both to ensure that security and to steer the various measures through parliament. There is a very real sense in which most of this legislation was non-partisan. Grey's reference to Conservative principles could be seen as an attempt to gain support from the Tory-dominated House of Lords for his measure, as to a degree it was. But as a result of the Whigs' unwillingness to do battle again with the Lords, two-party government was necessary if legislation were to pass. There is little, apart from clause 147 of the Irish Church bill, on which the two front benches in the Commons substantially differed. 'Look at the questions on which I have supported, and those on which I have opposed the Reform government', Peel argued in 1835; 'compare their number, compare their relative importance, and then decide whether I or the ultra-Reformers were the parties differing the most in views and principles from the government of Lord Grey.'[6] The important legislation of 1833–34 was inevitable, given the circumstances of each measure, and it is doubtful that a Peel–Wellington government would have offered legislation differing significantly in principle from that of the Whigs under Grey. Defending and strengthening the institutions of society through moderate reforms based on reluctant interventionism and mild *laissez-faire* attitudes was a programme that all but Tory ultras and the extremer Radicals could follow.

ECONOMIC AND SOCIAL POLICIES

Whig adherence to a pragmatic rather than doctrinaire approach was strikingly evident in the government's economic policy. This is scarcely surprising, for apart from a vague historical attachment to 'retrenchment', in itself a reference with more historic and political content than economic, the Whigs were not noted for a particular interest in economic questions. With the exception of a belief in the importance of free trade and a distaste for intervention in the market place, Whig grandees entered office with limited preconceived economic notions. Far more at home with discussions of political, foreign and church issues, they found themselves, as do all governments, the immediate target of economic pressure groups which argued for change or for the maintenance of the status quo. They learned quickly to forge economic policy from amongst the competing economic and political interests in a manner which seemed consistent with the maintenance of civil order. Moreover, if there had been any doubt that pragmatism would govern economic considerations under a new, reforming government, there would be none following the damaging defeat on Althorp's budget measures put forward in February 1831.

Althorp was one of the small group of Whigs who took a keen interest in economic matters; with Poulett Thomson and Francis Baring, he belonged to the Political Economy Club, where Ricardian economics formed the basis of discussion.[7] His budget was an attempt to introduce changes in commercial policy by reducing tariffs and shifting the incidence of taxation. Duties on 263 items were to be repealed altogether, and those on tobacco, newspapers and newspaper advertisements reduced; duties that gave preference to colonial wines and timber were to be altered in favour of non-colonial imports. The loss of revenue was to be offset by a duty on imported raw cotton and by a transfer tax of one-half per cent on landed and funded property. At the end of the day, there was to be a surplus of roughly £1 million. The budget proposals were an amalgam of views held by the leading exponents of David Ricardo's liberal economics. Poulett Thomson, Vice President of the Board of Trade, had a hand in it. So too did J. R. McCulloch.[8] Sir Henry Parnell's influence was clear. His *On Financial Reform* had, in the spring of 1830, set out the basic programme of reductions in the restrictive impediments to industry of customs and excise duties, together with increased taxes on 'unproductive' income in order to provide tax relief for industry and commerce. Althorp, who as Chancellor of the Exchequer was the leading architect of the budget proposal, had been heavily influenced by Parnell, and in fact declared in the Commons that the measure was framed on the financial views expressed in his publication.[9]

It is not surprising that Althorp, alone among government ministers who had taken great interest in economic measures while in opposition, should have taken the first opportunity to implement what he regarded as essential changes in economic policy. It was generally thought that he had been responsible for Thomson's post at the Board of Trade,[10] and if true, by doing so made provision for the only other Ricardian adherent in the government. What is surprising was the acquiescence of Althorp's colleagues in the plan. Grey, Brougham, Palmerston and Spring Rice were known opponents of Parnell's programme.[11] It can only be surmised that preparations for parliamentary reform left little time for discussions of the much less interesting and less important questions of trade. And the Whigs were new to office. More experienced ministers would have allowed Althorp his enthusiasm for financial reform less rein at the very time that the opposition forces were looking for any excuse to weaken both the new government and the gathering momentum for reform of parliament. The result was inevitable.

Led by Peel and Goulburn, the Tories viciously attacked the transfer tax on behalf of the fundholders who had made special, tax-exempted loans to the government during the Napoleonic wars and who would now be required to pay a tax on their redemption. Althorp's incautious response to the claim that the City was alarmed – 'That is its best recommendation' – did not help. The transfer tax was quickly given up. There was some talk of adding a property tax in its place, but this was not a solution that would have found favour with the landed classes, Whig or Tory.[12] Opposition to the weakening of colonial preferences was equally intense. The Cape wine and Canadian timber interests found sufficient support from the Tories to have the wine provisions given up, and by defeating the government in committee in March, to have the timber duties restored to what they had been. The budget was as unpopular for its exclusions. Many Radicals and ultra Tories had expected that the Whigs' taking of office under the banner of 'peace, retrenchment and reform' would lead to tax reductions and expenditure cuts. But if the 'personal rule' of George III had given Whigs a long-standing argument against sinecures, places and pensions, they were not prepared, by 1831 when the King's support was paramount, to adhere to Whig mythology where the King's station was concerned. There would be no 'interfering with the personal comfort of His Majesty or diminishing in any degree the splendour of his court', Althorp instructed the Lord Chancellor,[13] and it was no surprise, as a consequence, that the civil list remained largely unaltered. Tax reductions in fact were never contemplated. Althorp was dismayed at the growing popularity of the government from anticipated reductions which he thought impossible with the state of the country and Europe requiring an increase in the army estimates. He had spoken out against tax reductions in the spring of 1830 and refused to give in to the mounting demands until, in 1833–34, the political advantages were more apparent.[14]

The 1831 budget was the only Whig attempt to change the course of English commercial policy. Amended and chopped beyond recognition, the measures were finally passed by September. For the remainder of the decade, budgets were designed 'primarily to offer concessions to those who asked for them most loudly'.[15] By abolishing the duties on a large number of goods, the

Whigs began the process which Peel would be given credit for a decade later, but parliamentary hostility to doctrinaire policies taught the Whigs a political lesson. Most of the leading Whigs had not favoured major change. It was not clear to them that anything other than political reform and 'good government' was necessary to stem the tide of social discontent. Until the political will of more than the economists called for fundamental policy changes as necessary to ameliorate social discontent in order to provide for internal peace, there were few Whig magnates prepared to promote such changes. It was far from clear that much more than the contemplated political reforms were necessary to solve the 'condition of England' question, and equally unclear, given the limited sources of information, just how serious distress was. In any event, Whigs were no different from the other early nineteenth-century aristocrats, most of whom were not yet educated to the importance of the 'dismal science' in solving, or manipulating, social and political problems. 'I do not pretend to understand anything about these matters', Holland had once told Grey. 'Allen once made me comprehend the question between gold & silver as a standard, & though I have in some measure forgotten the reasons, I still retain the conviction that silver should in all prudence be our standard.'[16] The economic liberalism which characterised future budgets was no more than what most of the politicians vaguely regarded as useful and non-controversial. Competing interests made too great a change politically difficult. In that sense the 1831 budget fiasco was to teach the Whigs to follow the basic anti-dogmatic instincts inherent in Russell's description of political economy as 'an awful thing'. But more than that, the relative economic prosperity allowed them, until 1836 at least, to do not much more than tinker with the system as politics might dictate. Reductions in expenditures and further alterations of tariffs amounted to something less than a fundamental shift in policy. Most retrenchment took place in the Service estimates as a result of peace. The continuing strength of protectionism on both sides of parliament produced 'unobtrusive and non-controversial' policy which resulted in only a slight reduction of tariffs, a consolidation of existing duties, and a continuation of the reorganisation of commercial policy at the Board of Trade begun by Huskisson and Peel.[17]

For the remainder of Grey's tenure of office, his government's financial policies fell victim to the political pressures of the moment. It was not a particularly handsome sight. Despite the overwhelming majority which followed the 1832 elections, Le Marchant soon lamented the politically driven 'indecisive policy which will prove our ruin':[18]

> People complain, with justice, that it is impossible to calculate upon us. Stanley, one day, proposes a loan of £15,000 as a compensation to the W. I. planters, and then a few days after, without giving any reasons, he converts [it] into a gift of £20,000. The Bank Charter is undergoing similar modifications. In a great commercial country, this [is] intolerable. The announcement of a Government measure necessarily disturbs certain commercial interests. Speculations immediately take place which have the measure for a basis. The measure is changed and the speculators are ruined.

The Whigs' financial management during this period leaves little doubt that the government found itself in a weak position, at the mercy of several powerful interests. The business of parliamentary reform and a deficit for 1831–32 of over £1.2 million prevented the budget of 1832, issued in July, from being anything other than a stop-gap measure.[19] Within a year, however, that deficit had been turned into a surplus of nearly £1.5 million,[20] and Althorp found himself the object of several groups demanding reduction of taxes. His budget aimed at reducing taxes which could be shown to be pressing on commerce and industry; it included reductions in the taxes on newspaper advertisements, shopmen and commercial clerks, and in the house and window taxes as they affected shops. The tax on farm carts, which the landed interest had complained of, was repealed; the duty on raw cotton imposed in 1831 was removed as was the excise duty on tiles. Finally, the duty on marine insurance was halved. In total, a reduction in revenue of £1,000,000 was effected, leaving a proposed surplus of £500,000.[21] Althorp's prediction that the budget would satisfy 'all parties, Whigs, Tories and Radicals, with very few if any exceptions',[22] proved to be partly correct. The proposed measures did pass through parliament, but only after the severest protests and setbacks which were to influence measures taken in 1834. First to be dealt with was Attwood's troublesome 'Currency Club'. Althorp feared that some of the government's friends would support Attwood's currency motion set for 22 April in the hope that the government would 'take some half measure to catch some votes'.[23] A motion for an inquiry into public distress by Thomas Attwood in March had mustered 158 votes,[24] and there was talk of his brother Mathias' motion to enquire into the currency system defeating the ministry. This result was unlikely. Peel refused to support paper currency[25] and although 79 ministerialists deserted the government, the motion was defeated by 276 to 234.

Much more troublesome were the competing claims of the urban radical representatives for a reduction of the assessed taxes and of the landed interest for a reduction of the malt duies. Of all the assessed taxes, the house and window tax, by which the towns were assessed very heavily and the country estates practically not at all, came under heaviest criticism. Thirteen MPs from Middlesex, who it was said paid over half the tax,[26] had urged Althorp to abolish it altogether. A meeting of leading Radicals was held at the Crown and Anchor on 25 April to procure a total abolition, and a motion to that effect was announced by Sir John Key, one of the four City representatives, for 29 April. Hobhouse had already resigned his Cabinet post and seat for Westminster over the lack of an abolition measure, and with feelings running high, several Radicals joined in Sir William Ingilby's motion to halve the malt tax on the 26th. With the drop in the price of wheat from 63s. a quarter in July 1832, to 54s. in December,[27] the landed interest took up the cause of agricultural distress in the most forceful manner since early in 1830. Ingilby, a Whig baronet from Lincolnshire, proposed his motion a few hours after another by Chandos asking for relief for the agricultural interest had been narrowly defeated in a sparsely attended house. Wood, the Whig whip, thought that there would be no division and allowed members to leave for the weekend. Seeing this, Ingilby pressed for a vote and, with Radical support designed to pressure the government to reduce assessed taxes, the motion carried against the thinly attended treasury benches by 10 votes.[28] With their budget in shreds for the second time in two years, Althorp and Grey were all for resigning,[29] but when Grey went to see the King, he was persuaded to stay in office. Given the economic orthodoxy of the day that a government should balance its budget, Althorp realised that only by the imposition of a property or income tax could he adhere to the principles of Ingilby's successful motion. Although he was not personally opposed to such a course, Althorp recognized that public opinion was unprepared for it.[30] And, still smarting from the budget of 1831, he was unwilling to test his weak reputation as Chancellor by stepping again into untested waters. A tax on property and income was nevertheless not without its attractions. In September, Russell told Althorp that a budget based on such a tax 'will immortalise you'. An additional income of £12 million (£10 m. in England, £2 m. in Ireland), he noted, would satisfy every interest group.[31] Perhaps Russell was tilting at Stanley, who was opposed to a property tax, but although Ellice, Graham and Richmond favoured some form of property or income tax as well,[32] it was out of the question. Not only would the Tories have fought it; Grey told his son in 1830, when the question was first discussed, that he would lead the attack against it in the House of Lords should a measure ever succeed in the Commons.[33] What saved Althorp from further embarrassment was Peel's unwillingness to take office. To the great disgust of the ultras in his party,[34] Peel let Althorp know through Holmes and Ellice that he would support a motion to rescind the malt tax resolution.[35] With additional support from Hume, who assured the Whigs that all but a few Radicals had intended only to press for a reduction in the estimates,[36] Althorp was able to announce that the previous motion would be rescinded in order to avert a tax on property or income.[37] 'Your resolution will do', Peel quipped to Althorp on his way past the Treasury benches.[38] The government was spared. As a sop to the malcontents, Althorp announced the establishment of select committees to enquire into agricultural distress and the state of manufacturing, shipping and commerce, but in doing so, he warned that it would be wrong to expect that 'any great public benefit would arise from the Labours of these Commitees.'[39]

Unsatisfactory though the proceedings in 1833 had been, the government attempted to satisfy the competing agricultural and urban interests in 1834. In February, Althorp announced his intention to repeal the house tax, valued at £1,200,000. Organised opposition to assessed taxes in a number of commercial centres and the complaints before Althorp's recent select committee that commercial premises were unjustly taxed had obviously worked to good effect.[40] But Althorp's admission that this 'exceedingly unpopular' tax was to be repealed against his better judgement[41] brought on a storm of protest from the agricultural interest, which feared that its own reduction was thereby effectively shelved. As a consequence, a motion by Chandos to reduce the taxes on agriculture lost by only four votes when Peel, somewhat disingenuously, supported the motion that was in essence asking for repeal of the malt tax. Althorp refused to be drawn in. Distress in agriculture, he countered, was caused not so much by the tax system as by local burdens, the amelioration of which was being attended to by a poor law amendment and the commutation of tithes.[42] Despite the preceding year's surplus of £1.5 million, Althorp would not be persuaded to reduce further the government's revenue in a manner which might put the positive balance at risk. While poor laws and tithes would serve the landed interests, the budget surplus would do as much for the urban communities. He suspected that the budget as proposed was generally popular, and knew that neither Peel nor the country at large supported the currency schemes or reductions in the malt taxes which the agriculturalists demanded. He was undoubtedly wise in refusing to reduce indirect taxation further. Peel unfailingly pointed out the dangers of such a course should economic recession return, and could be counted on to keep the government afloat. Competing special interests could never be totally satisfied, and by steering a middle course, Althorp for the first time could take some satisfaction with both the state of the country and his budget measures.

Although the great commodity monopolies of sugar, timber and corn were not touched during this period, the great institutional monopolies of the East Indian Company and the Bank of England were. The absence of legislation dealing with the former and the acts regarding the latter reflected the state of public opinion. Free trade was not yet an issue. The institutional monopolies were. Although the Whigs took credit for what transpired in their pamphlet the *Reformed Ministry and the Reformed Parliament*, it cannot be said that they had much influence over the legislation brought forward. The future of the East India Company, whose charter was due for renewal in 1834, was all but decided before Wellington left office. By the Act of 1813, the Company had lost its trading rights to India. The only question left apart from its administration of British India was the monopoly of the China trade. Constant criticism from commercial centres in Britain left no one in doubt that the monopoly would not be renewed. In 1825, the Directors themselves anticipated and tacitly admitted the loss of monopoly rights by giving their China merchantmen short-term contracts which ended in 1834.[43] Wellington and Ellenborough, as one of their last acts of government, told the Court of Directors in October 1830 that it would lose the monopoly but maintain the governance of India.[44] A rush of petitions in 1829, as well as the belief that sound, economical administration of India rendered dependency on China profits unnecessary, had decided the issue. There was never any question of the Company losing its administrative functions. It had governed well, and as Charles Grant the Whig President of the India Board acknowledged, no government looked forward to the troublesome debate that would follow the Indian patronage being lifted from the Company's hands.[45] Although Grant's negotiations with the Company did not resolve a long-standing dispute between the Directors and the India Board, parliament seemed unconcerned. In the Commons, the bill was introduced with an apology for the time taken on such an 'uninteresting' and unpopular subject.[46] In the Lords, Lansdowne moved the resolutions but, noted Ellenborough, 'did not understand the subject'.[47] With little debate, and less interest, the monopoly was ended.

The Bank Charter proved more difficult. In 1832, a committee was struck to study the charter which was due for renewal the following year. Chaired by Althorp, it included the Whigs Russell and Graham and the Tories Peel and Herries. With all but the Ricardian Parnell agreed that the Charter should be renewed, Althorp negotiated an agreement with the Bank which was put to parliament in May 1833. Although the Bank was unhappy at losing its monopoly as a deposit bank in London[48] and agreed to accept a reduction of £120,000 per annum in the fee it received for servicing the National Debt, its powers were substantially increased by another provision which gave it a virtual universal monopoly as a bank of issue. Not surprisingly, the country bankers were irate when it was announced that Joint Stock banks would not be allowed to issue notes. According to Le Marchant, their clamour caused more anxiety and discussion than did Irish tithes.[49] Although Althorp was determined to withstand their pressure, the cabinet was not up to the fight and dropped all references to country banks from the bill. Mortified at this desertion by his colleagues, Althorp was again near to resignation, and announced in the Commons that 'he felt . . . or rather, he should say, his Majesty's Government felt', that it was not desirable to press forward with this part of the plan.[50] With expedience again overcoming principle, a comprehensive reorganisation of the banking system was delayed until undertaken by Peel's government in 1844. With no real support in parliament or the country, no government, and certainly not this one, was prepared to take on another unpopular measure at a time when the difficulties of the Irish Church provided sufficient strain for Althorp and his colleagues. New directions in economic measures, it was clear from the time of the 1831 budget, would not be pursued.

If the economic record of Grey's government can be regarded with some justification as 'unattractive',[51] there is little doubt that its legislative interference with the social and economic conditions of slavery, factories and the poor was at once attractive and innovative. And with the exception of the initial opposition out of doors to the new poor law, their record was popular with both parliament and the electorate. The abolition of colonial slavery and the Irish Church temporalities act were described by Russell as two of the 'largest and most important measures that were ever proposed'.[52] They were in several respects similar. Both arose from violence and outrage that gave the English government little choice but to legislate. Both were concerned with the sanctity and alienation of property and both with religious appeals. But unlike the Irish Church question, the abolition of slavery had wide support in the country and parliament and was brought, as a consequence, to a successful and speedy conclusion.

Since 1823, Britain had followed an ameliorative policy whereby the colonial legislatures were encouraged to alter the governing institution regarding slavery in return for economic advantages. However, in January 1830 the British Anti-Slavery Society abandoned its hitherto 'prudent' goal of gradual abolition by demanding that immediate emancipation be granted to all slave children born after 1 January 1830.[53] Wellington's government responded by reducing the duty on West Indian sugar in March in the hope that the West Indian planters would allow a better regulation of slave labour.[54] Although immediate emancipation was not considered, this budget measure boded well for the new, aggressive tactics of the anti-slavery movement. When it came to office, Grey's ministry followed the policy of resisting the demand for abolition. Before long, continued resistance was out of the question. By the time that the Reform bill was steered through parliament, sufficient pressure had been organised to force consideration of emancipation. A bill to emancipate the West Indian slaves was brought forward as one of the first measures of the reformed parliament, and by August, 1833, had Royal assent. There can be little doubt that the pressure of the anti-slavery movement prompted the Whigs to act. When Foxwell Buxton, its chief parliamentary spokesman, provided alarming statistics on slave mortality in April 1831 and moved that parliament should take up the question of abolition,[55] the government was unmoved. Grey was indifferent to the matter, and was in any case too busy with Reform. Though Ministers failed to persuade Buxton to postpone his motion, Howick, as Undersecretary of State for the Colonies, announced in parliament that the government had no proposals for freeing the slaves.[56] Grey also told Buxton that those who argued for abolition, as Howick himself had done, were 'too zealous' in their beliefs.[57] As a result of this failure of the Anti-Slavery Society to influence government, an Agency Committee was formed from among its more radical members to organise in an orderly fashion the popular agitation that had appeared at the elections of 1830. By the time of the elections in December 1832, these forces of 'immediacy' were able to influence several elections both north and south, urban and rural.[58] Greville was struck by the 'extraordinary and remarkable' passions of this 'rage for emancipation' which seemed to go beyond political interest; Althorp remarked that emancipation, would be 'more popular than the reform bill'. But though tentative preparations for a measure were hastily undertaken, the omission of any mention of it in the King's speech on the opening of parliament excited the abolitionists yet further. The government could best be described as 'lukewarm' to the idea. Althorp in fact, told Buxton that the cabinet's real wish was to 'defer it sine die'.[59] But by announcing that he would bring a plan of his own forward on 19 March, Buxton forced the government to announce in turn that it would have a plan by 23 April.

The Whigs' vacillation in doing what they were quickly coming to regard as inevitable was prompted by the contervailing pressure of the West Indian planters, whose property, it was argued, was in considerable danger. In 1831, the government had emancipated all slaves owned by the Crown as a concession to the abolitionists.[60] This measure was followed by rumours of further concession and, finally, by an insurrection in December that required the proclamation of martial law and the calling of the colonial militia for the restoration of order. The West Indian planters were incensed, blaming the revolt and distress in Jamaica on anti-slavery clamour that the government appeared unwilling to control. William Bourge, a leading planter spokesman, organised a popular campaign that succeeded in gathering 6000 supporters in London to call on the Lords to investigate conditions in the West Indies.[61] In April, the Earl of Harewood, a leading Yorkshire Tory, successfully moved a resolution to that effect on behalf of the planters. Common gossip had it that the Archbishop of Canterbury had forced this select committee on the government as the price of his support for the Reform bill,[62] a charge less indicative of its truth than of general non-conformist ire against the Church which was, in this case, seen to support slavery. In the event, the Whigs were not opposed to this manifestation of support for the planters' case. 'I am perfectly convinced', wrote Althorp following the uprising, 'that something must be done for the relief of the West Indian proprietors'.[63] When Buxton moved for a select committee of the Commons to counter the Lords' committee which included eight slave owners, Althorp acquiesced in it only at the last moment, and not before telling Buxton that such a committee would have to take into account the interests of all classes.[64] Goderich, the Colonial Secretary, was to learn somewhat painfully that his colleagues were not prepared to legislate against the planters' interests. In June 1832, he said in the Commons that the government 'ought to contemplate' abolition, and his dispatches to the colonies declared that the government was working to that end. Within a year he was replaced at the Colonial office by Stanley, who, it was thought, would not be susceptible to the abolitionist ideas rampant among the junior members of that office as the weaker Goderich was believed to have been.[65]

With the elections out of the way at the end of 1832, the cabinet began to debate a plan, drawn up at the colonial office by Howick, that called for emancipation in 1835, with a loan to the planters to compensate them for their loss. At the same time, it was decided that though the select committee of the Commons should resume its hearings, nothing would be submitted to parliament before the West Indian planters were 'consulted'.[66] Indications that abolition was planned had alarmed the West Indian and other financial interests. Amidst rumours of financial crisis, a Committee of West Indian merchants threatened to cease all trade in order to show its objections to abolition, and succeeded in having Howick's plan submitted to a delegation of planters and merchants. Howick was incensed with his colleagues' concern for the planters' interest. When the government decided further in March not to act without their consent,[67] he resigned. Stanley then postponed a government motion until mid-May, and began to negotiate directly with the Standing Committee of the West Indian planters and merchants. The resultant measure was made public on 14 May. It satisfied neither competing interest. Announced as a matter of 'doing some good, at the least risk of effecting evil', the bill proposed a twelve year apprenticeship with a loan of £15 million to the planters, who would pay wages to the slaves for one-quarter of their work time.[68] The terms of the bill had undergone substantial adjustment from Howick's early draft; the demands of the planters for greater compensation and gradual emancipation had worked to some effect. The abolitionists' fury at the changes was predictable. Buxton was nearly able to persuade the Commons to abolish the apprenticeship entirely, and when the government defeated his motion by the narrow majority of seven votes, a decision was made to reduce the apprenticeship to seven years but to compensate the planters further with an outright grant of £20 million instead of the original loan for the smaller amount. In this form it passed the Commons, and unlike any other measure of importance in 1833, was left virtually unchanged by the Lords.

The act which was to set more than 800,000 slaves free was, as Dr Temperley wrote, an 'amazing achievement' when viewed from anything other than the anti-slavery leaders' 'perfectionist standpoint', coming as it did only ten years after the crusade had begun.[69] It is important, though, to note that it was the uprisings in Jamaica which threatened the slave owners' livelihoods and property as much as the movement to abolish slavery which moved the government to action. The anti-slave crusade made emancipation the only possible course of action once the government decided to act, but Whig sympathies and initiatives lay generally as much with the slave owners as the slaves. Ellice, whose family fortune owed no small part to its West Indian interests, favoured a scheme that would take twenty years to implement, arguing that 'discretion must preside over our feelings'.[70] Holland was the most prominent slave owner among the Whigs. His largest source of income came from Lady Holland's Vassall estate in Jamaica, and his attitude towards abolition provides a good indication of the Whig dilemma in treating this issue. Although Holland had long been a leader of the West Indian lobby in parliament, he had vigorously promoted abolition of the slave trade which he had described as 'one of the greatest evils to which the human race has ever been exposed'. Although he supported in principle the abolition of slavery, he was convinced that the zealotry of the Saints who demanded immediate emancipation would lead to disorder and riots. The Jamaican rebellion which had ruined twenty plantations and caused the deaths of 2000 slaves was, he believed, a foretaste of further problems if adequate preparations could not be made for emancipation. If the plantation owners could not be protected against ruin and the newly-freed slaves ensured of co-operation from their former masters and the full enjoyment of newly won rights, the whole fabric of the island's society would be imperilled. It was with some relief that he welcomed Stanley's proposal for a seven year apprenticeship, which he considered necessary if both master and slave were to be prepared for the new economic and social realities.[71] Russell too was concerned with this practical as well as the moral issue; although the cabinet was sympathetic to the slaves' plight, he told Howick, it wished to move more slowly in order that there 'not be any sudden change in society'.[72] Howick, it should be said, had also taken the owners' interest heavily into account; his plan had been based on the belief that the masters preferred immediate emancipation, and included provisions which would force the freed slaves to work for their old masters rather than for themselves.[73] Graham, who owned that he was 'quite devoid of passion on this subject . . . and sincere to avert the ruin of the owners of slave property', expressed feelings similar to Macaulay's, who, though usually pictured as a stout abolitionist, told the Commons in 1845 that his obligations to slavery ceased when slavery itself ceased in the part of the world for the welfare of which he, as a member of the house was accountable. Macaulay's opposition to the apprenticeship scheme, in fact, was in deference to his father Zachary, 'for whose sake alone' he took part in the whole business.[74] None were so hostile to emancipation as Melbourne. 'They would have their fancy', he is reported to have said, 'and so we've abolished slavery, but it's great folly'.[75] At Holland House he exclaimed 'By God, you are ruining your empire', whereupon Lady Holland pointed at Brougham with the response 'Yes, and there is the chief sinner.'[76] The Lord Chancellor, of course, had been distrusted by his colleagues from the time of his popular victory over the traditional aristocracy at his Yorkshire election in 1830. He had argued strongly for immediate abolition on the eve of that election which he later acknowledged had turned largely on that issue, and was thought by most to have courted a personal popularity on it. Yet during the cabinet debates in 1833, he showed the same reluctance to act quickly, and did little more than to support gradual emancipation rather than concede to the abolitionists' desire for immediate freedom.[77]

Too much has perhaps been made of the influence of the Reform Bill on the granting of emancipation. William Knibb, the most celebrated of the dissenting missionaries who were exiled from Jamaica in September 1832 for their anti-slavery activities, announced, on hearing on the bill's passage, 'Thank God, now I'll have slavery down'.[78] He little realized that the measure was, by then, all but drawn up. Almost a year had passed since Althorp was convinced that something had to be done for the planters, and nothing since had altered Whig plans. Holland wanted a measure to prevent troops being necessary to restore peace, and looked on emancipation as a means of preserving property.[79] Goderich, who by February 1833 had been brought into line with government thinking, told Mulgrave that 'we are influenced by a desire to save them [planters] from a danger most imminent, and to raise them from a state of depression amounting, in some instances, at least almost to ruin.'[80] This overriding concern with the planters' interests, it must be remembered, came at a time when the Reform Act left the West Indian interest with much less representation in parliament than before.[81] It is true that the widespread support for emancipation in the new House forced a reduction of the apprenticeship from twelve years to seven, but at the same time, Stanley had pointed out to Buxton that without an apprenticeship clause, there would be no bill at all.[82] Abolitionist pressure did keep the government up to the mark, and amounted, at times, to what Holland scathingly termed 'the lash',[83] but as far as parliamentary considerations were concerned, the government was just as concerned with Tory opposition in the Lords. Wellington, it was learned, was planning to beat the government on the question 'with effect', and during the passing of the bill through the Commons, there was a great deal of concert between Wellington and Grey over its provisions.[84] Then too, there was the King's well known opposition to emancipation that had to be countered. Ellice did his best to assure him that the slaves were 'not sufficiently apt instruments' to assert their independence from plantation owners, but Stanley's assurances that property and colonial peace would best be preserved by the measure had more effect, and had much to do with the King's confidence in him.[85]

It cannot be denied, in the end, that the abolition of slavery was a great measure of reform. It was not a measure which Whigs brought in from any theoretical attachment to the principle of emancipation, and like so much of their reform legislation, would likely have been passed whoever was in office, and without the influence of parliamentary reform. If insurrection in the colonies and the crusade of the Anti-Slavery Society forced the home government to legislate, the Whig role was to conciliate the interests of the slaves with the slave-owners. There is some evidence, however, that many Whigs shared certain assumptions with the Evangelicals, and that the convergence of values was of some assistance to the anti-slavery movement in prompting the government to abolish the institution. Professor Kriegel has demonstrated, for example, that both groups accepted the need to provide an honourable liberty to the degraded slave; both Whig and Saint expected the freed slaves to accept with gratitude a subordinate position in a hierarchical society.[86] Whigs could not, and would not, preserve the institution of slavery, but they hoped that abolition, if accompanied by compensation to the slave owners and passed in such a form that would guarantee the maintenance of the sugar industry, would not interfere with the sanctity of property.

Within a few weeks of the slavery legislation, parliament also passed the act regulating the employment of children in factories. As Halévy has noted, both came in response to the demands of 'a humanitarian piety' that was difficult to resist.[87] The movement for factory legislation, revived so dramatically by Richard Oastler's letter on Yorkshire slavery to the *Leeds Mercury* in October 1830, accomplished an important victory in a few short years. Yet as was the case with the slavery abolitionists, the leaders of this movement were critical of the government's bill as a cruel and hypocritical measure designed to serve the master by putting off more extensive legislation. It was, charged Oastler, 'a trick of the government' to save 'their dear friends the capitalists'.[88] For this Tory and Church of England estate manager, whose paternalism had once prompted him to hope for a union of the aristocracy and people, 'and thus to save them both',[89] disappointment was prompted by the postponement of a ten hours bill, the movement for which had grown under his tutelage.

It would be wrong, however, to suggest that the measure, or the enquiry that preceded it, was nothing more than a cynical attempt to support capitalist friends. If Whiggery had a 'typical' attitude toward parvenu capitalist entrepreneurs, it would have been better described as one of mild contempt and fear for their influence on traditional society. What prompted the Whigs to take up their cause, like that of the slave masters, was not amity, but a rudimentary belief in *laissez-faire* economics and the traditional virtue of leaving well enough alone until political forces dictated intervention. It is true that the Whigs did not generally sympathise with the labouring poor whose unemployment was thought to be behind demands for shorter hours,[90] and in this gave a preview of their distaste for idleness that would surface in the debates over the poor laws. In 1818 Graham had denounced the signatories of a petition supporting Peel's restrictive bill as 'a set of idle, discontented, discarded, good-for-nothing workmen', and in the *Edinburgh Review* of 1830, Macaulay savagely denounced the anti-Malthusian writings of Sadler's, a man whom he later described as a 'hyena . . . imitating the cries of little children'. 'As Whigs', opined the *Leeds Intelligencer* during the reformed election, 'we have been accused of being levellers; but never did we contemplate turning the House of Commons into an almshouse for deranged tradesmen'.[91] But far from this distaste of intervention being a craven attempt to keep the unemployed in a state of degradation by propping up the profits of the entrepreneur, Whigs believed that intervention between masters and men would tend to the ultimate disadvantage of both. It was this 'progressive Liberal' argument that legislation would cause both economic ruin for the entrepreneur and lower wages and unemployment for the labourer that Macaulay had in mind when he insisted that 'however unpleasant it might be to work, it was still more unpleasant to starve'. What Palmerston still condemned in 1855 as the 'vicious and wrong principle' of restricting men was anathema not only to those of the government like Thomson and Althorp who were informed on economic matters, but also to those of the older Whig school who looked on legislative interference as nothing more than an attack on property. When Melbourne told Victoria that Ashley was 'the greatest Jacobin in Her Majesty's dominions' he was speaking for that great panoply of Whigs who knew little of economic questions, and cared for them even less. A ten hours bill, Graham thought in 1844, was 'a dangerous course . . . a Jack Cade system of legislation', an opinion with which none of his colleagues, eleven years earlier, disagreed.[92]

It was no surprise that the Whigs, governed as they were by this philosophical objection to interference, should oppose any attempt to do so. When Hobhouse introduced a bill at the instigation of factory reformers in February 1831, the government gave him no encouragement. Lord Morpeth presented petitions against the measure from Yorkshire masters, and with opposition from much of the north and Scotland, Hobhouse was forced to give way and accept all of the masters' amendments. Rather than a bill which would have limited severely the hours of children and young persons in all textile factories, reformers had to do with a much weakened measure that would affect only cotton factories, and provide no enforcement.[93] But the reform movement was given great impetus by this defeat, and before the end of the year Sadler, its new champion in the Commons, was given leave to bring in a factory bill that accorded with the views of the Ten Hour movement. Introduced in March, it prohibited factory labour below the age of nine, restricted the labour of those between nine and eighteen to ten hours a day, and prohibited night work for all under twenty-one. Althorp responded to Sadler's philanthropic and paternalistic approach with what one critic later termed 'the heartless haranguer of Whig political economists':[94] should the bill pass, there would likely be no children and fewer adults working at all in the factories; a detailed parliamentary enquiry would be necessary, he declared, and even if it should favour a measure, 'he did not wish . . . to pledge himself in any way to further the progress' of a bill.[95]

The parliamentary committee was rightly regarded by the Ten Hour movement as a procedural device to postpone its legislation, but despite the presence on it of declared opponents of Sadler's bill such as Morpeth and Thomson, the report which was issued in January 1833 was a massive indictment of industrial conditions which did a great deal to counter the damage done to the movement by the general elections. 'Two opinions could not be entertained' as a result of the Sadler Committee's report, thought Hobhouse. Yet the government of which Hobhouse was now a member remained unconvinced. When Ashley, Sadler's successor in the Commons, gave notice to reintroduce Sadler's measure, Morpeth told him that he would present a rival measure extending Hobhouse's 1831 Act to all textiles that would suit the interests 'of all classes'.[96] Morpeth finally withdrew his motion, but only after the government gave its support to a motion by the Conservative

Wilson Patten to set up a Royal Commission. Patten's motion, instigated by the hastily formed 'Association of Master Manufacturers' who wanted their views heard, was widely condemned as another shelving device, and an unconstitutional one at that. The opposite in fact was the case. Melbourne, who as Home Secretary was responsible for law and order and unhappy about the dangers that might follow delaying tactics, gave the Commission only six weeks to report.[97] The commissioners, several of whom were Benthamites, saw matters in a much less emotional manner than Ashley's friends; they were critical of his bill and its likelihood of restricting the hours of adult workers as well as children. Nevertheless, like the parliamentary committee of 1832, the Commission did nothing to hide evidence of the harmful effects of long hours in bad conditions on children in factories.

There can be little doubt that the Commission's task was not to stall, but to provide evidence for the government's view that legislation should not affect adults. In fact it was the known objection of Chadwick and his fellow commissioners to unnecessary interference with adult labour that prompted the Whigs to appoint them to a Royal Commission, which would be far more reliable than a parliamentary select committee. A rapidly drafted report might help to take the wind from the Ten Hours Movement's sails.[98] Even before the Commission reported, Althorp suggested to the House that restrictions should apply only to the youngest children, a conclusion reflected in the succeeding Report's contention that restricting the labour of young persons over thirteen, as Ashley's bill would do, would limit adult labour and harm the manufacturer. On 18 July, he carried by the large majority of 238 to 93 an amendment to Ashley's bill to limit restrictions to the age of thirteen so as not to 'curtail the profits of the manufacturer, and lessen his powers to compete with foreign rivals'.[99] Ashley's ten hour bill now in ruins, Althorp introduced the government bill on 9 August. It was prepared by Chadwick along the lines of the Commission's recommendations. Its education and inspection provisions were an improvement on Ashley's bill, but the main intent was, in Horner's words, to prevent the overworking of juveniles 'without interfering with . . . adults'.[100] By proposing an eight hour day for children, a provision which permitted the use of relays, limitations on the working hours of adults could be avoided. Although Althorp 'still entertained doubts' of the propriety of interfering between master and servant, he admitted to the house 'that if children were placed in a situation in which they could not protect themselves, it was the duty of the House to afford protection to them.'[101]

The appointment of the Royal Commission and Althorp's bill which came from it were shrewd measures, for despite the tendency of the Reform Act to enfranchise opponents of factory legislation ('the people do not live in £10 houses', commented Oastler)[102] and the disastrous defeat of Sadler in Leeds, the Ten Hour movement had managed to gain the support of a significant number of MPs on both sides of the Commons. Furthermore, with added support from the Church and Tory paternalists, a ten hours bill would likely have carried the Lords. The treasury secretary Charles Wood explained to Halifax liberals that whether the eventual bill was good or not, it was the only course that the government had in its power to pursue 'to avoid a much greater evil'; at the beginning of the session, a large majority would have carried a ten hours bill.[103] The advantage of the Commission report was to have expert criticism of Ashley's bill make Althorp's amendment and his own subsequent bill politically acceptable. Wood might also have mentioned the Radical support which made Althorp's bill possible. Lacking the personal interest that prompted so many industrialists to oppose Ashley, several Radicals nevertheless accepted the economic orthodoxy that intervention was dangerous. But the passions aroused by the ten hours campaign rendered opposition to a 'people's measure' impossible. Several were caught between personal principle and political sensitivity and dared not speak on the issue. Characteristically, Hume was one who did. By his own later admission one who condemned 'mawkish humanity' and 'humanity mongers', he found himself forced to support Sadler's bill in 1832 despite his declared belief that 'it was essential to the welfare of the country at large that as little legislative interference as possible should take place between master and servant'.[104] Cobbett, too, objected to such interference which 'always failed',[105] but the Commission and Althorp's bill allowed him and many Radicals to support both their principles and the people. Hume led a large number in supporting Patten's motion for a Commission of Enquiry and Althorp's wrecking of Ashley's bill on 18 July. Radical support was significant. It helped secure passage of the final act, and made the cries that the Whigs were deserting the people ring hollow.

The Whigs, then, made the best of a difficult parliamentary position to prevent what they considered harmful legislation. Their bill, it was admitted in the *The Reform Ministry and The*

Reformed Parliament, was successful because it was 'less dangerous to the commercial prosperity of the country' that all persons depended on for peace and security.[106] There is little doubt that there would have been no measure had it not been forced on them, a fact which, as was the case with slavery abolition, must temper the estimated effect of their supposed overwhelming victory in the 1832 elections. Ironic too was the effect of the Reform Act on this measure. Without the passions which the struggle for the Reform Act stirred, movements like Oastler's might never have succeeded. But the striking effect of the Act was to weaken the factory reformers' parliamentary position. It was among the more traditional groups in and out of parliament, the Church and Tory paternalists, that support for factory reform emanated, and it was only by the most strident efforts of middle class dissenters, the supposed benefactors of Reform, that a more far reaching factory act was averted. Wood concluded that it was only by the exertions of the representatives of the newly enfranchised towns that Ashley's bill was rejected in favour of Althorp's.[107] In the end, Whig paternalistic sympathies for the children's plight allowed them to give way to limited interference, but their equally strong support for property and the vulgarised ideals of Adam Smith prevented gross intervention.

Where the need to preserve urban tranquility had prompted factory legislation, the pressing requirement for rural peace led to the new poor law of 1834. It had been evident for some time that the old poor laws were manifestly unable to provide for rural stability. Pauper indiscipline was a problem of long standing, and the extraordinary rise in the rates which it was believed followed implementation of the 'Speenhamland' relief methods prompted the landed classes to call for substantial change in the system. As landed proprietors themselves, the Whigs were determined to find an effective remedy to the problem. Because this was an issue which affected them personally, they had few of the doubts concerning intervention which had attended their factory endeavours. In this sense, their poor law measure more closely resembled the Reform Act than it did factory reform. Indeed, the Tory *Annual Register* praised the new law as 'their true Reform Bill'.[108] As had been the case with reform of parliament, and unlike factory reform, the Whigs did not react to insuperable pressures which allowed them only to alter inevitable measures to suit their principles as much as possible. Rather, they saw that an institution designed to maintain social harmony required amendment. Halévy criticised ministers for 'very cleverly' introducing the bill as a measure of 'agricultural relief',[109] but this, in fact, was how they viewed it. In every discussion of agricultural distress since the Napoleonic wars, the increase in agrarian poverty was attributed to the operation of the poor laws. Public relief, which Brougham described in 1816 as a 'cancer in the state'[110] was widely regarded as a cause of idleness, vagrancy and agricultural depression. By 1830, poor rates and agricultural distress had risen correspondingly to alarming levels, and with the incendiarism and Swing riots that broke out at the end of the year, the case for an alteration of the system was obvious. No 'movement' for poor law reform was necessary, and no parliamentary pressure group forced the issue. The landed classes regarded the problem as their own, and through parliament possessed the power to effect a remedy. Although the Poor Law Amendment Act of 1834 has been described as Benthamite centralisation designed to reduce the power of the magistracy and local vestries in favour of the middle class professionals in Somerset House, it seems clear from recent studies that the Whigs were motivated by a desire to 'maintain the economic and social ascendency of the landed interest', as Professor Brundage has written, 'to reorganize and strengthen the power of the country's traditional leaders over their localities.'[111]

If the financial burden to the landed classes weighed considerably on the aristocracy's deliberations, such consideration was secondary to the need for social harmony. In Russell's account of the question, the extraordinary increase in the rates since the introduction of the 'Speenhamland System' is contrasted with the 'remarkable' decrease following the passage of the 1834 law, but it is clear that his prime concern was for legislation 'to prevent the total absorption of property by the sturdy beggar and idle vagabond'. Without a change, 'all property was in danger'.[112] Althorp, too, was concerned about the landlord who was 'ultimately the suffering party' as a result of maladministration which tended 'directly to the destruction of all property' in the country. Hence, he refused to exempt from the act those parishes like Manchester where rates were comparatively low, arguing that such an exemption would make the bill what the government had been accused of wishing to make it, namely a plan to save the pockets of the ratepayers only. Strengthening the role of the landed magnates as magistrates in the local administration of the poor, it was thought, would best provide for social harmony which alone could safe-guard property. In the belief that lax administration had arisen through vestries which had too little landlord influence, the government sought a remedy which would give landlords who hitherto 'had not the power of influencing the management of the poor or of voting at the vestry' a more direct influence.[113] In 1831, a select committee of the Lords set up by Wellington's government to investigate the problems of poor relief interested itself primarily in the magistrates' powers and legality of relief.[114] The Royal Commission established in 1832 was also concerned with these powers. The assistant commissioners were instructed to ascertain what influence should be given to the landlords in the vestry, and to determine where magisterial interference was unwarranted. The phrasing of this second instruction suggested that magisterial influence was to be reduced only where magistrates lacked a strong local connection.[115] The bill which followed the Commission's report addressed itself in large measure to this question. The role performed by the magistrates was made direct, rather than appellate as before, a plural voting system for the vestries gave them a weight dependent on the size of their property, and the union boundaries were left to be drawn up according to local ownership patterns.[116]

The desire of the landed classes for a more direct control of local administration was premised on the belief that poverty had been fostered by too little control over relief. Only those who had an interest in local society would be vigilant in reducing harmful payments. J. R. Poynter has termed the new act 'revisionist Malthusian' at best, pointing to Malthus' desire to abolish poor relief altogether,[117] but there is no question that a stricter control over relief was thought to be necessary for the salvation of the agrarian system. There was some debate over the effectiveness of the workhouse test which in the end was to be only partially applied, but few dissented from Brougham's view that Tudor legislators 'were not adept in political science, they were not acquainted with the true principles [and] could not foresee that a Malthus would arise to enlighten mankind.'[118] Although Malthus' principles of population held little sway by 1830, there was a widespread acceptance of his attitude that misery and insecurity were necessary for virtue. His belief that the poor laws were 'strongly calculated' to eradicate the spirit of independence of the peasantry, and that 'hard as it may appear in individual circumstances, dependent poverty ought to be held disgraceful',[119] guided the thinking of the Poor Law Commissioners. They reported that the system tended to destroy diligence, honesty and skill in the labourer, and asked, 'what motive has the man who is to receive 10s. every Saturday . . . who knows that his income will be increased by nothing but by an increase of his family . . . what motive has he to acquire or preserve any of these merits?'[120] The government too, accepted this concept as a truism. Before the Commission had reported, Althorp told the Commons that improper administration of the poor laws had worked to the detriment of the labourers, where 'feelings of independence . . . had been almost entirely extinguished in many parts of the country.'[121] In 1821 Russell had proposed the remedy of eliminating relief entirely; two years later, he had come to the view that strict adherence to such dogma was wrong: 'The poor laws must be pruned, not rooted up; the knife, and not the axe, must be used'.[122]

The Whig remedy, then, was based on wise pruning which, it was believed, would be most likely adhered to by local magnates. Castlereagh had argued in 1817 that the Scottish system of control by local proprietors should be copied in England, and in 1834, Brougham explicitly stated that the purpose of the act was to approximate English practice to that of Scotland. Howick, too, pointed out that the Scottish heritor [landowners], having votes, had been productive of 'the most beneficial effects in the administration of the Poor-laws'.[123] Nassau Senior did his utmost, through the Royal Commission of Enquiry, to provide the government with a centralist Benthamite plan that would give local proprietors little control, but it is doubtful that ministers had any intention of listening to him. It is likely in fact that the Commission had been the chosen vehicle of enquiry in order to provide the government with an anti-centralist report. Graham later told Peel that the Whigs had used the Commission to pave the way for a specific change in the laws.[124] And although Senior was an ardent Benthamite centraliser, the majority of the seven Commissioners were not. Chadwick, who drafted the eventual report, rose to prominence as one of twenty-six Assistant Commissioners not simply because of his undoubted talents. He had made it clear that he would not let his own attachment to Benthamite principles interfere with the Whigs' known desire for increased local control, and was brought into the Commission to counter Senior's more stubbornly held vision. Senior himself was forced to conclude that because the local magistrates would be the most influential members of the Board of Guardians, 'the bill does not take away their power but enables them to exercise it in a more beneficial manner'.[125] That the Whigs regarde the increase of local landed influence as a central feature of their measure can be seen in their later rejection of Chadwick as a permanent Commissioner to oversee the implementation of the Act; he was known to sympathise with the notion of centralisation and would, it was feared, work to establish what he had realised could not have been part of the bill itself.[126] In 1837, Russell made the point publicly. In response to John Walters, the Berkshire magistrate and proprietor of *The Times* who had opposed the new law and now moved for a select committee to investigate the harmful effects of the new law, Russell declared all descriptions of the loss of local initiatives as a 'gross misrepresentation' of the act; the 'real object', he claimed[127]

> was to establish self-government – a principle to be found so useful in all matters of local concern . . . The magistrate was now a member of the Board of Guardians . . . The consequence was, that a kind of local government was established, acting certainly under such general rules and general directions as the intelligence and experience of the Poor-law Commissioners had prescribed, but with respect to details, acting according to the judgement of the magistrates, country gentlemen, the farmers and the ratepayers connected with the district.

Of all their important legislative acts, poor law reform was the one on which Whigs had no substantial doubts concerning the propriety, form, or success. The main features of the bill are well known. Three central Commissioners were to advise and supervise the Boards of Guardians who were to be elected locally by the ratepayers of the newly created Unions. The cabinet committee which consisted of Richmond, Ripon, Graham, Althorp, Melbourne and Russell debated at length the wisdom of the workhouse test and the abolition of outdoor relief to the able-bodied, but in the end maintained this central principle.[128] There was little doubt that the measure would be generally well-received. Bishop Blomfield, a member of the Royal Commission, had been on guard for the interests of the Church, which was particularly pleased with the provisions for religious instruction in the workhouses.[129]

Dissenters supported this feature of the bill as well, although they later became bitterly opposed to the universal practice of Boards of Guardians paying the salaries of Anglican workhouse chaplains from the rates. Introduced on 17 April, 1834, the bill was supported by most of the important Radicals and all but a few Tories. 'It was our support . . . that enabled government to pass it without fearful resistance', Peel later told Croker, and with Hume in the Commons and Wellington in the Lords speaking out in favour of the measure, there was every reason to support Lansdowne's view that 'it has not been treated as a party question – it is sure to pass'.[130] By August it had Royal assent.

The Whigs had much reason to be pleased with the Act's reception out of doors. The mixed acceptance in the country and the difficulties of its implementation were predictable, and if the setting up of the central commission was an attempt to put the local administration of the poor laws beyond the pale of party politics, that hope was dashed.[131] Yet, time and a judicious allowance by the Commissioners of local circumstances in the provision of relief overcame most local resistance to implementation. The discontent of the labouring classes and their leaders was something that the government understood and expected, and though, through Chartism, the protest was rather more than predicted, serious dissatisfaction proved to be less dangerous than many had feared, and certainly less alarming than the incendiarism that preceded the act. In any event, the unpopularity and hardship of the workhouse were counted on to reduce pauperism and make the measure work, and with no working-class franchise, the act was not expected to do either aristocratic party much electoral damage. Among the middling and upper orders, more especially the latter, the new law was a popular success. It pleased the King, whose obsession for a coalition government of Whigs and Peelites led him to congratulate Althorp on the 'conservative proceedings of the Government',[132] and his delight at the influence given to the traditional leaders of society was matched by those leaders themselves. 'So far as my observation goes', wrote Althorp to Brougham in 1837, 'the new Poor Law is the most universally popular measure I can remember'.[133] Perhaps this popularity was due to what Cobbett referred to as the role of the central Commissioners 'stuck up here in London to bear all the blame'.[134] More likely, however, was the success of the new measure in fostering what it was designed to do. Althorp had remarked that 'The landed interest were looking for immediate relief',[135] and within five years of passage, the act had provided many salutary benefits for this interest. Ninety per cent of the country had come under the pale of the new law, the poor had found it far more difficult to receive indiscriminately administered relief, and the rates were down considerably. With encouragement from Russell, the local boards were given discretion to provide some outdoor relief where necessary and to relax the strictest codes of workhouse living, measures which helped to overcome some local resistance to 'centralisation'. By the end of the decade, most peers and gentry were involved or co-operated with the new system which, Brundage concluded, 'enhanced a sense of community as well as the leadership of traditional elites'.[136] In 1852, when Disraeli was toying with the idea of national rather than local taxation for poor relief, Nassau Senior was told by a friend that 'The country gentlemen would not bear to have the management of their parishes and unions put into the hands of Government officers.'[137] That the local magnates continued to dominate poor law administration for most of the century was not accidental. 'We owe you an eternal debt of gratitude', wrote the Tory Lord Western to Russell in 1841. 'The Poor Law was necessary to our salvation.'[138]

THE WHIGS AND THE CHURCH

In the midst of the crisis brought on by the Lords' rejection of the Reform Bill in October 1831, Lord Holland met with Bishop Blomfield of London to discuss the controversial role taken by the Bishops who had voted against the bill. 'If he will support what you deem right in the state', Holland wrote back to Grey, 'he may reasonably expect you to co-operate in allaying the public cry against the Church and to confine reforms and regulations . . . in the Church to such objects as will leave the establishment untouched.'[139] This letter points out the two fundamental political attitudes held by the Church at this time. First, it was worried about the prospects of its own reform as much, if not more so than of parliament. Indeed, it refused to give the Tories in the Lords further support against Reform in order to avoid hostility that might provoke a reformed House of Lords and a damaged Church. Secondly, the Church did not trust Whigs.

By 1830, the Church was as much in need of reform as was parliament. Critics and Church reformers, with varying degrees of hostility and amity, had made persistent calls for changes in the Establishment. Among all but the most blind of the high Tory politicians, the need for reform was obvious. The Primate Archbishop Howley had talks with Wellington on the subject in 1828, but the change of Government in 1830 prevented a measure from being brought forward.[140] Howley and Blomfield both recognised that moderate reforms affecting preferments, pluralism and non-residence would strengthen the Church and weaken the cries of its enemies. To this end, Blomfield worked closely with Peel on reform programmes and strategies almost from the time Grey took office. But the great fear of the Church, which lacked the autonomy to reform itself, was spoliation at the hand of its enemies. With widespread demands for a radical reduction in the wealth of what was seen to be a socially exclusive monopoly, it was important that the Establishment be reformed by friends. And it was on this score that the Whigs were found wanting. In January 1828, during the last weeks of Goderich's ministry, Bishop Phillpotts termed Whigs 'disgraceful'. Supposing a Whig ministry were to follow, he asked, who are they to be? 'Lord Holland, his wife an atheist, and himself not far from it. Lord Lansdowne, a confessed Unitarian, Brougham a Deist . . . '. He later was to scribble on a scrap of paper his description of the new Whig government:[141]

```
g  R  ey
m  E  lbourne
d  V  rham
h  O  lland
a  L  thorp
r  U  ssell
s  T  anley
r  I  chmond
g  O  derich
.  .  .
```

That Grey's government brought in legislative changes which increased the rights and liberties of Dissenters, Catholics and the

Commons only added to Church concerns. Whigs, it seemed obvious to Churchmen, preferred to support its opponents. The view that Peel's ministry of 1834–35 was the first 'friendly to the Church' since Wellington's[142] fails to take into account the Whigs' actual attitudes, but there is no question that Church prelates thought in these terms. And even if the Whigs as individuals wished no harm to the Church, it was clear that many of those who counted among their parliamentary supporters did. The Church noticed with dismay that it was the Radical Hume who moved for the Commission of Enquiry into Church property in 1832,[143] and no matter how well constructed the Commission, or however moderate Whig proposals, the Church would not feel safe until a Tory government, eschewing Radical and Liberal support, would take up the question.

The Whigs were not insensitive to the Church's fears, and indeed, shared many of them. They too believed that the Church ought to be reformed by Churchmen, and to that end, saw that the Commission was composed only of conservatives. The result, wrote Professor Chadwick, was 'a low bulwark against hasty change'.[144] In October 1832, Grey advised Howley that because of the government's desire that the Church be reformed voluntarily, the Bishops themselves should evolve a scheme of reform to protect the Church. A few months later, he stressed publicly the need for 'calm and dispassionate consideration' of the subject, and added that if even he were to propose any reform, 'it should only be with a view of adding to its efficiency, promoting the security of the Church itself, making it more respectable [and] placing it completely in safety.'[145] Grey's attitude was shared by his colleagues. Church reform was necessary for the same reason as parliamentary reform had been: the system was plainly unpopular and was in need of reform if it were to be saved. Grey blamed the delay in granting Emancipation for the 'power acquired during its agitation by some of the popular leaders & the use they seem inclined to make of it'.[146] Similar dangers accompanied the difficult passage of parliamentary reform, and the Church's own recognition of the need for change made it imperative that it be done safely without undue delay. Church reform was necessary, Melbourne later told Queen Victoria, for the 'cry . . . came from the Bosom of the Establishment itself'.[147] The cry was also coming from the country. Morpeth told Grey that though the general feeling in Yorkshire was for a measure of Church reform, there was no wish to destroy the Establishment; he advised that it was 'essential to the welfare of the Church' that a 'decided measure of Conservative reform' be undertaken. Althorp told the Prime Minister that to do nothing would 'be doing infinite mischief', and called for measures to abolish sinecures, reduce Church rates and commute tithes 'to save the Establishment'. Graham, who would soon join Peel in opposition, was most forthright. 'No time is to be lost', he wrote to Holland,[148]

> in taking decisive measures of large Church Reform, and in giving to the people some substantial fruit of the great changes which have been effected in the Government of our country . . . patience is nearly exhausted . . . if we do not quickly and freely give up that [which] can be safely granted . . . [there will be] no limit to the demands which will be made, and to the concessions which will be extorted.

However necessary Church reform was for its own salvation, and however acceptable the concept of reform might have been to the Church or to the Tories who had, and were, to devise plans for its improvement, Whig religious attitudes generally earned the Churchmen's distrust. Those attitudes were derived from eighteenth century notions of rationalism and liberty. To the Whig mind, the Christian virtues of justice, benevolence, temperance, patience and self-denial were the unique civilising attributes of Western society.[149] If left untrammelled by ignorance and intolerance, human progress and enlightenment could not be better served than by rational religion. The Whig preference, as Melbourne termed it, was for 'cool and indifferent' religion,[150] a view which perhaps ironically generated greater sympathy at times for the Church than for overzealous Dissenting sects and Roman Catholics. Russell, who 'suffered from dogmatic anti-dogmatism' in his opposition to bigotry and superstitious clergy, was notoriously anti-Catholic;[151] his opposition to dogma was aimed as much at the religious opponents of the Establishment as at the Church itself. Holland recruited Anglican priests for his Jamaican plantations to counteract the passions of Dissenting missionaries, and by so doing, recognised the usefulness of the Church in restraining the zealous appetites of those who, Macaulay wrote in defending the Church as a bulwark against fervour, 'are placed above all earthly fears'.[152] Whigs were Erastian from a belief that educated men could provide for enlightened legislation, a rational step removed from clerical passions and prejudices. Only to the extent that religiosity and clericalism were too often intertwined were Whigs anti-religious. The cause of civil and religious liberty was the cause of the liberty of conscience from the tyranny of dogma and intolerance. Thus, though the Bishops doubted it, the Whigs did support an Established Church, albeit for the reason that the state could, by virtue of its control, ensure that it did not discriminate against other religions by claiming a monopoly on truth. An Established Church, in other words, was useful, and on that ground alone could be defended.

Although the Whigs did not set out to reform the Church, they could not violate their Foxite principles of toleration when circumstance made reform necessary. Nor could they set aside their intuitive Erastian concept of government intervention in Church matters, a concept which came directly into conflict with the Churchmen's strongly held notion of an independent Establishment. It was one thing for Grey to ask Howley to draw up reform plans, but the prelates were not as confident of such assurance when they saw the Whigs devising their own strategies for the first reforms of the Establishment in Ireland. Long before the Commission of Enquiry into Church property was struck, that *damnosa hereditas* had prompted the Government to make assumptions about church property which, in the Church's eyes, augured little good for the English Church. The Irish Church, wrote the Tory Croker, was 'the field of battle in which we are to fight for all property and all our institutions'.[153]

What made reform of the Irish Church inevitable was the Whig belief that the social unrest manifested by the tithe wars was largely a religious problem. In a sense, the Whigs were dragged into Irish Church reform against their will. When they took office, increasing Irish resistance to the payment of tithes prompted some response. Within six weeks Grey reported 'thinking of nothing but Ireland night and day.'[154] Resistance to tithes was largely a protest against agrarian economic conditions, and in several areas was accompanied by the refusal of tenants to pay rents and taxes. The tithe wars were therefore viewed as an attack on property, and it did not require much perspicacity in 1830 to see the revolutionary spirit of France and Belgium crossing the channel to Ireland. 'You may rest assured', Melbourne wrote to Stanley, 'it is all the same spirit which influences all Europe at present'.[155] Daniel

O'Connell, for one, made no secret of his admiration for the Parisian revolutionaries, and in an open letter to the *Dublin Morning Post* exclaimed that France 'has set the great and glorious example, and it only remains for every other country . . . to imitate the precedent'.[156] O'Connell was a particular thorn in English sides. Not only did he transform the campaign against tithes into a movement to eliminate the Protestant Establishment, but it was thought that the tithe war itself was the result of his oratory. Irish Attorney-General Crampton repeated in the Commons the statement of the Lord-Lieutenant of Donegal that the peasants of his country were resolved to pay neither rents, tithes, nor taxes, until O'Connell 'got new taxes for them'. Few Whigs doubted Althorp's opinion that the Irish agitator would have to be put down 'whatever may be the means necessary'. Unsuccessful attempts to buy O'Connell with office and, alternatively, to prosecute, together with the serious nature of Irish unrest, forced the Whigs to realise that the roots of the problem required attention more than O'Connell. 'How to take O'Connell's strength from him', wrote Holland, 'is the problem to be solved'.[157]

The course to be followed in Ireland produced a great division within the ministry that could not be healed and was to end with the resignations in the spring of 1834. The smaller section, led by Stanley and Lansdowne, regarded the problem as one of 'law and order'; as long as tithes remained unpaid, the Church would be unable to function, and the triumph would go to O'Connell and the peasantry whose reward for agitation would be the inevitable destruction of the Establishment. Chief Secretary Stanley, who was as high-handed as he was high-minded, was particularly convinced of the necessity for stern action by the constabulary and army organised under the Peace Preservation Act. In July 1831, within a week of his promotion to the Cabinet, he astounded his more liberal colleagues by announcing in the Commons an arms bill that included provisions for the transportation of any person found with unregistered arms. Most of the cabinet, which had not been shown the offending clause, were 'appalled and disgusted' by it; Althorp termed the provision 'one of the most tyrannical measures I ever heard proposed'.[158] Stanley was forced to drop the offending clause, and for eighteen months the government did its best to govern Ireland with no substantial additional powers. Stanley's insistence on coercive reaction to Irish unrest set him directly against the majority of his ministerial colleagues, who were determined, in Althorp's words, to 'fight to the last to prevent any vigorous laws [from] be[ing] enacted for Ireland'.[159] Holland, Brougham, Durham, Althorp, Russell, Duncannon and Graham formed the nucleus of this group. All regarded the Irish problem as basically religious in origin. The Church of Ireland, with fewer than a million communicants in a population nearing nine million, owed its wealth to a state protection that was increasingly assailed by its critics. Unless reformed, the Protestant Establishment would be unable to survive. These more liberal Whigs did not have complete faith in Anglesey, the Irish Viceroy, but their instinct was to give general support to his constant proposals to reform both tithes and the Church in Ireland.[160] They believed that moderate concessions to the disaffected Catholic population would reduce the antipathy to England and its Church in Ireland. If coercion was necessary, so too was reform.

In viewing the Irish *hereditas* as a religious question, the Whigs shared the common English ignorance of Irish affairs. Few recognised the economic problem in the tithe wars. Stanley's coercive reaction to the question was in fact the single Whig attempt to think in non-religious terms. In their determination to reform the tithe system, the Whigs failed to grasp the economic plight of the peasant or his dependence on the landlord. They were doubtless correct in assuming that commuting tithes to a land or corn tax payable by the landowner would save the Church from embarrassing 'pecuniary collision' between clergy and peasant, but it made little difference to the luckless Irish occupier who would ultimately be forced to bear the brunt of any tax.[161] Whigs were particularly susceptible to this English blind spot, for their historical attachment to civil and religious liberties and support for Catholic emancipation had conditioned them to associate justice for Ireland with justice for Catholics. Stanley's insistence that both select committees set up in 1831 to study the tithe question should have nothing but Protestant members, prompted Holland to regret that 'the distinction of Catholic and Protestant is still so much considered';[162] it could be argued that his objection to the exclusion of Catholics reflected by way of a reverse bias the entrenchment of that very distinction in Whig thought. On a different, but no less significant level, the Whigs were captive to the belief that without a middle class to guide them, the ignorant Irish peasantry were too easily swayed by O'Connell's oratory. Melbourne was not alone in thinking that the Irish were 'persons totally unfit . . . unable to speak English, and in short half or rather whole Barbarians'. Althorp wondered if, without increased wealth and intelligence, the Irish were fit for free government; Russell concluded that 'the physical wretchedness and the moral ignorance' of the Irish, led by poorly-trained priests and O'Connell's sedition, was the cause of 'blind ignorance in all that concerns religion and a sympathy for political violence and popular agitation'.[163] This prejudice helps to explain the importance of appropriating surplus revenues to Irish education. It also led Whigs to accept O'Connell's public association of Irish discontent with the need for tithe and Church reforms. Acceptance of O'Connell's premise was not based so much on his parliamentary support, which was necessary in 1831–32 but not in 1833, but on the view that Church rather than land reform was the patriot's goal, without which agitation would continue to the detriment of the Establishment.

In the end, the tithe wars had to be regarded as a Church question. Most of the Whigs were opposed to coercion alone. Without Church reform, they would not have agreed to coercive measures, a solution to the problem which would have left the tithes unpaid and violated what was fast complementing civil and religious liberty as basic Whig dogma – the sanctity of property. Among the Whigs, Stanley, Palmerston, Spring Rice and Duncannon owned large Irish estates, but this factor was peripheral to the issue. All Whigs were property-holders of one form or another, and to attack the patrimony of property was politically and morally unthinkable. Refusal to pay tithes, rents and taxes produced notions, Russell argued in the Commons, which 'if acted upon to their full extent, . . . would lead to the destruction of all property, to the revolution of all society, and to the annihilation of all order in the community'.[164] Though Russell and his colleagues did not favour the forced collection of tithes, they regarded such income as a form of property to which the Church had a right. Tithes, Melbourne said, were 'a mode of payment belonging to earlier times',[165] but tithe reform was intended only to render the Church's patrimony politically acceptable and more easily collected. In its most extreme form, tithe reform meant commutation to a tax on land that would provide for the Church, a course that Duncannon, one of the most liberal Whigs, regarded as 'very just and fair'.[166] The Irish problem, it was clear, was to be solved not by land reform or the extinction of taxes, but by tithe commutation and Church reform. The basic Whig notion of Irish Church reform was in itself fairly unobtrusive: if the grossest 'abuses' were left unchecked, the Protestant Church, Russell opined, would be 'too large for its own permanent stability.'[167] On this point all Whigs could agree. But before the ink on the Reform Act was scarcely dry, the details of Stanley's proposed Church reform bill brought to the surface what Althorp had termed 'dramatically opposite principles' that could not be reconciled; 'the case is too important and too urgent to admit of much compromise'.[168] The two main points of dispute concerned the relationship of the Irish Church to the English, and the question of appropriating surplus revenues to Roman Catholic or lay purposes.

Stanley's reform plan, which did abolish 10 of the 22 Irish bishoprics, left untouched a number of parishes, with little or no protestant congregation, where a clergyman would continue to be paid. His opponents in the ministry objected to the maintenance of such posts, on the grounds that it would be pointless to provoke Catholics by forcing them to pay for a parish that existed in legal form only. In effect, they were arguing that a protestant priest should be appointed on the principle of 'representation by population'. With the growth of protestant non-conformity, the danger to the Church of applying such a principle in England was obvious, and the supporters of a more extensive measure were forced to argue that Ireland was a special case. This argument necessarily led to a review of the nature of the Establishment. Althorp told Grey that though Stanley's position on the indivisibility of the Churches of England and Ireland was a legal one to act on, such a principle would 'destroy the Church Establishment of England'. 'I think the time has come', he added, 'when we must look at the two Churches as separate Churches as they are in fact and in reason.' Grey agreed.[169] When Althorp threatened to resign in October 1832 unless Stanley's plan was altered,[170] Grey was able only with some difficulty to reach agreement on the clause that empowered a Board of lay and ecclesiastical commissioners to suspend appointments to parishes where no religious services had been performed for three years. But if Stanley and Graham were able to convince themselves that the principle of proportion was not admitted by this clause, nor that of a unitary Establishment violated, they were unable to accommodate themselves to the principle of appropriation.

The liberal Whigs' advocacy of appropriation was not the product so much of O'Connell's pressure as their own belief in the need for the education of the Catholic populace. An educational system need not have been financed by the Church's surplus revenues, but the alternative, direct state-funding for a comprehensive system, would again have repercussions in England, where Radicals were calling for just such a plan. The traditional view that education was more the duty of the Church than the state was one that Churchmen could understand. More important was the Whig view that the Church had failed to discharge its responsibility to provide moral and religious instruction to the people.[171] The moral ignorance of the 'miserably barbarous' people led them, as a result, to follow demagogic prejudice aimed at the protestant Church.[172] The English prejudicial attitude, in turn, assumed that a more enlightened people would learn to tolerate protestantism. Howick thought that because the Church had failed to extend its religious principles among all of the Irish people, its surplus revenues should be used to educate them.[173] This position was taken by most of his colleagues. Appropriation, then, was a means by which the Church could educate the people, could be seen to be doing something for non-Churchmen, and could help to overcome the hatred generated by the Protestant Ascendancy. Althorp argued that 'the best chance Protestantism has in Ireland is the education and civilization of the country'; in the House of Lords, Melbourne traced many of the Irish problems to the laws and religion of England that had been forced on Ireland 'without any previous preparation of the minds of the people'.[174]

The proponents of appropriation argued that the measure was designed to strengthen the Church Establishment, but their opponents regarded their view of that Establishment as especially dangerous. Appropriation was seen as an attack on Church property, and the appropriationists' conception of the Church seemed to their opponents as allowing the evil that appropriation was designed to prevent. Just as swamping the House of Lords had suggested to the opponents of peer creation an attitude of mind on the part of the creationists that seemed to accept for the Lords a smaller role in the constitution, so did appropriation, in the eyes of Stanley and Graham, suggest that the appropriationists had in mind a much weakened Church Establishment for Ireland. Thus Ebrington could argue in 1833 during the debates on the Irish Church bill that the government had no intention of overthrowing the Irish Church Establishment, but when he added that 'nothing had been more injurious to the security of the Establishment in this country . . . than the attempt to bind together the separate Churches of England and Ireland',[175] his opponents considered the practical effect of such thinking the virtual abolition of the Irish Church. There was some ground for their belief, for most of the appropriationists would have agreed with Melbourne's later comment to Howick that the Protestant Church in Ireland was 'a great anomaly'.[176] Not all Whigs were as forthright as Sydney Smith, who thought the government absurd not to take 'bold measures for the destruction of the Irish Protestant Church', but there was widespread support for his view that the state should pay the Catholic clergy.[177] The division, noted Holland, was between those who wished to preserve the character of an established and endowed Church, and those who thought it should be reduced to a stipendiary one, on an equal footing with the Catholic Church. Although Althorp, angered when the Lords opposition to the 1833 bill threatened the government's existence, thought that the Irish Church Establishment would 'fall to the ground, and by doing so will save the Church Establishment here', no one actually favoured disestablishment. As Holland wrote in his diary, pressure by O'Connell and his Irish followers to adopt resolutions tantamount to the subversion of the character of an establishment left the government no alternative but to defy them.[178] But the concept of 'an' rather than 'the' Establishment did give their opponents room for doubt. Russell, who would soon argue that all three religions in Ireland should be provided for by the State, and thus be 'established', attacked Stanley's defence of a single large Protestant establishment. 'I presume you do not dissent from Paley's doctrine', he wrote angrily to the Irish secretary, 'that a church establishment ought to be judged by its utility, & I presume that you would not think of planting a glebe & a church in every parish in Hindustan or even attempt like Charles the 2d to make the English liturgy prevail all over Scotland'...[179] But if Russell and his like-minded supporters had reason and a sense of toleration on their side, they did not have the law. During the appropriation debates in 1835 when Russell, again quoting Paley, argued that the Irish Church neither promoted religion nor maintained good order, Graham answered that there could be only one undiminished Establishment, and that 'so long as Union continues, the Protestant religion is the religion of the majority'. Before the Irish Establishment could be treated separately, he charged, you must first dissolve the Union.[180]

The appropriationists did not have the support of Grey, who regarded the diversion of revenues as unpopular in England and unlikely to pass through the Lords. Stanley's intransigence on the question, moreover, left Grey with no option but to support his plan. Grey feared the consequences in Ireland of a ministerial split that might put the Tories in office, and was probably correct in assuming that resignation threats from Russell, Althorp and Brougham were to be taken less lightly than Stanley's.[181] Although Stanley's emotional and intellectual inclinations attracted him to coercive measures, he was not insensitive to the need for Irish reforms. In 1831, he had superintended a successful scheme to provide for a nondenominational system of Irish primary education, and in that same year sent Grey a tithe reform plan designed to make the Church less unpopular, and without which there was 'no hope for the continuance of the Protestant Establishment in Ireland'.[182] Indeed in December 1831 he pointedly asked the Bishop of Limerick to[183]

tell me how the Primate of Ireland can gravely declare his conviction that all that is necessary is . . . enforcing by Police and military, the full rights of the clergy; and that though he [Primate] had heard of various schemes, he could see no reason for making any alteration in the existing system.

But Stanley had to be dragged into reforms. In June 1831 he argued that if tithes were proposed during the Reform Bill debates the Tories would be afforded 'the cry of Revolution in the Church following up Revolution in the State'.[184] Though events in Ireland soon persuaded him that reform was necessary, he did his utmost to keep it to a minimum. Largely through Stanley's influence, Anglesey's plans for a poor law, a labour rate, tithe reform, state salaries for the Catholic clergy and appropriation were rejected by the cabinet in February 1832.[185] As these questions recurred in cabinet, he relented only when unavoidable. But with the support of Graham, Goderich, Lansdowne, and Richmond, who would not accept that an Irish Church could be considered as separate from the English by divesting it alone of its property, Stanley refused, with Grey's concurrence, to allow an appropriation clause. The 147th clause which was widely regarded as encompassing the principle of appropriation was in reality a compromise. By this clause, a fund of £2–3 million, raised from the selling of the

Bishop's lands to tenants in perpetuity, would be applied to non-Church purposes if, after the Church's needs were met, a surplus existed. Stanley agreed to the plan on the grounds that because the fund was a new creation of parliament, it would not affect existing Church property.[186] But he could not have been very happy. Although all in the cabinet agreed that the clause did not admit the appropriation principle, it was understood outside as an indication of Whig intent. Charles Grant's aside to Littleton that the clause was added on the representation of the 'government's friends',[187] was doubtless an overstatement given the passionate defence of appropriation in cabinet, but in the sense that Stanley's coercion plan would never have passed the Commons without an extensive Church reform, Grant was substantially correct. The clause was the price Stanley paid for his intended coercion bill.

Grey's plan was to introduce simultaneously the coercion bill in the Lords and the Church bill in the Commons. This course was virtually forced on him a year earlier, when, after he had announced in the Lords that a bill to remedy Irish grievances could only come after the law was upheld, a number of the cabinet strongly objected. Graham, Durham, Holland, Ellice and Anglesey argued that without ameliorative legislation, coercive measures would fall in the Commons and provoke further outrage in Ireland. Within a week, Althorp announced in the Commons that 'extraordinary powers . . . ought not to be granted unless accompanied by an efficient remedy for the grievance which occasions the demand'.[188] But Grey's diplomatic nicety was not, by itself, sufficient. Wood, the whip, warned Stanley that unless he had Ebrington's support for both measures, he would lose up to 250 votes. It was in order to secure Ebrington that Stanley gave up his attempt to move Anglesey from Ireland. That done, Ebrington fulfilled his part of the bargain in following Althorp's introduction of Church reform with an announcement that he would support both measures.[189] Althorp introduced Stanley's Irish Church temporalities bill on 12 February 1833. O'Connell's support in the House, following hard on the heels of Ebrington's, removed any doubts that the ministry might have had over its passing. But before it came to a second reading and the important committee stage, the coercion bill came down from the Lords, who had dealt with it extraordinarily quickly. Grey introduced it on 15 February and by the 22nd it was sent to the Commons, accompanied by a hastily arranged change of venue bill which allowed trials to be moved to adjoining counties or to Dublin.[190] The coercion bill was the work of Stanley, with strong support from Grey, Richmond, Graham and Lansdowne.[191] It was an embarrassment to the appropriationist ministers. The failure of Stanley's 1832 Tithe Arrears Act to bring an end to tithe and rent protests made some coercion necessary, but if the Church reformers were unhappy at the 1832 coercive measure, they had greater cause to dislike the new bill. In addition to empowering the Irish government to ban or restrict public meetings, the bill allowed the Lord Lieutenant to suspend habeas corpus and substitute court martials for ordinary courts. Le Marchant assumed that Stanley had forced the sternest provisions on his colleagues as the price of his support for those parts of the Church bill which he did not like, and he was probably right. Even Melbourne had argued for more than a year against suspending habeas corpus, and Palmerston described to his brother the irony of Whigs passing 'the most violent bill ever carried into law. . . . Few absolute governments could by their own authority establish such a system of coercion'.[192]

A meeting of government supporters in Althorp's rooms prior to the first reading in the Commons convinced him that the coercion bill would not pass, and his introductory speech was lethargic and apologetic in tone. 'If' he could prove its necessity, he declared, the House should support the bill.[193] Fortunately for the government, a series of particularly violent speeches by O'Connell and the Repealers turned several opponents into supporters, and after strong speeches by Stanley and Ebrington, it carried with little difficulty.[194] But Holland's reaction to Stanley's speech reflected the reforming Whigs' dissatisfaction with the bill and its author; his speech, he wrote, was 'a philipic . . . and breathed a haughty spirit of defiance in defence of our coercive measures, without any counteracting sympathy with the feelings of the people in describing those [measures] of a conciliatory nature'.[195]

While the coercion bill was still in the Commons, the Conservative MP Charles Wynn successfully put off second reading of the Church temporalities bill on a procedural question. This delay allowed the coercion bill to become law before the controversial 147th clause of the Church bill came before parliament. As a consequence, the opponents of appropriation had nothing to lose by forcing the clause from the bill. The government were made painfully aware that the measure could be in some difficulty when the House of Lords flexed their muscles by passing the censure motion against the Minister's Portugese policy on 3 June. Although there was talk of forcing the Lords by creating peers, Grey told the King that no such proposition would be made.[196] The King, for his part, sent an unfriendly letter to the Cabinet, indicating that as the Government had declared their readiness to stand or fall on the Irish bill, he would gladly accept its resignation. He urged a coalition with the Tories, which, he added, would make for the 'happiest day of his life'.[197] In order to save the 147th clause from the wrath of both King and Lords, it was decided to amend the clause at the committee stage to the effect that any surplus revenues would be left only to religious and charitable purposes rather than to any which Parliament saw fit.[198] But unbeknown to all but Graham and Grey, Stanley announced in the Commons that the clause would be dropped altogether. Holland thought the press reports of this surprising announcement incorrect.[199] Stanley, of course, was involved with the King in the attempt to form a 'union of the two Conservative parties' described earlier. The Ministry's supporters were furious. But for a strenuous whip, there would not have been fifty Whigs in the majority according to Le Marchant,[200] and as Stanley had been wishing for all session, the Whigs had to canvass the Tories as much as their own supporters. Although the government had decided to resign if defeated in the Lords, Stanley's insistence that the King ensure Tory support for the reduced measure secured its passage. When the news came in that the Tory diehards had transferred their meetings from Apsley House to that of their own leader the Duke of Cumberland, the bill appeared to be safe.[201] With only one important amendment, by which the funds of a suspended benefice would be taxed in order to build a church and glebe house, the bill passed through the Lords by the end of July. Without appropriation, and with the suspended benefice clause made meaningless by amendment, the Act provided for only a mild reorganisation of the Irish Church. In 1857, Stanley claimed that abolishing ten bishoprics had saved the Irish Establishment, a doubtful conclusion given the Irish people's lack of interest in the number of bishops.[202] But what Stanley had done was to win the opening skirmish in the battle he would soon lose: to keep the principle of appropriation from Whig policy.

Neither Church reform nor coercive laws struck at the heart of the original tithe problem, but parliamentary difficulties made a meaningful solution to the problem impossible. Until 1838, by which time everyone was heartily sick of the issue, the disease proved resistant to treatment. In 1832, Stanley's Tithe Composition Act made composition for tithes compulsory and permanent; the tithe composition was set on the lower corn prices for the years 1823 to 1830, and chargeable to the landlord rather than tenant. But though by 1834 nearly all parishes had compounded, there was general opposition by landlords in the south, who passed the charge to their tenants in the form of increased rents.[203] More importantly, Stanley's full tithe plan was withdrawn in the face of Irish opposition. Based on a report sent to Grey in 1831,[204] this bill intended to commute tithes to a charge on land. Tithe payers would redeem their obligation to the Church by a single money payment which would provide the Church with capital to invest in land. It was expected that diocesan corporations would get a fixed return on their investment of at least 85 per cent of the tithe, and in doing so bring to an end collision between clergy and peasant.[205] But the Irish members, who wanted tithe income to be used for all religious and charitable purposes, greeted the plan with a howl of protest. Stanley had little option but to leave the commutation scheme out of his bill, given the Irish politicians' opposition and the Whig theory that only by a satisfactory political situation would the tithe wars be ended. When E. J. Littleton succeeded Stanley as Irish Secretary in May 1833 he found that there were no plans for dealing with tithe. Althorp suggested that the cabinet furnish him with at least a plan to provide the Irish clergy with much-needed funds. Although the government had given the Lord-Lieutenant £60,000 for disbursement to impoverished tithe-owners in an 1832 tithe arrears act, the provision of the bill which empowered the Irish Attorney-General to collect arrears was a signal failure. At a cost of £26,000, only £12,000 of £116,000 owing was collected, and a considerable portion of the clergy in Roman Catholic areas was in need of relief.[206] In June 1833, arrangements were made to ask parliament for £1 million for the relief of the clergy in return for a government pledge to consider a new system of tithe revenues for the clergy. The money was to be loaned to the clergy and repaid, as of November 1834, by a temporary land tax. By this Church Million Act, the 1832 provision for the enforced collection of tithe arrears was given up. The government's initial drafting had included the collection of arrears, but Graham thought it 'madness'. Moreover, Althorp, with the cabinet's authority, had pledged in the House that no more arrears should be levied, and a number of Irish members had been induced on that assurance to vote for coercion. As a result, arrears were given up.[207]

During the recess, Littleton and Wellesley, the new Lord Lieutenant, worked on a plan which it was hoped would settle the tithe question. The plan which they produced, based on Stanley's bill of 1832, proposed commuting the existing compositions into a land tax which could be redeemed by a money payment on land. Landlords could add the tax on redemption payments to the tenants' rent; the Church, as tithe-owner, was to invest the income in land.[208] O'Connell attacked the bill in the Commons in a strong speech which argued that the landlords, as tithe-proctors, would earn the odium previously directed against the clergy. The hard-pressed peasant, understanding nothing but his taxes, would agitate increasingly against rent as well as tithes.[209] Unlike Stanley, Littleton refused to give way. Commutation was a popular approach, for few were willing to understand the economic aspect of the tithe war. And O'Connell's poison was meat to the Whigs. The virtue of this plan, thought Littleton, was its likelihood of relieving the clergy and peasantry at once from pecuniary collision. Church property 'is saved', he told Wellesley, 'by the passing of an act for its realization by redemption'.[210] What the bill also did, of course, was evade the two questions which were dividing the ministry: was the Church's revenue unnecessarily large for its maintenance, and should a portion of its funds be appropriated to other uses? Holland recorded growing disgust and impatience at Stanley's 'somewhat nice, subtle and unintelligible' distinctions between ecclesiastical reform and a diversion of Church revenues.[211] Littleton thought the divison of opinion so strong that no other measure was possible. The desire to keep the government together alone prevented an open split before parliament met. Still, the strength of feeling on either side made Littleton 'fear the result'. Althorp told him in January that 'at no very distant period' the question would dissolve the Cabinet; 'it can only be postponed for a very short time', he wrote, 'and whenever it is really forced on [us], we shall be obliged all of us to take our line'.[212] By May, the expected pressure for appropriation by the Irish members produced the open split, but it had little effect on the bill. Grey, in fact, thought that O'Connell's invective was advantageous to its passage. But in the end, the bill was scuttled by the arch-Conservative high-flyers among the Tory peers led by the

Dukes of Cumberland and Newcastle, who refused to agree to an amendment put forward in committee by O'Connell and accepted by the new Melbourne government; they were able to persuade Wellington that the bill was 'abominable'.[213] There was little doubt that Grey would have refused his assent to the amendment, preferring the original bill, but Peel wanted it heard in the Lords and, if necessary, amended. But Wellington would not have it.

If, by the end of 1834, the Whigs' legislative record in Irish Church matters was largely inconclusive, achievements in English Church reform were yet to appear. It could hardly have been otherwise. The Ecclesiastical Revenues Commission, set up in 1832 and twice renewed, had not reported by the time the Whigs left office. Because the government had encouraged voluntary reform by the Church itself, there was little that could be done. To do otherwise would have appeared as a gratuitous attack on the Church, a charge which the Whigs were careful to avoid. What the government did hope, though, was that other less contentious legislation might remove some of the cause for hostile attacks on the Church. To this end, preparations were made for legislation on English tithes and to settle Dissenters' grievances. Although opposition to tithe was not as widespread in England as Ireland, the Swing riots in 1830 emphasised the growing unpopularity of these payments. The general substitution of cash for payment in kind, arranged between tithe owner and payer, had by the earlier part of the century alleviated much of the discontent which arose from the difficulties of payment. But the more recent antipathy to tithes was of an economic rather than logistical nature, and could not be eradicated without a fundamental alteration in the tithe system. The unpopularity of tithe was due to its regressive nature as a tax, which, when applied to total produce rather than profits, was most harmful to the farmer with little or no pre-tax profits. This feature meant that capital improvements in agriculture served the tithe-owner before the farmer, who because of tithe, was not likely to realise the increased profits which the capital outlay was expected to generate.[214] Not surprisingly, the dissatisfied agriculturalists tied the cost of tithes to reduced agricultural improvements, profits and employment. The Church, as largest tithe-owner, came in for a certain amount of criticism; it has been suggested, in fact, that friction between clergy and farmers accounted for the spread of Dissent in rural areas.[215] But apart from the most violent critics of the Church Establishment, the tithe problem was not connected with Church reform. Where the Whigs were unable to understand the economic grievances of Irish tithe reformers, they had no difficulty with the English case, and it was on that basis that the government undertook a reform of English tithes.[216] The tendency of the English tithe reformers to support the Church probably accounts for its being regarded mainly as an agricultural economic question, making all the more striking the English failure to understanding the economic aspect of the Irish tithe dispute.

On the grounds that 'this measure was pregnant with . . . great advantage to the landed and agricultural interests of the country' and that 'nothing should prevent those good feelings and fellowship which ought to exist between [clergy] and their parishioners', Althorp brought forward a tithe bill in April 1833. The principle of his plan was to effect a voluntary arrangement between clergy and tithe-payer for the perpetual commutation of tithes to a corn rent tied to the price of corn. If after a year this was not done, the tithe-payer could apply for a compulsory commutation arrived at by independent valuators on both sides. By July, opposition from the Church forced Althorp to drop the compulsory commutation and the measure was in effect postponed.[217] In April, 1834, the principle of making the tithe vary with the rent was introduced, as well as provision for the redemption of tithe at twenty five years' purchase. In addition, there was to be assessment of the rate of a national average land value, a provision that reduced even further room for conflict between landowners and truculent clergymen.[218] Leave was given to bring the bill to parliament, but the time lost by the change of government, and the more pressing need to amend the poor law, caused the government to shelve the measure for another session.

The political strength shown by the Dissenters during the 1832 elections and subsequent anti-slavery debates convinced their leaders that the Whigs would be susceptible to pressure for redress of their grievances. But a meeting with Grey in May 1833 gave the Dissenting Deputies little reason to hope that much could be expected at a time when Irish affairs and the English social legislation dominated the government's agenda. The resultant Dissenting dissatisfaction led to a violent attack on the Church itself. Thus, what had been a more modest demand for religious liberties gave way to calls for reduction and disestablishment of the Church.[219] This shift in tactics came at the wrong moment and did the Dissenters' cause great harm. The Whig party historically had faithfully supported Dissenters' causes, and was indeed 'their natural home',[220] but it was not a party of disestablishment. At the very time that the party was attempting to persuade King and Church that its Irish Church plans were not meant to subvert the Establishment, support for the now openly destructive aims of the Dissenters' Deputies was an increasingly unattractive proposition. Grey was incensed that the Dissenters should raise their sights at the Church itself; he told one Churchman that he had been 'humbugged'.[221] Holland, who with Russell and Lansdowne was in regular contact with the United Committee, hoped that moderation would prevail to the Whigs' political credit. But holding the Dissenters to a moderate course was difficult. In January 1834, Holland prepared Grey for a deputation from the United Committee by passing on the sentiments of a leading Presbyterian who represented 'a large and respectable minority' of moderate Dissenters who disagreed with the committee and did not want to see 'all' the Church establishment attacked. After the meeting, Holland argued that the deputation did not represent the 'great body' of Dissenters, who were not being heard, and who would be satisfied with moderate marriage and universities' admission bills.[222]

Holland's optimism was soon dashed, Russell's marriage bill, which offered dissenters a marriage in chapel but kept banns and registration in Church, was not a promising start. The comprehensive registration of births, marriages and deaths which Dissenters had been demanding was rejected on grounds of cost, and a fully separate marriage on principle.[223] To what extent ministers were weary of further Church opposition and concern for Tory support for their other legislative measures is difficult to gauge, but there is little doubt that the Whig abhorrence of passion and dogma provided little sympathy for what were regarded as changes of little significance. The Dissenters, Russell told Grey, had no cause to complain 'if you subject them to no other hardship than having their names called three times in Church'. This Whig attitude was not simply one of insensitivity to another's religious views. Russell himself was unconcerned with the 'petty superstition' of confirmation, which he never received, and held no brief for those who looked on such detail as important.[224] The Dissenters were outraged. They refused to support Russell's bill, and went into opposition against Attorney-General Campbell's unsuccessful re-election attempt at Dudley.[225] Russell withdrew the bill. Althorp fared no better. In March, a private motion to abolish compulsory Church rates was put off when Althorp promised a forthcoming plan.[226] But when, in April 1834, he announced a bill to replace the rates by an annual charge of £250,000 on the land tax, 140 Dissenters and Radicals objected to a national tax for repair and upkeep of an unnecessary Establishment.[227] The government could not accept this argument. In August, Russell told Holland that Whigs could not assent to the abolition of Church rates, and 'far less to the principle announced by Dissenters', who, like all others, should pay for a national church.[228] To exempt them might only encourage the unscrupulous to declare themselves Dissenters. But before the division took place, Althorp sensed that his bill had not satisfied, and he warned Dissenters that anxious though he was to remove their grievances, 'he would only do so on one condition . . . that he did not go so far as to destroy the Established Church'.[229] Without waiting for second reading, he dropped his bill.

The Whigs' failure to see justice for the Dissenters' claims was one occasion in Grey's government where the *via media* did not succeed. Prevention of extremism by salutory and moderate reform had generally worked. Even O'Connell had shown willingness to accept half loaves. Perhaps the Whig anti-clerical mind misunderstood the religious convictions of the Dissenters, who in the end appeared bent on humiliating rather than reforming the Church.[230] The Whigs certainly felt deceived by ungrateful plaintants. 'If they choose to drive things to a contest between them and the Church', Grey told Holland, 'they must take the consequences . . . I have done all I can'.[231] Holland's hope that moderate Dissenters would prevail proved groundless as soon as Russell's marriage bill was made known. Within a month, despair reigned, and it was 'generally understood', wrote Le Marchant, 'that nothing would be done for the Dissenters'.[232] The government allowed a Dissenting motion giving equal rights to university admission to pass the Commons with 'indecent haste and indifference', but they knew and cared little that a Dissenters' bill could not pass the Lords.[233] Abetting a church rates measure had met with rebuff, and the Lords' expected rejection of the universities' bill must have been sweet revenge. Militant dissent had caused the Whigs to question their support before the session began.

Once ministerial measures met with Dissenting opposition, they were dropped for the Poor Law bill, which Le Marchant described forty years later as, next to the Reform Bill, 'the most valuable if not the most brilliant achievement of the Whig ministry'.[234]

7

Melbourne and Opposition, 1834–35

'Well, here's another hoax!'
Lord Holland over the morning newspaper which announced
his government's dismissal, 15 November 1834.[1]

There can be little doubt that the disintegration of Grey's fragile
cabinet had been prompted by the single issue of the Irish Church.
Those who had been persuaded that the Church was too large for
its own stability carried on; those who resisted any reduction in
its size resigned. Reducing the Irish Church and appropriating
surplus revenue for Catholic purposes was seen by the one group
as essential to the preservation of the Establishment, and by the
other as destructive of that Establishment. Despite the charges
levied by the defectors, by Peel and by historians since, the
government that carried on until 1841 was not fundamentally
different in outlook from Grey's but for the difference on how to
save the Church. The King's dismissal of Melbourne's ministry
and electoral defeats in 1835 and 1837 would force the new
ministry into a parliamentary alliance with Radicals and make the
job of resisting any but moderate and timely reforms more
difficult, but post-Grey Whiggism was neither Radical by nature
nor Radically led. The determination to steer a moderate, safe path
between 'destructive' reform and the Tory reaction that would
provoke such destruction characterised Melbourne's government
as it had Grey's. The difference between the two lay in the
definition of the boundary on that one question. The picture of the
new government painted by Peel and Stanley has Melbourne
leading a group of aimless wanderers who were prepared to desert
all of Grey's principles in order to hold office. But the reality was
quite different. As soon as the King's experiment in personal
interference was over, Melbourne's government would act with
Peel's consent as much as Grey's had done. Melbourne had little of

his predecessor's dogmatism, but it would be a mistake to confuse his lapses into indecision with indolence or lack of purpose. His was the role of the arbitrator. Few politicians in the 1830s were reformers by nature, and it is a measure of Melbourne's statesmanship that he allowed reason to overcome prejudice when convinced of its necessity.[2] He spoke little at cabinet meetings,[3] preferring to chair rather than direct, and the result was to restore the harmony and discipline that Grey's cabinet had lacked.

The King's reason for choosing Melbourne is unclear. Brougham claimed to have put his name forward in a letter to the King suggesting a purely Whig administration,[4] but it was Grey who had recommended during his audience on 9 July that Melbourne succeed. According to Lady Holland, the new government was a legacy from Grey, 'made and urged by him'.[5] Althorp had been Grey's choice for more than a year, but his resignation and the King's known dislike for his liberal politics ruled him out. Grey had not been allowed to choose a successor when he broached with the King the possibility of resignation in May, and it is likely, knowing as he did the King's preference for a coalition with the Tories, that he regarded Melbourne as least likely to offend the King's predilections.[6] On this latter score, there was no doubt where the King stood. 'As he values the peace and the protection of property against spoliation', Taylor told Brougham,[7]

he must be anxious to resist the admission into places of trust and authority of those who aim at the destruction of those blessings, and who would not only readily yield to, but might feel disposed to invite and encourage pressure from without, tending to violent changes and to the introduction of frightful differences and collisions between the various classes of society. . . . His Majesty is justified in seeking a broader basis than that to which your lordship would seem disposed to confine him.

In the circumstances, Melbourne proved of sterner mettle than bargained for. He refused the King's request to attempt a coalition with Wellington, Peel and Stanley, on the grounds that as the Tories would not accept the Irish Tithe bill or the Commission of Enquiry, which he regarded as 'vital and essential', no common ground existed. When asked a second time to meet with the Tory leaders and Stanley, he again refused, and told the King, moreover, that Althorp would have a difficult time with an impatient

Commons if an administration were not settled quickly.[8] Having boxed the King into a corner, Melbourne became Prime Minister, a position described by his secretary Tom Young as 'never occupied by any Greek or Roman',[9] on his own terms.

The King was in trouble and knew it. He had accepted Stanley's resignation in May 'with tears running down his cheeks'[10] and now, instead of his much hoped for union of parties, had another Whig government. It was, in addition, headed by a man who had told him that though he was not a reformer by choice, 'the times and the people of the country would not leave it alone', and that 'all that was consistent with justice' would have to be done to adapt the institutions to the 'real opinion' of the country.[11] Nor was it reassuring to be told by Melbourne that the new cabinet included Duncannon, a known appropriationist, and Hobhouse, who had resigned his seat in 1833 in deference to the wishes of his Westminster constituents. William tried to talk Melbourne out of both appointments, but without success.[12] His plans in ruins thanks to Melbourne's insistence that the royal prerogative did not extend to the choice of ministers and measures, the King waited only for an opportunity of effecting a coalition of parties. On 11 November, Althorp's removal to the House of Lords on the death of his father, the Earl Spencer, presented the King with that opportunity. He told Melbourne that Althorp's removal made the government's position in the Commons precarious; no additional support in the Lords could balance the weakness in the lower house. Without an accession of strength from those 'who would urge and advocate extreme measures', the ministry could not hope to stand. He had, Melbourne was informed, 'always been told' by Grey that Althorp's loss to the Commons would be sufficient reason for breaking up the administration; had not Melbourne himself 'laid the same stress' on Althorp's services when he succeeded Grey in July?[13]

Of course the King was justifying an action that he had been waiting to do for some time; his attempt to pretend that his view of Althorp's importance corresponded to Grey's and Melbourne's was specious. Grey regarded Althorp's leadership of the Commons essential only as long as he was Prime Minister, but he had more than once suggested that Althorp be called to the Lords as his successor, and had in fact said as much to the King in July. Melbourne, it is true, made a point of Althorp's service, but he had only done so *at the instigation of the King*.[14] Melbourne had sent the

King a letter when Spencer died stating that as the government was 'mainly founded on the personal weight and influence' of Althorp in the Commons, it was for His Majesty to decide whether the government should continue,[15] but this was a *pro forma* response to the King's own letters to Melbourne. Three days before the death, Melbourne had informed the King of Spencer's failing health as a preamble to a letter concerning another matter. Taylor responded that same day to record the King's 'deep concern' at the 'embarrassment' that Spencer's death could cause, and on the 11th, the King wrote Melbourne a lengthy letter on the importance of Althorp's services in the Commons. Melbourne's letter the following day, in the context, cannot be seen as anything but a formal restatement of the King's view and its logical implication.[16] The King had hoped that Melbourne would be made to feel it his duty to resign, but during their discussions at Brighton, it was evident this ruse had failed. Melbourne did not think that Althorp, having experienced the parliamentary difficulties of the previous two sessions, was of crucial importance in the Commons. He told the King that too much stress had been placed on Althorp's skills as speaker and debater, 'these being advantages which Lord Althorp did not possess'.[17] He informed the King that Russell had been chosen to succeed as leader of the Commons, and gave no hint that the government would be unable to manage. William was left with nothing but his own prerogative. The ministry was dismissed.

Spencer's death came at a fortuitous time for the King, for a number of events in the autumn of 1834 had increased his desire for a coalition of parties that might bridge the gap between the two houses of parliament. A major worry was Brougham, whose sanity was by now suspect,[18] and who spent much of the autumn engaged in a public quarrel with Durham. In an article in the *Edinburgh Review*, the Chancellor attacked Durham for his part in the committee of four which had drawn up the reform bill in 1830; he charged him, unfairly, with having proposed a £20 rather than a £10 qualification.[19] Brougham apparently wanted to put himself foward as a radical champion at Durham's expense. He had considered prosecuting Durham for a 'revolutionary' address at a Glasgow reform meeting, but used equally radical language himself during several public appearances in Scotland during September and October. He was reportedly 'conservative at Inverness; but changing his opinions as often as his horses, by the time he got to Dundee he was downright revolutionary. Here he was at the full.'[20] Grey thought Brougham was determined 'to make it impossible for the Government to go on', and told the King, who had noted his 'concern' at the impetus given to radicalism, that the quarrel would lead to 'serious consequences'.[21] When the privy council met with the King on 17 November to surrender their insignia of office, Brougham's audience was short, and he appeared mortified in the ante-room as he left. Melbourne would have little to do with Brougham thereafter, telling him that his conduct was 'one of the principal causes' of the dismissal.[22]

If the King was concerned that Brougham's conduct was destructive, the government's Irish policy gave him greater concern. In the week preceding Spencer's death, the Lord Lieutenant of County Down, the Marquis of Downshire, called a special Protestant meeting of the county 'to give His Majesty's subjects' an opportunity of expressing their opinions on the subject of property. The liberal press was quick to condemn Downshire and other Lieutenants 'who abet such Orange gatherings'. Wellesley, who protested to Downshire, considered removing him from his position.[23] The King's reaction was to have Taylor inform Melbourne that the subject was of the *'deepest importance'* and that dismissal of Downshire would be *'a very strong'* step, 'unnecessarily and inconsiderately severe'. It was in the interest of Wellesley and the government, he warned, 'to conciliate rather than to irritate those who stand forward in support of the Established Church; which is so furiously assailed in Ireland by M. O'Connell and other lawless agitators and Revolutionists. Surely', the warning concluded, 'this is not the moment to stir up a first flame in Ireland'.[24]

Indeed it was not the moment, for the King had undergone a worrying fortnight, one filled with misgivings about the state of his nation and his ministry. He had written to Melbourne about the disturbing prospects of unrest among the rural population, symptoms of which had already been apparent in his own 'neighbourhood' and in Suffolk, and though Melbourne replied that the cause of unrest lay in a temporary reduction of agricultural wages, the King's concern was not so easily assuaged.[25] Taylor's memo to Melbourne concerning the Downshire affair, which included the King's first reaction to the news of Spencer's imminent death, instructed the government to 'look to the *general* situation of affairs': 'Lawless agitators and Revolutionists' in Ireland and agricultural unrest in England, together with a rumoured call for troops from the colonies and the 'possible effect' of another government crisis in France, were issues more important than an Orange meeting in County Down.[26] It mattered little that the government did not support Wellesley's plan to dismiss Downshire. The tone of Taylor's warning was harsh, much more so in fact than any to be found in the seven years' correspondence between the King and his ministers. William was clearly upset, and Melbourne thought that Wellesley's precipitous conduct was a major influence on the King's actions three days hence.[27] The *coup de grâce* came when the King learned that same week from Duncannon that the long-dreaded plans for the Irish Church were being proposed. In September, Duncannon had drawn up a plan of reform that called for reductions in the Church and an appropriation of surplus revenues. Although the plan had not been considered by the cabinet, there was little doubt that it would be approved.[28] In two audiences with the King, Duncannon opened to him, 'prematurely' and with some 'imprudence', Melbourne thought, the proposed measures. Although the King had agreed to a commission of enquiry on the Chuch when Stanley had resigned, he instructed Melbourne in July not to pledge the government to measures with 'speculative' value that ran counter to the general feeling of the nation, which was 'in favour of the more moderate and safe course, and of the Principle which advocates *letting well alone*'.[29] The King had no option now but to rid himself of the government. It was not so much apprehension of what would happen with Russell as leader in the Commons, as despair at what had already happened with Althorp and Melbourne at the helm, that prompted the King to dismiss the Whigs.[30] To approve of Russell's appointment, Taylor told Stanley, would have placed the King 'in the equivocal situation of appearing to sanction designs which he had formerly pledged Himself to resist'. Whenever the measure should be submitted to him, the result would be 'concession after concession, and exhibition of weakness and inconsistency' damaging to the King's character and claim to confidence. A ready comparison is obvious. Once the King had agreed to parliamentary reform, Grey had extracted one concession after another. William would not again submit to a similar process. He would only be forced to dissolve the government later, Taylor explained, and preferred doing it sooner.[31]

Late on the evening of 14 November, 1834, Melbourne returned from Brighton with the dismissal notice in one pocket and the

King's sealed message for Wellington in the other. Although he planned to inform the cabinet the following morning, he told those whom he saw before retiring – Brougham, Palmerston and Duncannon – that the government was out. Brougham detected the hand of the Queen at work and quickly dispatched one of his people in a hackney cab at half past midnight to the offices of *The Times* and *Morning Chronicle* with the story that appeared in the morning: the ministry was out, Wellington was with the King, and 'The Queen has done it all'.[32] The last British ministry to be dismissed by the Monarch thus learned of its fate in the newspaper. It seemed scarcely credible. Brougham, who detested the Queen,[33] had most of the story wrong. The Duke was preparing for a hunt at Stratfield Saye and would not be asked to Brighton until later in the afternoon on the 15th. It is moreover unlikely that the Queen had an undue influence over the King. The mission of the Queen's Secretary Hudson to Peel, in Italy during the crisis, evoked suspicion, but the choice of 'Hurried Hudson' was Taylor's, not hers.[34] Holland believed the Queen to be one of the ingredients in the resolution, and Althorp that the dismissal had not taken place in July because she was 'absent then and present now',[35] but there was, in general, little support for the extreme nature of Brougham's view.

The King dismissed Melbourne's government on the assumption that Stanley would join a new mixed administration which would have the confidence of both houses of parliament.[36] Although he no doubt overvalued Stanley's importance and following, his use of the royal prerogative was a legitimate attempt to arrange an alternative majority from the one on which Melbourne's government had theoretically depended. In that sense he failed not when Peel's government was defeated in the Commons in April 1835, but as soon as that government was formed. The prominence of place given Wellington, surely an error of judgement given the King's earlier stated wish to exclude the extreme Tories from a Peel–Stanley coalition, sealed the fate of his hoped-for junction. Stanley would have nothing to do with Wellington, who had opposed most Whig reforms, and whose speech in the Lords on the occasion of Grey's retirement had been ungracious and condemnatory. 'It is quite clear', he told Richmond before Peel had returned from Italy, 'that this is an Administration which *we* cannot touch.' Peel's own ultra Tory appointments convinced Stanley more than ever that he could not take part until the ultra influence was abated: 'He cuts our ground of support from under our feet.'[37] William regretted that Stanley's scruples prevented his 'applying his shoulders to the *Conservative* wheel', but he could scarcely have expected otherwise. Taylor admitted afterwards that the King had acted more by immediate circumstances and the dread of embarrassment resulting from indecision and delay than by any calculation of the support he might receive.[38] He might have given a coalition a greater opportunity of success had he called on Peel directly rather than expect that Stanley would join forces with Wellington and Lyndhurst. Allowing Wellington the preponderant influence[39] until Peel returned was an act of folly which brought to an end any hope, however slight, of a union of moderates.

Precipitous as William's action may appear, it did not cause a great stir at the time among the established political classes. There was some Radical opinion which regarded the dismissal by 'His Highness, the Dictator'[40] as unconstitutional, but on the whole, it would be wrong to suggest that what had occurred was generally looked upon as a serious breach of constitutional principle. The more Whiggish members of the new opposition found little cause to blame the King. Grey came close to outright vindication of William. 'I cannot blame his decision', he told Russell, 'and for your own sakes . . . I do not think there is much cause for regret'; Melbourne was fortunate to be relieved from the difficulties of maintaining a unified administration with its internal dissensions and outside pressures. Grey found the King's determination 'a very natural one in the circumstances in which he was placed', and was 'not at all sure, everything considered, that it is not the best.'[41] He was not alone in this sentiment. Melbourne, not 'personally aggrieved', considered the change justifiable; 'I am not surprised at his decision, nor do I know that I can entirely condemn it.' Grey's impression, he added, 'entirely coincides with my own'.[42] Lansdowne held to the same view, and Holland agreed that the change was 'not altogether *unjustifiable*, though very foolish'.[43] Russell also accepted Grey's reasoning. Although he felt that some notice or warning should have been given, that there appeared 'a want of discretion and fair dealing in the whole proceeding', he did not think that the King exceeded his privileges, and later told Mulgrave that 'the King has always behaved very fairly by men'.[44] Further Whig support for the monarch's role and rights was manifested in January during discussion of the nature of the proposed amendment to the King's speech, when there appeared widespread opposition to publicly disapproving the dismissal: 'to do so', it was thought, 'would open the door to a great deal of declamation . . . on the impropriety of interfering with the King's prerogative'.[45]

If there was some acceptance by the ousted ministers that the dismissal was not improper, there was almost complete agreement that Whiggism would be forced to a more radical posture by forcing an 'unnatural alliance' between Whigs and Radicals. It seemed a foregone conclusion that elections would be required by the new government and that the Whig majority, unnaturally large due to the first reformed elections in 1832, would be reduced. This would serve to the advantage of both Tories and Radicals. The old ministers would return sooner or later, it was thought, but able to withstand Radicalism less than in 1834. Palmerston had foreseen the difficulties when the King sought a Tory government in July; elections would be necessary, the press, political and trade unions would come alive, and though the Tories might return fifty more members, the majority would be Radicals and 'pledge-bound Whigs'. The dismissal, he was certain, would have just that effect, and the Radicals, he told Melbourne, would be the great gainers from 'this attempt to force Toryism into power'.[46] Thus, ironically, those Whigs whom the King feared most thought that the dismissal was 'full of formidable consequence' and the 'great struggle between contending principles' unavoidable.[47] Throughout the autumn, Russell had consistently resisted O'Connell's overtures of reconciliation. He complained that Wellesley, the Lord Lieutenant of Ireland, had been too prepared to consult the Agitator, and thought that no government member should 'seek any intercourse or ask for any truce' from him. He found the *Morning Chronicle* too willing to join O'Connell in condemning Grey, whom he thought, 'extremely just and reasonable (in being) . . . glad to find that we do not truckle to O'Connell as he imagined'. Out of office Lord John faced a new situation; the change would greatly serve the Radical party and do disservice to the Whigs, he told Grey: 'The Whigs and Radicals together can, I believe, at any time defeat a Tory government, but I fear no liberal government can be formed which will have such a hold over the popular party as at present – or rather late'.[48] Even Brougham, his politics feared by the King and distrusted by his colleagues, had foreseen the difficulties in the summer: 'The formation of a Tory government will of course end after a few months in an ultra-liberal and almost a mob government – with 100 new peers made to prevent collision' he told Melbourne. 'Nobody with much reflexion can think that a very desirable *euthanasia.*' His *Edinburgh Review* article which caused such a storm was actually a warning to Melbourne not to assist the formation of such a government by being 'hustled' into rashly-framed and unworkable radical proposals, brought on by popular clamour, which would necessarily fail and reduce the government's stock in the country.[49] Duncannon thought that the King had not acted wisely and prudently, as only the late government could have prevented 'such a concession to popular feeling as which amounts to revolution'. 'You must become associated with *Radicals*', he wrote to Wellesley, 'or as a party you are left totally powerless'. It was, none the less, to be deprecated:[50]

> a thorough change must come and the measures which have led the King to adopt the course he lately took will be adopted either by yourself moderately . . . or by some other in a manner that will carry with it the overthrow of Protestantism in Ireland and consequently strike a hard blow at the Church here . . . the course taken by the King has given an importance to Durham he never had before, and has imparted an almost sovereign sway to O'Connell . . . the Whigs alone cannot form a government that would stand a week.

The jubilation of radicalism bears Duncannon out. Within a fortnight, John Stuart Mill considered that the dismissal had done more good than the Whigs could have in a twelvemonth: a 'unanimous declaration' from the whole country in favour of the ballot, triennial parliaments and a further extension of the franchise meant that there 'would be no more now of the "final measure" '.[51] At the Bull's Head in Halifax, the local reform society resolved on 19 November 'that in the present crisis of affairs' reformers 'should bury all minor differences and take prompt and decided measures to drive the Duke from his newly-acquired post.' Similar meetings throughout the country reflected the heady atmosphere which prompted Radicals to rally to the cause. On the 18th, the United Dissenters called for friends of liberty to flock to the standard to attack 'the mitre and sword Administration'. Reformers of all shades were exhorted by newspapers and pamphlets to unite. Fonblanque's *Examiner* typified the reaction: 'We shall not affect regret at the dissolution of the Grey Ministry – we regarded its reconstruction with derision', he had written in July. Yet he told Bulwer after the dismissal that 'tho' the past may not be explained to his own satisfaction, he shall never recur to it in the *Examiner* – Amnesty & Union being Cardinal policy'. 'From this moment all the discussions among Reformers are at an end. . . . Let us not dwell on our family quarrels when we have the enemy before us' commanded the *Morning Chronicle*: 'England expects every man to do his duty'.[52]

Radical manifestations of support and solidarity were generally unwelcome to the leading Whigs who were nevertheless condemned throughout the elections for their alleged association with Radicals. On 12 Janury, *The Times*, which had come to a quick accommodation with Wellington,[53] criticised the sacrifice of principle involved in the 'Union of Reformers'. But the Whig leaders' fears that radicalism would be the great gainers by the dismissal prompted them to eschew public solidarity with Radicals. Melbourne, Russell, Grey and others spoke out actively against Radical proposals for further constitutional reforms, and as described earlier in Chapter two, they pointedly refused to work closely with the more liberal members of the election committee who were involved with Joseph Parkes. Yet Tory electoral success[54] made partners of these hostile antagonists. Believing that peace both in England and Ireland required their return to office, the Whigs recognized the need for Radical support in parliament. Lyttleton's comment to Melbourne – 'Surely it is more essential than ever to keep out Radicals . . . Common enemy indeed! – Why the wolves are worse than the Foxes',[55] was a sentiment with which no Whig could find fault. But the main Whig objection to Peel's government was not that Peel would govern in a manner that they were openly hostile to, but that a popular reaction to an unelected Tory government would produce an immense cry for extreme reforms in Church and State, both English and Irish, which no government would be able to resist with safety. The Whig leaders' main objective, as a consequence, was to remove Peel from office as quickly as possible. They were not unaware of the danger of the paradoxical use of Radical aid to render the Radicals less effective; in the case of the Tories being beaten, Melbourne suggested, '*God knows what will happen*'.[56] But as reports came in of Radical losses in the elections, Melbourne's advisers were convinced that they were in no position to drive a hard bargain. Holland impressed upon Melbourne the Radicals' aspiration 'to be led by those they formerly reviled' and the need to use their aid to turn out the Tories. Howick was of a similar opinion. Certain that the Radical strength had been shown to be overrated, and that the acquisition of power·by the Radicals 'is what we have most to fear', he thought that Radicals should be used in the battle against Peel before they had time 'to disgust and alarm' more moderate men.[57]

There can be little doubt that Russell played a leading role in the shaping of Whig policy during this period of opposition, and, to the extent that the policy of the parliamentary leaders represents 'party' views, of the Whig party in the post-Grey period. The most commonly held view of Russell's thinking, and *ipso facto*, of the Whig party, is that put forward by Peel's biographer, who regarded the Whigs as turning to Radicalism as soon as that conscience of historical Whiggery, Grey, and to a lesser extent Stanley and Graham, had deserted the fold. Despite Russell's initial reservations about an alliance with the Radicals, this argument holds, he had 'no doubts at all about the need for a more radical policy'. When a meeting of Whigs, Radicals and O'Connellites took place at Lord Lichfield's house before parliament met, an alliance took place on the basis of a radical policy.[58] Taking the view that Lord John looked forward to an accord with the Radicals 'with excitement', Russell's biographer held to the same opinion, as did O'Connell's, who stated that Russell plotted behind Melbourne's back to work a union with the movement.[59] None of these views accord with Russell's or the Whig government's policy from 1835 to oppose Radical demands for constitutional change by governing in a scarcely covert alliance with Peel. A closer inspection of Russell's views during these weeks in opposition suggests that neither he nor his colleagues planned to move the party in a radical direction. In answer to Grey, who argued that the Whigs should offer no opposition to Peel, Russell asserted the necessity of holding 'our own Whig course'; leaving the game to the Tories or Radicals would be neither honourable nor safe.[60] This was a clear expression of the 'juste milieu' philosophy of Baring's body of men standing between the constitution and revolution. Russell believed that the removal of Peel's government was necessary for the peace of Ireland, without which there could be no safety for the English Church and institutions, and he was prepared to accept Radical assistance to that end.[61] He made it clear to his colleagues that the constitutional changes being demanded by the Radicals would be resisted, but at the same time had enough self-doubt about this course to warrant the advice from Duncannon that opposition would be fruitless if he 'trembled at shadows' and 'quaked' at the name of O'Connell and every Radical who was willing to turn Peel out. 'Consider well', Duncannon urged, 'whether you will not give additional strength to the Radical party by separating yourself from them, instead of making them subservient to a certain degree which they are now prepared to be.' This argument, in the end, was persuasive. Refusing to act with the Radicals where their opinions agreed would throw in Radical ranks all those members pledged to moderate reforms who wished 'to adhere to the Whig party'.[62]

There was an important tactical consideration in reaching an accommodation with the Radicals. H. G. Ward had let it be known that he would move an appropriation resolution shortly after the session began. This was the type of motion that the Radicals were counting on to unify the opposition and defeat the government. But Russell was acutely aware that many moderate Whigs might support Peel's government if it was not given an opportunity to govern; a premature attack would give in to the 'cant' of the 'fair trial men' and help to establish the government it was meant to overthrow. What Russell termed the 'danger' of the 'Whig course' was clear: premature hostility or lack of hostility could both strengthen Peel's position and, simultaneously, the Radicals'. In twenty years as leader of the party, he recollected in later years, the task of keeping the majority together was never so difficult.[63] The way out of this dilemma was to imply a want of confidence without expressing it and to gain the confidence of sufficient moderate Radicals in order to discourage the more extreme colleagues from establishing their credentials by pressing Peel too early. The Speakership of the Commons provided the first such opportunity.

By converting the choice of speaker into a covert choice of party, a tactic never before done, the Whigs meant to imply want of confidence in Peel's administration. Amid widespread feeling that Manners Sutton, the Tory incumbent, had acted partially during the change of administration in November,[64] a number of the Radicals and more eager Whigs suggested that Abercromby stand against him. Abercromby's name appears to have come from Warburton, who was trying to organise a unified Radical response to Peel at the same time. Although Melbourne had some doubts about opposing the Speaker whom the Whigs had appointed in 1833, he agreed to approach Abercromby, who promptly rejected the offer.[65] Spring Rice, who had wanted the chair in 1833, asked to have it again, and for a few weeks the issue remained undecided. But though Russell and several of his colleagues favoured Rice personally, several considerations weighed in Abercromby's favour. Rice's conservatism, it was thought, would lose the support of several Radical and liberal members who were putting pressure on Abercromby to reconsider. As the election results became known, it seemed certain that Rice could not win.[66] Renewed application was made to Abercromby, who finally accepted for the sake of the party a position which he had described to Melbourne as a 'purgatory'.[67] Rumours, and the Tory press, had it that the Whigs had chosen the more liberally-minded Abercromby in deference to O'Connell who would not have Rice, but the charge was groundless; O'Connell had told Duncannon that he would vote for anybody the party put up.[68] Moreover, a number of the leading Whigs pressed Rice to leave himself free to accept a ministerial post in a future Melbourne administration. Rice had sought refuge in the chair because, among other reasons, he could not go to the length of organic and constitutional changes that several of the Whigs' 'friends' had pledged themselves on, and it was just this quality that made him attractive to most of the leading Whigs. His patron Lansdowne wanted him part of an administration in principles 'similar to the last'; Russell, whose opinion decided the issue, thought his being in the chair would be too serious a loss in debate to the 'Whiggest part of the Whigs'.[69]

The choice of Abercromby was a sound tactical move which satisfied the Whigs' supporters and left Rice free to work towards what he termed a 'real Whig government', but tactical considerations in a game which the Whigs had not wanted to play were not an encouraging prospect. The Whigs might be adamant in their determination to resist 'the movement', but there could be no denying the fact that they were scarcely free to choose their own candidate to face Manners Sutton. 'It is quite clear', Holland admitted, 'that Abercromby and Abercromby *only* gives them a chance of success.' Rice observed that it was not the staff so much as the 'corps d'Armée' that caused alarm.[70] As the meeting of the new House approached, it became increasingly obvious that positive steps would have to be taken to curb what the Radicals considered a sense of power and the Whigs their power of mischief. This determination to curb Radical influence ran counter to the Whigs' embryonic party 'machinery' at Cleveland Square, which had been most active in support of Abercromby's candidacy as the first stage of a more formal junction of opposition parties. For more than a month before the meeting at Lichfield House, Parkes, with the active support of Thomson, Mulgrave, Duncannon and Durham, had been busily arranging a meeting in conjunction with Warburton, who was simultaneously trying to organise and unify the 'Radical brigade'.[71] Holland had given some encouragement to a unified opposition, but most of the Whig leaders had not. Neither Russell nor Melbourne agreed with the calling of a meeting at Lord Lichfield's, planned for 18 February, fearing disunity as much as unity.[72] When it became obvious that the meeting would be held in spite of their views, Lord John went in an effort to prevent the Radicals from taking the lead on the opposition benches. Leadership did not come easily to Russell. It was with some relief that he had been saved 'from being sadly pummelled' by Peel, Stanley and O'Connell by the dismissal in November,[73] and he was slow in picking up the reins which Grey had dropped and Melbourne seemed loth to touch. Hobhouse had warned Melbourne earlier in January that without more and wiser heads in charge than those in Cleveland Square, the Radicals would be given too much headroom; someone, perhaps Russell, he urged, should take charge of the opposition.[74] It was not until faced with this Radical challenge that Russell was pulled out of his lethargic mood, which had no doubt been encouraged by Melbourne's wait-and-see approach, but his attendance at the Lichfield meeting should be seen as more than an appearance of one who was dragged there against his will. That he was at such a meeting against his wishes there can be no doubt; but having heard of the meeting, he took positive steps to tame the Radicals. The organisers of the meeting had planned to have Russell chosen as a joint leader of the three main opposition groups and to frame a general course of action that would be reflected in an amendment to the address embodying the Whig, Radical and O'Connellite 'platforms'. But a few days before the meeting, Russell hurriedly drew up an amendment that censored the dissolution, the only act for which Peel's government was responsible, and called for legislation to deal with the Irish Church, Protestant dissenters, and English corporations. Significant by its absence was any mention of appropriation and constitutional change. Peel was to be given a chance to govern. Russell knew that the Whigs would support this more moderate amendment that made short shrift of the extreme Radicals' plans. Hobhouse had assured him that Grote and the moderate Radicals would be satisfied with the wording,[75] and he went to the Lichfield meeting to disallow any discussion between the Whigs and Radicals. He told the 130 members present, more than half of whom were Radicals, that they were neither to abuse Sutton nor cheer Abercromby on the Speakership, that there were many present with whom he could not concur in other subjects, and that the affair was not to be considered a meeting of a party who were generally to act together. He avoided all mention of an amendment, allowed no one else to speak, and agreed with Melbourne afterwards that there should be no further meetings. He needed to attend such a meeting, he told Melbourne beforehand, to ensure that the opposition would act with rather than against him.[76] Thus, although there was a sizeable group of party organisers who favoured a close working arrangement with the Radicals, Russell spoke for the leaders who were strongly opposed to any arrangement that would give the Radicals security of place. Notice of a second meeting was put in the *Morning Chronicle* by Thomson, but Russell disallowed it. When Morpeth introduced the amendment in the Commons, its provisions had not been made known to the bulk of the Radicals.[77] It seems clear that the Whigs had intended to accept Radical votes to weaken Peel's ministry on important divisions, but in such a way that the Radicals could be under no illusions that promises had been held out to them. In acting as they did, the Whigs tried to make the best of a bad bargain forced on them by the King's actions the previous November.

During the opening day of debate in the new House, Stanley gave a scarcely concealed hint that he would have supported the Whigs if Rice had been a candidate for the Speakership. Rice was annoyed by Stanley's speech, for he had suggested to his colleagues that his taking the post might facilitate a rapprochement 'between those who have been unfortunately for the public separated', but had been unable to press this claim when Stanley told him privately that he would not, as Rice had requested, support his candidacy.[78] There were few who disagreed with the idea of a reunion with Stanley and Graham, but as long as the appropriation issue remained unresolved, the cause was hopeless.

In November, Melbourne had been hesitant to have any of Abercromby, Rice or Russell succeed Althorp as leader of the Commons, thinking that they would shut the door on a reunion with Stanley. Speaking at Melbourne Hall in Derby a few weeks later, he stressed the need of reconciliation and union.[79] But the appointment of Russell to the leadership, together with the subsequent dismissal and elections, made him aware of the practical difficulties of pursuing a course that the bulk of his party would not accept. He told Holland, who had suggested Graham's name for the Chair as a first step toward reunion, to think of the difficulty, unpopularity and jealousy of making an arrangement with Stanley, whose conduct during the elections he added, had angered the liberals. Russell, not surprisingly, was opposed to reunion. Although Grey urged him to agree to postpone appropriation in order to effect a reunion with Stanley and Graham, Lord John told Melbourne that he could 'take no share' in such a government. Melbourne had little choice but to agree:[80]

> You are quite right to be explicit about the Irish Church. You know, that in general, nobody is so much for shuffling over differences of opinion and getting over matters as well as one can, as I am . . . But this is really an important moment, and a great start and it is nonsense now but to understand one another at least upon matters so important and so urgent. Would you be satisfied with Duncannon's bill and leaving future measures to future discussion and consideration?

Melbourne assumed, as had Grey, that neither Whigs nor Stanley and Graham would change their views on the Irish Church; an agreement to disagree would have been the only possible basis of reunion. Howick was the one Whig who thought otherwise. Prompted by his father's insistence that Whiggery could never stand up to the Radicals without the support of the two ex-ministers, Howick took the view that they and Peel could be persuaded to join a union of moderate Whigs and Tories committed to appropriation. If Peel, 'in reality, in opinion and feeling much more of a Whig' could disentangle himself from the ultra Tories and 'do with a good grace what is altogether inevitable', Howick saw no obstacle to a junction. Although he understood that appropriation was the only point of principle on which he differed from Stanley and Graham, he thought that Peel was looking for a way out of his pledges against the measure and would break with the extremists in his party if faced with a Whig attack in the Commons on that principle.[81] Because none of his colleagues was prepared to follow a course that would provide Peel with little chance to govern, Howick tried to persuade Stanley and Graham to accept appropriation, thinking that Peel might follow them. On 9 March, he sent Graham a paper on the Irish Church which argued that both Peel and the Whigs were becoming captive to their parties' extremists; Stanley and Graham's reunion with the moderate Whigs, with the inclusion of Peel, would produce a liberal administration supported by the moderate and respectable nation. Their response to Howick's inquiry is indication that their differences with the Whigs on the Irish Church question were irreconcilable and that they were right to have left in 1834. Although Stanley and Graham both agreed that such an administration would be 'most desirable', neither was prepared to discuss appropriation.[82] They held fast to the view that the bulk of the Whig leaders were captives of Russell, who in turn was bent on power with O'Connell's aid. There is little to support this view of the Whigs. Russell did not force the principle on an unwilling party that would have been prepared to drop it for the sake of a partnership with Stanley. It was not only those like Holland, who doubted the prospect of regaining Stanley 'till the Irish Steeple which he has raised between us is shortened or removed', who were pressing for an appropriation measure. Lansdowne, who had written to Stanley expressing an ardent desire to be brought together again, nevertheless was adamant in his belief that surplus revenues should be applied to Catholic education, and that until that question was resolved, reunion was an object 'to which it is vain at present to do more than speculate'. Spring Rice had also told Stanley that though the Irish question was the only wall of separation between them, 'on that I think you are wrong'.[83]

Stanley's views, on the other hand, bore little resemblance to Whig concepts of civil and religious liberty. He told Howick that the failure of the Church in Ireland to improve the moral welfare of the people lay with the Church ministers. He was not certain, he added, that enforced payment of tithes would not work and he doubted that violence generated as a result of enforcement would harm the Church's reputation. Graham's reference to Whig principles that necessitated a 'jealous fear' of a dominant Catholic

Church was based on his own view of seventeenth century Whiggery which, by stressing anti-Catholicism to the exclusion of civil and religious liberties, had little relevance for the Whigs in the 1830s.[84] At a time when the Church, like parliament, was in need of reform in order to be spared, Whigs could not accept the same kind of defence of the old system as Wellington had in opposing parliamentary reform. For most of them, it seemed clear that Stanley and Graham would be more at home with Peel, whose prejudices had recently led him to attack the admission of dissenters to the universities as 'without exception, the most extravagant demand which had been advanced in modern times'.[85] This was an emotional defence of a system of privilege that Stanley might have regarded as moderate Conservatism, but it was not a view to which the party he had left could subscribe. That the difference in outlook was fundamental, and did not apply only to appropriation, can be seen from the arguments that Peel, Stanley and Graham used against the government's bill to reform the Irish Municipal corporations in 1836. Aware that the proposed bill would place the corporations in the hands of the Catholic majority, they moved for the abolition of corporations and their replacement by direct government rule. This, it was argued, would give the most satisfaction to the Irish Protestants who had, by all justice, to give up their indefensible hold on the corporations.[86] By abolishing rather than reforming the corporations, Peel, Stanley and Graham were trying, in effect, to nullify the repeal of the test and corporations act, a process that could scarcely have been called Whiggism.

The important reason why Stanley and Graham did not rejoin the Whigs was the simplest. They did not want to. For almost two years, Stanley and William IV had discussed an infusion of Whigs into a Peelite government, and by 1835, Stanley's political and intellectual future lay with Conservatism. There is no doubt that he would have welcomed an appeal from the King to form a 'government of the centre'[87] and for this reason took extreme care not to offend the moderate Whigs and Tories; but it is unlikely that he placed much hope in this possibility, knowing as he did that Peel was unlikely to accept anything less than the leading position in any arrangement.[88] Thus, while the Whigs thought in terms of Stanley and Graham rejoining them, they, in turn, meant by reunion the garnering of moderate Whigs for a Stanley–Peel partnership. The point of the Derby 'dilly' was not to wait for the

Whigs to rearrange their priorities in such a way that would appeal to Stanley and Graham, but to keep its leaders in a powerful, centrist position that would help Peel to dish Wellington and the ultra Tories. In stating publicly that he might have supported the Whigs if Rice had been their candiate for Speaker, Stanley was being less than honest, for, as he told Graham, he had advised Rice to withdraw, thinking that the Whigs would put up another candidate which he could then oppose; 'We should (then) have a beautiful opportunity of saying that if there *were* to be an opposition, Rice was the person who had the best claim.' By thus encouraging Rice to withdraw to force the Whigs into a less moderate position which he could more easily oppose, Stanley's protestation of neutrality had little meaning. He had decided in November not to oppose Peel's new administration, and was awaiting only an opportunity of supplanting Wellington as Peel's lieutenant. Graham had reportedly been eager to join with Peel in December; unlike Stanley, he had not paid even lip service to a union of moderates.[89] Unfortunately for Stanley, Peel's inability to free himself from the ultra Tories, and the continued conviction of the Whig moderates for appropriation, rendered void his plan to build a large centre party. When the dilly split over Russell's appropriation motion on 7 April, it was obvious that Stanley had too little following to make any demands of Peel. Thus, when the dilly died out as a centrist force, something its founders had in fact never believed in, Stanley and Graham had no other refuge than a Conservative party not at all shorn of its Tory extremists. When Melbourne's second administration was formed and Stanley led his party from below the gangway to sit with Peel, it was with cap in hand.

The circumstances of the Whigs' dismissal and elections left the relative position of parties and groupings in a confused state in the few weeks preceding the meeting of parliament. There was no certainty about the size or direction of the Stanley 'party', and it was not known how many members who would normally be classed as Whigs or Whig supporters would refuse to oppose the Tories either from the view that Sutton had been an able Speaker or that the Tories deserved a chance to govern. The Whig whips were far from optimistic that the opposition could mount a majority when parliament met; on 24 January, Wood predicted a margin of no more than twenty-four, with thirty returns not yet in. He and Howick both told Spring Rice, who appeared to be the leading candidate at that point, that contesting the chair at all appeared doubtful; a few defections from personal regard for Sutton would give the government a majority.[90] Estimates of party strength of course varied enormously according to one's political views. Howick and Wood did not want Spring Rice to be lost to the Whigs by contesting the Speakership. Ellice and Duncannon, on the other hand, hoped that Abercromby's taking the chair would signify a positive Whig attitude toward the Radicals; they predicted much larger opposition majorities.[91] Unlike their position two years earlier, when it was necessary to suggest that because of the closeness of the party strengths, Whigs needed to rely on Radicals to survive, Ellice now argued that the majority was sufficiently large that the fear of moderates being driven to the Tories by a reliance on Radical votes was unfounded. Howick and Wood were closer to the mark; their estimates of a narrow majority were matched by the Radical Warburton's, who predicted a close race for the Speakership.[92] It was decided by Russell and Melbourne that the opposition members should be whipped in by sending letters to everyone who was not an obvious Tory supporter. It was not clear however that the members would put party before any other consideration; Russell was prepared to let Sutton stand unopposed if the case were desperate.[93] Within a week of the opening, hopes were raised; the 'doubtful' had nearly all responded to the call, and though it would be a 'very pretty race', Abercromby seemed likely to win. The way was therefore clear to press ahead with the nomination. During the opening debate, Sutton defended his conduct in a strong speech that caused even betting in the lobby. On the division, Sutton lost a majority by 316 to 306, the first and only Speaker to be turned out by the party that had put him in.[94]

The opposition's victory gave Russell the confidence to go ahead with the amendment to the Address that he had drawn up with Melbourne. The motion called for legislation dealing with the corporations, dissenters and Irish Church, but left Peel free to do as he liked on those matters. Although Grote had assured him that the moderate Radicals would accept an amendment that would not drive Peel from office immediately, there was no assurance that the extreme Radicals would acquiesce. The narrow majority in the Speakership left little margin for dissatisfied Radicals who might support the Tories as a show of strength, but Russell was convinced that the first victory made an attempt at a moderate amendment necessary. He was concerned that a Whig administration, if formed too quickly, would give Hobhouse, Thomson and Mulgrave the influence necessary to carry 'violent measures'; a few weeks later he explained to a gathering of Whig supporters at the Freemason's Tavern why Peel would also gain from sudden defeat:[95]

> I am sure that if we had succeeded in throwing out the present Ministry at the commencement of the struggle, it would have been said that there was no difference of opinion between us – that we had availed ourselves merely of a party superiority, and that, if the present Ministers had been allowed to continue in office, they would have shown . . . that they were better qualified than any other men to conduct the affairs of this country.

Russell's gamble seemed to be successful. Although E. J. Stanley, the new Whig whip, thought that they would be 'very hard run indeed, if not beaten' by a superior Tory whipping-in,[96] a majority of 309–302 on 26 February gave some hope that the Radicals would not ruin the Whigs' moderate approach. Of the nineteen Whig supporters who voted for the Tories on the amendment, only one, G. R. Robinson of Worcester, was a Radical. Two days later, Melbourne, Rice, Thomson, Mulgrave, Hobhouse and Wood decided at a meeting at Russell's that after the two 'victories', there would be few obstacles to the opposition's remaining quiet for the moment to see what Peel would produce. But , ominously, it was also planned that at the end of March, when the report of the Commission of Enquiry into revenues of the Irish Church would be laid before the House, Russell was to give notice of a motion on that subject; there seemed no other way of overcoming the Radical Ward's threat to redeem his election pledge of moving an appropriation resolution.[97]

It soon became apparent that some of the Radicals were becoming impatient at what they considered to be Whig connivance at Tory governance. Disappointed that his fellow Radicals had forced him to concur in Russell's weak amendment by their own support for it, Joseph Hume decided to put pressure on Peel, and the Whigs, by moving that supplies be granted for only three months.[98] Russell realised at once the danger of such a motion. No matter how the Whigs decided to act on it, a unified opposition could scarcely be maintained. It was decided to canvass all opposition members to test their support for Hume, and when it became clear that large numbers would not support his motion, the Radicals feared 'power of mischief' was evident: support for Hume would cause a large number of moderate Whigs to support Peel's position; opposition to him would as certainly increase the Radicals' price of support for turning Peel out. The King's earlier preference for Althorp over Russell was made ironic by the fact that Hume's motion, which was designed to wreak havoc with Russell's moderate opposition posture, should have the support of Althorp, who pressed Russell to show solidarity with the Radicals by supporting Hume even if defeat were likely.[99] But Russell would not. A suggestion to make the motion less objectionable by having Hobhouse move it failed when Hume publicly restated his intentions. The only course left was to persuade Hume to back down. As a consequence, and against the wishes of Russell and most of the Whig leaders, a second meeting of all shades of opposition was called for 12 March at Lord Lichfield's house. With great difficulty, but with the threat of mass desertions from his ranks, Hume was persuaded to drop his motion.[100] Many Radicals were dejected. 'The game is up, as we say', wrote John Stuart Mill a few days later. 'The Tories will remain in place . . . the attempt to expel the ministry has been abandoned; they now only harass them in detail.'[101] Whigs obviously took a different view. The Whig party was not sufficiently strong to defeat Peel on a partisan issue that gave him little chance to make public his legislative intentions. There was good reason to doubt that his promised reforms would satisfy a majority of the House, but fairness dictated that he be given a try. And as Russell told Grey, who had condemned the second Lichfield meeting as roundly as the first, a meeting was necessary to weaken Radical influence by averting the danger of Radical motions. 'Everything is now to depend on my motion upon the Irish Church', he added. 'It is a great question of principle, and must be decided in one way or the other.'[102]

By the time that Russell moved for a committee of the House to consider the Irish Church temporalities on 30 March, Peel had introduced a measure of civil marriage for Dissenters and an Irish tithe plan. The tithe bill was closely modelled on Littleton's bill of February 1834, and supported by the Church despite the fact that it involved a larger reduction in clerical incomes.[103] But without appropriation, there was little hope of its passing the Commons. With it there was less chance for it in the Lords. Two days after

Peel's plan was made known, the Whigs prepared for what Ellice termed the '*commencement de la fin*' by settling that there should be an opposition 'cabinet' every Sunday – surely the first 'shadow' cabinet.[104] By the 26th, Greville was speculating on Peel's successor. Russell's subsequent motion did not refer to the appropriation of temporalities, but its implication was clear to all. Peel had Hardinge inform the opposition, through Rice, that though 'the game was up' as soon as Russell's motion had carried by 33 votes on 2 April, he would not resign until his own bill was either altered by a principle to which he could not agree or was defeated.[105] At the Sunday 'cabinet' on 5 April, the decision to turn Peel out, largely decided at Brooks's the previous day, was therefore agreed upon. Once the resolution of the committee of the House had been reported and moved, a second resolution would be moved stating that appropriation formed part of any Irish tithe bill.[106] The resolution was accordingly carried on 6 April by a majority of 25 and the appropriation resolution on 7 April by 27. On the 8th, Peel resigned. The ball was once again in the King's court.

It was no secret that the King would summon Grey to attempt the coalition of moderates that neither Melbourne nor Peel had been able, or indeed willing, to arrange. This was the assumption at Holland House where the leading Whigs gathered to discuss Peel's resignation; indeed Richmond, still Whig enough to be allowed entry to Lady Holland's, claimed to know before the day was out that Grey had already received the call. In fact, it was not until 9 April that Grey went to the Palace. He told William that he could come back as leader only of a cabinet composed of the heads of all the moderate parties, but that such a combination was impossible after the resolution of the House of Commons in favour of appropriation. A note to Stanley quickly confirmed this opinion.[107] 'Rome was not built in a day', Taylor wrote to Stanley to express his own, and the King's opinion that union 'at no remote point' was not unlikely. This episode signified the last such attempt. Graham told Greville, at the same time that Grey was seeing the King, that he and Stanley had 'no leaning' towards the Whigs and looked only to a junction with Peel. And the Conservative leader, Taylor himself conceded, would have refused for however short a term to join a Grey government or 'to play second fiddle in any combination or concert.[108] The King was left with Grey's advice to call on Melbourne and Lansdowne. When they in turn rejected as impossible a final appeal to seek a junction with Stanley and Peel, William summoned Melbourne, alone, to form a Whig administration. 'I said to him', Melbourne recounted to Queen Victoria four years later, 'I hoped he would give me his confidence, and he answered, "Good God! I wouldn't have sent for you, if I didn't mean to do so"; but he seemed a good deal annoyed, so that I stopped and didn't revert to it again.'[109]

Coming a month after Peel had refused office over the bedchamber crisis, it is not surprising that Melbourne's story did not include the hard bargain he had driven with the King. William had certainly not wanted to accept what he had rejected in November and it was only by the greatest effort that the Whigs were able to pursue their own course against the Royal prerogative. On 15 April, two days after the King had invited him to form a government, Melbourne wrote to claim the powers respecting peerage, household and other matters which would mark the Crown's confidence in its advisers. The King's reply was hostile and curt; nothing but the household was accorded, and along with pointed objections to individuals who might make up the new government, he suggested his unwillingness to support the principle of appropriation on the grounds that it might violate his coronation oath. The objection to individuals was accompanied by a disclaimer of the principle of exclusions from the government and did not, as a consequence, cause further dispute. The King had already told Grey that should Melbourne be summoned to form an administration, no Radical could take part, and had received the response that although the Whigs could not accede to a principle of exclusion, they would not propose O'Connell or Hume. The King's 'conscience' proved more difficult to overcome, for Melbourne told him that the choice was between the principle of appropriation or another set of ministers. The issue dragged on for four days. Melbourne would have nothing to do with a committee of fifteen judges who might rule on the connection between the oath and appropriation, and it was not until Lord Lyndhurst, still the Tory Lord Chancellor, refused to offer his services for the same purpose, that the King retreated. He fell, claimed the Duchess of Gloucester, 'the crown tottering on his head'.[110] Two days later, on 19 April, the second Melbourne administration was sworn in.

Allowing Wellington a central role in the formation of the new administration in November was an error on the part of the King

which made Stanley's participation impossible. In the same circumstance five months later, instructing Melbourne not to appoint
Radicals to office was less a blunder than an indication that
William's perception of the Whigs had been greatly distorted
under Stanley's tutelage. A less-jaundiced adviser would have
perhaps allowed the King to understand that the intention of
Melbourne's colleagues was, as Russell had stated, to hold 'our
own Whig course'. Appointing Radicals to office was as anathema
to aristocratic Whigs as it was to the King, whose advisors,
ranging from the high Tory court party to Stanley, immunised him
from the view that Whiggery could follow a moderate course
devoid of Radicalism and Toryism. Whig principles demanded
that the King's exclusion policy be opposed in theory but, at the
same time, the Whigs had no difficulty agreeing to a request that
was largely meaningless. The resumption of Radical activity in the
autumn of 1834 and Whig losses in the elections had already
convinced Melbourne that there could be no simple reconstruction
of the ministry bequeathed to him by Grey. 'We now stand upon
new ground', he told Spring Rice in December, 'and if ever called
upon again, I have a right to consider afresh upon what principles
and with whom as associates I will re-engage in the public
service.' Although this sentiment, and his Derby speech, led some
to think that he was hopeful of a reunion with Stanley and
Graham, Melbourne had too fine a grasp of political realities to see
any future in that course. A month later he made his intentions
clear: 'I will have nothing more to do with Brougham' he told
Grey, 'I will have nothing to do with Durham . . . my third
peremptory exclusion . . . is O'Connell.'[111]

None of these exclusions met with any resistance from the new
ministry. Holland had been willing to offer the Irish Attorney-
Generalship to O'Connell, and Russell suggested to O'Connell that
he would resign his own office if he felt an injustice, but there was
never any disagreement over his not being offered a post. Indeed
O'Connell's single request, that the Irish Attorney-Generalship be
given to the Catholic O'Loughlen instead of to the Protestant
Perrin, was rejected by the Whigs.[112] Durham and Brougham had
even fewer supporters. Durham had hoped that he would be
accepted back into Whig circles after Grey had retired, blindly
thinking that his quarrel was with Grey alone. In fact, his
father-in-law was one of the few who had any sympathy for him at
all.[113] His arrogance and personal attacks on Grey were never

forgiven by his colleagues, and though he expressed a wish to be employed 'as a means of regaining his own friends', Melbourne would not have him. In 1831, Melbourne reportedly said of Durham's outburst at a cabinet dinner, 'If I had been Lord Grey, I would have knocked him down', and by 1835, Durham's more recent involvement with the leaders of the Radical movement lost him all chance of a reconciliation. Ellice thought it would be best to send him to Ireland to have the gloss taken off his reputation, and before the summer was out, he was sent as Ambassador to St Petersburg, office in England out of the question. 'If the Great Aristocrat can make up his mind to receive Lord Durham', quipped a good-humoured King to Melbourne, 'His Majesty . . . is quite ready to admit that this country and its Government . . . will be benefitted by the absence of Lord Durham.'[114] Brougham's career as a minister had ended with the dismissal. Melbourne would not forgive him for his role in the events that led to Grey's retirement or for his speaking tour in Scotland that upset the King in the autumn. Brougham retorted with some justification that the court had made his proceedings in the north a pretext for doing 'what you all know it had resolved to do', but his erratic and wild nature was too much for his late colleagues, of whom all but Grey argued against his reappointment. 'Suppose Brougham' wrote Sydney Smith, 'who has tried all things, were to take to truth and honesty? Who knows, he has no practice, but his versatility is endless.'[115] Like Durham, Brougham's cavorting with the Radicals made him even less attractive. Although the King was willing to have him back, the Whigs were not. At a painful three-hour meeting, Brougham got very angry at not being made Lord Chancellor. 'God damn you', Melbourne burst back, 'you won't get the Great Seal and that's the end of it.' As a sop to his feelings, the seals were put into commission, but Brougham's ire had been raised. 'My life will henceforth be devoted to vengeance which I shall exact most fully against the creatures that have disgraced themselves and abandoned me' he wrote to Melbourne; 'the low rabble . . . at Brooke's . . . I certainly must touch no more.'[116]

Hobhouse, appointed President of the Board of Control with a seat in the cabinet, told Melbourne that the new government seemed to him less liberal than his former administration, and despite Melbourne's reply that some had told him it was too Jacobinical,[117] there was some substance to Hobhouse's opinion. Durham and Brougham were arguably left out for reasons other than their radical views, but because they had been courting, and were courted by, leading Radicals, their exclusion from the government was not without significance. Moreover, as Hobhouse pointed out, the new government had fewer balloteers than Grey's governments. Hobhouse was pledged to household suffrage and ballot, but the absence of Spencer (Althorp), Ellice, Abercromby, Durham and Brougham, all balloteers, gave this issue less prominence than Grey's personnel would have. Melbourne was aware, in fact, that Radicals were unhappy with the 'conservative' make-up of his administration; at a cabinet dinner on 22 April, he told Holland that their 'discontentment at arrangements' would pare the government's scanty majority more than it already was. The opposite view, that the new government was more liberal than its predecessor, was taken by Grey, who was known to be unhappy with the appointment to the cabinet of Thomson and Hobhouse, and whose refusal to join the administration was likely the cause of Melbourne's reference to the view held by some that his government was too Jacobinical.[118] On the same day that he was asked to form a government, Melbourne, together with Holland, Palmerston, Rice and Lansdowne, sent Grey a letter requesting his 'active support and assistance in office', if not as Prime Minister then as Foreign Secretary.[119] Grey had good reason to decline the offer. It was clear that differences over Irish policy had alienated Grey from Russell and Althorp to the point where they could not be expected to sit together. Althorp refused a post on the grounds that Grey had too much influence even though he was not a member;[120] recognition that Russell and Grey were equally far apart prompted the signatories of the request to say that Russell had not been informed of it. Russell, for his part, wrote to Grey the following day to say that though he had not signed the communication because he knew that Grey had no wish to be Prime Minister, he wished him to accept the Foreign Office in order to save everyone the embarrassment of having to give the position to Palmerston, who had threatened to resign if he could not have it.[121] Besides giving lie to his colleagues' claim that he had not been consulted, Russell's letter made it obvious to Grey that Palmerston was a less than genuine signatory to the invitation and that his own inclusion in a new government would produce disagreements and revive animosities that no man of his age and temper could wish for. But Grey's response to the offer was indicative less of his distaste for political conflict than of his disagreement with the direction which the party had seemed to him to have taken in the previous year. He could not, he told Melbourne, join his administration unless Irish appropriation, the obstacle to Peel and Stanley's joining it, were chopped.[122]

Grey was opposed not so much to appropriation as to the effect of its introduction: to attempt the question in the face of the Lords' resistance would give the Radicals in the Commons and the country too much prominence; it would also prevent a reunion with Stanley and Graham. Stanley, it seems clear, was hand-picked by Grey to succeed Althorp, if not Grey himself, and the Prime Minister had usually taken Stanley's part in cabinet quarrels. Following the break in 1834, Grey was convinced that Russell's new-found prominence, together with his impatience, indiscretion and inability to 'direct and control' men, robbed the party of an efficient leader with the authority to withstand Radical pressures.[123] He also felt let down by his party's apparently unconcerned acceptance of Stanley's, then his own, resignation. There was no doubt a clash of egos as well as of principles. The 'flippancy' with which Russell treated his opinions 'nettled' him,[124] and Melbourne's increasing preference for Lord John's counsel was an embittering experience. Against his strong warning of certain failure, the Speakership had been contested. Though it was clear that most of the Whig leaders thought Sutton's partisan conduct warranted his replacement, Grey regarded the contest as a measure which Russell had foolishly been led into, against his own judgement, by Radicals intent on widening the breach with Stanley.[125] Grey's conception of the Whig course, 'to work out the necessary reforms which the state of our institutions may require, upon safe and moderate principles, in accordance with the constitution of our mixed government and with the spirit of the Age', was similar to any statement of faith that Russell could adhere to, but in Grey's view, Russell's foolish adhesion to a Radical position destroyed the possibility of following that course.[126] He could not have known, of course, that Stanley had done all he could to have Abercromby chosen as the Whig candidate in order to widen his breach with his former colleagues, and he consequently held to the view that the Whig party, 'if such a party still exists',[127] was too weak, without Stanley, to support itself against Radicals and Tories. Grey's misjudgement of Stanley and Peel is not surprising, for with neither did he have regular contact. But his judgement of Russell betrayed a vanity that did not allow him to take lightly his own and Stanley's lack of influence. Russell was not duped by Radicals or the less Whiggish section of his party into an extreme course. Hobhouse, in fact, opined that he was 'too much led by Lord Holland and Lord Grey'.[128] Despite Howick's assurances to his father that Russell intended to make captives of the Radicals rather than be taken hostage himself, Grey would not believe it. 'I did not expect that you would approve of a meeting at which O'Connell was present', Russell answered one rebuke from Grey, 'but as I do not swerve from my path in the least to please him, I do not see so much harm in it . . . you did not disclaim his assistance in carrying the reform bill.'[129] There is no doubt that Russell was impudent. There is as little doubt that he was right. Melbourne's new ministry, in many respects less committed to the movement than Grey's, would quickly reestablish the pattern of governing with Peel in order that they both might subvert the goals of both parties' ultra followers.

8

Office Once More, 1835–37

I know it is disagreeable to be stuck up in that manner, bu
consider what are the imputations upon our Government &
consider the observations to which it would give rise & the
impression it wd make, if the custom or costume were to be
discontinued for the first time by a Government which is avo
wedly Whig & which is accused of being radical.

> Melbourne to Wrottesley, who had asked to be excused from
> wearing full dress for the Address to the King, 1836[1]

If Grey had little faith in the government's prospects, Hobhouse
was no more sanguine. The position, he wrote as the new
administration prepared to face parliament, was 'anything bu
encouraging . . . the King is against us, the court also, a majority
of nearly a hundred Peers . . . The Army, the Navy, the Church
the law, the squires, the magistracy, against us . . . To balance thi
we have a precarious majority of about 30 in the House o
Commons.'[2] What Hobhouse was coming to realise was wha
Grey knew all along. Despite the Reform Act, the electoral systen
was one still dominated by traditional eighteenth-century force
which were bound to be re-established without the enthusiasn
for Reform which had dominated the elections of 1831 and 1832
The Whig leaders were concerned not so much with the predict
able re-establishment of traditional influences as with the exten
of Conservative gains and the issues which they perceived to be
responsible for their own heavy losses. Although the actual caus
of voter preference in any given contest is notoriously difficult to
evaluate, the Whig leaders based their future conduct on wha
they believed to be the underlying reasons for discontent. Mos
prominent was their conviction that Radical, Irish and Dissentin
support had helped them in neither counties nor boroughs. Grey
told his son that the Whigs were wrong to have supposed tha
Church reforms could do anything other than 'have against you
the Whigs of the country',[3] but there is no doubt that the Whig

were surprised by the strength of feeling against all such reforms. Despite the similarity in programmes for English Church reforms put forward during the campaign by both Conservative and Whig leaders, the 'violent' attack on property encompassed in appropriation, and, more importantly, the type of support that it generated, was thought to have damaged the Whig cause generally. Many Conservative candidates had stated that the only meaningful division was between 'destructives' and 'upholders' of property, order and government,[4] a charge that featured prominently in several leading Whigs' own contests. Abercromby, Campbell and Fox Maule were all struck by the alarm in Scotland at appropriating Church revenues for Catholic purposes.[5] Palmerston considered the 'cry of the Church in Danger' of some importance in his defeat in what he had thought a 'pretty safe' Hampshire seat: 'the squire & the parson never had such a poll before'.[6] The 'wild language' of the Radicals who supported Church and other reforms was particularly disturbing to Howick, who discovered such reforms to be 'contemptible' not only in Northumberland but also, as Wood and Morpeth reported to him, in 'even' the manufacturing country. 'There really is', he was forced to concede to his father, 'much more of what the tories call reaction than we had the slightest notion . . . we have very much overrated the strength of the Radicals & underrated that of the Tories.'[7] Holland came to the same conclusion. 'It is equally clear', he told Mulgrave, 'that there is no inclination to go either too fast or too far & that those who bid highest for popularity are much more likely to forfeit than to obtain it by such a manoeuvre'.[8]

It was natural, in these circumstances, for Whiggery to incline its course to what was viewed as the mood of the electorate rather than to that of Radicals whose parliamentary strength seemed out of proportion to their strength within that electorate. As soon as Melbourne's second government was formed, its members tried to re-establish the relationship with Peel that had been so successful in 1833–34. The advantage of getting Peel 'back again',[9] as Lansdowne termed it, was two-fold: without his accommodation, nothing could pass through both Houses of Parliament; with it, Radical initiatives could be stifled. The attitude to be taken toward the Radicals was set out at the very beginning in a letter which Ellice sent to Hume, who had asked that consideration be given to Radical proposals. Melbourne's late government was replaced because it was supposed by the King to have leaned to 'impracticable objects and visionary schemes' he told Hume; the elections confirmed this suspicion. 'The union of parties in opposition to Peel's Government', Ellice continued,[10]

> as far as it tended to remove a Tory Government, was approved of by the country, but moderate men would be alarmed at the idea that its success was to lead to an acceptance of the extreme opinions of the 'côté gauche'. It wants a steady, middle government , having the left and the right equally opposed to it.

Thus, although the Whigs would not discourage the Radicals from providing support, they made it clear that they would not court them. Nothing was held out to the Radicals beyond those reforms already contemplated – municipal corporation reform for England and tithe legislation for Ireland. This was not an unattractive package. The corporation commission was known to have had a majority of Radicals and Radical sympathisers amongst its members and could be expected to propose a meaningful reform of the old oligarchies. Although few expected the Lords to allow a decent Irish tithe measure to pass, the prospect of the government going to battle with the Peers was one to whet most Radicals' appetites. But neither of these measures was sufficient to give full satisfaction to the Radicals who had called for further constitutional reforms throughout the elections, and neither, the Radicals knew, was inspired by their pressures. Municipal corporation reform was in reality decided upon early in 1833 when the Royal Commission of Enquiry was set up; Irish tithe reform had an even earlier history.

The Whigs' reaction to Radical proposals was given further, and public, voice early in June during the debate on Grote's annual ballot motion. Against Grote's call for an end to corruption and bribery, Russell stressed the tendency of the Reform bill, if given time, to establish 'freedom of election'. Although large numbers out of doors, and an increasing number in parliament, had been won over to ballot, Russell would not allow the government to be drawn to it. Moreover, he went beyond what was necessary by not only arguing that ballot was not the panacea its proponents expected, but by shutting the door to further demands for shorter parliaments and an extension of the franchise. Although even the most conservative Whigs had contemplated a quinquennial parliament in return for abolition of the need for re-election on appointment to office, an expensive nuisance of which Russell's bye-election defeat was the most recent example, Lord John spoke out firmly against any constitutional change by arguing that 'this House is now the fair Representative of the people of this country.'[11] Given that his speech made more than one reference to the bribery and intimidation that created an undue influence at elections, and considering that he had the previous week announced the government's intention to introduce a corporation reform that was designed, among other things, to reflect the weight of the middle classes in the corporations' parliamentary elections, Russell might reasonably have been suspected by the Radicals of telling less than the full state of his mind. What mattered for the Whigs, however, was the necessity of putting the Radicals firmly in their place. To make a demand was to delay any prospect, however slight, of its being implemented. Discussion of the growth of a two-party system must therefore reflect the general tendency of the governing party to legislate in accordance with its own thinking rather than with that of the smaller Radical group that helped to provide the 'party' solidarity on divisions of confidence. Behind the two-party system that seemed to be developing was a Whig government increasingly prepared to act in an unofficial and oftentimes phrenetic alliance with Peel and the moderate Conservatives.

If a corrective is needed for the view that the 'Lichfield House Compact' solidified a party behind a radical policy,[12] one need only to look at the manner in which the two front benches co-operated on the municipal corporation bill to the exclusion of their respective extremist supporters. At first glance, it appeared to the Radicals that the Whig ministers had been won over to a radical reconstruction of the corporations. Indeed, there was much truth in this impression. Although Spring Rice found difficulty in accepting a ratepayer instead of a £10 householder franchise, there was eventual agreement that the plan presented by Joseph Parkes' commission would be presented to parliament.[13] Parkes could scarcely conceal his jubilation. 'I never thought . . . we should spoon them with it' he wrote to Durham in St Petersburg; 'But it stays in their stomach . . . and tonics I hope will keep it down till the bill is fairly launched in the House of Commons.' Thinking that a 'united party' would force the measure past a reluctant Tory party, Parkes regarded his 'smasher' as safe. When Peel followed Russell's introduction of the bill on 5 June with a speech approving its main features, there seemed little doubt that reformers would 'sufficiently long stick together' for the plan to succeed.[14] But the 'union' of reformers which Radicals made great play of was little more than propaganda which Radicals hoped would force the Whigs to accept their cause. Parkes himself realised that if it came to a matter of serious constitutional principle, the Whigs would sooner look to the Tories for support than to the Radicals. Only a week earlier, for example, during a parliamentary discussion on Church rates, Peel made a point of saying that Russell had argued for state maintenance and repair of the fabric of the Church; when Hume called out 'No, No', Russell interjected as loudly in defence of Peel with 'Yes'.[15] Parkes was pleased that the Whigs had swallowed his corporate medicine, because Peel '*must*' denounce it; the Whigs, he told Durham, would discover that Peel's 'proper' anti-reforming position would render co-operation less likely or attractive. In the circumstances, Peel's inability to control Lord Lyndhurst and his fellow Tory extremists in the Lords forced him into an adversarial role in order to save his position in the Conservative party, but if Parkes and the Radicals thought that Peel's support for amendments to a bill that had passed easily through the Commons would find the Whigs in a fighting spirit, they were to be mistaken.

Melbourne's initial reaction to the Lords' mutilation of the municipal measure was to warn the Lords not 'to trifle with the public opinion'; according to Holland, the Prime Minister would direct his efforts at 'animating, gratifying and recruiting his support in the Commons and the Country'.[16] Not surprisingly, such an untypically popular course was overturned by cooler heads. It was no secret that Peel was furious with the violent Tories. Their obstinacy put his leadership in question and threatened the unity of the party and, more importantly, the alliance with Stanley and Graham that had only within the month taken public form.[17] The papers commented on his disgust with the Lords, and, through Stanley and Spring Rice, the Whigs were told that the course adopted by the Lords was entirely without his concurrence and against his judgement.[18] But it was equally obvious that Peel would not side with the Whigs in a 'free for all' with the House of Lords; a more judicious course that might have Peel's approval would be better. As a consequence, the government decided that some of the Lords' insertions, most notably that which allowed for the partial continuation of the old Aldermen for

life, would have to be radically altered, while others, such as the
property qualifications of the town councillors, could be accepted.
On the afternoon of 31 August, the day the Commons was set to
debate the Lords' amendments, Russell explained the course to be
followed to a meeting of all government supporters at the Foreign
Office. Hume spoke out for the Radicals who were against any
form of compromise, but when Russell persisted, and was supported by O'Connell, the Radicals, wrote Howick, 'piped down'.
Speaking in the Commons that evening, Lord John spoke in tones
of great conciliation, suggesting at one point that he would
acquiesce in the altered qualification clause because Peel had
suggested it.[19] Peel answered in a speech equally remarkable for
its spirit of compromise. According to Greville, he 'threw over the
Lords' by agreeing, to the great dismay and rage of his own
backbenchers, to most of Russell's amendments.[20] 'We are never to
have a storm again', Morpeth wrote to Mulgrave in Ireland; 'Peel
and J. Russell completely fraternise'.[21] Two days later, Lyndhurst
gave in at a meeting of the Tory Lords at Apsley House, and the
policy of conciliation appeared to have triumphed. He would
accept the bill which Russell and Peel were sending up from the
Commons for a second time, but not without some face-saving
amendments.[22] This final hurdle showed Russell's determination
to compromise at the expense of the Radicals. Although many of
his colleagues in the Lords, Holland in particular, advised him to
stand firm in defence of their supporters in the Commons, Russell
decided to acquiesce in some of the Lords' changes in order to
avoid a collision between the two Houses. 'Very doggedly and
obstinately in appearance' wrote Holland, 'but in truth most
sagaciously, judiciously and successfully, [he] adjourned the
House over Saturday and gained 48 hours in which to prevail on
his hot partizans in the Commons to check their impetuosity and
acquiesce in his more temperate course'. For the second time in a
week, he persisted against the Radicals' insistence that ministers
stand firm, and though Thomas Duncombe furnished a list of
peers who would allegedly give in to such pressure, the Radicals
were ignored. To Holland, it seemed clear that important as Peel's
compromising attitude and need to dish his 'hot partizans' was,
Russell's actions were not less important and deserving of praise.
Without his persistent determination to steer a moderate course,
there would have been no compromise offered to Peel to accept.[23]
   The Whig difficulties of pursuing a middle course involved

more than what Holland described as 'great caution, temper and circumspection'.[24] In following the path which they did, the government was counting on the Radicals' preference for a Whig to a Conservative government. Events were to prove their hope justified. There was little doubt that the government's majority on a trial of strength between the two front benches was small enough for the Radicals to cause its fall, but for a number of reasons their support for the government was nearly unanimous. Not least of these reasons was the extremely low number of Radicals unwilling to give the government an opportunity of re-establishing its reforming credentials. Joseph Hume, as much a leader of the disorganised Radical brigade as any, played an important role in moderating Radical demands. When urged by Francis Place to press Radicals into a campaign to repeal the stamp duties rather than wait for the Lords to throw out the government's Irish tithe and English corporation legislation, Hume refused to take an antagonistic posture until Ministers had a chance to show what they might do. He told Place that conversations with Rice, Ellice and Brougham left him hopeful that 'our friends' would be useful in 'formulating reforms of every kind'; though lectured by the Radical Tailor that ' "our friends" indeed, they are not our friends – never were our friends – never will be our friends', Hume would not be drawn in.[25] This reaction, it should be remembered, came after he had been told by Ellice that the government could not consider the opinions of the *côté gauche*; there appears to be no other conclusion than that Hume was unconcerned about temporarily refraining from Radical politics. The word ballot had not appeared in his address to the electors of Middlesex, and perhaps Place was right when he told Hume that Whig kindness and attention had disarmed him and infected him with 'Lord John-ism'. There is no doubt that Hume was genuinely worried about the consequences of Radical hostility to the ministry. If the events of November 1834 had not been sufficient to warn the Radicals against precipitate action, Ellice had made a pointed reference to the King's distaste for the movement; when Hume first responded to Place's pressure a few days later, he told him that he did not want to bring on 'any reaction'. The government had counted on this docility; an entry in Holland's diary during the formation of the new ministry records their readiness to answer Radical demands by saying that the King might throw them out again. The effect of the change, Holland concluded, had been to convince them that there were greater obstacles to rapid progress 'than their ardent minds had hitherto imagined'.[26]

The possibility of the King again dismissing the ministry could not be entirely ruled out. From the time he appointed Melbourne, the King became increasingly irritated and erratic. 'Mind me', he warned the government's newly created Governor of Lower Canada in July, 'the Cabinet is not my Cabinet'; they had better take care, or, by God, I will have them impeached'.[27] Throughout the summer, rumours of a dissolution spread widely, and although Croker and Peel had both written to the King's secretary to express in strong terms their concern at the rumours and their insistence that no government could be appointed against the majority opinion of the Commons,[28] it would not have been unusual if Radicals gave credence to those rumours. Some of the more violent Radicals welcomed the reaction that further Royal interference would arouse, but most did not. What they feared most, as the Tory journal *The Standard* reported before the end of the year, was a reunification of Stanley with the Whigs, which, together with an admixture of moderate Conservatives, would spell the end of the 'Whig-Popish-Radical party'.[29]

For most Radicals, the possibility of a new combination of Whigs and Tories was extremely alarming. Assured of a majority of both houses of parliament, such a government would be as difficult to influence as to dislodge. It was in order to avoid this possibility that moderate Radicals were determined not to endanger the life of the Melbourne government. Joseph Parkes knew from his work with the fledgeling Reform Association that the electoral system would support a 'vile Coalition Cabinet' should a pure 'Whig and family' administration fail.[30] His contacts with Hobhouse, Ellice and Stanley, the Whig whip, and with Place, Hume and most of the Radicals, put him in an ideal position to temper Radical demands for the sake of a government which he admitted was controlled by an 'unnatural party standing between the People and the Tory aristocracy'. Convinced that until there was a further breach in the 'vile representative system', it was necessary, he told Place, to 'keep up a jury mast to get into port' and to goad on but not to destroy 'the rickety, brainless, opinionless Ministry'.[31] Parkes did what he could with those Radicals like Roebuck and Molesworth who thought otherwise. Thus, immediately after Russell's meeting with government supporters, at which the Ministry's reaction to the Lords' mutilation of the corporation bill was discussed, he dined with some of the more uncompromising Radicals at Grote's house in Dulwich before going up to Westminster to hear Russell and Peel speak. There he found Grote in a great rage, doubtless spurred on by Mrs. Grote, to the great glee of Molesworth and Roebuck. The Radicals Strutt and Gaskell were also present. He preached peace. He knew, as he told Stanley afterwards, that it was better to have 'such a bird in the hand than a better in the bush', and though unpopular for doing so, told them to accept Russell's amended bill.[32] When the popularity of peerage reform increased following the Lords' handling of the bill, Parkes told Easthope not to overdo the peerage question in the *Morning Chronicle* lest the 'temperate class of Liberals' be 'dog barked into Peel's fold' by 'intemperate scribblers'. He also told him not to give in to an 'ill judged provocation of a Church cry'. At the same time, he told Stanley that though there was 'as yet no fulcrum for a lever against the House of Lords', the government should not unnecessarily provoke the Radicals by setting themselves against so strong a current of public opinion as peerage reform.[33]

Parkes was clearly a mediator, and as far as it is possible to judge, an important element in holding the Whigs' parliamentary majority together. In the summer of 1836, when he thought privately that the session had ended in 'absolutely nothing' and that the Whigs would have to leave ballot and triennial parliaments as open questions if the concern were not to go to pieces, he told Rintoul, the editor of *The Spectator*, that the government had done all in its power to serve reform.[34] His battles were not always successful. He did not succeed, for instance, in having Thomson and Hobhouse carry more of the government's speaking in the Commons. He considered this pair idle, having 'reached the top of the tree', and thought that they left too much to Russell, Rice and Howick, whose anti-Radical tendencies threatened to provoke Radical tempers that could endanger the ministry.[35] There can be little doubt, however, that the 'unnatural alliance' could hold together without the bonding agent of a Parkes. But if individuals like Parkes and Hume had an important role to play in the preservation of that union, it was almost certainly in their ability to moderate wilder Radical demands that might have otherwise driven the 'temperate' Whig government supporters to the Conservatives; they were unable to apply similar pressure on the Whigs by threatening to withdraw Radical support. Although the

Radical press continually would have the world believe that the 'movement' held the balance of power between the two large parties, the claim was grossly exaggerated. It was one thing for the Radical members to help the Whigs into office by voting against Peel, but quite another to engineer the new government's defeat. There was little likelihood of defeating the government on an issue like ballot, for if enough government supporters voted against the cabinet's view, the Conservatives, who had no wish to climb into office on the strength of a Radical issue, could be expected to support the government.

The government's willingness to alter the English corporation bill in 1835 to suit the wishes of Peel and the Lords, and its acceptance of the Lords' rejection of Irish corporation reform in 1836 with apparent equanimity, left the Radicals with the single threat of withdrawing support on Irish tithe legislation. Yet this was unlikely to happen in light of the Radicals' secular views. Withholding support from the Irish Catholics involved a crisis of conscience, moreover, that most English Radicals were not prepared to consider. For much of the nineteenth century, a tie of fellow feeling and shared grievance bound the Irish nationalists and English Radicals together. Despite the all-pervasive, scarcely latent English anti-Irishness, there was usually mutual support for each others' issues. In a style reminiscent of Lady Holland, Mrs Grote took great delight at never having had O'Connell to dine. She blamed Hume's 'comprehending the Irish tail' and his concern for the offensive proceedings of the Orange Lodge (when 'everyone' was 'sick to death' of the question), for the lack of Radical unity.[36] But the adherents to this view, if there were many, did not allow their private prejudices to overtake public policies. When the less compromising Radicals like Place urged that Irish legislation should not take precedence over English or 'National' issues,[37] there was usually little positive response. Typical was the reaction to Roebuck's pamphlet campaign, at the end of 1835, which called for an end to Radical support for Irish legislation without government concessions on ballot. Grote (no doubt out of domestic earshot) told Hume that he could not identify himself with Roebuck's 'ultra and startling reforms'; Wm. Tait used the columns of his *Edinburgh Magazine* to urge the 'good sense and forbearance' of the English Radicals. 'To them', he argued, 'it would be self-immolation to desert, upon any occasion, the objects of their fellow-labourers, or to withhold support from the Ministry, merely to mark their increasing consequence and weight in the State'.[38]

With such sentiments prevailing, it is not surprising that the Whigs were little concerned about the trials of strength in the Commons. By the end of the first session of the new parliament, their earlier expressed fears of an uncontrollable Radical power appeared unfounded; with few exceptions, the government was again free from undue Radical pressures for most of 1836. On the eve of a crucial appropriation division in August 1836, *The Examiner* put the view of the moderate Radicals: 'Any professed Reformers absent from their posts' it cautioned, 'would betray the people to a Tory Government.' The division, in reality a confidence vote, carried without Radical defection.[39] O'Connell continually embarrassed the Whigs by intemperate language in Ireland, but his conduct in parliament gave no cause for concern. His support for the government's English corporation bill helped to stem the Radicals' ire during a meeting with Russell on 31 August, when even Hume was losing patience; he made it clear that because of his respect for the government's work in Ireland, he would do all he could to keep them in office. 'I do not support the ministry from any love of Lord John Russell or for the Whigs', he told one correspondent, 'but simply because they are standing between Ireland and the Orange faction and doing something to improve our condition.'[40] The Whigs had good reason to be pleased. According to Ebrington, O'Connell did the government more good by his general support in 1835 than 'any other' five men not in office. By April 1836, once 'Danophobia' had subsided after his annual demagogic recess in Ireland, Holland told Lord Lieutenant Mulgrave that he 'neither fawns nor bites, but runs in the pack quietly' as 'one of the best Irish hounds in the race'.[41]

If the combined group of English and Irish Radicals posed little problem for the Whigs by its realisation that the government, in E. J. Stanley's words, 'could not afford to play tricks' or to be 'trifled with', the Whigs on their part acted with Radicals where their own view of collective interests allowed. 'We are *not* led by those whose support we do not deny to be essential to our existence', Howick told his doubting father; 'they give that support because they dread the return to power of our opponents, but we never have and never will purchase it by going beyond that which we ourselves think to be just and right'.[42] Melbourne and Russell's support for Hume's attack on the Orange Lodges, a coalition of interests which resulted in the dissolution of the Lodges described in Chapter 12, is a case in point. So too was the reduction of the stamp duty in 1836, a measure which did a great deal both to secure and to tame the Radicals. For a number of years, the abolition of 'taxes on knowledge' had been a stock in trade of the Radical platform. Within a month of Melbourne's return to office in 1835, a delegation led by Place, Grote, Roebuck and Hume met with Spring Rice, the new Chancellor of the Exchequer, to press for the abolition of the duty on newspapers. If the delegates hoped to reap the rewards of helping the Whigs back into office, they were quickly disappointed, for Rice told them that they should never have the stamp duty repealed as long as he had the power to prevent it.[43] But Rice's innate anti-Radicalism, which led him to make short shrift of the delegates' demands in their presence, also moved him to consider, albeit from a Whig perspective, the merits of reducing the duty. That same day he received a letter from Brougham expressing the conviction that repeal would put an end to the 'obscure and blasphemous' radical press by taking away its illegal but successful advantage of being sold without stamps.[44] As Chancellor, Rice could not contemplate the complete loss of revenue from the duty, but he did see the merit of a reduced duty which, if strictly enforced, would provide some revenue and allow the stamped press to compete on equal terms with the unstamped papers which the government had failed to control. With its experience and higher quality, a rejuvenated stamped press might do what the Home Office had tried and failed: to drive the radical unstamped out of business. In July 1835 Rice therefore proposed that the government meet the Radical Bulwer's repeal motion planned for August by reducing the duty from fourpence to a penny. He was given strong support from Howick, who was worried that respect for the law was being eroded by papers like the *National Gazette* which had a weekly circulation of 40,000 and boasted in its pages about not paying the duty. Unless the government altered the law to keep up with practice, he urged in a memorandum to the cabinet, there would be a general refusal to pay assessed taxes; the stamped press would be forced into refusing payment of the stamp duty, and 'all we will do will be to fill the jails'. Russell agreed to Spring Rice's proposal, as did Poulet Thomson, who supported the plan as an example of Ricardian orthodoxy. Although Holland agreed that the duty should be repealed, or lowered to make it scarcely worth a trader's while to evade it, he, like Hobhouse who preferred doing nothing for the moment, supported Melbourne's opposition to the proposal from the conviction that the exchequer could not sustain the loss of revenue.[45]

Thus, although the government decided in 1835 to meet Bulwer's challenge with a direct negative, there was growing support for a reduction of the duty on the grounds that because it was impossible to control the unstamped press, a penny duty might ruin its competitive edge. By the spring of 1836, as the public campaign to repeal the tax mounted, the Whigs saw the increasing attraction of a measure that would at once weaken the prospects of the 'scurrilous' unstamped and pacify the demands of those whose shortsightedness had led them to overvalue the benefits of reduction. In February, Melbourne admitted to a deputation of thirty Radical MPs and fifty others, led by Place, that the duty could not be defended on 'so mean a foundation' as the state of the revenue; the previous August, Rice had defended it on just, and only, those grounds. Now, in mid-March, he announced to a meeting of all government supporters at the Foreign Office that the duty would be reduced to a penny.[46] Place tried to mount a campaign against the last penny, but the bulk of the Radicals supported the government. Wakely, who termed the measure a penny 'gagging bill', had with Hume and Baines asked in a weak moment at the end of debate the previous August if the duty might not be at least reduced to a penny; Bulwer in the same circumstance had asked that it be two pence.[47] Fonblanque's *Examiner* exhorted the Radicals not to receive the government's proposal 'in a churlish, thankless spirit', and when the bill came before the house on 12 April, it passed without division. The government had good reason to be pleased with the outcome. Although a few Radicals realised, and argued, that a penny duty was a sham reform that would favour the established legitimate press over the unstamped,[48] most accepted a bill which, from the government's view, had an object and design diametrically opposed to their own. By a peculiar convergence of interests, the penny stamp act helped to cement the 'unnatural alliance' and weaken the extreme Radicals' case that the Whigs were uninterested in reform.

A further example of the Whigs' turning a Radical initiative to their own advantage was the foundation of the Reform Club in 1836. The idea of a large club for Whigs, Liberals and Radicals was first put forward early in 1835 but failed from a lack of Whig interest. By the end of that year, a second and this time successful attempt was made by Stanley, Parkes, Hume and Molesworth. The success of the Conservatives' Carlton Club led them to think that the Westminster Reform Club, with only Radical members, and Brooks's, with Whigs, should be supplanted by a single club which would bring all reformers together. Parkes and Stanley thought that a new 'Liberal Union' club would prevent the 'old dissension and sores' from splitting the Whigs and their Radical allies by 'humanizing the Radicals and liberalizing the Whigs'.[49] Most of the Radicals, on the other hand, hoped that such a club would be to their benefit rather than the Whigs', who would be forced, by the common consent of their supporters, to adhere more firmly to Radical thinking. Ellice understood the Radicals' motives. When approached by Hume and Molesworth, he refused to co-ordinate Whig support for a new club that was patently designed to put pressure on the government. It was his opposition that had scuttled the earlier attempt, and when approached for a second time, he told Parkes that while he would 'march with the mass if only to guide it', the growing moderation of the Radical members would be undermined by a club that was likely to be hostile to the ministry.[50] Hume, Molesworth and Parkes nevertheless decided to go ahead, and on 4 February, the day before Ellice returned from his recess in Paris, and in order to prevent him from dissuading them or others of their plans, the three issued circulars announcing the formation of a new club. Ellice was naturally annoyed at the proceedings, and in an angry exchange of words on the way out of the House on the 6th, asked Molesworth 'if the Radicals intended to lead the Whigs' or to 'break up the party'. Obviously trapped into pledging Whig support or risk an open quarrel that could damage the government's majority, Ellice and Stanley agreed to assist in the formation of a club only after Parkes persuaded them that it would not be a Radical organisation.[51] Molesworth was ecstatic. 'We had them now', he told his mother,[52]

It will be the best club in town, and the effect will be to break up the Whig party by joining the best of them to the Radicals . . . and augment our power immensely . . . I don't fear their influence; some few they may seduce, but very few, whilst we shall gain many of them, for in all arguments we are their superiors.

This young Radical baronet, who was soon to lose the Whig gentry's support in Cornwall and seek a safer haven in Leeds, then Southwark,[53] could not have been more mistaken. He had admitted that the Whigs' only hope was to join the club in such numbers as to have a predominance; though he thought they would fail, Ellice saw to it that they did not. By the time the club began on 24 May, its outstanding features were a French *gastronome*, Alexis de Soyer, and a Whiggish membership. Ellice worked hard at swamping the club. Within the first fortnight he had Melbourne's name down, followed shortly by the Dukes of Norfolk and Sussex, all of the cabinet and some 250 MPs.[54] The club, as a result, resembled the government side of parliament by being far more Whig than Radical. As the liberal H. G. Ward told his cousin Mulgrave, 'no one wants to be brought into too close contact with [those like] Whittle Harvey or Wakely, who cannot, however, be excluded and must consequently be merged in the mass'.[55] By joining in the formation of the new club, the Whigs were able to maintain a cordiality with their Radical supporters, but the composition of the club, which chose the name Reform in preference for Fox, Grey, Milton and Hampden, reduced it to something less than an organized Radical pressure group. The Whig leaders themselves continued to frequent Brooks's. In a comment as applicable to Whig–Radical relations in general as the Reform Club in particular, one historian has concluded that 'if Molesworth and Parkes had seriously envisaged the Reform Club as a kind of Trojan horse within the Whig camp, the horse was soon docilely eating from the Whig manger'.[56]

If the steady erosion of the Radicals' power allowed the Whigs to pursue a moderate course with impunity, Peel's continued unwillingness to take office and his continued practice of supporting the government against Radical motions and revolts was an important factor in that moderation. The Conservative *Quarterly Review* made a point of eighteen divisions in 1837 where Conservative members saved ministers from defeat, but this was in fact a pattern that Peel had followed since 1830 and would continue until the Jamaica division in 1839. It is misleading to argue that the government would have gone down to defeat on these motions without Tory support, for the divisions took place in near-empty houses. If there had been any expectation of defeat, the Treasury could have whipped in enough votes to defeat the motions with little difficulty. Even on those divisions where a relatively larger

number of members voted, such as Harvey's attack on government
pensions in April 1836, there were never enough Radical voters to
seriously threaten the ministry had the Tories not voted at all.
Peel's support was nevertheless a clear indication that he was
unwilling to take office on these questions, and that if the Radicals
wished to dislodge the government, they would have to do so
themselves.

Of more significance from the ministry's point of view was
Peel's determination to serve notice on his ultra Tory colleagues
and the King that he was unwilling to renew the experiment of
1834. In a sense, the King's gift of office had been a political
setback for Peel, whose plan for a Conservative party bereft of
ultra Tory influence was necessarily put aside for the sake of a
government that had no prospects. Holding office by Royal fiat
was moreover an embarrassing irony for the author of the Tamworth manifesto, a document which argued for the reconciliation
of the Tory party with the Reform Act and the House of Commons.
Shortly after Melbourne returned to office, Peel spoke out. In a
speech in the City on 11 May which reiterated the basic tenets of
the manifesto, he referred pointedly to the need for government to
base its authority less on the Crown and peers than on the
Commons and people.[57] By July 1835, as rumours of a second
dismissal gained wide currency following the King's notorious
rudeness towards his ministers at a meeting of the Council, Peel
and Croker each wrote to Taylor expressing their concern at the
rumours and insisting that the King and Lords could not maintain
a government without the backing of the lower house.[58] Later that
month, when he was asked by Ellenborough how he would react
to drastic amendments to the Whigs' English corporation reform
in the Lords, Peel dismissed the changes out of hand. He had
agreed to the measure in the Commons and would not later
change his position. More importantly, he did his utmost to dispel
Ellenborough and his circle of the notion that he would lead
another Conservative ministry formed by the machinations of
Ellenborough and Lyndhurst and supported by the ultra Tory
court.[59] In a mood of despair at Lyndhurst's perseverance and
subsequent mutilation of the Corporation bill in August, he kept
to himself at Drayton as a sign of annoyance; when he came up to
London at the end of the month, it was to support Russell's
outstretched hand. Just as Russell found it necessary to show the
Radicals that he would prefer Peel's support to theirs, Peel was

determined to let the ultra Tories know that he would not be their captive. If the government were to resign on the Lords' obstinacy to as popular a measure as corporation reform, a not unlikely result in his view, fresh elections might very well wipe out the recent Conservative gains. Peel's return to office would be more remote than it already was. It was important therefore that Peel do all he could to support the Whigs' measure and to prevent their resignations. His disposition to 'throw over the Lords' thus should be seen as less an act of non-partisan statesmanship than a desperate attempt to stifle ultra Tory control of the fledgeling Conservative party that was so closely intertwined with his own political aspirations.

Peel was not to be entirely successful in quelling his party's ultras. At the opening of the following session, for example, he unwillingly moved an amendment to the address because the Tory peers had done so unexpectedly in the Lords. To his dismay, the government's majority of 41 was larger than on any important division the previous session.[60] But the tone of Peel's relationship with the Tory peers and the King had been set in 1835, and though he found it necessary to alter his views on a number of questions to suit the demands of party, there was a widespread conviction that he would not be party to a prepared defeat of the government. To emphasise the point, he told a gathering of Conservatives at the Carlton Club in February 1836 that it was hopeless to expect a return to power. By May, Ellice could report to Grey the general view that Peel was 'as anxious as the most selfish adherent of the Treasury to keep the Government in office'; as the King was 'more afraid of change than of his ministers – hating both', the government could count on a state of indifference and apathy in the Commons.[61]

If all was well in the Commons, it was not so in the Lords, where by 1836 the most important measures were emasculated with disappointing regularity. The failure of the Irish tithe and corporation bills was particularly disturbing. Few expected the Irish tithe plan to succeed as long as it contained an appropriation clause,[62] but there was a great deal of annoyance at the Lords' rejection of the Irish corporation bill. The Whigs' disappointment stemmed from the Lords' apparent unwillingness to extend the spirit of compromise that had characterised the passage of English corporation reform. During the recess, the Irish corporation bill which had passed through the Commons at the end of the 1835 session was altered at Russell's suggestion to make it 'similar to the [English] act which passed both Houses'.[63] But when Peel argued that the corporations had been founded on exclusively Protestant interests and as such should be abolished rather than reformed,[64] alarms were raised that the bill could not pass. Peel had allowed the 1835 measure to pass through the Commons without division or comment. That bill was eventually dropped owing to the lateness of the session, and when Stanley later expressed his view that the corporations should be extinguished, Peel's support for abolition was governed to a large extent by the need to develop his alliance with Stanley and Graham.[65] The attack on the Whigs' measure fitted in well with the ultra Tory opposition to what was viewed as an O'Connell-inspired bill; this peculiar convergence of Peel and ultra Tories sealed the fate of a measure. When the bill reached the Lords, Fitzgerald's successful instruction to abolish the corporations was the first of a series of mutilations. Faced with a chorus of demands that the government should resign or dissolve in protest, Russell held out for compromise by proposing that only eleven new towns be granted new corporations. Seventeen others would have public utilities commissions under an 1828 act, and twenty-two would be entirely extinguished according to the wishes of the Tory peers.[66] It was to no avail. The Lords would not accept Russell's offer of compromise and at the end of June the bill was dropped.

The government reacted to the Lords' emasculation of the municipal bill with a mixture of resignation and despair. Although the cry went up out of doors for a reform of the upper chamber, Howick was the only government member who advocated 'organic' change; his purpose, he told his father, was to prevent a dangerous Radical reaction.[67] Russell was angry. After the Lords had first amended the plan he expostulated somewhat icily on the contrast between the most popularly elected assembly, which evinced the 'greatest degree of calmness and temper', and the hereditary branch which 'betrayed less temperance of conduct in its proceedings'. But in June he sent Melbourne a memorandum which admitted that unlike the Tories and Radicals, who had a settled policy on the state of affairs, the Whigs were caught in the middle, 'confessing the evil and not consenting to the remedy'.[68] In a public speech at Plymouth in November 1835, he reacted strongly to the suggestions of reform of the Lords which had been proposed as soon as the peers altered the English Corporations bill; the divisions and convulsions that organic reform would bring made him 'stand pledged', he affirmed, to the constitution in all its branches. He also argued against a large creation of peers; making dull country gentlemen duller Lords would fulfil no purpose. He was prepared to create a handful of peers as a demonstration of the government's intention, and received some support on this from Holland at a cabinet at the end of June, but neither was very insistent, and creation was deemed 'inexpedient'.[69] Frightened that the King would again dismiss the government, Melbourne had already argued against such a 'serious step'. Moreover, he wisely decided that the circumstances were a far cry from those of the Reform crisis of 1832. He knew that there was too little support for Irish measures in England to justify a reduction in the power of the Lords; the clamour against that body was 'factious transient and temporary'.[70] Although he found it 'directly contrary to the spirit and meaning of the constitution' for the government to stand only upon the support of the Commons, he argued at the cabinet meeting that there was no point in the government resigning as it would ordinarily do, because the ministry had come in with the declared opposition of the Peers and because the Peers had declared from the beginning of the session against the Irish corporation reform: 'we know nothing now that we did not know before'. To be censured by the Lords, he stated further in the Lords, was insufficient ground for the resignation demanded by several Tories. His government had the support of the Commons, which in turn was supported by the people. Its duty was to stay.[71]

The reaction of all but the most rabid of the Radical press suggests that Melbourne's view of the transitory nature of the demand for Peerage reform was correct. Fonblanque's *Examiner*, for example, which accused the Commons of being 'not a disagreeable body to quarrel with' and thought peerage reform 'the grand essential', nevertheless admitted that it could not be assumed that the great mass of the nation demanded reform. But if all but the least moderate Radicals thought, like Fonblanque, that no one could expect the Ministers to reform the Lords 'for they are Whigs and not Radicals',[72] there was growing opinion at the end of the 1836 session that the government had not done enough for its Radical supporters. Nothing is more indicative of this trend than the impatience of *Tait's Magazine*, which had so steadfastly supported the Whig–Radical union earlier in the year. In October it gave prominence to a speech by the moderate Radical MP Wm. Hutt which emphasised his weariness of supporting reform proposals ending in nothing, and his decision to abandon automatic support for the government. By December, Tait wrote that though 'we still raiiiise the old cry, "Keep out the Tories!" . . . let us know why it is worth our while . . . there is no longer time for trifling.'[73] This newly found aggressiveness was to a large extent a journalistic campaign. Rintoul's *Spectator* joined the attack on the 'Whig pride or stupidity' that would be to blame if terms of a new Whig–Radical union were not settled, and *The Constitutional*, the first new paper to appear under the penny stamp, asked what right the Whigs had 'to expect from the Radicals an unconditional renewal of the alliance'.[74] A good deal of the Radicals' frustration was directed against O'Connell, who had himself engaged in a bitter quarrel with those Radicals who were threatening to sever the union with his Whig allies. The English Radicals were doubtless infected by both anti-Irish sentiments and a jealousy of O'Connell's success in having his reforms at least put forward. By making overt what had been simmering under covers for a year or more, they evinced a reduced desire to support the ministry for the sake of Ireland. Tait, who had described equal justice to Ireland as the one question on which all men were agreed, reacted to O'Connell's 'rash and ill-advised' censure of the Radicals by warning in December that though English Radicals would not lose sight of their 'suffering fellow-subjects of Ireland, . . . for the sake of both countries they will no longer dally in the dark'.[75] The appearance in January 1837 of Molesworth's article 'Terms of Alliance between Radicals and Whigs' in the *London and Westminster Review* was the high-water mark of the campaign. Anxious to be 'at war with the Whigs' and convinced that no good would ever come of the Radicals until they had broken with the government, Molesworth organized an aggressive opposition in conjunction with Roebuck, who was equally determined not to support the ministry 'on past emotions'. J. T. Leader, Charles Buller, the Grotes, J. S. Mill and Place were the other leading members of 'the Camp', which planned to hold a series of dinners at the opening of the new session in order to co-ordinate a number of resolutions that would test the Whigs' intention. In his article, Molesworth argued that the Whigs 'have no party' in a nation divided into Liberals and Conservatives; he called for the withdrawal of the Radicals' life-giving support unless a programme of ballot, triennial parliaments and household suffrage were adopted. The Radicals would be better off under a Tory ministry, he argued, for though there would be the same amount of liberal legislation – none – a new popular liberal crusade could be mounted.[76]

Radical discontent at the pace of reform threatened the Whigs' parliamentary stability in two ways. If the Whigs refused to give in, and if the Radical group held to its threat to secede, the majority on a trial of strength could disappear. It was in order to stem this Radical tide that Melbourne had threatened to resign if defeated on the appropriation division in August 1836. If, on the other hand, the government were to go some way to meet the Radicals' demands, there was every likelihood, as Stanley told Parkes in a letter asking him to restrain the press, that sufficient Whigs would withdraw support, thereby turning the government's majority into a minority.[77] It was as much to prevent this latter possibility, in fact, that Parkes began to mediate between the Whigs and Radicals. Although he thought that the symptoms of dissension were 'all Moonshine, of no moment', the press being unable to deliver the fatal blow that only disunity in the House of Commons could, he went round to several papers to have the Radicals denounced as a small and uninfluential clique. The problem of disunion, he told Mrs Grote, with whom he began 'clawing like wild beasts', was that the Whigs, aristocracy and electors would desert for ever the liberal cause. The Whigs would refuse to fight in the counties against the moderate Tories who would be their open allies, and Radical weaknesses in the corrupt urban constituencies would ruin any hopes of liberal interests prevailing.[78] Knowing too well that disunity was a double-edged sword that had to be blunted on both sides, he met and advised Melbourne to choose between the Tories and Reformers. If ballot and shorter parliaments were made open questions, and an improved and popular Irish corporation bill brought back, failure in the Lords followed by dissolution would produce a gain of fifty to seventy seats in new elections.[79]

Parkes had hoped to persuade the Whigs to assume a more liberal posture, that might allow the 'wiser councils' in the Radical circle to prevail, in order to save the union on which his political aspirations and beliefs rested. His hopes were quickly dashed. Melbourne had little confidence in those who placed too much electoral value on liberal measures. He had already told Parkes that he did not share his belief in the strength of the liberal party in

England, or in the impossibility of the Conservatives governing, and was shortly to tell Mulgrave, who also advised a dissolution should the Lords again reject an Irish corporation measure, that 'it is not 1831 over again. Ireland is not the popular question Reform was.'[80] He reminded Parkes of Whig difficulties at Court, of his colleagues' opposition to ballot and disgust at the press campaign for peerage reform; at a meeting with him he stated his strong objection to any course that would make him vulnerable to the Tory charge that he was a Radical-led Prime Minister. Forced to choose, Melbourne let Parkes, and through him the Radical malcontents, know that he was more concerned with Tory than Radical taunts, the latter of which would be far better ignored. Ellice too warned Parkes that the Radicals should not put too much pressure on the government; 'these people sadly miscalculate their own strength', he told Parkes in what was a well-planned campaign to convince the Radicals of the futility of their course;[81]

> Let them put an end to party – and drive the two centres to coalesce to govern the country – you will find the ten pounders give such a Government more power than will be good for any of us or than can easily be thrown off again . . . Do they think the . . . peace and order-loving people of England and Scotland have quite made up their minds to overturn the throne, the aristocracy, and other institutions of the country, to seek for better Government from Sir W. Molesworth, Mr. Leader, Mr. Roebuck and Mrs. Grote? Let the case be fairly stated, and you will see into what insignificance these people will shrink when they have separated themselves from the more reasonable divisions of the popular party.

There was less optimism in Whig circles than Ellice's piece of bravado would suggest, but in the end it was this view that prevailed. Opening ballot and duration of parliament would give rise to too much internal division and would, moreover, elevate these questions to an importance which they did not possess. It was assumed as well that most of the Radicals would reject 'these Radical crochets', as Russell termed the Molesworth group, and that the 'good sense of Englishmen' would point out the unpopularity of the questions.[82] If, as Bulwer Lytton told Melbourne, conceding open questions was 'of no importance to grant and only of importance not to grant',[83] the government took the opposite view. Although Thomson supported ballot, and Duncannon and Hobhouse thought that opening that question would be a harmless concession for the sake of parliamentary unity, Russell and Melbourne would have neither. Russell proposed a compromise on the duration of parliament that would have accepted quinquennial parliaments in return for the abolition of elections on the death of the crown and of re-election of officeholders, but this was a cynical ruse which reflected his low opinion of Radical strength. Even Melbourne pointed out that the Radicals would regard the proposition as a Tory measure without value, and the idea was quickly scrapped.[84] It was obvious that this issue had far less support in the country than ballot; rejecting it offered little danger. But such was not so with ballot, which gained support both in and out of government each year. Melbourne was prepared to admit the force of the balloteers' arguments and could see the logic of an open question,[85] but two considerations militated against this procedure. In the first place, there was an already adulterated system of openness which allowed government men to abstain. 'I have never insisted on official men who wished to stay away, voting against ballot', Russell told Spring Rice, 'but I have always asked such to keep away quietly and not make a parade of leaving the House.'[86] This system, which Melbourne termed 'winking' at absenteeism,[87] was not the same as an open one which would have allowed officeholders to vote for ballot. The second consideration was the most important. Opening questions, it was believed, would be the first in a series of demands. Ballot, moreover, was a popular question. Had the issue arisen on a less popular subject, concession would not have the same pernicious effect. Molesworth's open challenge to the Ministry had greatly increased the difficulty of settling the question, for once his article in the *London and Westminster Review* had appeared, the government could not make ballot an open question without giving credence to the charge that it did so under the threat of losing Radical support. It would lose as many supporters as it might gain. 'I do not know whether I could have stomached this open question of ballot in any shape,' Melbourne told Mulgrave, 'but I am sure that I neither can nor will swallow it in the manner in which it is now mixed and presented to me.'[88] At the same time, Melbourne's innate sense of fairness made him feel the difficulty of binding government supporters to a position which they found uncomfortable. Wishing to incite as little irritation as possible, he ordered the government not to go out of its way to offend its supporters by railing publicly against ballot. The disastrous effects of Wellington's declaration against Reform in November 1830 convinced him that a strong declaration against ballot would strengthen rather than weaken the influence of its supporters.[89]

On the eve of the new session, the government's course was set. 'We shall act towards the Radicals just as we have done, opposing ballot and triennial parliaments', Russell wrote to Grey in Northumberland, 'more especially as these seem but the advanced parts of a new army of demands'. To Mulgrave, who was fast becoming a sounding-board for his colleagues in England, he explained that 'if we begin to indulge the resentment of one party against the other, we may wish to stop when we have no longer the power to do so.'[90] Russell clearly felt as provoked by the Radicals as Melbourne did; when he began the session by issuing a strong warning to the Molesworth group that the government would not put up with a Radical tail wagging the Whig dog, he was staking out the 'finality' position which is generally associated with his speech the following November. Where Radical and Whig opinions clashed, the government would accept only support, not guidance, from the Radicals.[91] He had good reason to mount an offensive; already there was clear indication that 'the Camp' would fail to detach the Radicals from the government. At the Bath dinner on 5 January designed to open the Radicals' campaign, General Palmer defended the Ministry; while Roebuck and Molesworth spoke of withdrawing support, Leader suggested that Radicals would support a Whig in preference to a Tory government.[92] What is more, 'Hume and the prudents', as Roebuck disparagingly termed the moderate Radicals, undermined the extremists by staging a grand dinner of Middlesex electors at the Drury Lane theatre designed to support 'unity among reformers'. Roebuck and Molesworth were not invited, but Lord Grey, who declined, was; the dinner was chaired by Lord Russell and the list of stewards was notable for its concentration of Whig peers.[93] By the time the session opened, the Whigs' tactic of holding fast against what they thought to be a small group of disaffected Radicals was handsomely rewarded. Parkes reported that Mrs Grote's *coterie* 'are all drawing their brewing milder and aware of the insanity of kicking over the milk pail'.[94] When Roebuck attacked the Whigs in a speech which, according to one observer, 'threw the word democracy in the very teeth of the

House of Commons', Hume spoke out strongly against his colleague, who was deserted by every Radical in the House. A series of
weekly dinners, to be held at the Clarendon Hotel as part of the
Radical campaign, was hastily abandoned. The first was financed
by Roebuck on the Sunday before his speech. The second, paid for
by Leader, was dismally attended.[95] The Radicals' 'power of
mischief' abated.

Within a few days of Roebuck's speech, Russell announced the
government's intention of standing or falling on the 'vital' Irish
corporation bill. His declaration confused and annoyed several of
the moderate Whig supporters, who had thought from a statement
of Melbourne's at the close of the previous session in the Lords
that the government would not mount a campaign against the
upper house.[96] But Russell's statement did not indicate a change in
policy. It is true that he had decided to take a stand on the Irish
corporations, 'our Cheval de Bataille' as Mulgrave termed it, but
he did so on Aberdeen's understanding that the peers had only
stood out in 1836 'for dignity's sake' and would pass the measure
when it came before them again. He had made his mind up as
early as September 1836 that an Irish tithe bill shorn of appropriation would give the Lords reason to allow the corporation and
Irish poor law bills to pass. To emphasise this determination to
clear the Irish legislation from the desk until 'a better day and a
better parliament' could make appropriation possible, a compromise with which several cabinet colleagues disagreed, he closed
the introductory debate on the corporations bill with the announcement that he was 'ready to consent to a considerable sacrifice' on
the tithe bill; 'no personal feeling of mine, no false pride on my
part, shall stand in the way of a settlement of this great question'.[97]
Melbourne, too, thought that the Lords would make all this
possible by allowing the corporation bill to pass, but the mood
was not shared by all. Greville reported the general attitude that
the government was in considerable danger; Hobhouse was sure
that Russell's pledge was 'le commencement de la fin'.[98] Indeed,
when the government learned from E. J. Stanley within a few days
of that pledge that the Lords intended to move the adjournment of
the second reading for two months, there seemed every reason to
doubt Russell and Melbourne's optimism. Reports from Mulgrave
suggested that feeling against the Lords' hostility to Catholics was
running high in Ireland; without the bill, which had acquired an
artificial importance, government by force would be necessary.

Postponement was regarded therefore as tantamount to rejection and as less dangerous. There appeared little alternative to resignation.[99] There were signs as well that Peel was once again prepared to govern. Lord Francis Egerton's motion to abolish the corporations was defeated on 23 February by eighty votes, but this evidence of Tory hostility, coming soon after Russell's pledge, suggested that Peel was instructing the Lords to pursue the same destructive course followed in 1836. When he further announced his willingness to take office, on the very day that the bill was sent to the Lords, the suspicion of many Whigs that he had been seeking a return to government seemed confirmed.[100]

A few weeks of this unusually partisan atmosphere convinced most of the moderates on both sides of the Commons that the co-operation that had served so well should not be thrust aside on an Irish issue. Among many Conservatives, there was little inclination to risk an election on a question that was demanded by justice and rejected by the Lords. If Ireland was not a popular issue in England, there was good reason to suspect that a recalcitrant peerage would, on this issue, redound to the Whigs' advantage. This argument was felt most keenly by Stanley and Graham, who regarded Russell's veiled compromise as a good opportunity for getting rid of the Irish issues on which Peel and the Tory peers never failed to draw mutual sustenance. Peel demurred when first presented with their suggestion that the Lords postpone their rejection of the measure to await the Whigs' tithe bill, but gradually saw the wisdom of waiting to hear what amendments the Whigs might accept should he be called upon to govern. By 23 April, a few days before the second reading was due in the Lords, Peel and Wellington persuaded Lyndhurst and the ultras to postpone the bill for a short period only. Second reading was duly accorded, and on 5 May, Wellington adjourned debate until 9 June.[101] 'No question of dissolution, nor of resignation', Russell wrote to Mulgrave the next day. In fact, Russell and Melbourne had been determined all along that neither course would be followed. Melbourne was not opposed to a good fright that would keep his troops to the mark, but his scruples would allow him neither to desert those same supporters nor to stir up the agitation that resignation or dissolution on this question might generate. Russell had decided that the Whigs' resignation over the Lords' defeat would have to be circumvented, if only to prevent the trouble that the Tory Orange ascendency in Ireland would provoke, and his announced willingness to sacrifice appropriation virtually forced the Tories' hand.[102] He had hoped to have a tithe bill, without appropriation, tabled in the Commons before the second reading of the corporation measure in the Lords, but the unwillingness of Duncannon, Glenelg and Hobhouse to agree to this step made it impossible. He did get the cabinet to agree, however, that Morpeth should give notice of a new tithe bill on 1 May. This was at least a morsel to keep the chance of compromise alive.[103] When the Lords again postponed debate for a month and the cabinet seemed unlikely to accept Howick's advice to regard the Lords' decision as a tacit compromise, Russell refused to accept his colleagues' inclination to resign. He urged the cabinet at a second meeting to follow Howick's advice, and when they could only agree, somewhat put out, that he should do 'what he thought best', he announced in the house what he had told Mulgrave before the cabinet had discussed the issue: the government would not resign while it had the support of the Commons.[104]

On the face of it, Russell's announcement on 8 May appeared to proclaim the primacy of the lower house in constitutional affairs, but as everyone knew, it meant no such thing. Russell refused to be drawn in by the extremists in his party who were bent on throwing down the gauntlet to the Tories and the Lords; his speech was a significant indication that the Whigs would not be swayed by the Radicals or coaxed by the Tories into a Radically inspired resignation. A week later, Melbourne told the Tory Wharncliffe that 'things are soothing down' and that although he could not say so publicly, the government would give up appropriation 'without much difficulty'.[105] Compromise appeared to have, just, a chance. On 9 June, the question of making it through the session was put aside with the first public announcement of the King's illness. Lyndhurst used the occasion of an obligatory second postponement of the corporation bill to attack Peel's willingness to compromise; were it not for the King's impending demise, his speech would have undermined Peel's success in harnessing his horses and made it difficult for Melbourne and Russell to keep theirs under rein. But on 20 June, William's death put all speculation, and the life of his government, at an end.

On reflection, Melbourne had much to be pleased with after two years in office. A year earlier, he had doubted the propriety of going on against the majority in the Lords, the increasing hostility

at Court and his government's unpopularity in the English constituencies.[106] Now, with every prospect of seeing the Irish legislation through, his government could not be accused of battling on
against unreasonable odds. Although the volume and importance
of his legislation could not hope to match the unusual record of the
first reformed parliament, his government's record on the English
corporations and the Church measures, on the attendance of
dissenters' grievances, on the reduction of stamp duties and the
promise of Irish legislation to come, was no inconsiderable achievement. By virtue of his and Russell's direction of day-to-day
policy, the government had managed to emasculate the power and
leverage that the Radicals acquired after the King's dismissal of his
first government. Apart from hopeful Radicals and Tories who
looked for gain at the Whigs' expense, few could argue that
Melbourne's ministry had been dominated by Radicals. Tory
reaction that would have made Radical pressures intolerable was
prevented, an achievement in itself which gave pleasure to the
Whig mind. There were, to be sure, reasons for doubt. The
economy was well into the downward trend that would plague the
Whigs until out of office. With the perceived unpopularity of Irish
and Church reform in the English constituencies, there was little
to suggest that the elections made necessary by the King's death
would strengthen the Whigs' parliamentary position. In these
circumstances, while Parkes and the electioneering experts busied
themselves with preparations for the coming contest, Melbourne,
Palmerston and several of the Whigs kept a close watch on
Windsor. The death of the King and the age of the young Queen
lifted at once an enormous cloud of uncertainty. Parkes himself
had seen the opportunity for tutoring the new monarch in
something other than Tory ways as early as August 1836. 'It is of
the first moment', he wrote to Durham in St Petersburg, 'that the
young Princess on her accession should find a Liberal Cabinet
in.'[107]

9

The Queen's Government, 1837–39

Take care that Lord Melbourne is not King.
Duchess of Kent to Princess Victoria, June 1837[1]

I trust in heaven we shall have a majority for us and that the present government may remain firm for long.
Queen Victoria, August 1837[2]

The Summer of 1837 was one of tranquillity and promise for the Whigs. Harvest prospects were favourable, there was talk of an autumn trade revival and, as Melbourne quipped to Russell, 'Lady Holland is out of town'.[3] Above all, the young Queen on the throne had shown a decided preference for Whigs. As Princess, Victoria had been advised by her uncle, the King of the Belgians, to keep her ministers but to gain time in order to assess the political world without anyone being hurt, and although she told him on the eve of her accession that she had 'real confidence' in the incumbent administration and in Melbourne in particular, she claimed to 'belong' to no party. Within a week, all pretence to disclaimer had vanished: 'the present Ministry is the best and most moderate we can have' she told Leopold. By the end of the summer, the Duke of Bedford's bust had been restored to the plinth in the Castle from which it had been banished a year earlier; 'pleasant and instructive conversation . . . with clever people such as Lord Melbourne, Lord Palmerston, Lord Holland, etc.' she wrote in her diary, had convinced her that Whig politics 'are the best there are'.[4]

It is not surprising that Victoria began her reign as a Whig. If Leopold's decided warning against ultra Toryism had not influenced her,[5] Melbourne and Palmerston's admixture of moderate but opportunistic Whiggery, which led them to stay at Court for much of the summer, could not have failed to impart its message. There is little doubt that Melbourne's devotion to the Queen was a sincere, almost grandfatherly response to an affectionate but impressionable young woman in need of advice and guidance, but it is as clear that the Whigs were not unaware of the political advantages of a friendly monarch. They were determined to acquire what for them was an unfamiliar influence at Court. In September 1836, Melbourne had felt his temper giving way at being 'fretted' by the King's intolerable opposition to 'every little matter'. That same month William was reported to have told one of the Coburgh family to stay in England until the 10th in order to witness a change of government, 'always a curious event for a foreigner'.[6] The King was no longer able to choose his own government, as the events of 1834–35 attested, and it is doubtful therefore that the Whigs' term of office was prolonged by his death, but he had certainly been able to make life difficult for ministers by public displays of disapproval that encouraged ultra Tory obstructionism in the Lords. It was not unnatural, in the circumstances, that Melbourne would look for the advantages enjoyed for so long by his Tory counterparts. It was also very Whiggish. The Rockingham and Foxite Whigs had welcomed the regency of the Prince of Wales because they saw him as their entry to office, and since that day, Whigs paid scarce lip service to the 'abuse' of royal authority. They welcomed the short-lived support which William IV gave them in 1830, and their refusal to regard as unconstitutional his role in the dismissal of 1834 is evidence of their acceptance of the monarch's legitimate influence. Ministers with longer Whig pedigrees than Melbourne and Palmerston had little difficulty in having the Prime Minister take the post as a very Bute-ish private secretary to the Queen. In the autumn, Howick recorded his hope that Melbourne's daily attendance at Windsor and Brighton had given him 'a good deal of influence with her'. Holland opined that if the impression spread that the government had the real confidence of the Queen, it would have authority enough in parliament to do good, to carry measures and to go on. 'Our little Queen has made courtiers of us all.'[7]

Though the King's death brought welcome relief to the Whigs, the elections made necessary by that event gave scant room for optimism. The government gained on balance in Scotland, Ireland and the English boroughs, but heavy losses in the English counties gave the opposition a net gain of from twelve to fifteen seats. Although the Conservatives' victory in the English counties, which seemed due to a combination of superior activity and the unpopularity of Church and Irish reforms, was not an unexpected result, Russell's complaint that the government had overcompensated the landed classes in the Reform Bill[8] did not suggest that an improved electoral position could be expected to follow. Moreover, the issues which appeared to account for successes in Scotland, Ireland and the English boroughs were those on which the English counties were lost, and insofar as legislative measures influenced the results of elections, it seemed clear that the counties could not have been won back without throwing urban Dissenters and moderate reformers into Radical arms, or Irish constituents into the Repealers' camp. 'The sum total', Russell told Melbourne, 'is perhaps that very old difficulty of Whig administrations, that their friends expect them to do more than is possible; so that if they attempted little, their friends grow slacker, and if they attempt much, their enemies grow strong'.[9]

If there was universal acceptance that for one reason or other the Whigs' stock in the country had gone down, there was less than agreement on the government's prospects in the new parliament. Invigorated by his success at Court, Melbourne showed little despair at the losses. With a few minor exceptions all officeholders were returned and, more importantly, many of the extreme Radicals were not. The new Commons, he concluded, was likely to be composed of 'more steady and decided Party men' than the previous one. Parkes predicted that there would be little chance of a majority on the Church rates bill and scarcely one on appropriation, but Melbourne knew that neither would be proposed in their present form. With the increased prospect of reason and moderation prevailing in the Lords following the near compromise in the Spring, there was every reason to think that the Radical challenge was fully eclipsed.[10] Support for this view came from a number of colleagues. Baring, President of the Board of Trade, regarded the Whigs as 'a very different party, much more practicable and more ministerialist'; Wood, the ex-Whip, thought that with the 'cross-grained Radicals' like Roebuck, Hume and Ewart defeated, and others like Molesworth carried by Whig support, the Radicals would be 'humbled enough not to be mischievous'.[11] The more generally-held attitude, however, was one of alarm at the increased leverage held by a smaller number of impatient Radicals. Lansdowne put the gloomy view to Holland; it was fortunate that the Queen had not asked him what he thought of the government's parliamentary prospects, he wrote from Windsor, 'for I could not "consistently with truth" tell her I thought favourably of them'.[12] Russell held to the same view. He knew that despite an overall majority of twenty-five or thirty, the handful of extreme Radicals held the balance on Irish or Church questions; 'the first wind' of discontent could 'shake it down'. 'It is certainly of no use to conceal the difficulty of our situation' he answered Melbourne's optimistic note,[13]

> I do not at all think, as some do, that the members of the new House of Commons will be more steady to us than the last – on the contrary, the last was pledged to us from the first day and stood to its pledge to the last. On any new question the new House may take a view of its own, and adopt a character of its own, which like the late House, it will probably maintain.

Russell was not arguing for concessions that might appease Radical discontent. He did play with the idea of opening the ballot question to ensure the support of those members who were 'Whigs in party but Radicals in opinion', but he never actually pressed the issue, believing that the greater part of the Radicals were reasonable enough and looked for no grounds of difference. The handful of extreme Radicals who continued to press for constitutional reforms were a different matter. Here Russell was prepared to take the offensive. Roebuck's philosophic radicalism 'brought to bear upon the British Constitution', he wrote, 'would be like a cannon-ball let fly into the machinery of a steam engine'; the sooner Radical influence ceased, the better.[14] His election speech at Stroud repeated his determination to abide by the ancient constitution; when the Radicals attacked the ministry on the opening night of the new parliament by moving amendments to the address calling for suffrage expansion, ballot and shorter parliaments, he took it upon himself to put them in their place. In a speech which Holland termed an 'ungracious declaration . . . more repulsive than was prudent in a minister so dependent as he was on the occasional forbearance of the party he repelled', Russell breathed haughty defiance. The Reform Act, he argued, was framed to give the landed interest a considerable ascendancy over the boroughs, and it was right that it did so. He did not actually use the word 'finality', but there was no doubt that the spirit of the speech pointed in that direction.[15] Ward, a moderate Radical who had intended to oppose the franchise motion, angrily changed his vote after telling 'the noble Lord' that he had 'signed his death warrant'. Howick's account of the incident was more indicative of Whig thinking. 'I am inclined to believe they will vent their anger in abusive speeches for which I do not care one farthing, and continue to vote with us against the Tories.'[16]

Russell had not intended to attack the extreme Radicals as violently as he did, but found it 'impossible to be carried away in the flood of Wakley and Hume,'[17] the latter of whom had become their parliamentary spokesman. Yet it seems clear that he did intend to speak out; when Buller continued to press for constitutional changes on the second night, Russell repeated his views, albeit with less rancour. The purpose of 'finality' was two-fold: to defy the Radicals whose stock had gone down with the electorate, and to issue a challenge to Peel. This second consideration played an important part in Russell's resurgent aggression against his Radical opponents. The government's ability to withstand Radical proposals had always depended on Peel's support, without which a majority was often impossible. But rumours that the Conservatives meant to exploit the Whig–Radical division by opposing Abercromby's re-election as speaker added to Russell's suspicion that Peel was now willing to leave the government stranded. During the elections, Peel had been willing to allow the Whigs to bear the brunt of the Radicals' fury against the new poor law despite his full acquiescence in the measure. Russell thought his hypocritical conduct 'the most disgraceful of which one party was ever guilty', a view shared by Greville, who wrote at length about Peel's unprincipled willingness to profit at the expense of the government on a bill which he had supported as a good measure.[18] Russell doubted that Peel would attempt 'so desperate a game' as to seize the government with three-fourths or Ireland, half of Scotland and 300 members of the Commons against him, but he was quite certain that the Conservative leader was fully prepared to let the Whigs lose the confidence of the English electorate by running aground on its Radical and Irish support. As a consequence, he told Melbourne, he was fully prepared to have 'neither peace nor truce' with Peel, 'but to fight the battle out'.[19] He sent Peel a strongly written note to ask his intentions on the Speakership, and by speaking out strongly against the Radicals on opening night, told the Conservative leader in effect that the government would continue to rely on his support rather than be tied to the Radicals; if the Conservatives were determined to withhold that support they would have to accept the consequences and go to the country as something less than defenders of the conservative cause.[20] Peel could either put up or be quiet.

The need to re-establish the familiar triangular relationship with the Conservatives and Radicals was one that Russell regarded as an uncomfortable necessity. 'In the present House the loss of twenty two or three county members will be sadly felt on a radical question', he told Melbourne. 'We shall divide say 250 Tories, and 50 Whigs against 140 Radicals. This is an increase of what was already an embarrassment.'[21] His condemnation of the Radicals set the tone of ministerial relations with parliament for the next eighteen months. Much of that time was taken up with the increasingly difficult Canadian question, which made strikingly clear the Whigs' dependence on Peel's support and their refusal to succumb to Radical pressures. The long-simmering Canadian problem boiled over in November 1837. On 22 December, news reached London by way of the American papers that rebellion had broken out in the two provinces of Upper and Lower Canada. As a military exercise, the revolt was a non-event; in Toronto it lasted for half an hour, in Montreal for two days. But the rebellion pointed out the home government's failure to settle colonial grievances, particularly those of French origin in Lower Canada. The roots of grievance lay in the constitutional structure of the provinces as set out by an act of 1791 which effectively checked any democratic aspirations that the colonists might have borrowed from their American neighbours. Attempts to settle the disputes, especially the French Canadians' opposition to parliamentary domination by the oligarchic upper chamber of English-speaking Canadians, had met with successive failures. It was clear that a new initiative was needed. Amidst rumours and reports of the state of the insurrection, the government held a series of hurried meetings to work out a plan for parliament's inspection. All could agree that strong measures were necessary; habeas corpus would be suspended, the military increased. Apart from Howick and Russell, who wished that 'measures of vigour should be accompanied by measures of amendment [of the constitution] and conciliation', as Melbourne told the Queen, it was agreed as well that the governor would rule not by the terms of the constitution, which would be suspended, but directly by the military and by the appointed council.[22] After a great deal of acrimonious debate, it was decided that separate schemes drawn up by Russell and Howick, which would have given the Canadians a role in amending the 1791 constitution, would not be proposed. To do so, it was accepted, would have been seen as a concession to the Radicals at a time when, following news of rebellion, a steady hand was thought preferable.[23] There was little reason to suppose that the Radicals, already upset at 'finality', would accept the government plans. When Russell asked that the parliamentary recess be shortened to deal with the crisis, Hume, Leader, Molesworth and Warburton took the opportunity to blame the government's mishandling of the colony for the outbreak of rebellion. Early in January, Hume organised a meeting at the Crown and Anchor tavern in the Strand, at which Roebuck, no longer a member of parliament, condemned the government in a violent speech given wide press coverage.[24] The first Radical test had arrived. It required a Whig response.

It was at this stage that the Whigs and Conservatives began a cat and mouse dance that was to last for the remainder of 1838. Because neither party wished to be trapped by the actions of their more troublesome and philosophically unappealing supporters, Melbourne and Russell on the one hand, and Peel and Wellington on the other, enacted a remarkable series of parliamentary manoeuvres designed to reduce the influence of both Radicals and ultra Tories. Both sets of leaders aimed to strengthen their own party's position; both understood that where circumstances warranted, mutual co-operation could aid their respective causes. For Peel, the need to deny a small group of Radicals the opportunity to defeat the government, when he was not yet prepared to head an alternative ministry dependent on ultra Tory support, required that the Whigs be maintained in office. Such tacit understanding was not, of course, new. Both parties deprecated the need for concert; they recognised the transitory nature of the phenomenon. But most of all, they recognised its necessity. Thus, when the Radical leaders organised a public assault on the government's Canadian plans, Russell was able without much difficulty to join with the Conservatives in an address to the Queen in order 'to unite all who are against Roebuck and Papineau in a decided vote'. There was no direct appeal to Peel; Russell's old nemesis Lord Stanley acted as go-between.[25] The message sent to the Radicals and ultra Tories could not have been more clear. Peel had answered Russell's note before the opening of the session in November with the assurance that he would give the government due notice of any intention to oppose; now he fulfilled Lord John's further hopes by offering 'cordial support' in the Commons for the Address to the Queen. When Russell followed by moving a few days later to introduce a bill, only six Radicals supported Hume in opposition. In the Lords, Wellington announced his support for any strong measures necessary to suppress the rebellion; when Durham complained about the size of force at his command, the Duke met with him and told him how to manage with what he agreed was too small an army.[26] Holland recorded the government's debt: 'the good sense of the Tory leaders and especially of the Duke of Wellington' he wrote in his diary,[27]

> directly or indirectly prevented that party from putting forth their strength in a way that might have dislodged us but could have given them no permanent or satisfactory possession of power. The Duke of Wellington openly refused lending himself to any factious opposition on the Canada question and expressly exculpated us from the charge which we were in appearance most liable . . . that of not reinforcing the military establishment of the two colonies tho' we had so many grounds for apprehending disturbance . . . it was quite clear that he was far from impatient for a change and both from public principle and private inclination unwilling to molest the Queen's government.

The decision to send Lord Durham as Governor helped to weaken Radical opposition. Russell stressed privately the importance of having someone like Durham suspend the constitution if it was the wish that 'our friends' were to agree; Holland noted that the appointment facilitated a 'quiet passage . . . by dividing or rather reducing to the very minimum of a parliamentary minority, the Radical opposition to it.'[28] Durham was reluctant to take the post. He was first approached in July, two weeks after he arrived back from St Petersburg, but twice refused. It was not until January, by which time the government realised the advantage of having him go out, that he finally accepted entreaties to help them solve the Canadian crisis.[29] But though the news of his appointment was received with 'great delight' by Radicals and 'sarcastic cheers' by Conservatives, the advantage of making an appointment agreeable to the Radicals, 'whom it is well to please when you can do it so cheaply', as Melbourne noted,[30] was not the sole reason for his appointment. Durham's return from Russia had resurrected rumours that he was about to head the 'movement' party; although the Whigs did not regard him as much of a threat, there was a feeling that his absence would prevent his joining in what Ellice termed 'political plays'. Given his 'fever for any employment', Melbourne told Mulgrave, 'it would be well to satisfy and dispose of him.'[31] There was certainly no chance that his suspected ambition for a cabinet post would be gratified. Old wounds had not yet healed, and none would consider it. Russell was still angry at Durham's attempt in 1834 to claim credit for drafting the Reform Bill. Melbourne, who thought him 'dishonest and unprincipled', told Russell that 'everybody, after the experience we have had, must doubt whether there can be either peace or harmony in a Cabinet of which Lord Durham is a member.' Durham was not far wrong when he told Hobhouse that he was sent abroad 'in order to be got rid of'. When the Queen mentioned in August 1838 that it was better Durham was in Canada than England, Melbourne replied '*that* was one of the reasons why he was sent there, but we mustn't consider *that too* much.'[32]

Radical ambivalence on the issue was of some benefit to the Whigs. The small group of dedicated opponents of the government's plan viewed the colonies as an expensive drain on the British economy. Led by the philosophic Radicals Grote, Roebuck and Hume, and drawing their arguments from the Ricardian theories put forward by Bentham and Mill, they put the case for a quick withdrawal from a system that served only its patrons. The majority of the more moderate Radicals, on the other hand, were attracted to the economic advantages that a well-planned system of emigration held out for both mother country and colony. Basing their theory on the ideas of Gibbon Wakefield, they argued for an intervention by the home government that would replace the feudalism, intransigence and ignorance of the French with the superior enterprise and intelligence of the English. James Mill himself had suggested as much in his *History of British India*; his son put the case forcefully in the *Westminster Review* by arguing that 'the dictatorship . . . of which Lord Durham is the immediate depository, admits of justification.'[33] This difference in theory gives only a partial explanation for Radical disunity, for the important motivation of either group was its domestic political consideration. Hume's group likened the colonists' cause to anti-aristocratic sentiment in England. The plight of the French Canadian, moreover, was similar to that of the Irish Catholic. Support for the Canadians and opposition to 'finality' were obverse sides of the same coin. But most Radicals were not willing to threaten the existence of the Whig government for the sake of the French Canadians. Whereas Hume thought that the government, by enforcing their injustice in Canada with 'force and sword', had forfeited their right to the Radicals' forbearance, several moderate Radicals were alarmed by the violent language used by his group in the Commons debates on Canada.[34] It was evident from their conduct that they supported the view of *The Examiner*'s Fonblanque, who charged on 14 January, that 'those who justify revolt in Canada to obtain justice, would, by letting in the Tories, deprive Ireland of the justice she enjoys under her existing government . . . [and] mar the cause of reform at home'. But satisfying as these sentiments might have appeared to the Whigs, they could in fact give little comfort. Reforms which moderate English Radicals contemplated were more than Russell would allow. Fonblanque's 'cause' was seen to damage the government's electoral position and was to be resisted when brought forward by either group of Radicals. A split among the Radicals reflected in reality only a question of tactics and pace. It was not Fonblanque, but Peel's forbearance and need to avoid governance, that would moderate the Radicals.

In March, a motion by Molesworth to censure the Colonial Secretary Glenelg forced Peel to come again to the Whigs' aid. Molesworth's motion was a shrewd attempt to get Tory support, for no one could doubt that Glenelg had cut a sorry figure in this, as in every, post. Brougham quipped that the crisis would cost the Colonial Secretary 'many a sleepless *day*'; Melbourne was prepared to remove him over the Christmas recess but for the appearance of a concession to the Radicals.[35] The Radicals had reason to suspect that Peel would support the motion. Although he had come to the government's rescue in January, he had been unsparing in his criticism of Glenelg. There was, in addition, mounting public belief that the ultras in his party were having some success in persuading him to take a more forceful role in opposition. On five occasions in the last week of February, Conservative whips reduced the government to a minority on a series of motions decrying O'Connell's use of violent language.

Peel himself thought that his own party seemed to lack control.[36] Sensing that the Conservative leader might be forced to vote with the Radicals if only to maintain the unity of his party, Molesworth and Leader issued special invitations for a series of preliminary Radical meetings. Although the government expected a close division, and was prepared, as Melbourne announced to the cabinet, to 'stand our ground, if we had a majority of one',[37] the Radical initiative came to nought. At a meeting at the Foreign Office on the eve of the motion, O'Connell spoke out strongly against the mischief makers; the Radical split broke out publicly when the moderate Warburton accused Molesworth in the Commons of playing 'nothing more nor less than party politics'.[38] More importantly, Peel refused to be drawn in. Concurring in Wellington's belief that forcing the Conservatives on the Queen on this issue and at this time would be the 'greatest evil', he refused an offer of union from Hume, made through Knatchbull. But in order to satisfy his more rabid followers at the Carlton Club, he took Stanley's advice of an alternate motion censuring the government's handling of the Canadian problem.[39] Lord Sandon accordingly moved such a resolution which gave Molesworth little choice but to withdraw. The Government prevailed with a majority of twenty-nine. Not one Radical supported Sandon, and the extremists' 'power of mischief', as the moderate Lytton Bulwer pointed out, was 'not as great as they supposed . . . and damp their ardour for a *coup de main*'.[40] Peel's extremists were also quietened. He had managed to keep his party together, throw the Whigs back onto the Radicals for support, and yet prevent a premature assumption of power that would have played havoc with his Fabian tactics. *Juste milieu* politics was a course which the Whigs were not alone in pursuing.

There was one further episode in this chapter of Whig–Conservative co-operation concerning both the government's Irish legislation and the question of Durham and Canada. At the end of July, Brougham attacked an ordinance promulgated by Durham shortly after his arrival in Canada. The ordinance was Durham's solution to the problem of dealing with the disposal of the political prisoners still in custody following the rebellion of 1837. It declared that if any convicts should return from Bermuda, where they had been sent, without the Governor's permission, they would be guilty of high treason and would suffer death.[41] There is little doubt that Brougham's motive was to weaken his arch-enemy Durham, and the government, in order to ingratiate himself with the Radicals who were now in need of a 'respectable' head since Durham's assumption of a vice-regal post. 'I heard Roebuck boasted of having Brougham in his pocket, and had said "As we are deserted by Durham, we must trot out the old horse",' noted Hobhouse. The Brougham–Durham quarrel dated from the summer of 1830, and according to Melbourne, the two had 'hated each other ever since'.[42] A jealous Durham complained that the Lord Chancellor's name was to be put on the Reform column, while 'mine, who drew the bill, not'; in 1834, their quarrel continued in the columns of *The Times*, the *Edinburgh Review* and in the infamous speaking tours each undertook in the north.[43] Melbourne's refusal to have Brougham back in 1835 and Durham's continued employment with the Whigs resulted in an embittered Brougham's increasing hunger for revenge. Durham's appointment to Canada was grist for his mill. He made a violent and intemperate speech when the emergency legislation was introduced, denouncing the government and by implication Durham for its illiberal Canadian policy. He was to be disappointed when Conservatives refused to join the attack. 'I am in wonderment at the extreme self-denial of your conservatives', Brougham wrote to Lord Stanley, 'I thought I had opened the door of the closet for them to put the gov't in a fire that would destroy them – when my friend the Duke steps forward and shuts the door in his own face and protects them from my battering.'[44] When he brought up the subject of the ordinance on 30 July, there was every reason to believe he was making a partisan attack. He had vowed in March, in a letter to the Delegates of the Emancipation of the Blacks, to do all in his power to rid the country of the ministry, and Russell had already warned the Commons at least once against his personal and party motives.[45]

Surprisingly, the government gave in to Brougham's taunts, a decision that prompted Durham's early and spiteful return to England. Although Melbourne had responded to Brougham's first denunciation of Durham by declaring it 'impudent and unpatriotic . . . sacrificing the interests of the country to the interested party', and had with Glenelg two days earlier sent letters to Durham expressing 'the most active approval and concurrence' in his decision,[46] the government disallowed the ordinance and agreed to Brougham's Indemnity bill, which protected Durham's officials who had innocently taken part in the 'illegal' proceedings.

Durham appears to have been let down. He had been instructed to transport the convicts, and the Law Lords' decision that the prisoners' banishment was illegal, the stated reason for the disallowal and indemnity, was almost certainly wrong. Although criticism in both houses of parliament was directed against the dictatorial manner in which Durham carried out his ordinance (not sending the prisoners to trial), the law officers, when asked, found only his instructions to detain the prisoners in Bermuda illegal. In fact, while that part of the ordinance which declared that prisoners would suffer death if they returned was clearly illegal, detention in Bermuda was within his legal rights, jurisdiction and instructions.[47] It seems clear that the legality of the ordinance had nothing to do with the government's decision. On 8 August, two days after receipt of the Law Lords' hastily formed conclusion, Hobhouse reported that the government had not made up its mind and would 'wait for discussion in the Lords'.[48] Following what Russell told the Queen was a 'very disagreeable' debate on 9 August, the decision was taken to support Brougham. Melbourne, Howick, Rice and Glenelg argued in defence of Durham, but Russell would not. Too 'utterly exhausted by the labours of this protracted session' to defend one who had made himself thoroughly unpopular by his conduct at home and abroad, Russell 'long[ed]' for Thursday, when . . . this troublesome session will close.'[49]

Russell's refusal to defend the ordinance was not for the reason given by Durham's first biographer and repeated since, that the government feared massive Radical opposition which might have brought it down.[50] All but a handful of Radicals had supported the government's Canadian legislation, and most supported Durham. In July, Roebuck advised Brougham not to follow the Tory Ellenborough's lead in attacking Durham's conduct, arguing that everything done by the governor was 'wise, prudent and humane'. The Radical press was generally hostile to Brougham's opposition to his ordinance. Leader was the one Radical who spoke against Durham's ordinance in the Commons debates; Grote, the only other Radical to speak, argued that Brougham's Indemnity bill would weaken the government's authority in Canada.[51] Russell shared Roebuck's belief that the ultra Tories were behind the surge of support for Brougham, and told Melbourne that the success of the Indemnity Bill was the result of a 'cabal of Tories'. The ultra Tories were unhappy at Durham's overly-liberal conduct, particularly his dismissal of Sir John Colborne's military government.[52] They were, more importantly, angry with Peel's virtual dictation of the opposition's support for the government's Irish policy, and used the occasion of Brougham's attack for a last minute revolt. In March, Peel had agreed to support the Irish poor law, corporation and tithe bills when appropriation was dropped from the latter.[53] The tithe and corporation bills had yet to pass the Lords when the news of Durham's ordinance reached England; though the Tory amendments to the corporation measure made its progress doubtful, it was thought that Peel's compromise had ensured the tithe bill a safe passage. But during the same week that the Durham affair blew up, the Whigs had to contend with the ultra Tories who seemed bent on embarrassing Peel and the government by 'wrecking-amendments' to the tithe bill. When Wellington voted for Brougham's censure of Durham on 9 August, Melbourne could see the hand of the ultras at work, for he had learned that the Duke had stated in the morning that he would oppose it. This caused the government to consider their tithe bill in danger on the very day when the decision to disallow the ordinance had to be taken. Melbourne told the Queen later on the 10th that though the government had been worried, the tithe bill would now pass because they had 'given way' on Brougham's bill.[54] Harsh language about an 'unscrupulous selfish' Durham at a cabinet on the 16th is further evidence that the Whigs' dislike for 'Radical Jack' left him with few defenders, but there is little doubt that he was a victim of the Whig–Conservative compromise. Tithe reform in Ireland took precedence over the defence of questionable actions by an unpopular and often pompous Durham in Canada.

Russell's end-of-session fatigue was more than a reaction to the longest session yet known that century. In a letter to Melbourne during the recess he wondered if there was merit in his brother Tavistock's 'laying upon Pitt the fault of the Corn Laws and every other difficulty we have or shall have: . . . (1) 500 millions of debt (2) a bad currency (3) bad poor laws (4) a bad law for Canada (5) swamping the House of Lords'. Russell was clearly in need of a psychological boost for a sagging morale prompted by his wife's recent death and the government's increasing difficulties.[55] The failure of the Irish municipal bill was the most recent example of the government's difficulties with the House of Lords, which had rejected a number of measures during the session, but Russell was as aware as any that the Whigs' difficulties could be traced to other than Pitt. Economic recession and an increasingly aggressive foreign policy had much to do with mounting budget deficits; in a memorandum to the cabinet in November, he set out the need to increase the size of the fleet, adding that though it might involve 'danger to the government', unpopular taxes might have to be imposed rather than leave the Navy weakened or dispersed. Moreover, like many of his colleagues, Lord John had little confidence in Glenelg's ability to handle Canadian affairs. 'I have never felt such embarrassment as when last year I had to defend the Canada papers' he told Melbourne. 'What Peel said of them was in many instances indisputably true.'[56]

Pitt's legacy or economic and personnel issues aside, the unmistakable cause of Russell's frustration was the government's inability to pursue its own policies in its own way. The need to balance Radical and Conservative support was bound to wear down the most optimistic advocate of the middle ground, and by the end of 1838, most Whigs were tiring of the struggle. There was no lack of confidence that the mounting problems could be solved, but there was a growing feeling that the political room among parliamentary and electoral factions was in an increasingly short supply. If Peel's support was not entirely welcomed, the threat of its absence was no less inconvenient. There had been concern in May that Peel might drive the government out before the coronation in order to wrest control of coronation patronage. On a number of further occasions, the apparent ultra Tory impatience for office pointed out the Whigs' precarious dependence on what seemed to be a weakened Conservative resolve to unite against Radical pressures. The government's supporters in the Commons were also showing less patience with a cabinet so obviously committed to 'finality'. By the end of the session, O'Connell's complete disgust at the government's ready acceptance of the Lords' continued rejection of corporation reform led to the foundation of his repeal-oriented Precursor Society. Claiming that the Whigs would have to undertake popular measures or forfeit his support, his obeisance to the government appeared to be at an end; Normanby's fears 'for the prospects of the Party which an open rupture with O'Connell might or would produce' needed scarce saying.[57] The English Radicals were no less concerned at the lack of 'real progress', and though few MPs were to support the 'physical force' Chartism of 1839, already by the end of 1838 there was concern that Radicals might be attracted to the growing popularity of the Chartists' nominal demands. There was little doubt, moreover, that the government had little choice but to repress the more violent aspects of Chartism, a necessary response unlikely to reduce the influence of the handful of less moderate parliamentary Radicals. Although Russell advocated the prosecution of Stephen and O'Connor, leaders of 'a scramble for property . . . a sort of Jacquerie', he knew, as he informed Melbourne, that to do so 'may lead to mischief'.[58]

Competing pressures led inevitably to internal disarray, and as the government prepared for their next parliamentary session, the peace and harmony that had characterised the cabinet's deliberations since the resignations of Stanley and Graham became a disappearing luxury. The difficulties concerned men as much as measures. It was generally accepted that the government benches in both houses were in need of strengthening if the government were to survive the coming year. The importance of the Canadian question rendered imperative replacement of the incompetent Glenelg, but discussions of personnel unearthed a series of disputes resembling the unpleasantries of 1833–34. Melbourne foresaw the 'fears and hopes and all sorts of wild schemes and notions' that changes would produce, and consequently managed, in August, to postpone making new arrangements which he nevertheless knew to be inevitable.[59] By October, pressures to remove Glenelg could no longer be avoided. Although Russell and Melbourne were still loth to give in to the Radical critics of their Canadian policy, Duncannon, Ellice, Abercromby and Ebrington pointed out the dangerous consequences of Durham's early return; should a number of the government's more liberal supporters sympathise with his position, the precarious majority could be lost.[60] It was perhaps fitting justice that Glenelg should thus be made the scapegoat for the government's difficulties, for he had instructed Durham to transport the prisoners out of the province but never once mentioned this fact in Durham's defence when the ordinance was being discussed. Spring Rice, who was first suggested as a replacement for Glenelg, was widely regarded as incompetent at the Exchequer, and unpopular with the Commons moreover as a result of his continual canvass for the Speakership; it was thought nevertheless that he might strengthen the government in the Lords. Yet Melbourne did not want to move him from the Exchequer. Thomson, his preferred candidate for that post, was unliked by many, and Baring, the general favourite, was unacceptable to Howick and Thomson. It was consequently decided to leave Rice where he was, a decision that dashed Abercromby's hopes of vacating the Chair.[61] But what to do with Glenelg? Normanby, the Lord Lieutenant, was the only candidate whose colonial views were liberal enough to suit Howick, who was prepared to resign himself if he or Normanby did not replace Glenelg. The difficulty here was O'Connell, who had the highest respect for the Castle administration. Were Normanby removed, it was feared that the Irish agitator would have an additional pretext for a rupture with the government and might drive his Precursor Society to more violent agitation for repeal. Thus Glenelg had to be kept at the Colonies until O'Connell's hostility ceased. At Normanby's urging, O'Connell dropped repeal by January,[62] but the interval had given Howick time to engage in a quarrel over Glenelg that came close to bringing down the government.

Howick's views on colonial matters were the most liberal in the cabinet. He was not happy with suspension of the constitution in Canada, nor in Jamaica where local difficulties were making that course increasingly likely. Glenelg bore the brunt of Howick's wrath, which was in reality symptomatic of his own disagreement with colonial policy. Howick's great failure as a politician was his habit of stressing unduly the importance of his own briefs, and with the characteristic Grey inability to brook opposition on the essentials of those briefs, he entered a stormy nine month period that ended only with his resignation in August 1839. Howick was not in charge of colonial affairs, but as Undersecretary for the Colonies for a number of years and most recently Secretary at the War Office, he had a better knowledge than most of colonial problems and remedies. When Glenelg ordered additional funds for troops in December, Howick started a row with Rice, who as Chancellor, refused to relinquish his department's allocation of military funds to the War Office. The government's decision at the end of January to postpone substantive improvements in the governance of the West Indies was more than Howick was prepared to accept. He argued that military power was not the basis for good government in either Canada or Jamaica, and threatened to resign if Glenelg were not removed.[63] Russell effectively scotched Howick's resignation attempt by threatening to resign as well, a move prompted, Melbourne thought, by Lord John's unwillingness to have Howick make his government appear unpopular at a time when the Radicals were threatening to withdraw support. Against his own wishes, Glenelg was made to resign and Normanby brought over from Ireland to take the colonies.[64] As a sop to O'Connell's feelings and in recognition of his decision to drop repeal, Ebrington was sent to Ireland as the one possible Viceroy whose sympathies were similar to the departed Normanby's. Yet Glenelg's resignation did not restore peace to the Whigs' inner councils. Melbourne had twice in the autumn warned the Queen that Howick's dissatisfaction made the continuance of the administration doubtful, and on 10 February, a week after Glenelg's departure, he was forced to say again that a 'most violent speech' of Howick's produced a 'very stormy and unpleasant' cabinet that raised doubts of his being able to hold the administration together.[65] That Melbourne did succeed was testimony to his own ability as a conciliator and, more ominously, a reflection of the government's need in 1839 to band together against its opponents.

By 1839, a combination of circumstances made the government's position extremely precarious. Peel's increasing difficulty in controlling the impatient ultra Tories would soon force him to re-evaluate his parliamentary tactics. Rather than govern in opposition by maintaining a strict neutrality, the Conservative leader was forced to quell open revolts in his party by acting in a more partisan fashion; he was prompted, for the first time, to support the government's Radical opponents. At the same time, growing economic difficulties rendered the government whips' ability to control their parliamentary support more and more doubtful. From this point on, it was becoming patently clear that while the government was Whig, its parliamentary majority was increasingly moving in the direction of the free trade and parliamentary reform which would characterise the nascent Liberal movement. Thus, while ministers wished to hold to the more moderate Whig course which their nature and their views of the electorate dictated, the more liberal of their supporters began to exploit their weak parliamentary position in order to pull them in an opposite direction.

At the opening of the new parliamentary session, Greville noted that with the 315 Conservatives forming the largest single party, the remainder composed of 267 Ministerialists, 66 Radicals, 5 'doubtful' and 4 vacancies, 'never did a Government hold office by so frail and uncertain a tenure'.[66] A year earlier, Melbourne had foreseen the predicament; 'If there are Rats, we are done'.[67] Greville's description of 267 'Ministerialists' was in itself misleading, for a large number were committed to free trade policies which the Whigs were determined to resist. Throughout the autumn of 1838, agitation for repeal or moderation of the Corn Laws led to increased fervour on the part of the League and its parliamentary supporters. Most of the cabinet held a timid view on what *The Times* described as 'the oppressive system of the Corn Laws'.[68] Melbourne reported 'a good deal of difference of opinion' at a cabinet called to discuss the free-traders' demand for a moderate fixed duty. Thomson and Howick urged the government to take advantage of the clamour by fixing the duty, but the majority thought that though such a change might be useful politically, it would be unwise to alter the current course of leaving the question an open one.[69] Russell in particular had argued that the advantages of alteration were 'much exaggerated', believing that foreign grain could be kept out with any duty, and that the government should not act on the issue.[70] It was not simply that support for the League, such as for example on Villiers' motion in February to hear evidence against the Corn Laws, would result in the landed proprietors in the Commons defeating the government. The fact is that with the exception of Thomson, most Whigs held to the view espoused by Ebrington, that 'my own prepossessions are all on the side of the land'.[71] For his part, Melbourne was in need of little convincing, being of the opinion that agriculture would be hurt, and that the 'property or the institutions' could not stand the 'agitation' necessary to destroy the Corn Laws: 'If the opinions and feelings are weak, we shall fail', he told his colleagues; 'If strong, we shall still only carry it by the same means as we carried the Reform Bill, and I am not for being the instrument of another similar performance.'[72] The Whigs, it was clear, were not at heart adherents to the free trade principles espoused by the large number of their supporters who were to support Villiers' motions in the Commons.[73] When the ill-fated budget proposal of 1841 was put forward, it was done so with the conviction that the agricultural landed interest would not be left without protection.

The growing militancy of the parliamentary Radicals was of far greater moment for the Whigs. Free traders, after all, were unlikely to threaten the ministry's existence when the alternative held no promise for their cause. But the impetus given to the parliamentary reform question by the circumstances of the economy, the anti-Poor Law movement and Chartism prompted Radicals to put pressure on a government which appeared unlikely to be able to count on Peel's support for much longer. Rintoul's *Spectator* vied with *The Times* in wishing the Whigs out; Fonblanque's pro-ministerialist *Examiner*, which had hitherto criticised the impatient Radicals for expecting Whigs to 'eat their words overnight', and had argued that 'you may raise the devil of Toryism, but you cannot lay it again', called on the government to moderate Radical influence by allowing an open question on ballot.[74] What the Radicals wanted was an end to 'finality'. Eighty-six members supported the Radical T. S. Duncombe's amendment to the Address calling for further reform of parliament; a year earlier, only twenty had supported a similar demand. When, a month later, a successful censure in the House of Lords of the Whigs' Irish policies forced the government to seek the support of the Commons, the Radicals seized the initiative. It was clear to all that Peel was in trouble with his ultra Tories. Sixty-five English and Irish Conservatives had opposed the government's Irish corporation bill in March despite, or perhaps because of, Peel's support for the measure. Their revolt was obviously planned in conjunction with Lord Roden and the ultra Tory peers who censured the government in the Lords. Realising that Peel could scarcely come to the Whigs' aid in the Commons, the Radicals demanded further constitutional reform as the price of their support for Russell's announced motion in the Commons. Duncombe let it be known that he would move an amendment to this effect, and the *Morning Chronicle*, reportedly the government print but increasingly influenced by Radical opinion, called on Reformers to take advantage of the government's weak position by demanding ballot, household suffrage and shorter parliaments. On 15 April, the day set for debate on Russell's motion, it argued that 'to revive the belief that the accession of Tories to power would be a national calamity, Ministers must show that they are distinguished from the Tories in something other than name. *Finality* is the grave of enthusiasm'. Finality was indeed a word which caused a great deal of dissatisfaction among all Radicals; there was little doubt that Russell was the object of their complaint. Captain Berkeley's remark at the Bristol Reformers' dinner in January, 'that Lord J. Russell took in sail too soon', expressed a sentiment put forward by an increasingly large number of Liberals, Radicals, and now Chartists, who were able to use to great advantage that part of his 'finality' declaration describing the preponderance of the landed interest as the intent of the Reform Act.[75] H. G. Ward, a moderate Radical whose notice of an appropriation resolution in 1834 had been intended to encourage Russell to take the initiative in Whig affairs, warned his cousin Normanby before the 1839 session that the government could no longer survive Lord John's guidance; '*he can never lead us again, being too deeply committed to retreat; . . . a reorganization of the government must take place before you meet Parlt again.*'[76]

Russell was well aware of the Liberal growth among his supporters and the 'permeation of the Whig mass by the Radical leaven' that caused dissatisfaction with his leadership. In the autumn he had wondered to both his brother Tavistock and to Melbourne if another leader who had not pledged himself against ballot might not have an easier time of controlling the party.[77] But after the recess, and despite Tavistock's chiding him about Tory principles being in the hands of other than Tory ministers, Russell was convinced that the Chartist challenge called for a determined stand against Radicalism. He and Melbourne decided on the eve of the session that the government would stand firm on ballot and let the house and country decide to 'stand by us or leave us'; when Duncombe moved his amendment to the address he made a point of declaring the importance of finality. 'The opinion of the majority of the people of this country, I do believe, is against progressive reforms in the representation' he answered Duncombe.' 'My opinion is that the general sense of the country was with me when I made that declaration.'[78] Russell seemed firmly committed to a collision course with the Radicals. When told by Ebrington in April that several Radicals expected some concessions when Duncombe's second amendment was to come up, he could say only that they would be 'much disappointed . . . I can only refer to all I have said on the subject'.[79] At the begining of May, he drove the point home by publishing his *Letter to the Electors of Stroud*. Although the view has persisted that his object was to conciliate the Radicals by side-stepping the finality speech,[80] there can be little doubt that neither Russell nor the Radicals regarded it as such, or that the pamphlet was not a carefully timed exercise in response to the general complaint among government supporters that the *Morning Chronicle* had misrepresented their opinions when it called for constitutional reforms at the end of March.[81] While Russell did admit that the extension of the franchise to the £10 householder in the counties would not contravene the spirit of the Reform Act, the whole tenor of the pamphlet was against change. He had told his father to await in print his opposition to further reforms.[82] Convinced of the danger which threatened the country and the necessity of opposing the movement's progress, he entreated his supporters not to think of 'lifting the anchors of the monarchy while the signs of a storm are black in the horizon!' With the spectre of Chartism making concessions not only unnecessary but dangerous, the electors were asked to support the government 'in the spirit of that true Whiggism' and to ponder seriously 'the dangers of the time, and the means by which they may be averted'. His description of ballot as an 'irresponsible and secret power' was to delight lukewarm balloteers like Roebuck or its opponents like Fergus O'Connor,[83] but the bulk of the Radicals were represented by the view of the *Morning Chronicle*, which regarded the pamphlet as harmful to the prospects of reform; after the government resigned in May, it declared that 'the policy defended in Lord John Russell's "Letter to the Electors of Stroud" has received its definitive commentary in the occurrences of yesterday'.[84]

If the Radicals had misjudged the Whigs' forbearance to support their demands for reform, they correctly gauged Peel's inability to come to the Whigs' defence. Although the cabinet's decision to seek the support of the Commons was based on the assumption that Peel would not play into ultra Tory hands by deserting the anti-Radical cause,[85] Peel shrank from supporting the government against the Radicals for the first time since 1832. To 'keep our party together' and 'not to annihilate our influence by shrinking from strenuous opposition', Peel had been forced to acquiesce in Roden's censure motion;[86] he could not, as a consequence, provide that support in the Commons which the Whigs had expected. Rather, he announced his intention of moving his own amendment to Russell's motion defending the Lords' right to inquire into the state of Ireland.[87] In March 1838, he had Sandon propose an alternate motion to Molesworth's censure of Glenelg's Canadian policy, but deliberately kept all knowledge of it secret from even his own party in order to discourage speculation by the Radicals and ultra Tories that it was anything more than a motion to weaken the effect of Molesworth's.[88] The contrast with his pointed announcement on 12 April, that he had given notice 'in order to prevent the House being taken by surprise', was striking. It is clear from their correspondence that Wellington and Peel thought that the government might be forced to resign, a tacit admission that they expected Radicals to support Peel's amendment; although they did not want to govern on the Orange principles of their ultra Tory colleagues, they were doubtless hoping to embarrass a weary ministry and to keep the support of those same ultras. Peel told Graham that he thought he had Russell 'at a great disadvantage and that the debate would afford him the opportunity of a signal triumph'.[89] The government's successful defence of their Irish government by 318 to 296 votes, Peel's subsequent abandonment of his amendment and the defeat of Duncombe's amendment by 299 to 81 allowed the ministry to clear the Irish hurdle again, but Peel's newly found need to cavort with the Radical extremists in order to weaken the government and strengthen his own party was a departure that did not augur well for Russell's determination to crush the movement.

The final diaeresis of the Whigs' tacit alliance with Peel was not long in coming. On 9 April, the government announced its intention to suspend the Jamaican Assembly for five years and to rule instead by Governor and Council. This decision was the home government's response to the Assembly's refusal to implement the provisions of an 1838 Prison bill which, by giving control of prisons to colonial governors, restricted the planters' ability to punish too severely the recently emancipated slaves. After the five year period, during which time the emancipated slaves would have acquired sufficient voting strength to assert their rights, the constitution would be restored with any necessary modifications.[90] The government had supported Glenelg's rejection of a more comprehensive plan of legislative reform for the West Indies, relying on the effect of suspension on the rebel planters. Russell admitted that government by council might be 'perhaps very mischievous', but like all of his colleagues, with the exception of Howick and Thomson who pressed for an immediate general measure of legislative reform, he agreed that suspension was the best course.[91] There was little to suggest that the proposed course would cause much controversy. The handful of extreme Radicals who had opposed the suspension of the Canadian constitution in 1838 could be expected to continue their hostility, but anti-slavery feeling in England was solidly against the Assembly. The Radical press denounced the opponents of the measure as supporters of forty-five 'jobbing oligarchs' and, as Greville noted, 'the country does not care a straw for the constitution of Jamaica'.[92] It was to everyone's surprise, therefore, when Peel followed Russell's introduction of the government's plans by announcing his opposition to suspension. In 1838, he had not only supported suspension of the Canadian constitution but forced the government to abandon a council which would have limited the Governor's dictatorial powers. But now, in the Jamaica case, he criticised strong measures. Holland noted laconically that the government was 'mistaken' in assuming the acquiescence of both sides of the House in securing the emancipation of the slaves.[93] Greville, whose Conservative sympathies did not preclude his criticising Peel's partisanship, noted that 'Nobody can well make out what Peel is at . . . and nobody will believe that the Tories are animated by any high constitutional scruples, or that they care about the question'. Greville suspected his motive was to 'fight another battle', and though Peel argued in the Commons that he had no wish to offer any opposition to the progress of the bill which he did not consider a party question, his decision to oppose the bill going into committee instead of offering an amendment was a direct contradiction of that sentiment. By deciding to vote with the handful of extreme Radicals instead of proposing an amendment, as he had done in 1838 and again in the Irish motion in April, Peel had as much as announced a significant alteration in his opposition strategy.[94]

Everything done by Peel once the government did resign suggests that he was not yet prepared to govern and was probably trying to weaken the government's parliamentary position in a way that would force it to seek Radical support on other questions. He neither expected nor thought that the Whigs would resign if defeated.[95] But the Whigs could not be faulted for thinking, as they did, that he meant to force them out. On 26 April they decided to stand by their measure as announced and not to amend it to suit Peel's wishes,[96] despite the possibility that sufficient extreme Radicals would vote with Peel to defeat the bill. On 3 May, Stanley reckoned on a majority of no more than 10 or 12. The next day, the cabinet discussed their prospects and whether or not it ought to resign if the majority on going into committee was small. Lansdowne and Melbourne were opposed to such a course, and though nothing definite was settled, the impression was left on Palmerston, who thought it a bore to leave office ('I like power, I think power very pleasant', he told Melbourne[97]), that the decision had been to go on with any majority at all. But on the morning of the 7th, despite the urging of Palmerston, Hobhouse and the Chancellor to try the third reading, the cabinet decided that the narrow majority of five the previous evening, on the motion to go into committee, was insufficient to carry the bill.[98] The government resigned.

Resignation had little to do with the Jamaica bill itself, which could not be said to have rated very highly in importance. There was little reason to doubt that the bill would probably yet pass through both houses, and indeed, none argued that it would not pass. Just as Peel acted on political considerations divorced from Jamaica, it would appear that the Whigs' resignation was based on other factors. The reason most commonly given then, as now, was the number of Radicals who voted against the ministry and the number of supporters who stayed away; the ministry, Russell told the Commons, 'could not count on that support which is necessary'.[99] But while the Whigs' disgust with the Radicals' increased pressure had a lot to answer for their weariness and resignation, Russell's explanation was specious. None of the ten Radicals who opposed the government's motion were considered anything but extremists whose support could never be counted on, and exceeded by only four the number who had opposed the suspension of the Canadian constitution. It is doubtful, in other words, that this unsurprising and expected opposition would have influenced the government's mind between 4 May, when no decision to resign was taken, and 7 May. The abstention of fourteen usual supporters did cause greater concern, and was the subject of some cabinet discussion, but the Chief Whip Stanley had done nothing to secure their attendance. Three of the fourteen were abroad and should have been paired off, and one of the others, T. Wyse, explained afterwards that he had never received the least intimation of the importance of the vote or of its likely to be run so near.[100] Whatever the cause, these abstentions would not have been important or decisive without Peel's patently partisan conduct which brought the ministry so near to despair.

Peel's support against a few well-known extremists was the test and the factor which made the government wait for the division before resigning. Melbourne had warned the Queen early in April that Peel's attitude was a threat to the administration; he told her after the Conservative leader's announced intention to oppose the Jamaica bill that if he persisted, the government would have no choice but to resign.[101] If, at a time of Chartist disorder and commercial distress, the Conservatives would not support the government's resistance to the small number of extremists who were bent on constitutional reforms, there was nothing to do but resign. Giving in to Radical pressure was anathema to all that Whiggery stood for. The same decision could have been taken a month earlier when Peel announced his amendment to Russell's motion asking for support for the Irish administration, but had the ministry resigned, as it was suspected Peel wanted, a new Conservative government would surely have called elections and forced the Whigs to face the English electorate on an unpopular Irish question. If Peel meant to govern over the Jamaica question, he would not have the electoral advantage of an Irish question and would be forced to go to the country defending what was considered a spurious opposition to the Jamaica bill. Indeed Greville thought it such a disadvantage to take the government on the Jamaica issue that he wondered if Peel had not meant by his opposition to put office out of the question and to keep the ultra Tories, who hankered after office, thereby at bay: 'No question could be devised on which the Whigs could resign so advantageously as a party, none of which would be less popular for their opponents.'[102] The government were clearly aware of this consideration, for as Ebrington told Melbourne a week before the resignation, a defeat by Peel on the Jamaica question would be 'an event which if I could be influenced only by a desire to place them in [the] most unpopular of all situations (in this country at least) I should almost wish for'.[103]

There was nevertheless good reason to charge Radicals rather than Peel with responsibility for the resignation. Whig reform legislation had been unpopular with large sections of the electorate in the elections of 1835 and 1837; in the elections that would follow Peel's accession to office, an anti-Radical posture seemed obviously necessary. Whatever the clamour from 'the people', the electorate was conservative. Neither the Whigs' ideological commitments nor their political aspirations were for union with Radicals, whose causes, as Hobhouse noted, 'were not those of our supporters in the country'.[104] It was not only the government which held to this view. Those fringe members who generally sympathised with Radical objectives warned against concessions. Parkes, for example, told Le Marchant that a tour through the country in the Spring had convinced him of lukewarmness and even aversion to the movement, especially in those places where Chartism had penetrated.[105] Ellice told Russell in the first week of May that apart from a few 'movement men' who were 'incurable by any reasoning', the doctrines in the recently published *Stroud Letter* would find general assent and popularity among the electorate.[106] There was thus a widespread feeling that whenever elections might be necessary, the Whigs should appear to be determined to oppose Radicalism. Chartism, and the danger of Conservative rule hastening a crisis by increasing the fury of Radicals out of doors, produced a scenario tailor-made for the Whig mind and one which was thought would do much electoral good. But there was more to laying the blame for the resignation on the Radicals than possible electoral advantage. If Peel, with or without elections, failed to govern and the Whigs found themselves back in office, it was imperative that the Radicals be brought to heel. Spencer had suggested as early as February that the ministry go out when beaten in the Lords on the Irish municipal bill, in order to put an end to Radical hostility; with an increasing amount of time spent on maintaining a slender hold on the Commons, the attractiveness of a Conservative attempt at office was clear. Russell had warned the Radicals at the Foreign Office meeting on 5 March that he would prefer Conservative government to a Radical-led Whig ministry.[107] The Radicals would have to be transformed from sinners into supplicants.

In the end, of course, the Whigs retained office. The story is a familiar one. When Melbourne offered his resignation, he advised the Queen to send for Wellington, who in turn asked her to call on Peel. But unable to agree to the Queen's request to keep with her all the Ladies of the Bedchamber, Sir Robert refused to take office in a weak parliamentary position without some public token of monarchical approval of his government. In response to the Queen's appeal 'to save her from thraldom', the Whigs returned to office. The historians' verdict on the Whigs' role in the 'bedchamber' crisis has not been favourable. 'Love of place', wrote one, 'went to their heads'.[108] 'Avidity for office' and being 'too reluctant to part with it', wrote another, 'was not the best public image.'[109] Holland himself admitted that it did not *sound* very Whiggish to make the household the great bulwark of their cause, but his defence, like that of all the Whigs, rested on their being honour bound not to desert the Queen.[110] Given the fact that the government actually did resign despite its having a majority in the

Commons, the suggestion that it was too reluctant to part with office does not seem warranted. Unless the Whigs meant before-hand to scuttle Peel's attempt to form a government, an unlikely presumption, it must be assumed that the Whigs did mean to go out. They might well have thought that Peel's attempt to govern would not succeed with the Commons, and that his appeal to the country would not gain him the requisite number of seats, but that is another matter. The important question is how the government allowed itself to be manoeuvred into the position where it had little choice but to support the Queen by retaining office.

The answer to this question does not impugn Whig integrity, but it does suggest a lack of judgement. As Prime Minister and private Secretary to the Queen, Melbourne was in a difficult position, one that smacked of conflict of interest. His advice that she should express the hope to the Conservatives that none of those in the household except those who were engaged in politics should be removed was not incorrect, for the Queen had made a point of that sentiment in her first letters to Melbourne after the government's resignation.[111] In April, during a conversation about George IV's household, he answered her remarks, that 'I would rather starve' than accept a change of household with every ministry, with the instruction that though it would be very disagreeable, 'I shouldn't think of that too much, as it must be'.[112] He also told her, after Peel had balked at her outright refusal to allow a change in the household, that she should realise that Peel had others to satisfy; it was not unreasonable for the Tories to make this request. While it was proper for her 'to urge this question of the Household strongly', if Peel was unable to conce-de, 'it will not do to refuse and to call off the negotiation upon it'. He added that she should not refuse Peel the possibility of a dissolution, as she had done, but should reserve her opinion until the circumstance arose. 'Lord Melbourne', he concluded, 'would strongly advise your Majesty to do everything to facilitate the formation of the government.'[113] There seem no cause to suggest, therefore, that the Prime Miniser's advice sealed Peel's fate before negotiations began. It is clear, after Peel met with her, that the Whig cabinet was incorrectly informed by the Queen that Peel had requested *all* of the ladies removed, when in fact he had only asked that there be *some* changes in the household.[114]

On the other hand, Melbourne could not have failed to under-stand his influence on the near distraught young woman of twenty, who had admitted in the earlier conversation about George IV's household that in case she was obliged to have a Tory ministry, she 'didn't see how with all fairness one could go on well, if my feelings (as they are) were completely opposed to them, and was wishing them out all the time.' He knew that his role as the outgoing Prime Minister prevented him from meeting with her as private Secretary, and told her at the outset that the 'greatest caution' would be necessary; in order to prevent 'the most vehement jealousy and suspicion', correspondence and communication would have to be terminated. But a touching reply from Victoria – 'Oh! if Lord Melbourne knew how *very very unhappy* and wretched the Queen feels! *All* her happiness is at an end. It is *too sad*', followed by a hurried meeting requested by the Queen who grasped his hand and sobbed out 'You will not forsake me' – found a beleaguered Melbourne quickly giving way. 'Oh! no', he answered, I was afraid this would happen.'[115] He agreed to discuss with the cabinet what course she should pursue. From that point until the 10th, when Peel gave up his attempt to govern, the retired cabinet was in the unusual position of advising the Queen on her negotiations with its successor.

If Melbourne had continued to communicate with Victoria at all, a dubious course at best, he should have done so as private Secretary and not have discussed Peel's communication with his cabinet. No Queen, moreover, who could stand up to as seasoned a politician as Peel, and tell Melbourne that she thought Peel's request an 'attempt to see whether she could be led and managed like a child . . . the Queen of England will not submit to such trickery',[116] was in as much need of succour as she suggested. Melbourne would have done better not to let his emotional attachment to the young Queen get the better of him. Perhaps there was nothing sinister about his remark to the Queen an hour before she first met with Peel, and in response to her stated conviction that the Conservatives could not stand, that 'our people all mean to go with us now . . . anything like this allays disagreement; it will be easier to form the Government again'. Perhaps nothing was meant by his response to Victoria's account of pressing Peel on the 9th, 'I hope you had the better of him'.[117] But it would not be difficult to argue that there was enough encouragement here to strengthen the will of an already determined Queen. There can be little doubt that Victoria had settled against the Conservatives long before 6 May and, by telling Melbourne that Peel wanted to remove all of the Ladies, was stretching the truth in order to get his sympathy. It might not have been possible to dissuade her from her course, but a more thoroughgoing attempt could have been tried. The Queen's final word to Peel on the matter, sent on the morning of the 10th, advised him that his demand was contrary to usage and repugnant to her feelings; the letter was dictated by the cabinet after a long discussion the previous evening.[118] At the meeting, Howick, supported by Morpeth and Melbourne, had suggested that in order to be certain that Peel had objected to *all* of the Ladies and not just to the continuance of the *whole* bedchamber, he should be asked to state his position distinctly in writing. But at the beginning of the meeting, Melbourne had read out two notes that the Queen sent during and after her interviews with Peel and Wellington, putting in poignant terms her disgust at Peel's behaving 'very ill' and her wish not to be left without her Ladies. The effect was to swing the cabinet against Howick's suggestion. To have asked Peel directly, it was thought, would have further harmed the Queen's feelings. It could be argued that the Whigs latched on to Victoria's sympathies as an excuse to make Peel's return to office impossible, but what evidence there is does not support such a view. Howick, who was soon to retire from an administration that he had been accusing for some time of lacklustre, mediocre and opportunistic tendencies, told Lady Howick that he had never seen anything in the Cabinet like the feeling excited by the Queen's letters; he shortly regretted the Whigs' being 'forced back into office'.[119] Grey, who met with Melbourne during the course of the cabinet and admitted that the Whig ladies 'must be naturally regarded with an uneasiness by the ministers called upon to succeed you', nevertheless was moved sufficiently by the two letters and Melbourne's account of Peel's behaviour to suggest that the government was bound to duty' to support the Queen.[120]

On the evening of the 10th, the Queen held the first ball of the year; according to one witness, 'people's faces were very odd . . . the Tories quite aghast . . . the Whigs more or less nervous'.[121] It is not surprising that the Queen danced 'better than anybody', for she had earlier that day received the cabinet's decision to surmount the difficulties which caused it to resign. She rejoiced, she told Melbourne, 'at having got out of the hands of people who would have sacrificed every personal feeling and instinct of the Queen to their bad party interests'.[122] We have no record of how well the Conservatives danced, but it is doubtful that Peel was dissatisfied with the outcome of the proceedings. He felt personally aggrieved; he had acted, according to Wellington, in a gentle and conciliatory manner with the Queen and was distressed that he should be publicly criticised for an overbearing and tactless manner.[123] But he could not have been sorry that office had eluded him, for neither the timing nor the circumstances suited his plans. Peel's strategy dictated a more decided hostility to the Whigs than he had previously shown, but he was not yet prepared to take office unless the government fell apart as a result of internal disarray. He had no desire, moreover, to dissolve a Conservative government in a position of weakness. He was taken by surprise. Wellington told the King of the Belgians that the Whigs' resignation was premature; 'if we had taken the government we could have done nothing'.[124] Victoria thought that Peel put the question of the Ladies as a pretext for refusing office, but this is a doubtful conclusion. Grey, Melbourne and Peel himself had all had household positions placed at their disposal by William IV, and though the distinction between Queen regnant and Queen consort introduced uncertainty into the constitutionality of the question, asking for the power of replacement was not unnatural. It is more likely that Peel used the Queen's rejection of his request as the pretext which saved him from an unplanned entry into government.

The Whigs could not view their return to office with anything but equanimity. It was satisfying to see a humbled Peel pay for his partisan conduct by being forced to back away from office. It was satisfying as well to continue in office. In that sense resignation prolonged the government's life. Russell would not 'have liked to have been out *long*', Melbourne told the Queen on 12 May; later he told her that the resignation was perhaps premature 'but I think it did us good.'[125] But behind any hasty euphoric feeling lurked an uneasy realisation that maintaining their positions for the Queen's comfort was a course doomed to failure. Spring Rice asked plaintively how the government could go on without the confidence of the Commons; 'will this affair give it to us?'[126] Melbourne in fact doubted that it would. 'I do not think that we have the least chance', he told Grey. 'If we go on, we shall only fail more completely and deliver the Queen more completely bound into their [Conservative] hands.'[127] What Melbourne was referring to was the parliamentary balance of parties that had not been changed by the affair. However much the Whigs' resignation and Peel's failure to form a government might moderate party warfare and prolong the government's life, there was little to suggest that government measures had a better chance of succeeding than before. It would be only a matter of time before the Radicals or Conservatives forced another crisis. Russell told the Queen that 'great difficulties' could be deferred until the next session, but there was little expectation that things could continue beyond that. 'I am tempted to regret', Ebrington wrote to Ellice from Ireland, 'that Peel did not form a government'.[128]

There was thus little optimism in Whig circles, for it was seen quite clearly that their party would be forced to endure humiliating weakness which would do their standing in the country little good. By allowing their personal feelings for the Queen to impede their judgement, the Whigs had been caught in a trap which they had themselves laid in 1837 when Victoria came to the throne. They had instructed her in the art of Whig politics, and wittingly or no, Victoria was able to exploit the emotional attachment that had developed between Queen and ministers. A more detached government, or Prime Minister, would not have been asked to stand by the Queen. Victoria made a pretext of the Ladies to spare her a Peel ministry. The embarrassment to her personally caused by the Tory press's sensationalism over the Lady Flora Hastings scandal no doubt stiffened her resolve. To be surrounded by Tory Ladies, whose sympathies would most likely be directed to the unfairness of the false accusations of pregnancy levied against Lady Flora, was more than she could bear.[129] Without Melbourne, she would be forced to face the affair alone. Peel could offer no comfort. She was comfortable with the Whigs. It was Melbourne as much as the Whig Ladies that she could not do without. The Whigs' inclination in 1839 was to let Peel govern or fail in the attempt, but the result of the bedchamber crisis was to allow Peel to strengthen his position *vis à vis* the Whigs. For two years, Melbourne's ministry struggled through what Dr. Southgate accurately if harshly described as a 'fag-end period'.[130] The Whigs were not entirely to fault for their legislative record during these last two years, but it is difficult to avoid the conclusion that a government less committed to the personal feelings of the monarch would never have allowed itself to be manoeuvred into a position of such impotence.

10

The Queen's Government, 1839–41

We have everything excepting a revenue and a majority.

Baring, February, 1840[1]

An assessment of the Whigs' final two years of office which stresses the inevitability of collapse in the face of a coherent Conservatism is one which fails to observe the uncertainty in Peel's own party. It has been argued that 'unphilosophic' people wanted strong government rather than weak, and that a 'fresh propellant' would have been more edifying that a 'declining parabola'.[2] An examination of the Whigs' final two years in office reveals, however, that the Whigs were not as divided or tottering, nor were the Conservatives as strong and poised for a triumphant return to office, as most accounts suggest. The great weakness of the Whigs at the end of the decade was not so much a lack of energy or initiative – what got them in trouble during their last session after all was a series of innovative budget proposals not entirely unlike those which Peel would later consider – as much as the absence of a majority sufficiently large to overcome the need for Peel's support on those occasions when the Radicals pressed for unacceptable reforms. Peel, unfortunately, no longer had sufficient control of his party to be free to offer support to the government; nor did he have enough confidence in his party to oppose constantly, as many of his followers wished. The combination of Conservative vacillation and Radical mischief, the second encouraged by the first, rendered 'strong' government difficult. Unfinished business alone could be transacted, and that only by the compromises and concessions necessitated by the absence of predictable support from Peel; 'fresh' propellants could not have survived.

If it was to fulfil its promise to stand by the Queen, the cabinet's first task was to make it through the remainder of the 1839 session.

This was a goal made possible only by a series of painful concessions to both Radicals and Conservatives. The weakness of the government's position was set out by Russell on 19 May. 'We need not bring in new measures', he told Melbourne, for if measures were proposed and failed to carry, 'Lyndhurst and the ultra Radicals will make it a ground of attack all the autumn.'[3] Clearly, the bedchamber incident had not strengthened the government's position in any material way. Within two days of retaining office,[4] Russell had been warned by Spencer that the difficulties with the Radicals were not diminished, and indeed the next day Melbourne received a letter from Hume requesting a meeting to discuss matters which 'may be important for you to know'. The Whigs had expected Radicals to set a difficult price for support, and planned to adjourn until after Whitsuntide in order to gain time that might work upon the Radicals' fear of a dissolution. But the meeting with the Radicals, hastily arranged within a few hours of Hume's note, made it evident that such a move would cause the very desertion it was designed to prevent. Hume put the Radical terms which had been worked out at a large meeting of Radicals held at Molesworth's; despite Russell's refusal to put forward any legislation inimical to the Lords, the Radicals would be willing to support the administration provided that ballot, shorter parliaments, household suffrage, equal electoral districts and single-member constituencies be considered as open questions.[5] Shortly before this meeting, Melbourne had received a note from Stanley warning him against the 'twelve fools' who dined at Molesworth's but who, 'Philip sober' being different from 'Philip drunk', had already repented of their course. Melbourne therefore put Hume off with a promise that though any commitment would be objectionable, he would consult his colleagues. When pressed a fortnight later for a response, he told Hume that 'I have no communication to make'.[6] Yet despite such bravado, it was understood by all that if the government could not negotiate directly with the Radicals, concessions would nevertheless be necessary. A few days before the Jamaica division, Abercromby had announced his resignation from the Speakership, and Peel's decision to contest the chair produced a trial of strength that forced the government to solicit votes from the whole of the Liberal party. The Whigs were finally prepared to let Spring Rice have his long sought after post, but Radical hostility made this change impossible. Baring, Rice's likely successor at the

Exchequer, reported his Portsmouth seat to be unsafe due to a body of dissatisfied Radicals who would oppose his re-election; Ward, the Sheffield Radical, told Russell that Rice would never get the Radicals' votes in parliament.[7] It was decided that in order to save the need for internal shuffling that might produce bickering among supporters, a new candidate should be chosen. At the suggestion of the moderate Radical George Byng, Shaw Lefevre, 'the only man we could place in the chair . . . if he would consent to stand', was proposed and subsequently elected.[8] The majority of 18 votes over the Conservative candidate Goulburn was a satisfying victory, but the Radicals' virtual dictation of events was less felicitous.

The following morning, the cabinet met to consider what concessions might be necessary to ensure Radical support. It had already been decided that the recently publicised demand for a penny post could not be resisted. Howick actually supported Rowland Hill's scheme, although no one else did. The main objection to a cheaper post, apart from its Radical origin, was the loss of revenue that a reduction of an indirect tax would produce. Rice and Baring argued against any change, but in the end the decision was taken to grant the uniform penny post in order to ward off Radical hostility.[9] Warburton, the Radical chairman of the select committee on postal rates, described the 'coup-de-main victory' over Melbourne's government as 'the consequent necessity of his doing something to conciliate the people'.[10] In fact, the decision to concede was taken at the same time and as an obvious counter poise to a decision *not* to allow an open question on ballot. Despite suggestions that ballot as a single issue was becoming less popular,[11] there was little doubt that those Radicals whose support was most doubtful still regarded the opening of the question as the important concession to be gained. It was on this question too that the government was most vulnerable, for as the results of Grote's annual ballot motion would soon show, three-quarters of the government's supporters supported Grote. Of all the constituencies of Wales, Scotland and Ireland, and all the English boroughs, the ministerialist members numbered only thirty antiballoteers among them.[12] The Whigs neither could nor would support ballot themselves, but the idea of opening the question had been discussed more than once. In 1837, Russell had argued that an open question might draw the Radicals towards the government, but he opposed adopting a 'shuffling policy' to help the government through its parliamentary difficulties which could only discredit ministers. When Melbourne suggested, early in 1838, that there might be a relaxation in the government's policy by leaving the question open, Russell proved 'very unbendable'. 'I am sorry to find the majority of the party differ from me', he told Mulgrave; 'I cannot depart an inch from the line I have taken.'[13] There is no doubt that having issued his 'finality' statement, Russell had no desire to be seen to go back on his public utterance, but his main objection to opening ballot, like that of his colleagues, was the fact that the Radicals were behind the demand. On this point, the argument was the same as that against ballot itself. 'The Ballot as an abstract question is *not* the point [or] the real object of the original chief supporters of the Ballot', Lord Western told Melbourne; 'the question to be decided is a question between our present constitution and a democracy'.[14] Opposition to an open question on ballot having been the backbone of his anti-Radical crusade, Russell was determined to maintain that policy. When the cabinet met to decide the issue after their return to office, Russell circulated a memorandum arguing against change. After a good deal of discussion, it was decided that the desertions to the Conservatives that would follow any concessions on ballot, and the strong opinions in the cabinet against the measure, necessitated the support of Russell's position. At the same time, it was agreed that support for ballot should not make anyone ineligible for office, a provision that would soon allow Macaulay to join the government.[15]

Russell was prepared to concede the prospect of a £10 householder franchise in the counties. As a sop to the Radicals for stressing finality, he had held out some hope in his *Letter to the Electors of Stroud* that this extension of the franchise might be conceded at some future date. As soon as the government returned to office after the bedchamber crisis, Sir Hesketh Fleetwood, the Tory member of Preston recently turned Liberal, tabled a motion calling for extension of the county franchise. Like the original Chandos clause which was regarded as the precursor of this demand, the proposal could be expected to have the support of the landed proprietors who would increase their electoral influence, and of the Radicals who supported any extension of the franchise. Of all the changes that had been proposed since 1832, this seemed less likely to abrogate the spirit of what, against Radical pressures, was fast taking on the appearance of a document carved in stone. Apart from Howick, who opposed any concession, the cabinet decided to resist the motion but to declare that it would be considered in the future. It was also decided that Howick could resign if unhappy with this declaration. Like most of the cabinet, Russell would not have been sorry to lose so quarrelsome a colleague, but he was concerned lest the Grey influence be lost to the government. He told Howick to 'look at a letter of Mr Canning's in the 4th volume of the Life of Wilberforce respecting the duties of a leader and the obligations of those who consent to serve with him as such',[16] but when he heard from Howick at the start of the debate that the elder Grey had been persuaded to come and declare against the government in the House of Lords, Russell backed down. With no time for explanations, he startled his colleagues by announcing that the government could not concur in the motion.[17] Ward immediately announced that Radical support for the government was at an end, and when 80 Radicals joined him in support of Fleetwood's motion, the Whigs' prospect of continuing in office looked grim. There seemed nothing left to do but concede an open question on ballot if, as Normanby told Melbourne, 'your first object [is] to protect the Queen from Peel and the Tories'.[18] Despite Russell's protest that open questions would be to the 'convenience' of the administration but not to its 'honour and glory', Melbourne allowed an open question on the grounds that it would remedy the mischief done on Fleetwood's motion, yet not affect the government's 'course and action'.[19] There was no 'shift in principle on the question of electoral reform' as Professor Gash has suggested. Nor did the Whigs think that organic constitutional reform was in the general interest.[20] During Grote's hastily arranged ballot motion, Russell and Howick spoke out strongly against ballot and made it clear that the government had not altered its fundamental attitude to that question. Howick's support for the open question signified a perverse reversal of his earlier position that was no doubt partly motivated by a desire to embarrass Russell, but his argument is telling evidence that the concession on ballot was political rather than ideological: opening the question would serve the Queen as it was all that the parliamentary Radicals wanted. At the same time, ballot as an issue might be effectively retarded, if not permanently shelved.[21]

Having guaranteed their parliamentary position by making concessions to the Radicals, the Whigs' next task was to salvage what they could of their proposed legislation. The difficulty here was the continued Conservative emasculation of almost every legislative proposal, domestic or foreign. The first legislative change forced on the government occurred on the education plan, although it must be said that the government did not regard the success or failure of the measure as a party question, and few of its members were sorry to see it altered. In February, Russell had proposed an increase in state control of education, an increase in the annual parliamentary grant and the setting up of non-denominational normal schools for teacher training.[22] As the representatives of the Established Church in parliament, the Conservatives successfully fought the proposals in both houses so that the final proposals represented only a small portion of what was proposed. The normal school project was dropped before debates began in June, much of the remainder after. In contrast to the education plans, it was very much against the government's will that their plans for Jamaica had to be given up. At the end of May, an entirely different Jamaica bill was brought in. Based on the proposals put forward by Peel in April, the measure allowed the colonial assembly to continue as long as it accepted the acts of the home government. Although Peel failed in the Commons to reduce even what limited powers were given to the government, the Tories struck out those powers in the Lords. The government had realised from the moment it retained office that it could not go on with its original measure; in July, Russell had no choice but to recommend acceptance of the Lords' amendments.[23] What finally passed was not the government's bill, but Peel's. On the two remaining items of parliamentary business, the results were scarcely better. Opposition from all quarters forced the government to postpone the bulk of its Canada measure, and what finally passed in August was little more than holding legislation. Peel's support of a government compromise on the Irish corporation measure in March had augured well the prospects of a final settlement of that question, but a set of sweeping amendments by the Lords sealed its fate. Russell and Melbourne had the support of the cabinet to try an amended bill that would take account of the Lords' amendments; O'Connell reluctantly agreed to support it, but evidence that Buller and some of the Radicals would object prompted the government to withdraw the bill for a better day.[24]

Few sessions ended with more relief. Russell used apologetic tones to inform the Queen that measures to increase the size of the army and to establish a police force at Birmingham would prolong the session. He had told her earlier that dissolution would probably not be necessary, given the 'reunion of the majority' on the Speakership and the reintroduction of the Jamaica bill,[25] and he did not now look forward to threatening that majority by taking necessary precautions against the threats of the 'physical force' Chartists. Yet it was during such tense moments when the Whigs were forced to walk a seemingly impossible tightrope that they drew inspiration from their elevated view of the necessity of a Whig government. 'What will become of the country with such a mass of inflammable discontented matter united with all Catholic Ireland, and the Irish mobs in our great English towns who have hitherto abstained from uniting with the English Chartists?' wrote Stanley to Ellice; 'and yet this must be looked to in the event of a Tory Government with the present excited feelings as to Popery and the rampant fear of the Church.'[26] Thus, if doggedly serving the Queen was not exactly a Whiggish justification for continuing in office, preservation of civil peace, and the social order, was. Even so, the basic tenets of Whig mythology were less able to sustain its adherents after nine years of office. There was a growing feeling that the *via media* lacked sufficient force, that Whiggery could not hold on to office much longer if based on that concept. With an increasingly conservative electorate, preservation of the narrow parliamentary majority by concessions to Radicals was a course with decreasing attraction.

On one point most Whigs were agreed: if the government was to accomplish anything at all in the face of increasing Radical and Conservative opposition, the government bench was in need of strengthening. 'You evidently want strength', Spencer told Melbourne in July, a view supported by Normanby, who wrote to Russell to say that 'except you and Melbourne there is [not] a single man in the government for whom at present the country cares a straw'.[27] It is an interesting commentary on the nature of political life at this time that 'men' rather than 'measures' could still be considered of sufficient importance to prompt changes on the treasury bench. Whether or not such changes affected the success of legislation, or the government's stock among the electorate, is a question not easily answered, but it is clear that they were thought to have had some influence. If one test of party is adherence to a set of principles, then the obverse must have meaning; the predisposition to change personnel in order to get legislation passed, and to give the appearance and perhaps the reality of strength, weakens the argument that party was important. If a steady hand could, or was thought able, to guide legislation through parliament where a lesser one could not, the pull of party could not have been considered to have been of overriding concern. The replacement of Normanby at the Colonial Office is a case in point. Reports from Under Secretary Labouchere and others at the Colonial Office that Normanby was as incompetent, dilatory and indecisive as Glenelg had been, prompted his colleagues to put him elsewhere. By his own admission, the Colonies were too much for him, but more importantly, Russell considered it necessary to have the Colonial Secretary in the Commons, the colonies now being 'the vulnerable heel of the Empire, as Ireland was in 1835.'[28] Thus, although Normanby had done little to affect government policy towards Jamaica and Canada, the latter area by most expectations the troublesome topic for the coming session, it was decided to put Russell at the Colonies 'to make the machine work much more smoothly' and to see the government's measures through.[29] The change had nothing to do with governing principles. Legislation in one man's hands, it was thought, had a greater chance than when left in another's.

If the debate and dissension that was to surround Normanby's transfer to the Home Office was any indication, the general shuffle at the end of the summer presaged a stormy and uncertain future. Normanby was first slated to be sent to the Admiralty, where it was thought he could do less harm. Russell's post at the Home Office was then to be given to the Admiralty Secretary Minto,[30] but the absence of an obvious replacement for the Home Office resulted in Russell and Normanby simply switching offices. Normanby's new posting was not popular. It was generally agreed that Russell's work at the Home Office had been one of the government's strengths; Normanby's indolence and inefficiency would do the party and the country damage at a time when Chartist disorders called for competence in home affairs. What was more, Normanby's principles were considered by some of his colleagues to be too radical. Melbourne thought his views too well known for the Tory Lord Lieutenants to have any confidence in him; Ellice shared this opinion.[31] But the Prime Minister overcame his objections. Although obviously liberal in his opinions on Ireland and the Church, Normanby was after all a 'finality' man. His opinions might secure liberal votes in the Commons, and as Russell told Grey, 'forward views' were harmless when possessed by the Home Secretary; Wellington, Wharncliffe and Lyndhurst had stifled his own moderate plans, and 'for real purposes of good, no Home Secretary of our party will have sufficient power'.[32]

Normanby's appointment provided an occasion for Howick to complain of his own position. Unhappily for the Whigs, he chose to make a public issue of the government's Radical intentions which, he argued, Normanby's prominence signified. Howick was clearly disgruntled. Early in August, when offered the Postmaster-ship and a seat in the Lords to oversee the introduction of the penny post, he gruffly rejected the offer as 'an insult'. He was after a more senior position, one, in his own words, connected 'with all the higher and more important duties of Government.'[33] Within a few weeks he brought up the old business of the war office control over colonial estimates and threatened to resign if his own position were not changed or the War Secretary's powers in-creased. When it appeared by the end of August that neither was likely, he resigned. The ostensible motive was the weight given to Radicalism in the rearranged cabinet. 'Rightly or wrongly', he told Melbourne, Normanby was identified with those who wanted changes in the constitution; his promotion was evidence of a shift from men of moderate views.[34] Howick was particularly annoyed with Normanby's influence in the offer of the under secretaryship at the Colonial Office to his cousin H. G. Ward, the Radical whose open support of appropriation had prompted Russell's 'upsetting the coach' speech in 1834. But he knew that Ward had rejected the offer, and his own acquiescence in Normanby's holding the colonial seals makes specious his objections. His real complaint was Russell's domination of government policy. He complained that the growth in the size of the cabinet, from 12 to 15,[35] would increase Russell's ability to decide issues prior to cabinet meetings and to treat some Cabinet ministers as less important; his being among the last to hear of the proposed changes was confirmation of their want of confidence in him. Lambton, he complained to his father, knew of the changes long before he did himself.[36] In a sense he was right. Despite the advantages of pedigree and talent, he was considered by Melbourne to be too violent, obstinate and indiscreet to be raised to a higher office.[37] But he was wrong to put the blame on Russell's 'love of doing everything himself' and on Lord John's supposition that he had a 'right to move us all about and to make use of us just as he pleased'. Few were prepared to please him, especially after his ill-mannered rejection of the Post Office, and his going was due as much to Melbourne, who confided to the Queen that though it would be 'rather a trouble just now', it would be a 'very good thing to get rid of him'.[38]

Howick's break with the Whigs was also due in large measure to his father's counsel. The elder Grey had told his son at the time of the contemplated changes a year earlier that any change which would raise anybody in the House of Commons over his head should prompt his resignation; when he heard of the Post Office offer, he sent Russell a very indignant letter.[39] Grey had never recovered from Melbourne's refusal to heed his warning against a parliamentary alliance with the Radicals and O'Connell in the Spring of 1835. Nor did he waver in his conviction that Russell's independence, vanity and inability to resist Radical pressures were largely to blame. Though still a Whig, he had small regard for any government which gave prominence of place to Lord John, and attributed his son's exclusion from higher office to Melbourne and Russell's attraction to a Radical programme. There was less vanity in Grey's reasoning than in his son's, but there was more than a little spite. Howick's resignation should be viewed as the Grey family's final revenge for what it regarded as a snub. Melbourne wondered if he had not thanked the Earl sufficiently for his help in drawing up an address to the Lords; Grey was angry, the Prime Minister thought, because 'I don't pay enough attention to him and don't go and talk to him.'[40] In fact, Grey's alienation went back to his own cabinet's rejection of Lord Stanley, his chosen political heir. Howick's resignation was an extension of his own. So was his son-in-law Wood's resignation which followed. Howick was convinced that Labouchere's promotion to cabinet as President of the Board of Trade (a post Howick coveted himself) was a gross injustice to Wood, his sister's husband, who had a stronger claim to cabinet status. Wood was not unhappy with his lack of cabinet status, although Howick was convinced that he should have been put in the cabinet ahead of Labouchere. He listed this 'manifest injustice' to Wood as a cause of his own resignation. He was convinced by Grey to resign, and told Spring Rice that he could never have ventured back into Northumberland if he had stayed in office.[41] The same consideration prompted Sir George Grey, the Earl's nephew, to reject the offer of a cabinet seat to accompany his post as Judge Advocate. He told Melbourne that 'as he had always looked up to Lord Grey', he could scarcely think of coming into the cabinet upon Howick's going out.[42] The Whigs could ill afford the loss of Grey support. 'It is the impression which really does the mischief', Howick had said to Melbourne,[43] and at a time when the Whigs were hoping to reassure the electorate of their moderate intentions, Grey's hostility could bode nothing but ill. Parliamentary prospects were no less affected. Wood's loss to the Treasury was not one that could be made up by Robert Gordon, who was thought to be an indifferent replacement; Stanley, the Treasury Secretary, warned Melbourne specifically of the government's increased vulnerability to sorties by Wood and Howick.[44] Howick was especially dangerous. His views on colonial policy were sure to find support from the discontented Radicals should he choose to argue against whatever policy Russell might bring forward. Any ministerial attempt to earn Radical parliamentary support on other issues by concessions was likely to find Howick persuading moderate Whigs to oppose. Either scenario was likely to bring the government down. Howick reconciled many of his differences with Russell by the end of September and told Ellice that he would refrain from attacks on the government, but few could believe him. Grey had been the force behind the break, and he continued to show his hostility by sending his ex-colleagues 'very very unfriendly' correspondence.[45] There was little prospect for a reconciliation. 'Fudge', exclaimed Ellice, Howick would be 'Brougham the 2nd'.[46]

Macaulay's inclusion in the cabinet was a direct consequence of Howick's resignation. Macaulay's name had been put forward shortly after he returned from India in 1838, but neither Melbourne nor Russell had favoured his candidacy. His popularity, Melbourne thought, was more the result of his support for ballot than anything else. Russell was adamant on this point. His inclusion, he argued, would make the course of government 'somewhat doubtful as to the movement policy – Macaulay having spoken on ballot and nothing else.'[47] But pressure from Stanley and Ebrington to make up for Howick's loss by bringing Macaulay's popularity into the government made Melbourne and Russell reverse their earlier decision not to give him a post. Ellice voiced the opinion of many Whigs by wondering if he would be as great as his literary reputation and oratorical skills promised. 'If so', he told Parkes, 'he will be the atlas on whose shoulders the Commons will be carried through.'[48] Russell agreed to Macaulay's having the War Office only on the conditions that Lansdowne be consulted and that Clarendon be added to the Cabinet to counter Macaulay's liberalism.[49] Clarendon, whom Russell earlier suggested for the

Presidency of the Board of Trade, had already rejected the Governor-Generalship of Canada and turned down a further offer of the Mint; in October he came into the cabinet as Privy Seal upon Duncannon's resignation.[50] To Howick's disgust, the cabinet now numbered sixteen.

The government was not robbed of all its Greys. Apart from Sir George, who stayed on *ex cabinet*, Lord Grey's brother-in-law Sir Francis Baring, and Henry Labouchere, Baring's brother-in-law, were added to the cabinet. Indeed Stanley worried that there would be a 'little family knot' of Grey connections to dominate.[51] Labouchere, promoted from a junior post at the colonies to President of the Board of Trade, was middle class by origin and Whig by marriage. His appointment set the tone of his fellow entrants. Like Baring, Macaulay, Clarendon and Grey, he was comparatively young. Like Baring and Macaulay, his interests were less aristocratic and landed than financial. He was a man of the Commons who complained to the Duke of Argyll, whose forebears died at Stuart hands, of the 'narrowness' of the old Whigs.[52] Howick exaggerated when he termed membership in a cabinet of fifteen, of whom eight were in the Commons, as less than a distinction,[53] for Melbourne's was a highly aristocratic government. But he had a point, and it was perhaps for this reason that the general shuffle inspired its authors with little confidence. Baring's unwillingness to accept the Exchequer until persuaded by his father to do so[54] was indicative of the lack of enthusiasm which characterised the changes. Melbourne had hoped to fill the vacancy created by Spring Rice's retirement to the Lords with Poulett Thomson, but Thomson would not have it. There seemed, in his view, little point in trying to balance a steadily worsening budget in face of Conservative opposition. He favoured, moreover, the Canadian Governor-Generalship, a post which both Abercromby and Duncannon had rejected, and which he would himself until promised a future peerage.

Few Whigs thought much of their prospects. Holland doubted that Russell could guide both the Colonial Office and the Commons, and thought that the government was fast assuming the 'fatal' character of mediocrity and narrowness; its want of energy, boldness and decision made him 'tremble' for its fate. Ellice too noted a lack of vigour and the need of a 'better lookout for rocks and quicksands'. In Stanley's view, the 'chopping and changing' would at best 'leave us where we are' and 'probably leave us in a much worse position.'[55] But their pessimism was as nothing compared to that of their two leaders. Russell thought the loss of Howick and Wood a great blow to the government's chances of conciliating Radicals and Tories in the House of Commons. He complained of the 'many *dumb dogs*' around him and regarded as hopeless any possibility of making it through the next session without the Radicals forcing a dissolution. 'I am sorry for it', he told Melbourne, 'but it is better than making bargains with Mr. Harvey.'[56] It is little wonder that Melbourne talked in terms of being 'obliged' to meet parliament. He doubted that his government could stand up to the Radicals with impunity, yet believed that to do so was more than ever necessary. 'We are like men sitting upon a barrel of gunpowder with a lighted candle stuck in it.'[57] The government's position, characterised in June by the now departed Thomson as one with 'so many . . . rocks on which we shall split',[58] pointed to nothing but trouble for the Whigs.

The first few months of the new session confirmed the suspicions of many that Whiggery was a spent force. The ultra Tories among the Conservatives were still smarting from their failure to take office at the time of the bedchamber incident; having come tantalisingly close to office, they hankered after every opportunity to vent their frustrations by partisan sorties against the government. A number of early opportunities to do so occurred on issues that found support, for one reason or another, from several of the ministry's usual supporters. The government, as a result, suffered a number of embarrassing defeats. The allowance to be granted to Prince Albert provided the first occasion. Melbourne had already earned opposition jibes at the omission of the Prince's religion from the formal declaration of marriage which the Queen had him draft. When parliament met, Wellington continued the Tory attack by supporting the royal Dukes of Cambridge, Sussex and Cumberland, who jealously opposed their loss of precedence, in Albert's naturalisation bill, to this 'paper Royal Highness'. In the Commons, the Prince's allowance provided the focus for Conservative opposition. Although Melbourne was lukewarm all along to a German prince, and Russell thought the cabinet's proposed £50,000 allowance excessive,[59] it was agreed that in deference to the Queen's feelings and to past practice, less than what had been given to Queen Anne's Consort could not be offered to Victoria's. The decision was greeted by a storm of abuse. Peel was sufficiently bad natured to exact revenge for his treatment by the

Queen the previous May; in the words of his biographer, he took a 'malicious pleasure' in demonstrating hostility to the Queen.[60] When the Conservative member for Lincoln, Colonel Sibthorp, proposed that the allowance be reduced to £30,000, Peel found support from enough Radicals and Liberals to defeat the government's proposal by 104 votes. Victoria could conclude only that had the 'odius' George Cambridge been her choice, the full amount would have been granted,[61] but it is likely that Albert's foreign blood was not entirely to blame. Russell angrily denounced the opposition's disloyalty, and it is not too difficult to suggest that partisanship was behind the parsimony.

The government's vulnerability to a combination of interests was again made evident in February when the Conservative financial gadfly, John Herries, moved for the production of papers concerning a number of budgetary matters. Mounting deficits, an obvious source of concern to ministers,[62] rendered widespread parliamentary support on a less important question of papers doubtful; a number of Radicals defected to Herries' side on the question, with the result that the government sustained a loss by ten votes.[63] Thus, within a fortnight of the defeat on the Prince's allowance, further embarrassment could not be avoided. Before the month was out, the Conservative Henry Liddell's opposition to a pension for Sir John Newport, comptroller general of the exchequer, and gift of his sinecure to Spring Rice, triggered yet another defeat. This particular setback had less to do with Rice's appointment than with the growing imbroglio over Melbourne's insistence that appointments to Albert's new household should be Whigs who were non-partisan. Rice was clearly partisan. Although his new post was not to be in the household, his appointment, and Newport's pension, came up just as Melbourne proposed that Anson, the Prime Minister's private secretary, serve the Prince as well. Radicals joined the Conservatives and the press in condemnation. Anson resigned from Melbourne's staff, but Liddell was able to sustain the momentum of discontent to have Newport's pension of £1000 defeated by 28 votes.[64] Perhaps the most irritating defeat occurred on a bill brought on by Lord Stanley to reform the system of voter registration in Ireland. Fictitious registrations resulting from the inadequacies in the 1832 Irish Reform Act had swelled the lists of Catholic supporters of the Whigs and Liberals. By calling for annual registration to replace an unusually lax octennial system, whereby electors had been able to amass several registration certificates with impunity, Stanley was clearly hoping to restrict the Whig franchise in favour of the Conservative.[65] There was, to be sure, wide agreement that the corrupt Irish registration system was badly in need of reform, and put on a footing more firmly comparable to the English system. O'Connell had called for a change in 1835, and in that year and the following, abortive attempts to pass an Irish registration bill included provision for annual registration and an end to the certificates. But by the Spring of 1840, the Whigs were forced to defend the abuses of the old system. Stanley's bill was a partisan piece obviously designed to strengthen the Conservative party in Ireland at the expense of the Whigs, a result which would have eliminated the government's majority in the Commons. O'Connell had already in 1839 warned the moderate Irish MP W. S. O'Brien against a potentially fatal registration reform; the ministry's unsuccessful registration bill the previous year had been accompanied by arguments against annual registration. If justice to Ireland required Whigs in office, a claim somewhat muted by the death of Thomas Drummond during the progress of Stanley's bill, the Whigs' opposition to the measure could be regarded as a continuation of the cause of civil and religious liberty.[66] But to most observers, their conduct was a contumely attempt to hold onto power. Charles Wood told Lady Holland, who had earlier quipped that, 'we have nothing to rely on but the Queen and Paddy', that 'it looks as if the great O. drove them to it'.[67] Wood's comment expressed Grey's discontent with Melbourne and Russell's leadership, but there is little doubt that the Whigs were put in an uncomfortable position in opposing a measure which they had to a great degree more than once proposed. They offered no opposition to its introduction, and suffered defeat on nine of ten divisions, including second reading on 26 March. The Whigs were hopelessly on the defensive. Graham added to the assault with a forceful attack on the government's waging of war in China, and though the Whigs were able to manage a ministerial majority of nine votes in a well-attended house, it took all the oratorical skills which Macaulay and Palmerston could muster to avert further troublesome defeat. Grey thought that no ministry in the past would have continued under such circumstances of weakness and discredit 'which to me would be intolerable'.[68] Melbourne himself told Hobhouse that 'the odds are ten to one we shall not be in office next year.'[69]

Grey's discontent and Melbourne's despair are insufficient for the purpose of providing an accurate picture of the Whigs' parliamentary position in the Spring of 1840. Their position in fact was much stronger than the division losses would suggest. Six bye-election victories since September 1839 had augmented the government's position on any trial of strength to the point where it was in a virtually unassailable position on any matter where its existence was in question. In the wake of the troublesome 1839 episodes, broad ideological and tactical disputes among the Whigs and their more Radical supporters were given up in recognition of the Conservatives' apparent wish to govern. If the Whigs had made moderate concessions to their Radical supporters after the bedchamber, it was clear that they were unprepared to do more. Only a few Radicals, moreover, were to press for further concession. The result of this accommodation was a strength and unity such as had scarcely existed for three or four years. Whig strength had been evident from the outset of the new session when Peel, misled by Bonham and overzealous Conservatives, allowed a motion of confidence in the belief that the opposition would overturn the ministry. But unlike the Conservatives, who had difficulty in whipping up enough support from a surprisingly lukewarm backbench, the government was able to count on the attendance and support of all those whom Bonham had classified as doubtful ministerialists or Radicals likely to support the Conservatives.[70] The result was a majority for the Whigs of 21 on 21 January, a far cry from Bonham's prediction of a Conservative victory of 26. Peel was from that point restrained and the government safe. 'The prospects of Ministers brighten every minute' wrote one Whig to Lord Granville.[71] Stanley's registration bill could scarcely be considered as a damaging defeat. Although most Whigs agreed with much of the bill, there was little expectation that it would pass through both houses. When the Canada bill came up, the first matter of any political significance, the government were in a majority. Stanley in fact let his own Irish measure lapse in recognition that the government was beyond a successful assault.[72]

The Whigs were increasingly aided by the confusion and uncertainty on the Conservative benches, which made it far from obvious that Peel could, or would, take over. Greville described the scene on the eve of the new year as one in which parties were violent and nobody saw their way clearly before them. The government had 'not at all a bad case to bring before the country'; it had 'a much more respectable appearance than it has heretofore' had, containing as it did 'men of character, of experience, and of great acquirements . . . very united, agreed in general principles . . . as Conservative a Cabinet as possible'. The Conservatives, on the other hand, had too many members 'full of bitter animosity and an impatience for party victory . . . revenge and triumph'. To allow the government to remain in office, he thought, was 'the best thing that could happen in the present situation of the country.'[73] Greville was no Whig partisan, and because his views were not usually formed without the benefit of much gossip and advice, his opinion was presumably one that had some currency. There was little doubt that cloudy as the Whigs' future was, the bedchamber and its aftermath had caused much disruption among the Conservatives. When Peel took the sense of his party during the recess prior to the 1840 session, he had found a party that lacked a sense of common purpose. Wellington and Stanley doubted that the government should be turned out; Graham and Goulburn questioned if the conservative party could hold together much longer without a direct attack on the government.[74] It was above all this fear of dissolving his party that prompted Peel to take Graham's advice to attack. It was undoubtedly to his advantage that the confidence motion had failed, for no party that could talk in terms of dissolving unless a particular parliamentary procedure were followed could have much hope of governing. There was no coherent set of principles to overcome wrangling over tactics. It was largely in recognition of this lack of harmony that Stanley moved his Irish registration bill. By raising the one issue that would cause little discomfort, and by avoiding discussion of difficult issues on which there was no agreement, Stanley hoped to avoid splitting his adopted party. Thus, if the Whigs were not certain how they might retain office, the Conservatives were not certain how, or indeed whether, they should turn them out. An assessment of the Whigs' final two terms of office which stresses the inevitability of their collapse in the face of a coherent Conservatism is one which fails to observe the strain and uncertainty in Peel's own mind and party.

Peel's failure to gain a majority on the confidence motion made it 'all along evident', thought Greville, 'that the Government would not be turned out [and] that the leader of the Opposition did not want to turn them out.'[75] The result was a continuation, however phrenetic, of the mutual spirit of concession and compromise which had characterised Whig–Conservative relationships previously. In Greville's opinion, such a spirit was a 'counterbalancing good' to the 'evils and disadvantages incident to a weak Government'; with neither party strong enough to have it their own way, each was conscious that the other had a fair right to require some sacrifice. Certainly it was clear that Peel had little desire to push the Whigs from office before the paramount issues of the session were settled. On Irish matters in particular there were significant differences within his own party. Peel's own inclination was to clear the Irish hurdle. There was also a tactical imperative, for as Graham had advised as early as 1837, the opposition had every interest in an acceptable compromise solution; 'this Irish Municipal question constitutes after all, the principle difficulty which a Conservative Government, once formed, must overcome'.[76] The Whigs were aware of the problems within the Conservative party. Stanley told Ellice before the session had opened that the 'no Popery' people were a source of greater trouble to Peel than to the government; Russell was 'very glad not to be in Peel's shoes', likely as the Conservative leader was to 'displease half his party or three-fourths of his supporters in the country'.[77] There could be little doubt that the Whigs were just as eager for compromise solutions to long-standing problems. Peel held out against his ultra Tories on the Canada bill, but the Whigs were not prepared to scuttle the Irish corporation measure when those same ultras amended out of all recognition the bill which passed the lower house. O'Connell's revival of the Repeal Association in the spring made a defence of the original measure unattractive; the session had been as difficult as lengthy, and the time had come to get on with the business. When Lyndhurst told Duncannon by letter that the ultra Tories could not possibly agree to anything other than their version of a corporation bill, Melbourne rightly supposed that Russell would not insist on improvements.[78] Continual defeats on Stanley's registration bill had convinced Lord John that the Commons could not be depended upon for firm support on Irish motions. His wish was to get through the session without a decision of any vital question going against Ministers;[79] if Peel was unprepared to stand up to Lyndhurst, the Whigs were no longer willing to wait for a better day. Their conduct was a far cry from that of 1835, when a parliamentary majority did much for the government's confidence. In June 1840, when the government lost by four votes a division on one of the clauses in Stanley's Irish registration bill, Russell whispered to Hobhouse that it was 'almost impossible' to go on with so slight a majority: Robert Gordon, a government placeman, had been caught sleeping in the Speaker's room; two other government supporters had been shut out; three had taken ill. Lord John was able to inform the Queen that it was 'probable' the ministry would make it through the session, but he warned her that the House could not be 'depended upon for a firm support of any Administration.'[80] Yet the problem was not only one of discipline or desertion, and there is some force to Professor Gash's view that 'it would be a mistake to lay the emphasis on the laxity and indiscipline of party life'.[81] The impression one gets is that parliamentary attendance was generally more rigorous than it had been ten years earlier. The question was one of numbers. The session of 1840 was got through, but though Parkes thought in August that the government should 'rough thro' another session 'unless ill luck in dead MPs and vacancy in risk seats' made the position worse, his caveat that 'political predictions are not very discrete' proved to be distressingly true.[82]

On the eve of what would be their final session in office, the Whigs were guardedly optimistic. A long and quarrelsome internal debate over eastern affairs, during which Holland, Palmerston and Russell all tendered resignations, ended surprisingly well. The dispute concerned Palmerston's support of the Turkish empire against the overthrow of Syria by Mehemet Ali, who in turn was supported by France. When Palmerston's insistence that Mehemet Ali, and France, back down, threatened war with the French, Holland's Whiggery prompted him to take up the French cause. An Anglo-French entente was the best means of preserving liberty; Russian influence in the eastern Mediterranean was preferable to an English–French war; a Muscovite was probably preferable to a Musselman as guardian of minimal standards of morality; the commercial and strategic concerns of the east were tiresome when pitted against the struggle for liberty in the west. The Palmerston–Holland quarrel ended only with Holland's death in October 1840. There was an element of tragic irony here; he closed out his life in the defence of his great passion for the French and liberty, and in doing so, in turn 'exhumed the ghost' of his Foxite origin.[83] Yet Palmerston's great triumph was not to be achieved without further acrimonious debate with Russell, who objected to Palmerston's reluctance to make overtures to the French, and complained of the Foreign Secretary's high-handed insistence that he alone should shape foreign policy. It took all of Melbourne's skills to settle the quarrel. In August 1840, he could 'neither eat nor sleep properly' from the pressure; Holland's death in October was the 'heaviest blow, both personally and politically' he had yet received.[84] Greville characterised him as having lost control over his cabinet, 'a picture of indecision, weakness and pusillanimity',[85] yet Philip Ziegler, whose recent biography generally holds to the same view, gives Melbourne uncharacteristically high marks for his skilful diplomacy and judicious forcefulness which averted a cabinet crisis. 'More sapient than Mr. Micawber', Melbourne in turn backed Palmerston, warned the French to back down, conciliated Russell and did all in his power to avert a government crisis by maintaining a balance of power within the cabinet. Palmerston settled his differences with Russell, and with this 'little cloud blown over', Melbourne was said to be 'like a boy escaped from school . . . at having got out of a scrape', confident 'that all difficulties are surmounted.'[86] A few days after parliament opened, Greville reported that 'everything promises a very easy session, and the Conservatives are confessedly reduced to look to the chapter of accidents for some event which may help them to turn out the Government and get hold of their places.'[87] Greville's ink was scarcely dry before the chapter began in the form of bye election losses. Defeat at Walsall and Canterbury on 2 and 3 February 'has made us tremble in our places', wrote one Whig.[88] The week following, Monmouthshire fell to the Conservatives without a contest. Together with the loss of Carlow the previous December, and losses at Nottingham and Sandwich shortly to come, the government's working majority was all but eliminated.

Walsall was significant in that the contest appears almost certainly to have prompted the second, and fatal, chapter of accidents, Russell's proposal to amend the corn laws. The contest was marked by the influence of the Anti-Corn Law League, whose decision to intervene in the cause of total repeal wreaked havoc on the liberal side. Despite the presence of Joseph Parkes, who arrived six weeks early to manage the campaign for the government cause, Spencer Lyttleton, the Earl of Spencer's nephew, fell victim to the pressure for repeal. When he refused to agree to more than an enquiry into the effects of the corn laws, the League opposed his return. A canvass showed that he could not win. Under pressure from Spencer and Lord Lyttleton, Hatherton, who had considerable influence in the borough, informed Parkes that Lyttleton must withdraw.[89] Although Hatherton, at Parkes' and Melbourne's urging, used his influence in support of J. B. Smith, the Leagues' candidate, the liberal side was split. To no one's surprise, the Tory Gladstone won. Hatherton's agent, a lime merchant dependent on the farmer's custom, had been lax in registering where Tories had been assiduous.[90] The wonder was that Smith did so well. He took more votes than any victor at Walsall had previously done, and would do until 1859, losing by only 27 votes. The League would claim that their efforts helped Smith; the Tories argued that registrations and anti-League feeling produced the Tory win. Whatever the cause, Smith's unexpectedly strong showing appears to have had a considerable impact on the Whigs' thinking. Once the *Morning Chronicle*, hitherto critical of the League's activities, was influenced by Parkes and C. P. Villiers to declare the corn laws a 'hustings' question,[91] Smith's narrow defeat made corn an attractive issue.

It is difficult to conclude other than that Russell's decision to tack a revision of the duties on foreign corn to Baring's budget proposal was a calculated political decision, designed to do the Whigs as much good among the electorate as possible. Although the Whigs' growing budget deficits were a problem, Baring's plan to reduce the duties on imports of foreign sugar and timber was expected to clear most of the deficit. Russell's concern was with the Whigs' weak position as much as with the unpopularity and inefficiency of the 1828 sliding scale. At the end of the 1840 session, he pressed Melbourne to consider seriously the state of the Corn Laws, not for the revenue, for which he had not much fear, but because the current regulation impeded commerce and 'breeds discontent'.[92] In his memo to the cabinet which argued for a lowering of the scales and a reduced tariff, he put forward the same case. His paper was put together quickly; he had not had the time to calculate the effect on revenues, 'supposing' an increase of £600,000 to £800,000.[93] The timing could not have been accidental. The Walsall and Canterbury elections, he had told Victoria, brought parties 'nearly to an equality';[94] it was a few days later, when East Surrey and Monmouthshire fell, that he hastily scribbled the corn law memorandum. Elections, whether called for by the Whigs or by Peel, could not be far off. As far as Peel entered

Whig thinking, it is doubtful that Russell expected Conservative support for the proposal. It is true that he proposed a revision of the sliding scale, rather than a moderate fixed duty, in order to meet the 'principle proclaimed' earlier by Peel and Graham,[95] and it could have been no secret that Peel would have preferred the question settled before taking office. But the circumstances militating against Peel in 1846 were already in evidence; no measure could have passed through the Lords without Peel's approval, but with his support the measure would have ruined his own chances of office. Russell must have known this; his reference to his colleagues, to Peel, and the maintenance of the scale, was more likely a means of making the proposal acceptable to those colleagues. There is also sufficient evidence to suggest that Russell knew of Peel's innermost conviction that the corn laws were in need of revision; by bringing the question into the open, a calculated decision that could not fail to increase its urgency, Peel would be forced to declare himself for or against, and in doing so, run foul of either his party and the electorate or of his principles.

Whatever Russell's motives in proposing the revised duties on corn, there can be no doubt that his colleagues' acceptance of the proposal was due to the understanding that the issue was one for the hustings. The decision was taken quickly. Lansdowne claimed that the alteration was the subject of less discussion than far less important questions; Russell intimated in the House that the Cabinet had decided by 11 March.[96] Other correspondence among ministers would suggest that Russell's dating of the agreement was probably early, that there were doubts until well into April. But the decision was taken when it was obvious that the Conservatives could not be counted on for any support, and that the proposal had no chance of passing through the Commons. Despite Peel's speech on 12 February giving general support to free trade notions, his party's opposition to the government's Irish registration bill and his inability to control his followers on the extension of the 1834 poor law bill made it clear that the opposition was preparing to mount a campaign to defeat the government. 'We all allowed', noted Hobhouse at the end of a cabinet meeting the week before Russell anounced his intentions in the House, that 'the corn law amendment . . . had no chance of passing.'[97] In taking the decision to support Russell's proposal, the Whigs were not much convinced that the principles of agricultural protection were thereby violated. They generally held to the view that a moderate fixed duty, which was substituted for the first proposal of a revised sliding scale, would maintain protection for agriculture.[98] The consideration was political. Would a proposal to alter the corn laws be advisable, given the strains likely to be placed upon aristocratic government by this encouragement of Radical movements out of doors? Was there any reason to think that Melbourne's earlier concern for the 'very severe struggle' necessary to carry such a measure was now less urgent? The answer, apparently, was yes. Although Russell had in 1839 argued against any change in the government's policy rather than to 'take advantage of the clamour',[99] he was now persuaded to do so. Melbourne himself agreed to support revision if discussion revealed there to be 'such an increased disposition towards it as is supposed to exist'.[100]

The growing alienation between the Chartists and the more middle class League undoubtedly had much to do with the increasing respectability of the question. Walsall did not suggest that the issue was potentially revolutionary. The belief that Peel was to some extent amenable to the free-traders' arguments was evidence as well that advocacy of a revision of the tariffs would not be dangerous. Finally, there was the electorate. If stout maintenance of an anti-movement posture during the six years of Melbourne government did little to prevent the conservatively natured electorate from supporting the Conservative party, it would be necessary to beat Peel to the Tamworth punch by appealing to the moderate middle classes. To be sure, there was an element of duplicity in this position. To believe that tampering with the duties would not significantly weaken agricultural protection, but would win the votes of a middle class electorate which wanted to see an end to that protection, was to be less than genuine. But it is clear that an attempt was being made. While it appeared that free trade principles would do the Whigs little good in the counties and smaller boroughs, fears for the Church and discontent with the government's Irish policies had long left Whigs with little hope in these constituencies. A new programme might do the party some good in the larger boroughs. It would force Peel to take a position which would hurt either himself with his party or his party with the people. 'The discussions *must* injure them', wrote Sydenham from Canada. To Macaulay, the undertaking was clear. 'All the chances of our party depend on [it] . . . We shall play double or quits.'[101]

There had been some hope that Baring's reduction of the sugar and timber duties might pass,[102] but Russell's announcement on 30 April that the government would propose a moderate fixed duty on corn ensured defeat. Peel's strategy was to avoid corn by attacking sugar; Lord Sandon's motion condemning the proposed lowering of the sugar duties would bring the anti-slavery and colonial sugar forces together.[103] After eight nights of debate, the government lost on Sandon's motion by 317 to 281, when fifteen of its supporters voted with Sandon and eighteen others stayed away.[104] The game was over. Defeat on the Conservatives' non confidence motion was still to come, but this piece of partisan play-acting was nothing more than Peel's continued strategy of avoiding a damaging debate on corn. The government had in fact decided to dissolve the day after the loss on Sandon's sugar motion. Ministers had for a fortnight expected defeat;[105] it remained only to choose between turning the government over to Peel or appealing immediately to the country.

Dissolution did not at first appear attractive. It was expected that the budget would work to the Tories' advantage in the counties and agricultural boroughs, but the Whigs were not counting on the unexpected turn of events at the Nottingham bye election of 28 April, where the Conservative Walters took the seat on an anti-poor law campaign that won support from the Chartists. What hope for the boroughs that Walsall had given, Nottingham appeared to take away. When the cabinet first met on May 8 to decide on dissolution or resignation, only Palmerston, Hobhouse and Cottenham favoured elections.[106] Melbourne told Anson – who had been sent round by Prince Albert to inform the Prime Minister that he must not violate the Queen's constitutional position by seeing her on any subject – that Nottingham inclined him towards resignation; he and Russell both informed the Queen that the Conservative use of the anti-poor law cry would carry too much weight in elections to think of dissolution.[107] But the tide was turned to dissolution once Russell announced his fixed duty to the House. The government's followers had reacted with dismay at indications that the Ministry might resign without an appeal to the country on the basis of free trade. Hatherton noted that reticence towards elections was a concern 'more with Whig parents than with Whig sons, & that the Purse may have entered with the considerations of the former.'[108] Reports of a favourable response to the budget measures were quickly generated from all parts of the country.[109] Although Parkes advised that the corn laws would not greatly affect the final tally, there was growing opinion that the government could not disappoint its followers, who were buoyed for a contest, by giving up the fight at the first opposition in the House. Palmerston was able to make great use of these reports with his colleagues, and as one minister after another swung round to dissolution, Russell was finally persuaded. Perhaps his reaction to Nottingham was overly hasty. The industrial counties were reported to favour a reduction of the corn duties; his announcement of a fixed duty had quietened the Chartists. Not least in his consideration was his cat and mouse game with Peel, whose Huskissonian principles, he noted, were opposed by Buckingham and those whom Russell would shortly term the 'bumpkins' of his party.[110] It was necessary that the country clearly understand the difference between the Whigs and the opposition, even though it was likely to opt for the latter. Melbourne was the last to agree. To no avail, Parkes had tried to persuade him that a Peel dissolution would be the inevitable consequence of resignation; 'our friends' would not fight for an opposition as they would for the Court and a Whig Minister. A contest out of doors between the aristocracy and the masses would produce such a rout in the favour of the former that Monarchy and 'gradual descent of popular politics' would be swept aside by demands for 'premature' democracy.[111] Melbourne was not one to be influenced by hyperbole. Torn between his conviction that elections would return a government 'smack against' the crown, and Victoria's plea not to desert her 'to those hated Tories',[112] he hesitated. Despite Russell's argument that the Queen should have 'the shield of responsible advisers', he sat fast until Lord John told him on the morning following the sugar defeat that he could no longer postpone a decision; 'no one could bear a further suspense'.[113] The party came first in Melbourne's opinion, but he was not sure that the elections it clamoured for would redound to its credit. Unconvinced, he gave way. Duncannon had the final word: 'If the country after crying out for measures of this description will not support us in them', he wrote to Melbourne, 'it is their own fault at least, and we shall have done our duty.'[114]

11

The Business of Government, 1835–41

the period of the Melbourne Government had witnessed the enactment of many important laws, useful in their general character and well suited to the condition of the public mind.

Gladstone, 1855[1]

the measures of the Melbourne Government were generally moderate, well-matured and statesmanlike schemes.

Disraeli, 1851[2]

That Gladstone would later characterise Melbourne's government as 'useful' and 'well suited to the condition of the public mind' is not altogether surprising, for he, after all, had taken part in the councils of the Conservative party which had, under Peel, lent its support to any measure which was ultimately passed. That the author of the *Vindication of the English Constitution*, which had castigated the Whigs as 'a small body of persons hostile to the nation',[3] would later describe Melbourne's measures as 'well-matured and statesmanlike', might well seem remarkable. Disraeli, to be sure, was never particularly known for consistency. Yet, the difficulty in characterising precisely the main features of Melbourne's government was not unique to him, and can be seen in recent attempts to define the essence of Melbournian Whiggery. One historian has written of the construction of 'a real Liberal party' behind a 'more radical policy'.[4] Another has described the Whigs under Melbourne as a 'party of conservatism' responsible for 'Liberalism in Decline'.[5] There can be little doubt that a government which relied on Radical support and Conservative forbearance was not one which could easily effect a well defined public *persona*. The Whigs, of course, understood this problem and approached the resultant electoral disappointments with a good measure of stoicism. At the same time, Melbourne's governments were in the unenviable position of following Grey's governments, which luxuriated in a well-defined programme of reform and, from 1831, in healthy parliamentary majorities. If Grey's *via media* was one of political and constitutional theory, Melbourne was forced to tread an additional careful path through the minefield of parliamentary and electoral insecurity.

For all of his difficulties, Melbourne's legislative record was substantial, rivalling that of all but a few nineteenth-century governments. His legislative programme was a legacy of Grey's; what was begun by the earlier Whig ministries was completed by the later. And in dealing with the essential reforms of Church and State, Melbourne's Whigs neither added to the list of measures begun under Grey's Leadership nor deviated from the guiding principles of moderate and timely reforms that would safeguard the institutions of the nation. Further constitutional reforms would not be countenanced; the traditional landed elites could not be emasculated. This need to steer a safe course between Radical and Tory reaction can be seen in the reform of the municipal corporations, the passage of which bore all the hallmarks of the Whigs' later legislation. In the first place, the groundwork had been laid by Grey's government with the non-compulsory elective principle in Hobhouses's vestry act of 1831, and by the establishment of a Select Committee and ultimately of a Royal Commission in July 1833 to investigate the corporations.[6] Secondly, and as described in Chapter 8, the measure was a compromise between the Radical goals of Parkes and the Commissioners, and the attenuated version as handed down by the Lords. Through compromise and negotiation, a reform was carried which brought gradual change to a system which, according to its historian, continued to represent and cater for 'men of property and not simply men'.[7] The most striking feature of local government reform, wrote another, was 'how much of the old order had survived'.[8] Thirdly, Peel's support allowed this reform to be carried against the views of the ultra supporters of both parties. Fourthly, as later described in this Chapter, the bill was a reform which touched the issue of Church and State by effectively providing Dissenters an increased role in goverance and representation. And finally, the measure did not have Melbourne's wholehearted support. Just as he allowed an education measure when he did 'not know why there is all this fuss about Education. None of the Paget family can read or write and they do very well', so too did he permit corporation legislation despite his admission that 'a man's being a Trader' was 'an objection to his becoming a Magistrate'.[9] But Melbourne was far from indolent. He was committed to holding his government together. He was prepared to allow Russell a prime role in legislative affairs. Above all, he was convinced that the legislative programme inherited from Grey was in need of protection from both Radicals and ultra Tories, and necessary for the maintenance of order and the supremacy of property. The middle road of moderate reform could ill afford to founder on the shoals of his own personal prejudices. The result was a statesmanlike, if not completely successful, record of achievement.

THE CHURCH

If the Church of England rested uncomfortably with a Whig government led by Grey, its unease was heightened considerably with Melbourne at the helm. Two days before Peel resigned office in April 1835, a friend of the Reverend John Henry Newman in Oxford wrote to say that 'everything, humanly speaking, seems darkening round the church'.[10] High Churchmen like Newman had particular cause to worry, for if Peel's government had shown itself prepared to have the state interfere in the internal affairs of the Church, would it not be likely that the Establishment could look forward to more interference, if not spoliation, at the hands of Peel's successor? The Archbishop of Canterbury and the Church leaders were scarcely more sanguine. Howley had agreed to an Ecclesiastical Duties and Revenues Commission in January 1835 because Peel and Bishop Blomfield of London, its promotors, could be counted on to bring about some much-needed reforms in the Church in a friendly, safe manner. If the Church were to be reformed, better at the hands of its friends than its enemies. Melbourne was feared not for his own views, which typically were not held as passionately as were his colleagues' and were known not to be, as much as for his suspected indifference. Unlike Grey, who was known to have struggled hard in defence of Stanley's more moderate plans for reform, Melbourne seemed to have an unending capacity for shuffling and trimming. 'Church in danger' was considered to have real meaning under a government which had a Russell as leader in the Commons and a parliamentary majority dependent upon appropriation, Radicals, Dissenters and O'Connellites. It was not so much that Whigs were thought to want the destruction of the Church; they were regarded as particularly dangerous under Melbourne and Russell because they were willing, where Grey had not been, to put themselves in a position where they were less likely to be able to withstand attacks on the Church from those who did favour destruction. The Church was particularly concerned that the new government would propose radical change which, when confronted with inevitable opposition, would provoke damaging popular hostility to the Church. In fact, the Church had little to fear in this regard, for the Whigs had been as alarmed as Howley and Blomfield at the public outrage over the Bishops' opposition to the Reform Bill in October 1831; they were not prepared for another such episode. At a meeting with Howley shortly after returning to office, Melbourne assured the Primate that no bill would be brought forward without the prior approval of the Bishops. For his part, Howley agreed that the government was honour bound to attempt to appropriate surplus Irish revenues, and to abolish Church rates in England.[11] Knowing that the Lords would reject the first, and agree to the second only upon terms satisfactory to the Church, Howley was persuaded that Melbourne's government would not be much worse than Peel's. He could continue to sit on the Ecclesiastical Commission.

True to Whig form, Melbourne's governments moved quickly to the middle ground. They took positions based upon their Whiggish principles of civil and religious liberty, or on the need to hold the coalition of parliamentary supporters together. And they trimmed. In the end, nothing of substance was done which Peel could not have attempted. It is true that Peel would not have appointed Dr Hampden to the Regius professorship of divinity at Oxford, as Melbourne did, but it is likely that the outcry following that appointment was prompted as much, or more, by fear for the doctrine of the Oxford Puseyites as it was the Church's unhappiness at another Whig appointee. Even so, Melbourne learned from the appointment. He had earlier refused to appoint the Whig Dr. Arnold of Rugby to a bishopric because of Arnold's supposed unorthodoxy which would offend high Churchmen; his adviser, Archbishop Whately of Dublin, had failed to warn him now that Hampden was suspected of unorthodoxy. Having more bishoprics to give, he had told Mulgrave, would not dispose the clergy more favourably to the government, for the influence of patronage, being overrated, gains only a 'few hangers on and scamps, who are not worth having.'[12] The row over Hampden's appointment was all the proof he needed that partisan Whig churchmen offered doubtful, because passionate, advice. 'Cool and indifferent religion', whatever its particulars, was more to his liking. Dissenters, being overly zealous, he told Victoria a few years later, made good gardeners at his home in Hertfordshire – 'they don't go to races, they don't hunt and they don't engage in any expensive amusements'.[13] If the Church, through too much religious enthusiasm, was to render the advantages of ecclesiastical patronage nugatory, he saw no point to a fight. 'I am most anxious', he wrote to Howley a few years later, 'not to advance any man, whose doctrines are not in union with those of the established church, or even whose promotion would be disagreeable to the great body of the clergy.'[14] Thus the principles of allowing the Church to undertake its own reform underlay the Whigs' Church policy for the remainder of the decade. The reconstituted Commission of April 1835 had ministerial lay members rather than Conservative, but, as Professor Chadwick observed, though they had the 'vice' of being Whigs, they had the 'virtue' of rarely attending meetings; unlike Peel, 'they were not interested and left the bishops to go their way.'[15] Thus, although it has been commonplace to regard the Commission as Peel's work, what in fact was carried out under its auspices was done by the Church or, more specifically, the higher prelates of the Church. By the spring of 1836, when the first three reports of the Commissioners had been issued, the Primate was able to conclude that, though 'it was in vain to talk of security in these times . . . the Church Establishment would be placed in a condition to resist the attacks of its enemies'.[16]

It was by now with little irony that the Whigs saw conservative reform measures vilified by those who considered a particular reform either too much, or too little. The Established Church bill introduced in July 1836 is a case in point. Based entirely upon the report of the Commissioners, the bill called for the augmentation of incomes of smaller bishoprics by reducing those of the largest, for the creation of seven new archdeaconries, two new bishoprics and the suppression of two bishoprics, and most importantly, for the establishment of a permanent Ecclesiastical Commission with executive powers whose recommendations would be carried out by King in Council. Parliament would be informed of the Commission's activities in annual reports.[17] Reaction to these details showed forcefully the difficulties of a government trying to placate both Church and Dissenters. While high Churchmen and ultra Tories regarded a permanent commission as an unwarranted intrusion of the State into Church affairs – an Elizabethan Court of High Commission – Radicals and Dissenters thought that the Commission, through its episcopally guided executive and orders-in-Council, had been given the power which parliament alone should possess. Leaving aside the high Church reaction, which was in reality an attack on Howley and Blomfield, there is little doubt that the measure was moderate, as well as the intention of both the Commissioners and government. But though the bill passed easily through both Houses, the government tried to allay the fears of both sets of objectors by postponing the other two measures proposed by the Commission, a pluralities and residence bill and an ecclesiastical duties and revenues bill, until passions had cooled.[18]

During the same session, the Whigs managed to clear away the Church tithes and Dissenters' grievance problems held over from 1834. Aided by Peel, who supported the measures and had proposed similar legislation during his short-lived ministry, the government's proposals passed with little difficulty. The tithe commutation bill had been drawn up by a committee of Russell, Lansdowne, Duncannon, Howick and Poulett Thomson, the latter almost certainly owing his involvement to the view that the tithe measure was a financial, rather than ecclesiastical question.[19] By commuting tithe to a rent charge the equivalent of sixty to seventy five per cent of the old tithe, and by making the scheme compulsory should a single tithe payer in the parish desire commutation, the measure guaranteed payment without fuss to the tithe holders. Although Holland was convinced that the bill was too favourable to the Church, and for 'that bad reason' was allowed to pass without division through both Houses,[20] many of the owners of tithes were in fact lay landlords who had inherited tithe ownership from the sale of monastic households. Nevertheless, the bill was thought by the Whigs likely to 'quiet the alarm of the friends of the Church', and was agreed to by the cabinet with so little interest that, Howick concluded, several had either never read or never considered it.[21]

Dissenting claims on the government met with less sympathy. Whig discontent with what was viewed as an intractable and uncompromising set of Dissenting demands had established for some time the view that there was little to be gained from the relentless pursuit of measures as laid out by Dissenting organisations. Although the Whig party had faithfully supported Dissenters' causes and was indeed 'their natural home', it would not allow itself to be goaded into destroying the Established Church.[22] In 1834, Grey was incensed that the Dissenters' failure to accept moderate compromise, on legislative proposals designed to aid the nonconformist cause, was prompted by what he viewed as a raising of their sights on the Church itself. He told one Churchman that he had been 'humbugged'.[23] In that same year, Russell regarded Dissenting opposition to his proposed registration measure as petty, and the Whigs lost interest in satisfying the claims of 'those who are not to be satisfied'.[24] Dissenting failure to show gratitude for the government's attempts to ameliorate their claims prompted a breach that would never quite be mended. Put simply, Erastian paternalism could not easily brook nonconformist passion. But politics, if nothing else, made it certain that the Dissenters would get another hearing. Their influence in the Commons and, more importantly, in elections, coupled with Peel's Tamworth principles and subsequent support for their claims, left the Whigs with little option but to attempt a settlement. It was this overriding concern with the Dissenters' power in the state which particularly motivated the Whigs.

The Municipal Corporations Act had served to increase the Dissenters' importance in the eyes of the Whigs. The Act overcame the thorny problem of Dissenting-dominated corporations possessing the right to Church patronage; the Corporations would sell their Church patronage under the direction of the Ecclesiastical Duties and Revenues Commission, a provision which pacified much Church opposition to the bill and reduced possible tensions in the boroughs. Corporation reform was nevertheless the single most useful piece of legislation for the Dissenters. Large numbers of Unitarians, Congregationalists and Baptists were returned in the first elections under the Act in December 1835; non-conformists were prominent in several corporations.[25] In the attempt to preserve the corporations by reform, the Whigs had not proposed the bill with Dissenters specifically in mind. Just as the Reform Act was designed to bring a greater proportion of the nation within the pale of the constitution, and thereby to save it, corporation reform was proposed in order, 'to give the whole body of the people some interest in the government of their towns . . . in preservation of the public peace, and the protection and good

management of public property'. Otherwise, as Melbourne told
the Lords, the self-electing, oligarchical corporations had 'no
community of feeling with the public'.[26] There was nevertheless
little doubt that the communities he had in mind were to a large
extent Dissenting. John Wilkes, the Dissenters' leader in the
Commons, told Russell before the Whigs had returned to office in
1835 that pressure for reforms would be withheld until a corporation bill was passed,[27] so important was it to the Dissenting cause.
Melbourne, in conversation with a friend shortly after it passed,
noted that[28]

> You may not see all of the consequences of this tomorrow, but
> you have given by law a permanent power in all the centres of
> industry and intelligence to the Dissenters which they never
> had before, and which they never could have had otherwise.
> They are the classes who will really gain by the change, not the
> mob or the theorists; every year their strength will be more and
> more at elections and their influence in legislation.

In 1836, three noted measures of relief were passed. Although
granting a charter to the University of London was not all that
Dissenters wished for, there was little hope of more. The Lords
had rejected the notion of Dissenters' admission to Oxford and
Cambridge in 1834 and 1835, and Melbourne, not up to a hopeless
and 'imprudent' struggle, had strong doubts himself about allowing Dissenters into the two ancient universities.[29] A marriage bill
was based on the measure put forward by Althorp in 1834 and Peel
in 1835. Marriages in chapels would be deemed legal if the civil
registrar was present and, almost unnoticed, simple civil marriage
was legalised. Finally, civil registration of births, marriages and
deaths was developed. These measures were compromises, and
represented what only the more moderate Nonconformists and,
more importantly, Russell and Peel could accept. The government
had refused to allow the University of London a denominational
character, thereby safeguarding the rights of the Church to mono-
polise degrees at Oxford and Cambridge; the marriage bill was
modelled to a large extent on Peel's 1835 proposal. The Dissenters,
as a result, were far from satisfied, and turned their attention to
what they viewed as the more important question of Church rates.
On this question the Whigs would have liked to effect a measure
of reform, but were uncertain how to bring the issue to a

satisfactory conclusion. There was really little hope that a reform of rates could be acquiesced in by all parties. The issue was of such importance to both the Church and its critics that compromise was unlikely. To the Church, rates concerned the very question of the Establishment itself; was the Church to be a voluntary body, responsible for its own upkeep, or was it a national Church which was to be supported by the people as a whole? Dissenters and Radicals, on the other hand, put the case that the Church should look after its own costs and that it was wrong for non-Anglicans to pay for a Church to which they did not belong. Despite the fact that the Church had allowed cess in Ireland to cease in 1833, it would not agree to a similar abolition in England. Rates became the focal point for dispute in England as appropriation had become in Ireland. The Whigs' position was by 1835 an odd one: the Lords would not allow appropriation, and would agree to the abolition of rate only under circumstances which the Dissenters would not accept, namely, its replacement by another form of state support.

At the conclusion of the unsuccessful attempt to satisfy the Dissenters in 1834, Russell had told Melbourne that Whigs could never agree with the Dissenters' dislike of a national land tax as a substitute for rates; the government, he added, would 'resist the separation of Church and state' which the Dissenters' opposition to Althorp's 1834 bill had implied, 'and all propositions having that end in view'.[30] When Archbishop Howley met with Melbourne in April, it was his understanding that any attempt to abolish the rate would be accompanied by a tax such as Althorp had proposed. This too was the government's view. As soon as the Whigs returned to office, they decided not to propose a rate bill. Their greatly reduced majority in the Commons rendered passage of Althorp's plan unlikely, but Russell's view, that 'it is the duty of the State to see that the Churches of the Establishment are left in proper and decent repair',[31] made it difficult to arrive at any conclusion satisfactory to the Dissenters' parliamentary supporters. A solution, moreover, would be costly, for as was the case with tithe, rates were notoriously unpaid; a land tax would have to make up what Landsdowne estimated to be a shortfall of at least £700,000, an amount far greater than what Althorp had anticipated.[32] The government was clearly in a quandary. There was some hope that Dissenters might agree to a land tax if Church reforms could be shown to have reduced the Church's surplus and

ability to maintain its fabric, but this line of speculation, unfortunately, required more time than was desirable in the formulation
of policy.[33]

When the Whigs finally took the question up, early in 1837, they
did so for political reasons. The Dissenters were as alarmed that
Church reform would wipe out a surplus as the Whigs were
hopeful, and continued to press for an abolition bill. But though
Russell suggested in February 1836 that the government's intention was to settle the rates question,[34] neither he nor his colleagues
knew how to do so, and postponed consideration of the issue.
When a bill was finally brought forward in 1837, it was not so
much the increased demands of the Dissenting Deputies and the
Church Rates Abolition Society which prompted a measure,[35] for
the Whigs were well aware of their concern. The government's
concern was for its own precarious parliamentary position. The
cabinet's determination to stand up to the Radicals' demands for
further constitutional reforms gave ministers little alternative but
to keep Dissenting support, by offering a rates abolition bill
without a compensating national tax. With very little planning –
Melbourne told Russell that he had 'never looked much into the
subject before'[36] – a plan was put together which called for a
special commission to take over Church leases; by charging a
higher, more realistic rent for Church lands, £50,000 would be
raised for the maintenance of the fabric of the Church. The
Establishment would get no support from the State. There was no
question of the bill passing. It was a foregone conclusion that the
Lords would never allow it. There was equally little expectation of
its passing through the Commons. In addition to the Tories and
Church, the government anticipated opposition from the holders
of Church leases and from many Whigs.[37] Melbourne's note to
Ellice explained the tightrope which his government found itself
treading.[38]

> The Dissenters in my opinion will overthrow the Ministry; they
> force us upon a measure which . . . will upset us. We can only
> get the money out of the Church leases, and this will give the
> Church, who will . . . oppose it, so much and such strong allies
> . . . that it [parliamentary support] will be too small for us. We
> can hardly deal with it alone.

Introduced on 3 March, the bill prompted the anticipated outcry.

Tories denounced the plan as sacrilege and spoliation; Archbishop Howley, who regarded the absence of a compensatory tax as a violation of his agreement with Melbourne two years earlier, refused to continue with the Ecclesiastical Commission unless the bill was withdrawn.[39] But as soundings were taken, the government's prospects looked less daunting. 'Any majority will I think do', Melbourne told Russell on the day of the resolution, 'and the way will then be [clear] to put off the bill.' The resultant majority of 23 he considered 'capital'.[40] A second reduced majority of five for second reading on 24 May made little difference, for the cabinet had already decided not to go on with it.[41] By thus proposing, then dropping, what could not pass, the Whigs avoided the more hazardous course of not proposing a bill and facing defeat and elections with the Dissenting interests in the towns against them. The possibility of elections weighed heavily on ministers' minds, for with the Radicals in an unfriendly temper and with suspected difficulties over the Irish legislation planned for the session, the likelihood of defeat or resignation was widely discussed in government circles. Greville reported that a government 'underwhipper' dropped the truth of the real cause of bringing in the measure when he said that had the government proposed anything less, they should have all the Dissenters against them at the next election'.[42] Melbourne's note to Russell discussing the election returns later in August suggested that there was something to this theory. 'I quite agree that it was necessary to bring forward our church rate measure', he wrote. 'The defection of the Dissenters, which would have taken place if we had not, would have been as injurious to us as anything that had taken place.'[43] As the two leaders went over those election returns with a view to Church questions, and it seemed likely the government were safe in the new Commons, a rate plan was all but formally abolished.[44] 'I am quite tired of reforming the Church', wrote Melbourne, with perhaps more relief than resignation.[45] It would be thirty years before another government would try.

Within two years, a further quarrel with the Church arose over the education plan announced by Russell in February 1839. Although the proposed measures are generally regarded as Radically inspired, taken up at the instigation of Brougham, who was himself strongly influenced by the Radical Roebuck, it would be more correct to regard the plan as Whig inspired, entirely in keeping with their views and policies on education as developed over five or six years. There is evidence, moreover, to suggest that the proposals were designed to stop the Church from advancing its own education programme. By introducing their measures in 1839, the Whigs anticipated the anti-Church mood which would emasculate Graham's education proposals in 1843. Although the educationalists, led by Radicals and Dissenters, had applied continued pressure on the Whigs to establish a national system of state-aided education, there is little doubt that the government was persuaded to act in order to pre-empt the efforts of its Church and Conservative opponents to establish a national system on the principles of the Established Church. Gladstone was particularly active. A member of the 1834 Select Committee on Education, usually misnamed the 'Roebuck Committee',[46] Gladstone was easily able to persuade Blomfield, and Tories like Sandon and Ashley, that religious education was under threat from the Whigs.[47] Peel also became involved following his experience on the Select Committee set up in 1837 to investigate the education of the poor. That Committee, which found a need to extend the 1833 grant system to the larger towns, had received a proposal from one of its members to establish a Board or Office of Education. Although the motion was defeated in committee,[48] Peel was persuaded that Church vigilance was necessary. In April 1838, a delegation of Churchmen and Conservatives met with Archbishop Howley to discuss the Church view of the matter; in May, a Committee of Inquiry and Correspondence was set up by the Church's National Society to press for immediate anticipatory action. The Committee accordingly devised far-reaching proposals to establish a teacher seminary in each diocese, a central college in London to be linked to King's College, and regular visitations by Church inspectors. In August, the Committee issued its plan in the expectation that Church supporters would do all possible to see it through.[49]

Nothing was more likely to prick the Whig conscience than the attempt of the National Society to assert an exclusive claim to the education of the nation's children. The issue, in a sense, was not one of religion as much as it was of Church and State. The Whigs support for civil and religious liberty was tempered by support for an Establishment which could restrain the religious zeal and intemperance of the Roman Catholic and Dissenting recipients of such liberty. Russell had supported appropriation in the belief that priest-ridden teaching was the cause of the 'moral ignorance of the Irish population.[50] He reacted to the National Society's proposal in the belief that the equally unrestrained attitudes of the High Church were behind the plan. What appeared to be an unhealthy connection between the Established Church and the growing influence of Oxford catholicity prompted Russell to fear now for English education. The fact that some of the educational proponents, such as Ashley, were not supporters of High Church Oxford principles, would do little to temper his dread. If the obscure and medieval notions of those whom he would later chide in his Durham letter as 'the unworthy sons of the Church of England' were to take control of the Church and its educational affairs, the utility of the Establishment would be immediately cast in doubt.[51] Not only would the National Society neglect the educational needs of urban children, but where they did have schools, the 'mummeries of superstition', resulting from the church's 'assumption of sanctity as the special depository of truth', would negate what he believed to be the liberal tendency in education.[52]

In holding to the view that the Church's claim to educate the nation would advance little more than the cause of institutional bigotry, Russell paid scant attention to the actual and expressed views of the 'Young Gentlemen'. Although the National Society plan called for a national system encompassing both urban and rural lower middle classes, Whig Erastianism had little regard for the ecclesiastical paternalism as espoused by Gladstone and his followers. Gladstone might wish for a strong Church and hence for a Church-sponsored education system to remedy social ills, but Russell and the Whigs were never prepared to believe that Churchmen alone could be entrusted with so vital a responsibility. To the extent that Russell knew of Gladstone's and his fellow paternalists' social views, he gave them little credence. Dr James Kay, the secretary appointed shortly afterward to the new Committee of Privy Council on Education, had been instructed to lay the foundation of a system 'in which the young might be brought up in charity with each other, rather than in hostile camps'.[53] The reference to hostile camps is instructive, for it points to the Whigs' belief in the social utility of education, and the view that the usefulness of the establishment would be sharply reduced if it pursued a system by which intolerance and bigotry led to social conflict; even more harmful would be a lack of urban schools. If the regulations promulgated in 1833 had appeared in the spring of

1838 to allow for the gradual, civilising growth of education among the lower orders, the National Society's attempt to manipulate the system appeared by the end of the year to threaten social chaos, and to necessitate change in the system. In both his parliamentary speeches and his correspondence with Lansdowne, Russell made constant reference to the need for religious and moral instruction and for the acquisition of habits of industry among those children who were most susceptible to vice, crime, and jail.[54] If his government was prepared to reject the extreme, secular Prussian or American solutions of the Central Society of Education as a violation of 'the habits and feelings of the people of this country', it could not, at a time of growing Chartist disorder, give its adhesion to another extreme system, lately propounded, whereby the Church, and the Church alone, should conduct the education of the country. Not only would such a system be equally 'at variance with the general spirit of our laws, and with the existing feeling of society', but it would also 'leave untilled this great field of instruction and education . . . and leave that class which formed . . . the seed of our criminal population without the protecting shield which religious and moral culture would throw around them.'[55]

Russell was without doubt the central figure in the decision to act. As vice-president of the British and Foreign School Society, he was aware that the National Society had received the bulk of the schoolhouse grants established in 1833. He was concerned as well that the grant system was not providing adequately for schools in the urban industrial areas, a concern borne out by an 1838 select committee report.[56] At the time of the 1837 elections, he had told Brougham that the state should interfere to make education more general; he clearly had in mind that further state encouragement to local organisation was necessary. But the results of those elections had convinced him that Dissenting and Radical causes could be neither desirable nor useful. He told Brougham in the autumn of 1837 that, though education should be more general, he had 'no wish to hurry the matter'; nor did he think it would be of use to the government 'in a party view'. He shrank from supporting a proposal of Brougham's for locally elected boards not simply, as has been suggested, because Brougham advanced a low, radically inspired franchise, but because he doubted the education question could be kept free from party and religious dispute. Anything seen to be harmful to the Church would bring on a 'pitless storm'.[57] As late as June 1838, he spoke against Wyse's petition in favour of a national education system and a motion for a central board of commissioners, arguing that Parliament need do no more than what it had already done for education.[58]

Russell's response to what he regarded as Church aggression was emotional and quick. A copy of the National Society's August circular, in his papers, is heavily scored in his hand.[59] Immediately, he began to discuss a counteractive plan with his cabinet colleagues. Until pressed by Howick, Lansdowne and Glenelg, Russell was not entirely committed to any bill;[60] at one stage, he toyed with the idea of abolishing the annual grant altogether rather than allowing the Church to continue to collect most of the grant as it had done.[61] The government plan, as announced by Russell in February 1839, called for an order-in-Council creation of a lay Committee of the Privy Council to supervise school inspectors, whose reports would be necessary for a school to receive educational grants. The grant of £30,000 was to be allowed for either of the school Societies, or for other reputable schools, and based on local needs rather than the old matching grant formula. In addition, a non-denominational state-aided normal school and a model school were to be instituted. The plan owed much to the work of Spring Rice and, to a lesser extent, to Lansdowne. Rice was the Whig most directly and actively involved with education. 'He alone', wrote one recent authority, 'planned Whig educational policy. He was central to the educational history of the 1830's'.[62] The 1839 education scheme appears, indeed, to be an amalgam of his policies. In 1828, the Select Committee on Irish education, which he chaired, proposed a state normal school superintended by an education board. As Secretary to the Treasury responsible for administering the annual grant, he increased, with parliamentary approval, the total allocation to £30,000, the extra £10,000 earmarked for school houses in Scotland and model teacher training schools in England. In 1835, as Chancellor of the Exchequer, he again allocated £10,000 for English model schools, and refused over the next three years to give any of this fund to the National Society, preferring to preserve it for an eventual state normal school. In 1838, he changed the terms of the original £20,000 grant to allow some of it to be spent on inspection. And in the preparation of the 1839 scheme, he argued strenuously against Russell's opposition to a central board.[63] Lansdowne's role was similarly influential. In 1837, he had recommended to Russell that the grant be increased and that a board of education be appointed by order in Council to supervise school inspection and to establish a normal school. Early in 1839, he corresponded with Russell regarding his views on such a plan, garnered support from the Whig bishops, and, in effect, produced the plan which Russell announced.[64]

As expected, the proposals were accorded a hostile reception. Voluntaryists of all religious shades opposed direct state support for education. Evangelical Anglicans and Wesleyan Methodists protested the availability of grants for Roman Catholic schools and doctrines. But the most forceful opposition came from an alliance of Churchmen and Conservatives, the group which had generated the comprehensive Church plan of 1838. Russell had preferred to support local schools through a local rate levied by the poor law boards of guardians, to provide the National Society with surplus funds from church leases, and to have inspection of schools, distribution of the grants and teacher training administered through the Home Office.[65] Fierce opposition from Howley and Blomfield forced him to abandon his preference. The revised plan was no less objectionable. The Church objected to state-aided normal schools and non-Church inspection. Most of all, Churchmen regarded the plan as aggression against its sphere of influence. Supported by thousands of petitioners[66] and the combined opposition, the education issue succeeded appropriation and rates as the Church *cri de guerre*. The government had no choice but to back down. In June, Russell announced withdrawal of the proposed normal and model schools; in 1840, the government reached a 'concordat' with the Church by which the old system of matching grants, favourable to the Church, would be restored, and which gave the Church essential control over school inspections. But the result was far from a complete Church victory. During the dispute, the Church had asserted the historic indivisibility of religion and education, and the claims, as Blomfield told Russell, 'of the Church to conduct the education of the people'.[67] 'We may fairly assert that we have the education of the people in our hands', declared the Bishop of Ripon; 'why should it be taken away from us?'[68] By thus holding to what, since the 1833 grants to the Dissenters' British and Foreign School Society, was no longer true, the Church was clearly attempting to re-establish its sole right to provide education. And in this it did not succeed. The Education Committee of the Privy Council, established in April

1839, was the first authority to rival the Church in the field of education. Yet the Church had only itself to blame. The government had shown itself unwilling to support Spring Rice and Lansdowne's wish to delve further into education until faced with National Society assertiveness. 'I understood the design of your Government', wrote Kay to Russell, 'to be to prevent the successful assertion on the part of the Church of the claim they put forth for a purely ecclesiastical system of education'.[69] Though able to withstand earlier Whig attempts to take away what it did possess, the Church was unable to gain for itself additional powers that it did not possess.

IRELAND

In October 1834, Lord Lieutenant Mulgrave wrote from Dublin to report the views of 'most of the gentlemen in different parts of the Country'; they desired 'to do the very reverse of O'Connell' by turning their attention to practical points, 'particularly to the tenure of land by the Peasantry on some alteration of which so much depends'.[70] But nothing of this nature was to be attempted, or even discussed. In the belief that a key to pacifying Ireland was O'Connell's support, the Whigs continued to overlook the economic plight of the Irish peasantry by attempting, through legislative reform and administrative fair play, to secure reasonable agreement among the tithe-owners, O'Connell, and the Church. When strong public concern was expressed at an invitation taken up by O'Connell to visit the Lord Lieutenant at Dublin Castle in October 1835, and at a series of violent public speeches by the Irish agitator which followed, Holland defended the approach. It was O'Connell's avoidance of the ticklish topics of Repeal and appropriation, he told Grey, that the Ministry 'owed thanks to the tranquility of Ireland'.[71] Russell was more forthright. Policies aimed at eliminating the need for 'angry desperation' by O'Connell, he told the King, 'will afford the best chance of preserving the ignorant and inflammable population of Ireland from disaffection and disturbance.'[72] Ireland, it was clear, would continue to be regarded as a religious rather than an economic problem. This is not surprising, for few in England understood the tenancy and economic problems in Ireland. O'Connell himself paid little attention to economic factors, and was convinced that Ireland's problems were due to political causes such as Catholic disabilities and Union.[73] Thomas Drummond, Undersecretary in Dublin, adequately described the need to encourage landlord benevolence and a reversal of the subdivision of land in the 1837 Railways Commissioners' report, but apart from an abortive attempt to provide a loan for the development of Irish railways,[74] the Whigs' legislative programme for Ireland – tithes, municipal corporations and poor laws – belied an ethnocentric notion that Irish problems were similar to English, albeit more difficult politically, requiring similar solutions. Prime among these considerations was Church.

Whig attitudes to the Irish Church had changed little since 1833, and with the departure of Grey, Stanley and Graham the following year, were attended with little self-doubt. Those attitudes were clearly set down in a paper which Howick sent to Graham a few weeks before Russell's appropriation resolution in the spring of 1835.[75] The paper, an unsuccessful attempt to encourage Graham and, perhaps, Stanley, to join a union of moderate Whigs and Conservatives, set out three basic principles: an established Church could be defended only on the grounds of its practical utility; no one could claim a right of assuming his own religion to be founded in truth and that of others in error; and the end of government and legislation is the good of the whole community without the favouring of one individual or class at the expense of the other. Howick added his objection to the Church of Ireland: its practical effect was not to 'promote', but to 'impede the moral and spiritual improvement of the people'. Believing it to be 'one of the first duties of a government to provide for the religious instruction of the people . . . the present state of things in Ireland is one which sh[oul]d not be suffered to continue'. By appropriating a 'large portion' of the revenue of the Church to the 'extension of the system of national education which has been commenced with so much success', and leaving the Church with sufficient support for the Protestant population, the Establishment would be rendered more useful. Like most Whigs, Howick preferred an Establishment to a voluntary system; he declared himself an 'enemy' to the voluntary principle, and thought that the most reasonable course would be to re-establish the Roman Church in Ireland. 'The Church here instead of being weakened by such a change would be strengthened', he argued, 'since the Establishments in each of the three divisions of the United Kingdom could then be supported on the irresistible grounds of their practical utility to the great bulk of the population'. This course being clearly impossible given the strong, popular prejudices in England and Scotland, he, and his colleagues, could do nothing other than treat the Irish Church as a separate body de facto, and reconcile its position with the Irish people.[76]

Russell's speech in defence of his appropriation resolution put forward the same case. Church Establishments, he argued, should be considered as the means of moral and spiritual instruction 'and nothing else'; the great object in establishing them 'was to be essentially useful'. The Irish Church should be considered as a separate entity, it should be reformed in order that it continue to provide spiritual instruction to its members, and it should be left with no unnecessary surplus.[77] Although the Conservatives attributed the Whigs' support for appropriation to the Radicals' wish for a voluntary Church, the Whigs had clearly taken their position of their own accord. The position had been formulated in 1833–34, when there was no Radical pressure to be brought to bear, and was based, moreover, on the desire to avoid or eliminate damaging tithe wars which might provoke serious attacks on property, Church or otherwise, and render defence of the Establishment increasingly difficult. It was the same principle as applied to the Church in England, and to the reforms of parliament and the municipal corporations. To allow the status quo without appropriation, which in the case of the Irish Church meant to tax the Irish nation at large with benefits to only a few, would be to invite an alienation of Church and State.

Everyone had known since Russell 'upset the coach' that political Whiggery meant appropriation. And everyone knew that it could not pass the Lords. But an attempt was necessary; after Russell's resolution, a tithe bill shorn of appropriation would have left the Whigs open to the charge of the grossest opportunism. There was a further reason. If any one thing sustained Whigs throughout the difficulties of holding to a middle ground between radicalism and reaction, it was the belief that a Peel government would, by catering necessarily to the intolerance of the ultra and high Church party in its ranks, provoke an outcry damaging to not simply the Church. And appropriation was an important issue which could hold the government's slender majority together. This was not because appropriation was the only point on which all of the Whigs' supporters could agree; the majority of the House had shown itself prepared to turn Peel out on the Speakership. In a sense it was Peel, by resigning over appropriation, who gave the issue a greater prominence than deserved as a suspected glue to hold the Whigs' supporters together. But by doing so, Peel made the new government's task of managing the Radicals and Dissenters, as well as O'Connell's tail, easier. As long as appropriation was considered essential to the government's existence, 'less important' legislation which the English Radicals could demand as the price of their support could be held off. This is what Normanby was later to term playing 'the game of the appropriation clause'; by keeping to it, the Whigs were able to hold the Radicals at bay.[78]

A tithe bill was accordingly introduced in June 1835. Although the King objected to the plan on the grounds that appropriating revenues of Protestant property was wrong, Melbourne secured his grudging support by writing a strongly worded letter stating that a religious establishment 'is eminently for population, not for property'.[79] The details of what Holland described as this 'difficult and tiresome subject' took up the better part of a week's deliberation, chiefly from the government's inability to find a surplus of revenue to be appropriated; the matter was got over by relying on the sleight of hand of a local rather than a national surplus.[80] The bill, as announced on 26 June, replaced tithes with a rent charge. By it, a surplus of £58,000 was to be raised by suspending the presentations to scores of benefices with less than fifty Anglican parishioners, and given for the 'religious and moral instruction' of the people to the education board in Dublin.[81] Archbishop Whately's concern that the education board would become a hotbed of Catholic dissent which could clamour for more vacancies if it got funds only from dispossessed benefices, prompted the government to change the bill in committee, by giving a sum of money directly to the board from the consolidated fund, and placing the surplus generated by the rent charge into the Exchequer.[82] Despite fears that this second sleight of hand might lose Irish support in the Commons, the bill passed all three readings without division; on Peel's motion to separate appropriation, the government secured a majority of 319 to 282, enough, thought Holland, 'to shew that our Enemies cannot conduct the government with this House of Commons'.[83] The Lords, as expected, approved the measure only after throwing out appropriation.[84] The bill was promptly dropped.

The tithe plan adopted in 1836 was similar to the previous proposal, except for a slightly larger surplus set aside for appropriation. A land tax scheme was considered by Russell as a replacement for the rent charge, but was rejected in deference to the High Church party, who, it was thought, would have regarded the plan with suspicion because of its likelihood of producing a smaller revenue.[85] There was no hope, of course, that the bill as it stood could succeed, and when the Lords passed it with several amendments, the measure was again dropped. Lansdowne had suggested that the government should avoid the charge of insincerity by 'suspending' appropriation,[86] but in the spring of 1836, he was alone in this view. Yet by the end of the year, with evidence mounting that O'Connell was willing to see appropriation dropped in return for a municipal corporations bill,[87] the government began to weigh the benefits of appropriation against their other Irish legislation. As the next step toward pacifying Ireland, corporation reform had a number of attractions. Although the government knew before the tithe bill was brought forward in 1836 that O'Connell was prepared to give up appropriation, there was considerable fear that such a course might be fatal in the Commons.[88] But continued reports that appropriation was of far less importance to the Irish people than corporation reform, prompted the Whigs to think of a compromise. Mulgrave told Russell that because corporation reform was considered to embody 'the principal of equal justice to Ireland', there was no other question on which there was such general anxiety. Appropriation, on the other hand, was considered important only by the violent party; giving it up might in fact increase the government's support among Irish moderates. Hints from Aberdeen that the Peers had rejected the corporations bill in June only 'for dignity's sake', and would probably pass it in the next round, were all that was necessary for an altered course. Throughout the autumn, the government prepared to take its stand on the question. 'We have clear justice on our side', Russell wrote to Mulgrave in Ireland. 'We have no religious prejudice *directly* involved.' A number of tithe plans which did not involve appropriation were considered, and there was talk as well of giving grants to the education board in Dublin quietly and separately. If the corporations could be reformed, and tithes commuted, reduction in the Church revenues could wait for a better day.[89]

From this point on, settlement of the Irish legislation was only a matter of time and parliamentary politics. And chance. Although it appeared that Wellington and Peel had, by May 1837, persuaded sufficient Tory Lords to acquiesce in Russell's offer, announced in February, to trade appropriation for the corporations bill and a poor law, the King's death and subsequent prorogation of parliament forced postponement of the compromise for a year. As ministers considered the details of yet another tithe measure, there was little internal debate on the merits of abandoning appropriation. Morpeth sardonically reported a cabinet in April at which it was 'established' that it was impossible not to bring in a bill, impossible to bring in a bill without appropriation, and impossible to bring in a bill with appropriation. Wellington's 'offer' that May, considered 'in principle a fair one', settled the question. It was decided to introduce a measure, with appropriation, but to drop the clause once the new parliament was tested on the issue, in order to pass a tithe bill through the Lords.[90] Thus, with some alteration, a tithe bill was finally passed in 1838. The Act provided for a rent charge equal to 75 per cent of the old composition, payable by the landlords. The result was favourable to the Church for, although arrears for 1834 to 1837 were written off, payment of clergy and tithe owners was to come henceforth from the consolidated fund. The clergy, moreover, were absolved from having to collect tithe from an unwilling populace. The landlords, who were rewarded for their trouble in collecting the rent charge with a bonus payment of up to 25 per cent of the charge, met with little hostility in the short run; their ability to evict freely and to collect higher rent charges would eventually lead, however, to the war of tenants against landlords.[91] For the Whigs, the results were reasonably satisfactory. Tithe wars were ended, the Church reprieved.

From a tactical standpoint, the government had less reason for satisfaction. Although a poor law measure was adopted, the corporation bill was not. Peel and Wellington might have been in a position to deliver on their offer of compromise in 1837, but by 1838, the refusal of the ultra Tories in the Lords to accept their lead caused a further two-year delay before passage of a measure. And what was finally approved in 1840 was a far cry from what was first proposed. If, as one historian wrote, the Whigs' Irish programme had a 'dreary' parliamentary history, corporation reform was particularly badly affected by the strategies of government and opposition, the latter of which was so badly divided on the issue that a compromise solution was difficult to achieve. First introduced in 1835, a corporation bill became 'a hardy parliamentary annual'.[92] The Whigs had intended to reform the Irish corporations from the time they took office in 1830, but it was not until 1835, when the 1833 Commission had reported on the state of the corporations, that a measure was brought forward.[93] The Irish corporations were originally founded for the protection and extension of royal power and Protestantism; in the words of one English source, the corporation was to extend 'the lights of true religion and the example of socialisation among the bigoted and barbarous natives'.[94] Following Union, several corporations lost their rights of parliamentary representation and, hence, any reason for existence; by 1835, only 60 corporations existed. Self-elected, Protestant and poor, the corporations were condemned by the liberal Commissioners as unpopular, exclusive, and in need of a general and complete reform. The Whig bill was introduced in July 1835 by Louis Perrin, the new Irish Attorney-General who had previously headed the Commission of Enquiry. Based on that report, the bill proposed to institute elected municipal councils based on a £10 householder franchise in the larger towns, £5 in towns of under 20,000 population; a property qualification of £1000 was set for councillors in the larger towns, £500 in the smaller. The councils were to have powers over local courts and the election of sheriffs, but local magistrates were to be appointed by the Lord Lieutenant either from lists sent him by each council, or on his own.[95] In proposing a measure modelled on their English bill, the Whigs' motivation was uncomplicated. The Scottish corporations were reformed in 1833, the English in 1835. Simple justice required equal treatment for Ireland. The proposed replacement of coercion by a local constabulary, the need to have an element of popular control over more efficient local government, and above all the need to preserve the Union, rendered corporation reform an essential part of the Whig strategy for the peaceful government of Ireland.

The 1835 bill passed the Commons, without division, but was dropped due to Lords' preoccupation with the English corporation bill at the end of the session. In 1836, a similar bill was emasculated by the Tory Lords, who did not want to create Catholic centres of agitation with the power of taxing Protestant property. A compromise bill, whereby the government would create corporations in the eleven largest cities and towns, the others being vested with boards under the 1828 lighting and watching Act, was rejected by the Lords as well. Amidst clamour for peerage reform, the government again dropped the bill. The government's insistence that Irish corporations would be the 'Cheval de Bataille' in 1837, together with the possibility of a compromise with Peel, raised hopes that the corporations would finally be reformed. The 1837 bill, eventually postponed due to the King's death, made an important concession to the Tories by weakening the councils' rights in the appointment of sheriffs. With hopes of a settlement high, Russell worked out with Peel a new bill which would have given corporations to eleven of the largest towns elected on a £10 franchise; in smaller towns a majority could apply to the Lord Lieutenant for a charter of incorporation. Persuaded by Graham and Stanley that settlement of the corporation question was in the Conservatives' interest, Peel overcame his earlier wish to abolish all existing corporations without any replacement. Because their party was so badly divided on the question, a hurdle which an incoming Conservative government would have to overcome, having an act behind them would give the ultra Tories less room for mischief.[96] Thus, during the debates in 1838, Peel expressed his 'earnest desire' that the Irish questions would be brought to an 'adjustment' before the end of the session.[97] But it was too late. Wellington had been persuaded in 1837 to get Lyndhurst's support, but by 1838, neither Peel nor Wellington was able to control Lyndhurst's ultra Tories. The bill was once again amended by the Lords, and again dropped, a pattern repeated in 1839. The difference in 1840 was not the pattern, but the result. It was clear that Peel and Wellington could not control Lyndhurst, and that if there was to be any settlement of the corporations, it would have to be on ultra Tory terms. Given their declining position in parliament and the country, the government now acquiesced in the Lords' amendments;[98] the Commons followed suit without division. The Act, which Professor Macintyre termed 'in reality a scheme of municipal disfranchisement',[99] was a far cry from the original proposals. Fifty-eight corporations were abolished, to be replaced by local commissioners appointed under the 1828 Act or by the poor law guardians, and in some cases by corporations pending application. Ten towns were given councils with severely restricted powers, elected on a comparatively high £10 franchise dependent upon the payment of local taxes.

Unlike the tithe and corporation bills, the third measure of the Irish compromise passed through parliament comparatively easily. The rather short parliamentary history of the Irish poor law was undoubtedly due to the fact that an Irish law was generally viewed as of benefit to England. As a consequence, it received reasonably broad support from both sides of both Houses. Irish poverty was one of the great certainties of the age. It was estimated that nearly two and a half million people of the total population of eight million were unemployed or distressed for thirty weeks of the year.[100] During the 1820s, political and economic observers in England and Ireland engaged in a wide ranging debate over the nature and causes of Irish poverty and population, the efficacy of various remedies, and the role of the State in economic affairs. Needless to say, there was no uniformity of opinion except for the view that the existing, largely private, schemes for relief of poverty were ineffective. But as is often the case, politicians respond not to the considered views of the 'experts', but to the public perception and opinion of their supporters; to a large extent, they share in those perceptions. The history of the Irish Poor Law Commission, its report and the subsequent poor law legislation, shows this clearly to be the case in the Whigs' treatment of the issue.

English public opinion on Irish poverty was described by Archbishop Whately as a 'mixture of revenge, compassion and self-love. They pitied the suffering poor of Ireland; they had a fierce resentment against Irish landlords, whom they hastily judged to be the sole authors of those sufferings; and they dreaded calls on their own purse.'[101] Although there was, typically, no noticeable concern for tenants' rights, there was no doubt that the English held the Irish landlord in low esteem. Thomas Drummond reflected a section of liberal thought which regarded landlords as 'cold-blooded and indifferent to the sufferings of their tenants'; they had allowed subdivision to take place and they kept pauper tenants from becoming independent labourers.[102] On the other hand, many English thought that the landlords, by more recently fostering the consolidation of smaller holdings, were encouraging grazing and evictions. And evictions, it was assumed, meant a ready supply of Irish emigrants – 'the sorest evil this country has to strive with', thought Thomas Carlyle[103] – who competed unfairly with English labour, crowded the cities, and overburdened the English poor rates. In 1828, a Select Committee on Irish and Scotch Vagrants concluded that if nothing were done, the Irish paupers would, 'in no very distant period', throw upon England the expense of maintaining the paupers of both islands. An 1833 committee reported that the evil had increased.[104] The most common publicly pronounced remedy was an Irish poor law system similar to the English. The rates would take care of the poor, keep them at home, and give the rate-paying landowner incentive to find labour for the able-bodied pauper by investing in labour as well as cattle. English prejudice against the tenets of the Catholic religion merged, moreover, with popular notions that a workhouse test would reduce both the birthrate and overpopulation. In 1833, Poulett Scrope addressed an open letter to the landowners of England to urge them to use their influence to get an Irish poor law 'in justice to themselves, their tenantry, and the labouring classes'.[105] In that same year, Althorp responded by setting up a Commission of Enquiry into the relief of the Irish poor. His acquiescence followed a proposal by J. Richard, MP for Knaresborough, who argued that the subject concerned 'the great injury sustained by England from the dreadful extent of pauperism in Ireland', which caused 'a drain upon the resources of England . . . [from] the vast numbers of labouring Irish . . . flying from beggary and want in their own country'.[106]

Headed by Archbishop Whately, the Commission was thorough. It produced three reports and, finally in 1836, its recommendations. But the proposed remedies were not at all to the government's liking. Heavily influenced by the orthodox economists like Nassau Senior, an ex-student of Whately's at Oxford, the Commissioners recommended against a poor law based on the English workhouse model; it was too expensive, it would lead to idleness, and it was unsuited to a country with no alternative employment. It recommended instead the creation of a board to supervise a wide scheme of public works: land reclamation, agricultural model schools, road building and state investment in such agricultural infrastructures. Only the infirmed would be given assistance; an emigration scheme would help to reduce overpopulation.[107] This was a bold and imaginative plan of state aid to improve the economy and increase the demand for labour. It was not what the Whigs wanted. 'The English landowner who objects to the unchecked inroads of Irish labourers' would be disappointed, Mulgrave wrote from Ireland. 'The provision to satisfy them . . . must be compulsory in its nature'.[108] There were no doubts where Whig sympathies lay. Accordingly, George

Nicholls was sent to Ireland to investigate the suitability of an English system. This English Poor Law Commissioner, who had earlier sent Russell a memorandum arguing that an Enlgish poor law should be extended to Ireland, wrote to Russell in September, after a hasty trip to a country which by his own admission he had not known. 'I am happy to assure your Lordship that I have returned not only with a full conviction of the applicability to Ireland of the Workhouse System . . . but also that Ireland stands in need of a system of Poor Laws based upon that principle, fully as much as England itself'.[109]

Nicholl's report was all that the government wanted, and a bill based on his recommendations[110] was prepared for the 1837 session. The only question to be decided was whether the Board of Commissioners should be predominantly English, Irish or mixed. Although several ministers preferred a wholly English board, they agreed with Mulgrave's view that the Board should be based in Ireland, though predominantly English. Ireland 'is a strange country', Russell wrote to Thomas Moore, 'but Mulgrave seems to have found out the way of governing it'.[111] Palmerston, Lansdowne, and Spring Rice were not in favour of a measure which would throw the burden of rates on the owners of land; Rice in particular objected to the harmful effect on the industry of the able-bodied pauper who received rate assistance.[112] These three Irish landowners were representative of the limited opposition to the bill, which received support from Stanley, Peel and most of the Conservatives.[113] O'Connell was to make common cause with the landholding Irish peerage in opposition to the measure. Although he gave early support to the experiment, his private views were similar to Rice's; unlike the Whig minister, he temporarily allied himself with the Irish Tories in rejecting the bill brought forward in the spring of 1838.[114] Postponed until that session because of the King's death, the poor law passed easily through parliament. Before the Whigs left office, most of the Unions had been formed and half the workhouses. The system would be unable to cope with agrarian Irish poverty and the famine, and would upset Rice's 'brother Squires, who of all parties and creeds are alarmed at the measure'.[115] Yet it had served its intended purpose of satisfying English opinion and was, moreover, popular in Ireland.

A central feature of the Whig programme to pacify Ireland was the application of fairness to the administrative governance of that country. In practical terms, this policy meant that Irish officials would attempt to show the Irish people that government would be guided by other than the whims of the Protestant Ascendancy. Patronage was an obvious means of allaying Catholic fears; in redressing decades of Tory patronage by appointing Catholics and liberal Protestants, where possible, the Whigs attempted to identify the Irish administration with the community.[116] Centralisation of patronage at Dublin Castle, combined with what Russell told the King would be 'caution and selection' in the appointment process, produced much more satisfaction in Ireland than hitherto. During the lifetime of Melbourne's governments, three of the six judges placed on the bench were Catholic, the other three liberal Protestants. The attorneys- or solicitors-general were similarly of either stripe; wherever possible, the whole range of patronage appointments from magistracies and assistant-barristerships to police and army appointments, came under this policy. The other side of patronage was the dismissal of officials, and here the Whigs evidently agreed with O'Connell's advice to Littleton in 1833, that the dismissal of an Orange assistant barrister or a dozen Orange justices of the peace would do more to strengthen the Union than anything else.[117]

The Whigs were able to gain substantial Irish confidence by their willingness to support the growing attack on institutionalised Orangeism. First founded in 1795, the Lodge system had grown to about 1500 in 1835. The government was concerned as well at the growth of rival Catholic riband societies which led to increasing bitterness and violence. There was particular alarm in England at the penetration of leading Orangemen into the army, the Irish yeomanry and magistracies. In the spring of 1835, Hume succeeded in having a committee of the Commons appointed to investigate the activities of the Orange societies. By July, three lengthy reports were completed.[118] The reports made it clear that a number of Tory peers were involved, most notably the King's brother, the Duke of Cumberland. Russell hoped that Cumberland, a field marshall in the army, would give up his Grand Mastership of the Lodge to avoid embarrassing measures being taken, but although the King added his weight to the wish by promising vigour in suppressing the activities of the Lodges, nothing was done.[119] In September, Hume sent Melbourne the committee's fourth report, which recommended that everyone who held civil or military office should be removed if he did not retire from any Lodge or Society which used secret signs or passwords.[120] Melbourne could not have failed to see the irony in Hume's reference to secret ceremonies, for it was by the use of the 1797 Unlawful Oaths Act that Melbourne had overseen the transportation of the Dorchester labourers. A further letter to Russell made it clear in fact that Hume was as concerned that something be done for the Tolpuddle martyrs. Russell told Melbourne that as he had already recommended to the Colonial Office that the Lovelaces be pardoned after three years in the colonies, he did not want to do more, for the government would then be in the Radicals' power 'instead of their being in ours'. Within a week, however, he told Melbourne that he would not want to keep the sentences in force the whole seven years, and in March 1836, announced free pardons for all six convicts.[121] As for the Orangemen, Russell doubted that the same laws reached them, but he did concede that they were *de facto* 'far more guilty' than the labourers. Melbourne would agree. He had urged Grey in 1833 to consider banning the Lodges under the terms of the Coercion Act. Though such a step would 'probably offend the Protestants', he told Grey, 'it still appears to me almost impossible to submit to the existence of societies which break the law in a manner so open and audacious'. Hostility to fanaticism of any type, and particularly of the religious variety, was central to Melbourne's beliefs.[122] By October, when Hume and Molesworth circulated fresh and convincing evidence that Cumberland was involved in a plot to put himself on the throne when William died,[123] the government decided to act.

Following a cabinet meeting on the subject, Russell saw the King. William agreed with his view that dismissing all Orangemen from civil office would be 'making a flame indeed', but agreed that none should be appointed in future, and all should be dismissed from the army and police. It was further agreed that the King would take steps to discourage the continuance of the Lodges, and that they would be thereafter disbanded.[124] When parliament met in February 1836, Hume arranged with Russell the terms of a motion which recommended the removal of members of all secret societies from all civil and military offices. It was agreed that Russell would follow in debate and propose an amendment, taking into account the terms reached with the King. This done, Hume withdrew his motion, and Russell's resolution was approved without division. Molesworth, as the seconder of Hume's motion, called for the trial of Cumberland, the Bishop of

Salisbury, Lord Chandos and Lord Kenyon as members of secret
societies; although the government agreed that there was substantial legal evidence of a misdeameanour, there was no intention of
undertaking such a 'harsh proceeding'.[125] The King agreed to
apply the necessary pressure, and within a few days, Cumberland
announced the dissolution of all Lodges.[126] Within three months,
Morpeth was able to announce in the Commons the dismissal of
ninety-six constables and sub-constables. The Castle also began to
remove all members of the Lodges from government service;
Orange magistrates, who encouraged violation of the law, were
deprived of the Commission of the peace.[127]

Impartiality in the judicial process was of vital importance. An
attempt to ensure its success led to the administrative reform of
the Irish police system, one of the lesser known but more successful measures in the Whig attempts to pacify Ireland. Since the
imposition of the first Coercion Act in 1833, the use of force to
collect what the government had viewed as an unjust tithe
violated Whig notions of tolerance and justice. Indeed, the necessity of coercion prompted Whigs to consider Church reform in the
first place. In 1835, on the expiry of the second Coercion Act, the
government decided not to extend the measure, but to implement
a policy of selective use of military force where the peace was
disturbed in the collection of tithe.[128] But though this new policy
of refusing to use force to collect tithes brought to an end the tithe
wars, agrarian violence continued. Led by the 'midnight marau-
ders' of the secret societies, violence against landlords and Unions
reached alarming proportions. Within a year of first taking office,
the Whigs, particularly Lord-Lieutenant Anglesey, Irish Secretary
Stanley and Home Secretary Melbourne, realised that the normal
instruments of peace preservation did not work.[129] Often reduced
in size due to economy measures or to military engagements
elsewhere, the Irish army was suspect even to its officers, who
feared subversion by Catholic soldiers. The local magistracy was
particularly inefficient; they were intimidated by the members of
the violent societies, and were continually accused of indecision.
Their control over the County Constabulary was weak. The Peace
Preservation Force, an organisation under Castle control, was
often effective, if expensive, but jurisdictional problems limited its
effectiveness as well. What made Melbourne's government
unusually effective in dealing with Irish violence was its readiness
to divest the Irish **magistracy** of its powers. Particularly important

was the advice of Thomas Drummond, Undersecretary in Dublin from July 1835 until his death in May 1840. A Scot who had learned of Ireland on the ordnance survey, Drummond combined good sense and administrative impartiality. Toleration and a concern for the Irish people produced one of the ablest of all Irish civil servants in the nineteenth century. He had little sympathy for protestant landlords, or for the operation of the Ascendancy through magistracies or justices of the peace, and came quickly to the conclusion that peace could not be maintained as long as partisan JPs controlled the appointment of the county constabularies.[130] Based on his suggestions, a new constabulary bill was drafted and presented to parliament in August 1835.

The Whig bill amalgamated the County Constabulary and the Peace Preservation Force into a single Irish Constabulary. The new force was placed under an inspector-general appointed by the Lord Lieutenant; two deputy-inspectors, four provincial inspectors and thirty-two sub-inspectors assisted. Police constables, appointed not by the magistrates but by the Lord Lieutenant (in reality by the Inspector-General), would be professionally trained and sworn to be impartial. Though the bill was defeated in the Lords at the instigation of the Irish peer Roden, who objected to the manifest desire to take appointments out of the hands of magistrates, the government persisted. It was supported by Peel, who argued that the force should be 'free from the influence of party animosity and party excitement'. When Wellington arranged a last minute meeting of ministerial and opposition leaders,[131] the measure passed through parliament early in the next session. The new force resembled an army more than a civilian police; it was soon larger than the old Peace Preservation Force and County Constabulary combined. Respected for its well-trained and impartial recruits, the Irish Constabulary became a popular force within a few years. Most of its members were eventually to be of Catholic peasant origin. By vesting policing powers with the central administration, the Whigs were successful in showing that the policy of fairness and efficiency could work. Ireland was to remain a violent society, but the ending of faction fights and Orange processions helped to bring about a significant reduction in the level and amount of disturbances.[132] By this example of administrative fair play, the Whigs earned for English governance a respect which their legislative programme could not. When they left office, a decade of administrative activity had given Ireland a

system of primary education, workhouses, municipal governments and a police force. In 1839, Sydney Smith claimed that the
Irish needed just laws as well as just administration 'such as they
have experienced from the Whig government'.[133] But whether they
had weakened the repeal movement by removing basic grievances
was doubtful.

THE ECONOMY

Since the disastrous attempt to introduce dogmatic reforms in
1831, Government economic policies under Grey had been guided
less by the economic views of Parnell and its adherents in cabinet
than by a pragmatic attempt to balance interests. Melbourne's
government was to follow the same well-trodden path until
recession in 1837 would force a different approach. It is not
surprising that economic issues were given little attention in the
mid-1830s. Annual surpluses continued; the 'condition of
England' question was noticeably absent. The Whig mind was, as
a result, left free to concentrate on its more natural agenda of
political and religious reform. The budget defeat of 1831 continued
to feed the Whigs' suspicion that serious attempts to alter the
economic patterns of activity were not worth the risks. At a time
when its parliamentary position rendered precarious the path of
political and religious reform, the luxury of balanced budgets and
the absence of any real conflicts in economic matters allowed
government to leave economic matters in the hands of those few
ministers responsible for such questions. The considerable issues
were not economic, but of party and religion, of Church and State.
Until the Queen's accession then, economic matters were of
comparatively, and apparently, less importance than other affairs
of state. The one measure during these few years which did
receive much attention was the newspaper tax reduction in 1836; it
was not, however, seriously regarded as a fiscal measure at all, but
rather as an attempt to muzzle the previously unstamped and
highly successful 'underground' radical press.[134] The anticipated
loss of revenue resulting from the reduction of the tax to a single
penny would be more than offset, it was thought, by revenue
gains which had produced surpluses of £1.2 million in 1835 and
£1.8 million in 1836.[135] Spring Rice, the new Chancellor, brought
forward his budgets without discussion or debate among his

colleagues. Although not closely associated with the Parnellite views as Althorp had been, Rice's appointment reflected the Whigs' attitude that economic matters were of lesser importance than other more pressing questions. Although Peel had argued with some force that surpluses should be used to reduce the national debt rather than to reduce taxes,[136] the latter was far more popular both in and out of parliament; it was a notion which Rice took as a matter of course. Howick and Poulett Thompson complained that Rice's budgets came forward without much discussion and 'upon his own sole judgement',[137] but on the whole, the relatively minor reductions on glass and paper duties were considered of too little importance to occasion debate.

As long as trade remained at favourable levels and expenditures controlled, Whig policies, such as they were, could be regarded as successful. But by 1837, revenues were already weakening. Dependence on indirect taxation appeared to be a reasonable policy during the years of expanding trade in the early 1830s, but the trade depression and crop failures which began simultaneously in late 1836 pointed out the weaknesses of this approach. The drop in cotton exports and the tariff barriers of the European protective systems caused the yield of customs duties to drop below the Chancellor's estimates for the first time in 1837. Simultaneous growth in expenditures brought on by instability in Europe and rebellion in British North America made the likelihood of continued surpluses doubtful. By 1838, with interest charges on the £20 million compensation due to the West Indian plantation owners added to the cost of suppressing rebellion in Canada, expenditure estimates stood at £47.5 million, nearly £3 million higher than in 1835. Already, the deficit reached £1.4 million.[138] Surprisingly, it was not until 1838 that the problem was regarded as particularly serious. The previous year, Rice had described in his budget speech the difficulty of predicting the Customs and Excise yield, or more accurately, the volume of trade. Unlike the revenues from assessed taxes which remained fairly constant, expansion or contraction of trade had a significant effect on the yield from these indirect taxes. In 1835 and 1836, revenues had considerably exceeded the predicted amounts. In 1838, Rice argued that the temporary reduction in imports was caused by trade recession. The deficit was an aberration.[139] Despite the widely held notion that the budget should show a balance, this explanation held, without calls for changes in the system. But in 1839, when Rice announced a deficit of nearly £500,000, despite a rise in Customs and Excise of a similar amount,[140] a new tax could no longer be avoided.

The Whigs, unfortunately, were in no position to take such an unappealing step. By the time that the budget was announced in July, the bedchamber crisis had reduced the Ministry's options to the point where little could be done which did not suit the views of the Radical members. It was this weakness of position which accounts for the surprising introduction of Rowland Hill's revolutionary Penny Post. Hill had argued in his *Post Office Reform* that the volume of business generated by a prepaid penny would offset any loss of revenue arising from the discontinued variable charge.[141] His scheme would be proven in the long run to be entirely correct; in 1839, verification of his figures was impossible. His claim that administrative efficiencies would increase net revenues was not enough to convince the Whigs that the scheme should be introduced. The 1837 Select Committee, which was set up to investigate the rates of postage, and which recommended a rate of twopence, did little to allay these concerns.[142] But the need to appease the Radicals in order to keep the government alive forced the issue. Place, Warburton and those who decried all taxes on knowledge generated hundreds of petitions in favour of the tax reduction.[143] Within a fortnight of returning to office, Russell agreed to grant the uniform penny post; he meekly coupled the concession with a pledge to make good any deficiency in the revenue. Though Rice and Baring disapproved of a 'measure of reckless daring' which added no new tax, the cabinet approved the scheme 'to keep the whole party together'.[144] The Penny Post would be an enormous success. Spencer Walpole was to mourn the brevity of the modern letter which sacrificed 'grammar, style and wit'; several others declared that there was 'no longer any use in being in Parliament' with the simultaneous abolition of free franking privileges.[145] But the social and economic advantages of better communications were not lost on the public; within a few years, the volume of Post Office business surpassed even Hill's predictions. Distressingly, however, the Whigs' fears for Hill's revenue predictions proved well founded, for the net revenues of the Post Office fell by more than £1 million in 1840.[146]

It was against this background of declining revenues and continued deficits that import duties were increased in 1840 for the first time in several years. Baring, who had replaced Rice as Chancellor during the recent reconstruction of the cabinet, proposed that the deficit, projected to be nearly £3 million, be made good by a loan. But Russell and Melbourne argued for surgery to the fiscal system by the imposition of fresh taxes.[147] Their view prevailed. The budget of 1840 included provision for an increase of 5% on Customs and Excise taxes and of 10% on assessed taxes.[148] Baring's proposal to borrow as a means of covering the deficiency was clearly designed only as a temporary measure. The new Chancellor had not favoured the new imposts. He thought that much of the increase in expenditures was temporary in nature, particularly that due to rising military requirements, and exhorted Melbourne to put an end to 'the reckless way in which the cabinet seem to go on'.[149] As reports began to filter in of lower customs income during the succeeding months,[150] Baring borrowed £600,000 from the Bank for the fourth quarter, and began in earnest to review the government's fiscal system in a systematic manner such as Rice never had. The result was the ill-fated budget of 1841.

When Baring read Melbourne's draft of the Queen's speech which would open the 1841 session, he reported to the Prime Minister that although the 'principles of economy' were mentioned annually in the Royal address 'and one never hears them again for the rest of the year in the Cabinet', attention to such matters 'can't be helped this year'.[151] He had already circulated a preliminary memorandum to the cabinet pointing out the failure of the taxes imposed in 1840 to realise the expected revenues, and warned that because the navy and ordinance estimates were to be increased, a 'heavy' deficit was expected.[152] Baring's approach to the deficit was as innovative as that taken in 1840. But now, instead of raising import duties, he proposed a combination of lowered duties on imported non-colonial sugar and Baltic timber with an increase on the duty of Canadian timber. Although he had also suggested that either a loan or an income tax would clear the expected deficit, he knew that a loan would not deal with the problem at hand, and that the support to be found in both major parties for an income tax was too insubstantial to count on.[153] There was good reason, on the other hand, to suspect that increased revenues resulting from an attack on colonial preferences would be popular. It was known that the colonial interests would be opposed; Baring had asked Melbourne only whether the cabinet were decided that the sugar question 'can be agitated'.

Would others oppose? Given the impetus for such measures generated by the appearance of the Select Committee Report on Import Duties, it seemed unlikely that the Whigs' parliamentary supporters would do other than find favour. The Committee had been set up in 1840 and was influenced heavily by the Board of Trade;[154] it produced a series of recommendations which found favour with both the commercial middle class and the Radical interests. An account of a meeting held at the Thatched House Tavern in St James's Street on 20 February was sent by its participants to Melbourne; it was clear that MPs representing the most important commercial and manufacturing constituencies supported measures to remove serious obstacles to trade, and wished for a 'prompt revision and extensive reformation of our commercial code'.[155] There was reason as well to think that Peel might support Baring's measures. Throughout the 1830s, he had placed paramount importance on the need for balanced budgets; he had, moreover, spoken out against an income tax and other basic alterations in the system of taxation. In 1840, he supported Baring's increase in indirect taxation, and again, in February 1841, supported a preliminary proposal to equalise the duties on East and West Indian rum.[156] It was widely known, in addition, that Peel was increasingly attracted to the principles espoused in Baring's plans; 'if you do not make' a move in this direction, Ebrington advised Melbourne, 'Peel [in office] shortly will'. Because the Conservative leader would have to force his views on unwilling supporters, it was thought that he might very well allow measures which would ease his own path in governance.[157] In the end, of course, Russell's decision to alter the corn laws and the Conservatives' apparent determination to see the Ministry out, rendered moot such deliberations and considerations. The government's proposals could not, or certainly would not, carry.

The budget proposal and debate of 1841 has been widely scrutinised in an attempt to discover the extent to which the Whigs were committed to the principles of free trade. Kitson Clark, Spring, J. T. Ward and Southgate have studied the involvement of Whig landed families in non-agricultural pursuits in order to assess the extent of the Whigs' abandonment of the defence of the Corn Laws. Southgate concludes that the landed interest had 'reason to be alarmed' at the number of Whig hierarchs with a strong financial interest in an expanding industrial economy.[158] There is little evidence, however, to suggest that the Whig leaders meant in 1841 to abandon protection for agriculture, or to usher in an era of free trade. The Whigs gambled that free trade supporters might provide support in elections, but in attacking colonial preferences and restructuring the Corn Laws, the evidence suggests that Whiggery was anything but a party committed to free trade. There can be little doubt, on the other hand, that in revising the tariffs on sugar and timber, free trade measures were proposed. Parnell had himself put the tariff case forward as a member of the Select Committee, and had written an article for the Spring edition of the *Edinburgh Review* demanding radical changes to tariffs.[159] Baring had suggested bringing on his tariff proposals 'with reference to our financial position and to our want of money and not with reference to the general principles of free trade',[160] but his was a political instruction to a cabinet which had hitherto reacted strongly to suggestions that the free traders' interests be supported. The Whigs clearly moved timidly in the direction of free trade by their tariff proposals, but it is important to recognise that the debate which would immediately take place over the permeation of free trade principles into the Whig party was not occasioned by the attack on colonial preference. In the highly charged, emotional atmosphere of 1841, *the* question of free trade concerned corn and the protection to be afforded land and agriculture. On this question, Whiggery had not yet altered its principles.

The Whigs did not propose to alter the Corn Laws in order to raise revenue. Baring's tariff revisions were calculated to cover most of the expected deficit; Russell's memorandum to the cabinet which suggested a revised sliding scale 'supposed' an increase in revenue following not much more than guesswork.[161] It was understood that the corn measure could not pass; the issue was one for the hustings. At the same time, it was believed by all that far from abandoning protection, a revision in the Corn Laws would benefit agriculture. Melbourne was the least convinced by the economic arguments. He answered Ripon in the Lords by stating that the alteration would proceed 'unquestionably' on the principle of protection,[162] but it was on this point that his cabinet colleagues had to be most insistent in arguing a case. Russell had long been convinced that the sliding scale of 1828 had failed to provide agriculture with sound protection. Although he first advocated a revised scale of duties, he quickly reverted to his own preference for a moderate fixed duty when representations were made to the government that frauds were too easily committed with sliding scales. By arguing for a fixed duty of 8 s. per quarter on wheat, which he 'did not see' as an 'absence of protection' but as 'sufficient protection', he stood on the same ground as he had two years earlier when he ridiculed the 'danger' of cheaper foreign grain which, 'if there is any duty at all', would be kept out. The sliding scale, he was convinced, increased high prices in dear years to the consumer yet decreased the low prices of cheap years to the producer.[163] Most Whigs readily accepted the argument that the sliding scale had not acted to the benefit of the agricultural producer. Not only had the price of corn failed to reach the expected level of 80s., but the sliding scale which produced severe fluctuations in price was grossly inefficient in promising anything like a steady or predictable level of income. Few would go as far as Spencer and Durham, who favoured total repeal in order to reduce the injury done to both agriculture and commerce by restrictive duties,[164] but when the cabinet debates on the subject took place early in 1839, most were already convinced that a moderate duty was preferable. As Howick had argued, five-sixths of the farmers in Hertfordshire wanted a change in order to afford protection to the farmer, who was forced to 'gamble' on the sliding scale 'which kept foreign corn out when it should be in and vice-versa'. The agricultural distress of the later 1830s, he was convinced, was the result.[165] Melbourne received reports that the farmers in Forfar-shire and Scotland 'generally' were unhappy with the laws, and by 1841 Ebrington reported that several Whig magnates thought corn better protected by a moderate duty: the Dukes of Sutherland, Devonshire and Bedford, the Lords Westminster, Fitzwilliam, Leicester, Spencer, Fortescue, Radnor and Carlisle, and a 'number of others'.[166] Lansdowne too pressed the expediency of a fixed duty which he 'always thought' preferable for protection. But it is doubtful that the Prime Minister was convinced. An alteration in the opinions of the landowners themselves 'is a thing which never happens', he had earlier told Russell.[167] Melbourne was driven to accept a proposal which could not pass in order to stake out an electoral position. The legacy of deficits would be Peel's problem.

12

'Just Out'

'The Country is tired of the old hands and wants to try a new doctor.'

Francis Baring, 23 July 1841[1]

On the eve of what would be their final elections while in office, the Whigs added Sir George Grey to the cabinet. A number of minor ministerial and household changes were made as well.[2] 'To me', wrote Hobhouse in his diary, 'it seems ridiculous to shuffle the cards at the end of the game. We should be beaten most assuredly at the elections. The only question is by how many. The Tories say 80.'[3] He was right on both counts. His pessimism, moreover, reflected the Whig consensus that Peel must govern. Although few were as alarmist as Spencer, who expected the contest to 'nearly annihilate the Whig party',[4] the fact that the cabinet had to be persuaded to dissolve rather than to hand the reins immediately to Peel suggests that its members did not expect to continue in government. It was hoped by many that the budget might help their sagging electoral fortunes, but none could dissent from Ellice's opinion that 'I never thought there was a chance of winning.'[5] It was not surprising, given this languishing attitude, that the leading Whig magnates were unwilling to provide much in the way of financial support for what appeared to be a hopeless cause. Ellice complained of the small amounts pledged by the leading peers; Lansdowne gave only £500, Portman 'not a shilling'. Spencer had 'not one farthing to dispose of'.[6] The important effect was to be seen not in the inability to raise funds for the relatively unimportant central election chest, but in the constituencies. It was at the local level, where funds were to be raised, electors registered and candidates arranged, that the lack of enthusiasm was most keenly felt. Russell noted early on in the contest that by resigning their seats, 'many members on the ministerial side' made prospects even less favourable. Ellice grumbled that there was 'neither zeal, qualification or energy' among those 'who ought

305

to attend to such things'; Howick and Morpeth bemoaned the lack of energy on the part of local party magnates which would account for unnecessary defeats.[7]

At first glance, the large number of uncontested seats would seem to give some credence to these views. Whereas 251 of the 401 constituencies had been contested in 1837, only 188 were recorded as contested in 1841. The difference between the 132 Conservatives returned without a contest in 1837 and the 217 in 1841[8] accounts for more than the 78 seat Conservative margin of victory. Unless a significant number of local studies suggest otherwise, however, Whigs like Howick and Morpeth must stand accused of hopeful thinking. It is often forgotten, yet important to remember, that 'uncontested' elections in Victorian Britain did not mean that there had been no contests. Rather, it most often meant that one or other party recognized the desperation of its cause and either refused to field a candidate or withdrew its candidate rather than risk unnecessary expense and defeat. Thus, when the Duke of Hamilton's Whig nominee in Lanarkshire, Sir Edward Colebrooke, discovered that defections of two of the leading families resulted in a disastrous survey, he was withdrawn by the Duke, who thought it better not to 'expose to the publick the extent of the failure'.[9] In this case, as with the Whig Townley in Cambridgeshire who withdrew when he found he had not the numbers he had 'hoped to rely on',[10] the canvass *was* the election. Although the losing party, in this case the Whigs, might choose to reflect on what might have been, the inescapable conclusion must be drawn that it was not a lack of candidates or cash which brought defeat in both of what might be more properly described as 'polled' or 'unpolled' elections, but the weight of opinion and the confirmed re-establishment of traditional Conservative-Tory strengths. 'Putting candidates in the field did not produce the Conservative revival', one historian wrote recently, 'it attested to it'.[11]

The Whigs' defeat in 1841 confirmed the trend established at the elections of 1835 and 1837. Indeed, it could well be argued that the trend had begun much earlier, and that after the unusually large Whig victory in 1832, the resurgence of Conservative strength could have been predicted once the traditional concerns and influence would no longer be overshadowed by the Reform issue. At the 1831 elections, Francis Baring noticed the 'wholesome, very loyal and very aristocratical' feeling of the country. 'Though they for that one time threw aside the Tory members', he wrote in his diary, 'my personal impression is that the first, or perhaps the second, reformed House will be very country-gentleman'.[12] A number of recent studies lends credence to the view that the Whigs' opponents were not, as a number of historians have suggested,[13] the 'broken and discredited minority' who 'faced extinction' by 1833. D. C. Moore, for example, has shown that the local alliances which brought Wellington's government down in 1830 scarcely endured beyond the Duke's resignation. As the local Tory leaders re-established the old local coalitions, increased vigour and confidence prompted them to 'reclaim' lost or uncontested seats. Altogether, at general elections and bye elections between 1832 and 1841, Conservatives won 79 of 103 such contested county seats; Whigs, Liberals and Radicals only 2 of 37 newly contested seats. Only 22 of these successful Conservative reclamations occurred in 1841. The 'logic of cohesion' underlying these re-established local coalitions, Moore argues, 'was generally phrased in terms of the need to defend the corn laws'.[14] Stewart too has pointed out that a significant number of county seats fell to the Conservatives on the first occasions that they were contested. In the nine leading arable counties alone, they reclaimed 14 seats in 1835, 19 in 1837 and 24 in 1841; in these nine counties, Conservative candidates stood when they regarded local conditions favourable for victory. They scarcely lost.[15]

There can be little doubt that the country gentlemen and farmers were to regard Conservatives as the party of land, and would, once Reform was passed, return to their normal patterns of electoral activity. Whether the issue was agricultural distress, malt and land taxes, Church or corn laws, the natural tendency was to distrust Whigs as protectors of property. Althorp had foreseen the problem while drafting the Reform bill, and had argued that the landed interest was being given too much additional influence in the counties as compensation for their losses in the closed boroughs. 'I always resisted John Russell on that.' By 1837 Russell would agree that by increasing the number of county seats and by conceding the Chandos clause, the government had indeed overcompensated the landed interest.[16] It is to this agrarian voter that Crosby refers in his study of the politics of English farmers. Conservative successes, he argues, were due to the party's capitalizing on the grievances and fears of this 'newly important electoral group'. By 1841, corn was paramount. Olney arrives at the same conclusion for Lincolnshire, where the percentage of straight party votes cast increased from 58 per cent in 1832 to 75 per cent in 1841. Farmers were now willing to accept the Conservatives as the friends of agriculture.[17]

Sydenham's prediction to the Conservative Fitzharris that 'of course *you* will get all the counties, we all the great towns, and the small boroughs will be anybody's money'[18] was not far wrong. In the non-Irish counties, 157 seats were taken by the Conservatives, 22 by the Whigs. Of the 45 manufacturing seats, the Conservatives won only 13. The English counties and smaller boroughs provided Peel with his margin of victory.[19] There was nothing remarkable in the Conservatives' recovery in the counties, where the combination of tradition and Whig policies gave them a certainty of success. But if, as Hatherton hoped, the populace would get behind the cry for 'cheap sugar, cheap bread, and the Queen, God bless her', the Whigs were mistaken. It is difficult indeed to think that they expected their budget to provide much more than limited additional support. Parkes had warned Russell, who conceded later that the tactical decision was an error, not to count on the corn law proposal in the boroughs. The Reform Act, as the Whigs well knew, had not given supporters of commercial reforms a preponderant influence in the boroughs, the large majority of which contained less than two thousand rather traditional electors. And it was also known, as Hatherton predicted, that 'all the Capitalists are Tories'.[20] Apart from the manufacturing seats, where Conservatives were able to count on a certain number of corrupt freeman voters and where the free traders and Radicals were at best lukewarm in their support of the Whig candidates,[21] there were few constituencies where the traditional concerns of Church and land did not redound to the Conservatives' advantage.

In the smaller and middle-sized boroughs, where the Conservatives recorded most of their gains, the Whigs' budget proposal dominated almost all of the contests. 'Shall the Corn Laws be abolished – aye or no?', asked the Conservative *Canterbury Journal* on the eve of the election. 'The Ministers, let it be remembered, go to the county upon THIS question!'[22] In Buckingham, where the liberal member Sir Harry Verney withdrew, allowing the uncontested return of two Conservatives, Corn was quite obviously the issue. Verney's position had already weakened in 1835 and 1837 as a result of his support for the Whigs' Church policies. In 1841, neither his old committee nor Mayor Humphreys, who had seconded his nomination in 1837, would support him. 'His votes with the anti-Corn Law government must affect him with the Electors', announced the *Bucks Herald*; 'the great struggle of the general election will arise from the question, of whether the Agriculturalists of the Empire shall or shall not retain that protection which is virtually necessary to their existence'.[23] Corn, concludes Professor Davis, broke the Whig party in Buckinghamshire. It caused Lord Nugent to withdraw in Aylesbury, leaving two Conservatives uncontested; it halved the Whig poll in the county.[24] Typical of the arguments put forward against the corn proposal was that of the *Kentish Gazette*, which informed the electors of Canterbury that the Whigs' budget was bound 'to overthrow the existing order of society, to trample down the agriculturalist and the farm labourer, and to pave the way for the downfall and destruction of all those great mercantile and commercial institutions by which the magnificence and superiority of Great Britain are maintained'.[25] It was not uncommon for Conservative candidates and papers to urge their supporters to withdraw their custom from liberal merchants and tradesmen. In Cambridge, for example, the farmers were urged to 'enlighten' the tradesmen on market day on the folly of voting for 'the total repeal of the corn laws'.[26] At Reading, where the Whigs lost both seats, the Conservatives played on the same fears. The milling of corn into flour for shipment to London would cease, warned the *Berkshire Chronicle*. Having already announced that 'the appeal to the country is to be on the corn law question', this Conservative paper concluded that just as the clothing trade had disappeared in the sixteenth and seventeenth centuries, 'the effect of lost milling on most of the tradesmen of the town would be ruinous'. When reports came in that local farmers and squires had awoken to their own interests by warning local traders not to vote Whig, the *Chronicle* argued that such practices were the right of the farmers and clearly defensible.[27]

The connecting of agricultural depression with commercial destruction and lower wages was also common. The argument had an obvious appeal in the north. In Wigan, it was alleged that repeal of the corn laws would lay hundreds of thousands of acres waste, cause distress to the manufacturing interests, and lower wages. Crosse, the Conservative candidate, took his stand on the existing corn duties. On the eve of the election, which gained two seats for the Conservatives by a margin of five votes, the local

Conservative organ advised the electors that 'if you want them [lower wages] vote with the Whigs'.[28] Sir Walter James, the Conservative candidate at Hull, argued that Whig free trade would ruin England: 'a greater quantity of poor land . . . would cease to be cultivated, and a great number of labourers would be thrown out of employment'.[29] The electors, concluded the *Hull and East Riding Times* after the Conservatives had gained a seat, have done their duty 'to the great commercial interests in which their town has so deep a stake'; free trade and cheap bread 'were the great turning points upon which the late contest hinged'.[30] John Hornby, who took the second seat from the Whigs at Blackburn, argued in his election address that 'if the cry of cheap bread means anything at all, it means low wages': the flooding of towns by agricultural labourers would produce a large oversupply for the manufacturers. Apart from the new poor law – 'a disgrace to humanity' – no other issue was raised.[31] In Halifax and Bradford, similar appeals were put forward.[32]

There can also be little doubt that the Conservatives' reputation as defenders of the Church was an essential ingredient in their victory. The 'Church in danger' had been a dominant theme in the 1835 and 1837 elections when Conservative candidates in both counties and boroughs had accused the Whigs of betraying the Church and national interests to the Dissenters and Irish Catholics.[33] Few Conservative candidates missed an opportunity to make use of this weapon. 'Mr Clay is a Whig', cried the Tory organ in Hull. 'He is ready to do the dirty work of the O'Connell ministry.' 'The Chartists', it continued in an effort to cement a Radical–Tory alliance, 'are honest men . . . They did not concoct the New Poor Law. They never were mean enough to lick the unsavoury feet of O'Connell.'[34] 'The people', the Conservative candidate Ferrand told the electors of Knaresborough,[35]

will never consent to become the degraded tools of Mr. O'Connell . . . Do not forget that the Protestant religion is to be defended by you in the approaching struggle . . . I have taken my stand by the side of 'the Crown, the Sceptre and the Bible' . . . I will meet you at the Poll, where you will have to defend your Protestant Faith against the Errors of Popery and the deadly sin of Socialism.

By thus tying the Bible to the Crown and institutions of the country, Conservatives appealed to the same instincts as those awakened by the issue of agricultural protection. The appeal was extremely powerful. In his first address at Knaresborough, Ferrand had not mentioned the Church issue; after two days of canvassing convinced him of the popularity of the question, it became the focal point of his campaign.[36] The *Berkshire Chronicle*, which had based its campaign against the government on the corn laws, reported afterwards that 'the most powerful instrument in changing the tone of political feeling is the subservience of the executive government to the sordid and mendicant papist'.[37] On the eve of the Liverpool poll, the *Liverpool Mail* warned of 'Popery, the great curse of the world'. The Conservative Lord Sandon concentrated his electoral address upon the Whigs' attacks on the protestant Church, and at his victory address, amid shouts of 'Down with Maynooth', he thanked the local ministers of the gospel who had 'not in vain . . . been teaching you that the good protestant and the good churchman ought to be at the same time the good politician and . . . support the men who are attached morally and religiously to the church themselves'. Mr Samuel Holmes, the local Tradesmen's Conservative Association representative who followed, praised the 'protestant feeling' which had caused both seats to fall to the Conservatives: 'I feel satisfied', he added, 'that the good, sound protestant feeling will have the effect of docking O'Connell's tail in the next parliament'.[38] It is not surprising that Ashley would make his point. He had argued that the party 'endeavour to get the Government out on a Protestant point', and wrote after the elections that 'Our great force has been Protestantism, we began the re-action with it; every step of success has been founded on it'.[39]

By the end of June, with scarcely one tenth of the results in, it was clear to all that the Whigs were 'Just Out', as one wag pencilled under a new likeness of Melbourne which appeared in a London print shop.[40] Nine seats had already been lost; when the cabinet talked of the probable majority against it, there were, noted Hobhouse, 'no signs of sorrow'.[41] There was in fact considerable relief. Although Russell would confess bitterness at Peel's chicanery of letting the Whigs founder on measures which he had supported or, in the case of free trade was known to favour, Lord John was comforted by the certainty that Peel must fall to the eventual 'insurrection' of the Tory 'blockheads'.[42] Reliance on support from some combination of Peel, Radicals or O'Connell had taken its toll. Parkes' judgement that the Whig–Radical 'coalition' was based on the desire of both 'to do without the other',[43] could have as well applied to the government's reliance on Peel. Ellice expressed the Whig view that because Peel had withdrawn support, it was better that they had not won the election; resignation was preferable to 'stumbling on to our fall' at the hands of 'radical coadjutors'. 'We could not have had a sufficient majority', he wrote, '& as the Tories must have their turn, let it be now.'[44] Russell in particular was consoled that the Whigs could rebuild on the strengths of their own supporters and their own programme; 'we stand better than if we had remained with a majority'. In 1846, he rejected the notion of joining with the Protectionists in a new alliance. 'I should not like to embark in a Government which rested on the support of any extreme party', he told Duncannon. 'This has been the case too much . . . with our Ministry of '35'.[45]

There remained only to hand over the reins. Improbable though it seemed, Russell was approached in August by the ultra Tory Vyvyan to consider a coalition,[46] but the Whigs' course had been by then set. With an eye to the principles by which they should be guided in opposition, the party's final debate concerned the means of resignation. From Althorp Park, Spencer suggested a simple announcement during the debate on the Queen's speech; although this would be an unorthodox method of resignation, he told Melbourne, 'by dissolving Parliament with the almost certainty of being beaten you have placed yourselves in a very unusual position.'[47] For a time, there was speculation that Peel would give in to his ultras by opposing Lefevre as Speaker; when Peel let it be known that he would not do so,[48] it was decided to test the House on the Address. Russell considered moving a resolution on the sugar or corn duties in order to make Peel commit himself, and in fact drafted a letter to the Conservative leader which was not sent. Ellice had prudently pointed out that some Whig county members would likely give Peel a larger majority than he actually possessed, and allow him moreover to duck the issue in the future with the excuse that the House had already offered its opinion on the subject. In the end, it was decided to go out if beaten on Peel's amendment to the Address.[49] Parliament was recalled 24 August. Although Russell had told Peel there would be no undue delay,

Lord John used the recess for betrothal, marriage and honeymoon. A terribly upset Queen made the rounds of several Whig country estates; Melbourne indeed was distressed as much at the Queen's pain as at his own losing office.[50] When parliament met, Ripon carried an immediate vote of non confidence in the Lords. In the Commons, the Whigs tried one final time to extract from Peel his views on duties and trade. He refused to budge. At the end of four days of fencing, the division on the Conservatives' amendment gave the opposition a majority of 91. Melbourne resigned. Entering upon 'my present heavy trial, the heaviest I have ever had to endure',[51] the Queen sent for Peel.

13

Postscript

a couple of years out of office . . . will do us all good in every way, both as to health and as to public favour. Ten years is a long innings to hold; and in order to know our value, the country must have a taste of our opponents.

Palmerston, 1 September 1841[1]

The history of any party which governed for more than ten years should be regarded as one of achievement. In the case of the Whigs, whose decade involved legislative acts among the most significant of the century, the history could be considered by all but their political foes as one of victory. To a large extent indeed it was, and has been, so regarded. Yet the electoral defeat which would follow, defeat which seemed inevitable for much of the life of Melbourne's governments, suggests that the Whigs to some extent failed. And, to be sure, comparing the Whigs' failure to Peel's success has become the commonplace view which this volume has attempted to alter. To some extent, the differences depend upon one's perspective; legislative success suggests achievement, parliamentary and electoral setback failure. It would be wrong, however, to dwell on those aspects of weakness which the Whigs were powerless to counter. Failure is a relative term. Had the Whigs set out to win support from those electors who turned increasingly against them in three successive elections, their story would properly be described as one of failure. If, on the other hand, their goal was to reform in a manner which would not turn the system over to the mob, those very elections provide support for the view that they succeeded. Neither goal, however, properly describes Whiggery's aims. Whigs took and left office as somewhat reluctant reformers. They were reformers in that they wished to provide moderate reforms timely conceded, but reluctant in the sense that they wished to steer a moderate middle path between the more violent forces of left and right. They wished to build what would be known as the Victorian consensus by refusing to make common cause both with those who opposed all change and those who wished for too much. Leaving office was to that extent neither triumph nor defeat so much as it was a disappointment.

The stoic equanimity with which the Whigs accepted loss of office reflects a certain degree of resignation which was justified. When looked at from both the parliamentary and wider political perspective, their loss was, by the later part of the 1830s, inevitable. They had governed by a parliamentary consensus which involved Peel, whose goals were more philosophically congenial than those of their more extreme followers. Whether or not 'party' developed during this period, the reality of Whig–Peel cooperation reflected the joint desire for moderate reforms in Church and State. But as the electorate began to reflect the political aims of the two extremes which both the Whigs and Peel had hoped to absorb, the governing consensus fell apart. The Whigs' problem was increasingly manifested in the Commons. The primacy of the House of Commons in parliament was an essential ingredient in the aim to balance the constitution, for it was in that House that the just desires and legitimate grievances of the people would be heard and the cause of civil and religious liberty – the ultimate 'safety valve' – promoted. Standing between the dangers of monarchical authority shored up by an intransigent House of Lords on the one hand, and mob rule on the other, the Commons would represent the views of moderate property owners who were entrusted with representing the people. Thus, when Holland and Melbourne observed in 1833 that the Reform Bill would 'throw the Government of the country into the House of Commons', the extremes of autocracy and democracy were considered to have been averted.[2] Yet by 1837, when the majority of the Whigs' supporters began to reflect views that could only be regarded by aristocratic Whigs as democratic in intent, the House of Commons became the problem rather than the remedy. Ballot and abolition of the corn laws, the two issues that had hitherto been supported by only a small number of Radicals, now found widespread acceptance. Melbourne told Russell that 'we must go by the elections and the House of Commons as elected. That is the principle of popular government',[3] but the Whigs were being caught in the net which Tory opponents of Reform had warned against laying in the debates of 1830–32. Where Whiggery had once been 'the beating of dissidence upon the shore of power',[4] its proponents now found themselves part of that shore. The issues which had sustained the Whigs until the accession of Victoria were those on which Fox and Pitt had pronounced in the 1780s and 1790s, but after a half dozen years in office, Whigs had done all they could to promote 'the old cause'. In 1839, Spring Rice told the poet Wordsworth that for twenty years he had acted on the doctrines of the Old Whig School and 'had not added to it nor taken therefrom [as] a friend of Reform and Catholic emancipation and of complete religious equality for the Protestant dissenters'. The year before, Russell attributed many of the Whigs' current problems to 'Pittite sins', and in the decisive nonconfidence debate in 1841, referred to 'the great cause of civil and religious freedom' and his determination, 'espousing the principles of Mr. Fox', not to desert that cause.[5] It is to be questioned if these professions of faith had much meaning by this time. Whig thinking has been described recently as 'static and embalmed in Holland House';[6] in the sense that Foxite principles had little relevance to the issues raised by Chartism and the League, there is much force in the argument. What the Whigs had to face was a new set of demands, put forward by the followers of a new Liberal creed, whose goals did not follow the old Whig determination to maintain the propertied interests in greatness and the system of deference on which that greatness rested. Foxite concepts of liberty had little in common with the competitive ideologies of Cobden and Bright.

More recently, Richard Brent has argued that a 'new modelled Whiggery', based on liberal Anglican values, supplanted both High Church Anglicanism and the Foxite inheritance as a dominant Whig principle. His study of Whig religion suggests that Russell and several other liberal Whigs were governed by a desire to establish a less nostalgic, more reform-minded party. Assisted by evangelical Whigs such as Althorp, the younger Whigs who came to dominate government after 1834 were guided by a 'constitutional moralism' which rejected the eighteenth century notions of the Foxites.[7] Brent is correct to reject the orthodoxy, established by Gash, Close and Beales, among others, which sees the Foxite inheritance as increasingly overtaken by Radical and O'Connellite influences. As has been argued throughout this

study, there was no cohesive Whig–Radical–Irish alliance confronting a united Conservative party. The Whigs who followed
Grey governed with Peel's assistance in order to reduce the
influence of each front bench's ultra supporters. On the other hand
Brent, like Gash, does argue that Whiggery entered a more
progressive or liberal phase once Grey and the High Church
Anglicans Stanley and Graham left office. It might well be wondered, however, if the evangelical religiosity which Brent, and to a
lesser extent Boyd Hilton,[8] has suggested as a philosophical basis
for Whig liberality has not been overemphasised. Both studies
offer an illuminating view of an aspect of Whig religion that is far
removed from the rational scepticism of the enlightenment, but to
what extent such religiosity can be accepted as the main principle
behind Whig government is less evident. Nor is it clear that
Whiggery under Melbourne was more progressive than Grey's
version. Melbourne, Holland and Palmerston, who were not
without influence, were not 'liberal Anglicans'. Althorp, who was,
had retired. Graham, who left with Stanley, was in many ways
more reformist in Church matters than several who remained. It
cannot be forgotten as well that Grey's retirement was in large
measure occasioned not so much by a philosophical dispute
between Foxite and liberal Anglican principles, or indeed between
age and youth, as it was a reaction to his loss of authority. And
here, the young Stanley's coquetting with an increasingly Tory
King had as much to answer for the breach as did differences of
principle. In many respects, the argument that evangelical liberalism guided Whig policy gives the same undue importance to the
appropriation issue as does Gash. It suggests as well that Church
matters were the most important topics in Whig councils, and
were, moreover, entirely religious in nature. But this was not
always the case. Holland, a Foxite atheist, was prominent in
opposition to Stanley and in support of Church reform. The
Whigs, it must be remembered, did not actively promote
appropriation on its own merits; it is doubtful that appropriation
would have been introduced without the tithe wars and the
resultant coercion measures. Church reforms, as the Church rates
issue indicated in 1837, were often prompted by as many political
as philosophical or religious considerations. Preservation of the
institutions of society was the goal of such legislation, a goal that
was unaffected by the change of leadership from Grey to Mel-

bourne. Whiggery's *via media* was just that. It is relied more on
Peel than on a coherent party and philosophical consistency. And
by so doing, it possessed a fatal weakness.

The problem of Whiggery seemed obvious to Russell. 'I always
thought', he told Melbourne shortly after the 1837 elections,[9]

> that the Whig party as a party would be destroyed by the
> Reform Bill. Their strength lay in certain counties and in close
> boroughs. The Tories, by the new construction of the House,
> were sure to beat them in the counties, and the radicals in the
> open towns.

This analysis offers a profound insight into the Whig mind in the
late eighteen-thirties, and provides, with the aid of hindsight, a
clue to the later disappearance of the Whigs. Whiggery stood for
property and the defence of the landed interest, but as its leaders
undertook reforms which they regarded as essential for the
preservation of that interest, property turned increasingly to the
Tories. At the same time, representatives of the urban communities grew increasingly alarmed at the Whigs' defence of the
constitution and promotion of reforms designed, to the urban
mind, only to shore up the traditional centres of authority. Before
1837, 'Radical politics' referred to the views of a minority of
government supporters; after the elections of that year, Russell
meant by that term the views of the majority of his supporters.
Whereas the ministry was previously supported by a large
number in the Commons whose political sympathies were similar
to its own, now it was not. Gradually, but undeniably, the
ministerial supporters differed from the government on a wider
range of issues. From 1838 there were scarcely 100 members whose
ideology resembled the ministry's. During Melbourne's first three
years as Prime Minister, Whig reforms were effected, or proposed,
on a basis which all but the Radicals considered sufficiently
extensive. Initiatives had been consistent with Whig beliefs.
Extra-parliamentary forces had often helped to secure passage of
these measures, but the government would not sponsor what was
not thought prudent and necessary. By 1838, with the exception of
unresolved business carried over from the old parliament, the
measures which the majority of the ministerialists supported were
regarded by the Whigs as either dangerous and unnecessary, or
indicative of a **democratic** tendency which would ultimately lead

to danger. The Radicals' attack on pensions, which greeted the civil list proposals in November 1837, is a case in point. Previously, Whittle Harvey's attacks on sinecures took place in thinly-attended houses which offered little support. Now, the Radicals' anger at the civil list which carried an additional £100,000 to pay off the debts of the Queen's mother, the Duchess of Kent, prompted the government to propose a committee of enquiry into pensions. Ministers hoped that a committee would shelve the problem, for they had no intention of meddling with existing pensions, but it was unnerving to find that had they resisted an enquiry, scarcely a person out of office would have supported them.[10] More alarming was the state of the ballot and corn law questions. The growing popularity of these two issues, and the increasing practice of candidates on the hustings to pledge themselves to change, put the government in the embarrassing position which Russell had forecast, for the centre of resistance to change was the cabinet. On 15 February 1838, only 60 of the 315 who defeated Grote's ballot motion were ministerialists; the 198 who supported Grote were the backbone of the Government's usual supporters. A month later, 221 of the 300 members who defeated Villiers' corn law motion were Tories; the majority of the voting ministerialists (90 of 169) had supported repeal. It was clear that what only Radicals had requested before 1835 was now considered by the majority of ministerial supporters to be worthwhile. In his decription of the ballot debate, Greville noted that the question was getting more popular in the country and was 'not regarded with much apprehension by many of those who are altogether opposed to Radical principles'.[11] He could have said the same for a repeal of the corn laws.

If Greville's comment suggests that Radicals were not the sole supporters of newly minted reforms, the Whigs grew increasingly ill at ease with the notion that, as the reform party, they should promote or become the depository for ballot and corn law reform. The electorate, they knew, was distinctly different from the 'country'; it was not attracted to these issues any more than they were themselves. They were committed to the 'finality' of reform and to a system devoted to the maintenance of the landed classes. 'My own natural prepossessions are all on the side of the land', wrote Ebrington to Melbourne on the eve of the 1839 session; 'I feel in myself no desire any more than you do to make friends with the Mammon of Trade & Manufacturers at the expense of that interest which I am exclusively connected by property as well as by the Constituency which I represent'.[12] Such a statement might well have been made by a number of Tories, but not likely by Peel. Here was the rub. Whigs were convinced that the new causes were not their own. They saw opponents of the new reforms rewarded at elections at an equal, if not more rapid, pace than advocates. But the number of MPs supporting the new reform agenda would make life exceedingly difficult for a government with a narrow majority. There was already a hint of resignation in Ebrington's words; two years later, he advised Melbourne that if Whigs did not move in such a direction, 'Peel shortly will'.[13] Political pressures would thus force an altered position by the end of the decade, but Whiggery did not succumb lightly. If at any time during these eleven years of Whig rule it was possible to say that a Liberal party began to emerge from its Whig cocoon, the session of 1838 would appear to be that time. Such a Liberalism, however, was of a ministerial parliamentary nature, not ministerial. Poulett Thomson was probably the first Liberal cabinet miniser, but his colleagues were Whiggish anti-Liberals to a man. The great divide in the Whiggism of the 1830s is to be seen therefore at the accession of Victoria, before which time it was in essential agreement with its parliamentary majority. Afterwards it was not.

As long as the tacit alliance with Peel continued, the governing consensus could nevertheless survive. By 1839, however, Peel's own difficulties with his extremer supporters allowed little room for .manoeuvre. Not surprisingly perhaps, many of Peel's supporters were as upset with his moderate course of governing in opposition as were Melbourne's. When the Conservative leader was forced by the ultra Tories to support their strategy of vigorous opposition, the government's preference was to leave office. The Whigs had never taken much comfort from Peel's support. Melbourne claimed not to mind by whom he was helped, as long as he *was* helped, but Russell, who termed Conservative support an 'embarrassment', was more representative of Whig thinking.[14] Peel's unwillingness to take office, and thereby to place himself at the mercy of his ultra supporters, generated two final years of the governing consensus, but the alliance was more phrenetic, if not splenetic, than hitherto. The Conservative leader's failure to moderate his own party's policies, a failure in large measure caused by the electoral success of the anti-Reform movement, produced further polarisation. The consensus was destined to disintegrate.

It was perhaps an irony, but one inescapably true, that while elections returned government supporters increasingly committed to reforms which the Whigs could not support, the electorate as a whole was profoundly conservative. The electoral trend which culminated in the Conservative victory in 1841 was based on concerns for the Church, land and respect for authority. Sydney Smith's brother expressed the general attitude of the country at the end of the Whigs' long tenure of office.[15]

> The country was tired of them, I think, and always will be after a short time. There is too much botheration in their politics for our people, who, though they have reformed more than all the nations of Europe put together, do not like scheming and planning reforms when the work is not in hand, and called for by some pressing occasion; they have something else to do, and talking about reform disturbs them.

Melbourne's governments were scarcely more prone to this reaction, which began before the ink on Reform was dry, than Grey's would have been. The Whigs were moderate reformers, but the 'botheration' which Robert Smith reported was with all reform, whether conservative or radical. Peel was no less immune, for he was no more in touch with this political nation than were the Whigs, with whom he had governed in one tacit manner or other from the day in May 1832 when he refused to support Wellington's attempt to regain power. It was not Peel who won in 1841, but the reactionary forces which deeply offended him. What triumphed in those elections were not his new Conservative principles, which were in many respects more liberal than those espoused by the Whigs, but those aspects of Toryism which he had unsuccessfully tried to subvert. Those who governed in the 1830s – Grey, Melbourne, Peel – could not, and did not, survive this reaction. Grey was the first to fall and Melbourne the second. Peel's parliamentary defeat in 1846 was only the final signal that what he represented had been similarly defeated in 1841. The process of reaction was inevitable. Reform, with its decade, was ended.

Notes

(see List of Abbreviations on page ix.)

1 'COLOURS AND CRIES, BUFF AND BLUE'

1. *Fortnightly Review*, March 1886: 'Only a few years ago the name [Whig] was a proud boast, a hereditary recollection, the appanage of a great party; now it is an historical recollection, recalling colours and cries, buff and blue'. D. G. Southgate, *The Passing of the Whigs 1832–1836*, 1962, p. xv.
2. T. S. Estcourt to Sir William Joliffe, 1 January 1856, Hylton MSS, 24/11. f. 13. I am indebted to Dr Angus Hawkins for this reference.
3. Earl Russell, *Recollections and Suggestions 1813–1873*, 1875 2nd edn, p. 51.
4. Southgate, *The Passing of the Whigs*, p. 197.
5. R. William, 'The Origins of "Whig" and "Tory" in English Political Language', *The Historical Journal*, 1974, vol. XVII, pp. 247–64.
6. Sir D. Le Marchant, *Memoirs of John Charles, Viscount Althorp*, 1876, p. 110; Le Marchant Diary, January 1832, in A. Aspinall (ed.), *Three Early Nineteenth Century Diaries*, 1952, pp. 175–6.
7. For two recent accounts of the Whigs' historical principles, see J. Clive, *Thomas Babington Macaulay*, (1976), chs. IV–VII and L. Mitchell, *Holland House*, 1980, chs. 2–4.
8. T. L. Erskine, *The Defence of the Whigs*, 1819, p. 23.
9. Quoted in J. Hamburger, 'The Whig Conscience', in P. Marsh (ed.), *The Conscience of the Victorian State*, 1979, p. 28.
10. *Edinburgh Review*, October, 1830, vol. LII, p. 277.
11. Russell, *Recollections and Suggestions*, p. 213.
12. A. S. Foord, *His Majesty's Opposition*, 1964, p. 453.
13. For the early Whigs, see F. O'Gorman, *The Whig Party and the French Revolution*, 1967; L. Mitchell, *Charles James Fox and the Disintegration of the Whig Party*, 1971; J. Derry, *Charles James Fox*, 1972; A Mitchell, *The Whigs in Opposition*, 1967; E. Smith, *Whig Principles and Party Politics*, 1976.
14. Mitchell, *Holland House*, p. 50.
15. Herbert Butterfield, *The Englishman and His History*, 1944, pp. 78–9.
16. John Carswell, *The Old Cause*, 1954, p. 20.
17. J. Boswell, *Life of Johnson*, 1969, p. 973.
18. *Cornhill Magazine*, 1907, in Bernard Mallet, *Thos. George, Earl of Northbrook, A Memoir*, 1906, p. 33.
19. Clive, *Macaulay*, pp. 211–14; Mitchell, *Holland House*, pp. 22–6.
20. Baring to Melbourne, August 1839, RA MP.
21. G. Le Strange (ed.) *Correspondence of Princess Lieven and Earl Grey*, 1890, vol. II, p. 278.
22. Mitchell, *Holland House*, pp. 46–7.
23. Palmerston to Melbourne, 30 October 1838, RA MP.

24. N. Gash, *Reaction and Reconstruction in English Politics, 1832–52*, 1965, p. 149.
25. J. Boswell, *The Journal of a Tour to the Hebrides*, 21 October 1773, (ed.), L. F. Powell, 1958, p. 235.
26. Sir H. Maxwell, *Life and Letters of the Fourth Earl of Clarendon*, 1913, vol. i, p. 220.
27. Joseph Parkes to Francis Place, 21 March 1836, Add. MSS 35150, f. 99.
28. In N. Gash, *Sir Robert Peel*, 1972, p. 717.
29. Hamburger, 'The Whig Conscience', pp. 19–38 (see note 9).
30. Ld. Aberdeen to Princess Lieven, 30 November 1837, in Southgate, *The Passing of the Whigs*, p. 78.
31. Lady Holland suggested as much. 'The fact is', she remarked in 1839, 'we have nothing to rely on but the Queen and Paddy.' C. C. F. Greville, Lytton Strachey and Roger Fulford (eds), *The Greville Memoirs*, 1938, 23 September 1839.
32. Curiously, Gash states that the 147th clause of the Irish Church bill was the single exception to this pattern. This same issue of appropriation he describes as one of the leading Radical attributes of Melbourne's governments. *Reaction and Reconstruction in English Politics*, p. 169.
33. Gash, *Reaction and Reconstruction in English Politics*, ch. VI.
34. Mallet, *Northbrook Memoir*, pp. 32–3.
35. J. Hamburger, 'The Whig Conscience', in P. Marsh (ed.), *The Conscience of the Victorian State*, p. 28.
36. A. Brundage, *The Making of the New Poor Law 1832–1839*, 1978, p. 182.
37. Southgate, *The Passing of the Whigs*, pp. 66–8.
38. W. Thomas, *The Philosophical Radicals. Nine Studies in Theory and Practice, 1817–1841*, 1979, p. 417.
39. Russell to Brougham, 18 February 1835, BrP 38142.
40. *Hansard*, 3 August 1836, vol. xxxv, col. 1309. On this point, see Mitchell, *Holland House*, pp. 66–8.
41. *Edinburgh Review*, 1837, vol. 65, p. 267.
42. Hobhouse to Holland, 1 October 1836, Add. MSS 51569, f. 83.
43. R. Brent *Liberal Anglican Politics: Whiggery, Religion and Reform 1830–1841*, 1987.

2 PARTY AND MANAGEMENT

1. Holland diary, September 1836, Add. MSS 51871, f. 971.
2. J. C. D. Clark, 'A General Theory of Party, Opposition and Government, 1688–1832', *Historical Journal*, 1980, vol. 23, p. 295.
3. Sir Lewis Namier, *Monarchy and the Party System*, 1952, p. 19.
4. Austin Mitchell, *The Whigs in Opposition, 1815–1830*, 1967, p. 1.
5. D. E. D. Beales, 'Parliamentary Parties and the Independent Member, 1810–1860', in R. Robson (ed.), *Ideas and Institutions of Victorian Britain*, 1967,. pp. 1–2.
6. N. Gash, *Reaction and Reconstruction in English Politics, 1832–52*, 1965, p. 126.

7. A. Aspinall, (ed.), *Three Early Nineteenth Century Diaries*, 1952, p. xxvi.
8. Brougham to Stanley, 18 January, 1830, DP 116/1.
9. *Morning Chronicle*, 12 July 1830.
10. *Tait's Edinburgh Magazine* 1833, vol. ii, p. 526.
11. D. E. D. Beales, 'Parliamentary Parties and the Independent Member, 1810–1860', p. 18.
12. Greville, *Memoirs*, 22 February 1833, vol. ii, p. 361.
13. J. Grant, *The British Senate in 1838*, 1838, ii, 272. Cf. B. Rose in 1835: 'A Conservative in principle, I have attached myself to no party'. D. H. Close, 'The formation of a two-party alignment in the house of commons between 1830 and 1841', *English Historical Review*, vol. lxxxiv, 1969, p. 263.
14. Brougham to Grey, 1 June, 1834, BrP.
15. Melbourne to Russell, 1 August 1841, RA MP, 15/48.
16. See B. W. Hill, 'Executive Monarchy and the Challenge of Parties, 1689–1832', *Historical Journal*, 13, 1970, 398. See too Frank O'Gorman, *The Emergence of the British Two-Party System 1760–1832*, 1982, p. 120: 'party alignments as such had dominated Parliament since the end of the Napoleonic Wars'.
17. Russell termed Stanley's speech one of the greatest triumphs ever won in a popular assembly by the process of oratory. Lord John Russell, *Recollections and Suggestions 1813–1873*, 1875, p. 138. George Byng told Lady Holland that 'neither Pitt nor Fox ever produced such an effect.' A. D. Macintyre, *The Liberator: Daniel O'Connell and the Irish Party 1830–1847*, 1965, p. 49.
18. Howick diary, 19 June, 1835, GP.
19. See Michael Brock, *The Great Reform Act*, 1973, pp. 217–20.
20. Gash, *Reaction and Reconstruction in English Politics*, pp. 167–72.
21. *Edinburgh Review*, vol. LXXIII, 1836, p. 249; Sir John Walsh, *Chapters on Contemporary History*, 1836, pp. 62–9. Cf. *Tait's Edinburgh Magazine*, 1836, p. 73, for the view that the term Whig-Radical was the favourite appellation of the Tory journals for Melbourne's government.
22. Harriet Grote, *The Personal Life of George Grote*, 1873, p. 109.
23. *Westminster Review*, vol. 28, October 1837, pp. 8–9. See Gash, *Reaction and Reconstruction in English Politics*, pp. 168–9.
24. Russell to Grey, 22 January 1835, Russell to Howick, 1 February, 1835, Howick diary, 28 November 1835, GP; Holland to Henry Fox, 17 January 1837, in L. Mitchell, *Holland House*, 1980, p. 54; Melbourne to Russell, 14 June 1840, RA MP, 14/127.
25. Beales, 'Parliamentary Parties and the Independent Member, 1810–1860', p. 18.
26. W. O. Ayedelotte, 'The House of Commons in the 1840s', *History*, vol. xxxix, 1954, pp. 249–62 and 'Voting Patterns in the British House of Commons in the 1840s', *Comparative Studies in History and Society*, vol. v, 1962–63, pp. 134–63; D. H. Close, 'The formation of a two-party alignment in the house of commons between 1830 and 1841, *English Historical Review*, vol lxxiv, 1969, pp. 257–77.

27. The sixteen divisions in the 1835 parliament were:

19 Feb.	1835	Speakership
26 Feb.	1835	Address
2 April	1835	Irish Church Resolution
7 April	1835	Irish Tithes Resolutions
23 May	1835	Peel Amendment—appropriation
4 Feb	1836	Address
8 Mar.	1836	Irish Corporations
28 Mar.	1836	Irish Corporations – 3rd Reading
3 June	1836	Irish Tithes – 2nd Reading
10 June	1836	Irish Corporations – Lords' Amendments
4 July	1836	Irish Church – Appropriation
2 Aug.	1836	Irish Tithes – Lords' Amendments
15 Mar.	1837	Church Rates Resolution
22 Mar.	1837	Irish Corporations
11 April	1837	Irish Corporations – 3rd Reading
23 May	1837	Church Rates Report

The eighteen divisions in the 1837 parliament were:

27 Nov.	1837	Controverted Elections Bill
6 Dec.	1837	Irish Elections Subscriptions
7 Mar.	1838	Canada Censure Motion
3 May	1838	Church Leases Comm.
3 May	1838	Church Leases Comm.
15 May	1838	Irish Tithes – Appropriation
19 April	1839	Irish Government Resolution
6 May	1839	Jamaica Suspension Bill
22 May	1839	Speakership
19 June	1839	Jamaica Bill – 3rd Reading
20 June	1839	Stanley's Education Motion
24 June	1839	Supply – Education Grant
31 Jan.	1840	No-confidence
9 April	1840	China War Resolution
20 May	1840	Irish Voter Registration—committee
25 Feb	1841	Irish Voters' Bill
18 May	1841	Sugar Duties
4 June	1841	No-confidence

Although a number of these divisions took place on government measures or policy issues, particularly concerning Ireland, they were all, in fact, regarded as trials of strength. As such, they should be considered as 'touchstone' divisions.

28. The three divisions were:

15 Nov.	1830	Civil List
22 Mar.	1831	Reform Bill – 2nd Reading
19 April	1931	Gascoyne Amendment

29. The eleven divisions were:

6 July	1831	Reform Bill – 2nd Reading
12 July	1831	Reform Bill – Committee
19 July	1831	Reform Bill – 1831 Census
21 Sept.	1831	Reform Bill – 3rd Reading
26 Sept.	1831	Scottish Reform – 2nd Reading
10 Oct.	1831	Confidence
17 Dec.	1831	Reform Bill – 2nd Reading
9 Feb.	1832	Portuguese Affairs
23 Feb.	1832	Reform Bill – 3rd Reading
10 May	1832	Address Crown
25 May	1832	Irish Reform – 2nd Reading

30. On 12 July 1831, fourteen Tories voted with the government in opposing the adjournment of debate on the Reform Bill. *Hansard*, Series III, vol. IV, col. 1146.
31. Beales, 'Parliamentary Parties and the Independent Member', p. 17.
32. Melbourne to Brougham, 13 October 1835, BrP. See too J. C. Hobhouse, Baron Broughton, *Recollections of a Long Life*, 1909, vol. iv, p. 86, for Hobhouse's view that but for Reform and Brougham's Chancery reform, the government would have been thrown out.
33. The absence of trials of strength during the 1833–1834 parliament made it necessary to establish government or opposition status for each member by reference to C. R. Dod, *Electoral Facts from 1832 to 1852*, 1852, and F. W. S. Craig, *British Parliamentary Results 1832–1885*, 1977.
34. The 24 divisions recorded in full by *Hansard* from the 1833–34 parliament are included. For the 1835–37 parliament, 38 divisions which took place on Radical reform motions, as well as on Legislative matters which were recorded in full by *Hansard* and on which a large proportion of the House voted, were included. Twenty-eight similar divisions for the 1837–41 parliament were included.
35. For purposes of tabulation, the Whigs' supporters are classified as government for the whole period. This practice does not, as a result, take into account the fact that Peel was Prime Minister of a Conservative government for the first two months of the 1835 session.
36. Peel, for example, supported the government in 14 of the 24 divisions analysed for the 1833–34 parliament, and opposed only 14 times, thereby giving the government more support than 87% of the government's ministerialist supporters.
37. Until 1836, *Hansard* usually recorded only the members who voted in the minority in these divisions. The basis for analysis is the number of times a ministerial member voted in opposition to the government.
38. Mitchell, *The Whigs in Opposition*, p. 66.
39. *Ibid.*, pp. 66–7.
40. *The Times*, 29 June 1841.
41. Beales, 'Parliamentary Parties and the Independent Member', p. 8.

42. Ian Newbould, 'Sir Robert Peel and the Conservative Party, 1832–1841: A Study in Failure?', *English Historical Review*, vol. xcviii, 1983, pp. 545–6.
43. Gash, *Reaction and Reconstruction in English Politics*, p. 126.
44. J. Morgan Sweeney, 'The House of Lords in British Politics 1830–1841', Oxford D. Phil., 1974, pp. 86–97; H. J. Hanham, *The 19th Century Constitution*, 1980, p. 180.
45. Wood to Grey, 3 July 1832, GP.
46. Ellice to Grey, 17 April 1832, GP.
47. Ellice to Grey, 22 July 1832, GP.
48. Wood to Grey, 3 July 1832, Ellice to Grey, 12 November 1832, GP.
49. Wood to Grey, 8 September 1832, GP; Althorp to Graham [n.d.] in Aspinall, *Three Early Nineteenth Century Diaries*, vol. liii.
50. Wood to Grey, 31 December 1832; Ellice to Grey, 9 January 1833, GP.
51. Hobhouse Diary, 24 February 1833, Add. MSS 56557, f. 108; Ellice to Holland, [n.d.] Add. MSS 51587, f. 28.
52. Aspinall, *Three Early Nineteenth Century Diaries*, p. 320 (Littleton's diary, 26 April 1833).
53. Wood to Grey, 6 May 1833, GP.
54. I. D. C. Newbould, 'William IV and the Dismissal of the Whigs, 1834', *Canadian Journal of History*, vol. xi, 1976, p. 315.
55. C. C. F. Greville, *The Greville Memoirs*, Lytton Strachey and Roger Fulford (eds), 1938, 25 February 1834, vol. iii, p. 16.
56. Greville, *Memoirs*, 25 February, 1834, vol. iii, pp. 19–20; Howick diary, 25 February 1834, GP; *The Times*, 26 February 1834. The meeting was held in Althorp's rooms at the Albany.
57. Greville, *Memoirs*, 21 July 1833, vol. ii, p. 399.
58. Wellesley to Melbourne, January, 1835, RA MP 39/69.
59. Stanley's papers have not survived. According to Miss Nancy Mitford, they were 'lost in the war'. There are a few letters in the Parkes' collection, University College, London, concerning electoral matters.
60. Parkes to Durham, 3 April 1835, LP. He added though that 'the Tories drill better'.
61. Holland asked Ellice on 5 January 1836, to exhort all travelling peers and MPs to be at their posts. EP/14, f. 168.
62. He was replaced in 1839 by H. G. Tufnell.
63. Ellice to Melbourne, 21 November 1838, RA MP 5/7.
64. Melbourne to Russell, 24 December 1838, RA MP 13/1 15.
65. T. Wyse, one of the government absentees, told Melbourne that he had never received the least intimation of the importance of the vote or the likelihood of its being so near. Melbourne to Russell, 19 May 1839, RA MP 14/31.
66. Durham to Ellice, 29 August 1832, EP/29, f. 64; Durham to Grey, 30 August 1832, GP.
67. Melbourne to Fred Lamb, 26 December 1832, in R. H. D. Custance, *The Political career of William Lamb, 2nd Viscount Melbourne, to 1841*, Oxford D. Phil., 1977, p. 24.
68. *Ibid.*, p. 25.

69. Ellice to Parkes (copy), 22 December 1832, EP/41, f. 13.
70. Ellice had gathered slightly more than £25,000 for the 1831 election. For the subscription list, see EP/75, f. 70.
71. Grey to Ellice, 12 December 1832, EP/18, f. 129.
72. Ellice to Grey, 10 and 19 September 1832, GP. Fleming was likely trying (unsuccessfully) to revive the Barony of Slane, extinct since 1726. Custance, *The Political Career of William Lamb*, p. 342.
73. Grey to Ellice Sr., 12 December 1832, EP/18, f. 127.
74. Ellice to Holland, [n.d.], Add. MSS 51587, f. 14.
75. Graham to Ellice, 21 August 1832, EP/18, f. 127.
76. See, for example, Ebrington to Ellice, 27 August 1832, EP/13, f. 203 and P. Thomson to Ellice, August 1832, EP/55, f. 1.
77. Althorp to Brougham (copy), 20 September 1832, SP, Box 7.
78. For evidence of Tory turmoil, see E. Herries, *Memoirs of J. C. Herries*, 1880, vol. ii, pp. 162–3: It was impossible, thought Herries, not to be struck by the activity of the Whig and revolutionary parties on the one hand, with the 'torpor, listlessness and Turkish waiting upon Providence' of the Conservatives on the other.
79. Melbourne to Mulgrave, 12 December 1834, MCA, MM/16.
80. 'I am glad you approve of my Newcastle manifesto', Durham wrote to Mulgrave. 'It occurred to me that it was just the moment for an amnesty – and for recruiting all Reformers.' 30 November 1834, MCA 0/293. For Durham's conduct, see W. Thomas, *The Philosophical Radicals, Nine Studies in Theory and Practice, 1817–1841*, 1979, pp. 361–2.
81. Robert E. Zegger, *John Cam Hobhouse*, 1973, p. 213.
82. Bulwer to Mulgrave, 14 January 1835, MCA 0/74.
83. Ian D. C. Newbould, 'Whiggery and the Dilemma of Reform: Liberals, Radicals and the Melbourne Administration, 1835–9', *BIHR*, LIII, 1980, 231–2.
84. Russell to Holland, 8 December 1834, Add. MSS 51677, f. 148; Grey to Ellice, 22 January 1835, EP/19, f. 50. See Palmerston to Russell, 22 January 1835, PRO 30/22/IE, f. 11, where Palmerston congratulated Russell on a recent speech in which Lord John attacked the 'absurd' ballot plan.
85. Howick diary, 26 December 1834, GP. Ingham, labelled a liberal by Dod, supported Peel on the important 'party' divisions, including the Speakership and the Amendment to the Address in February, 1835.
86. Zegger, *Hobhouse*, p. 214.
87. W. M. Torrens, *Memoirs of Rt. Hon. William, 2nd Viscount Melbourne*, 1878, vol. ii, p. 67.
88. Thomas, *The Philosophical Radicals*, pp. 251, 265.
89. Parkes to Durham, 26 June and 13 December 1834, LP, I–1.
90. Hume sent Francis Place a preliminary manifesto on 20 September 1834. Add. MSS 35149, f. 314. The Association was founded early in 1835, not 1834, as N. Gash, *Politics in the Age of Peel*, 1953, p. 404 suggests.
91. See Chapter 8.

92. Parkes to Stanley, 26 December 1839, PP, 25.
93. Parkes to Stanley, 7 September 1841, PP, 25.
94. A. Aspinall, 'English Party Organization in the Nineteenth Century', *English Historical Review*, vol. xli, 1926, p. 404.
95. Melbourne to Ellice, 17 November 1836, EP, 28, f. 43.
96. Holland diary, July 1834, Add. MSS 51879, f. 744. See too 'The Last Session of Parliament', *Edinburgh Review*, vol. 60, 1834, p. 248, for the view that members of parliament were determined not to give any countenance to 'those journalists' who opposed the poor law amendment bill.
97. See Kenneth Bourne, *Palmerston: The Early Years 1784–1841*, 1982, pp. 480–91.
98. J. C. Clarke, *The Fortunes of the Ellice Family: from business to politics, 1760–1860*, Oxford, D. Phil., 1973, p. 334. Aspinall, 'English Party Organization', p. 410. Grey refused Ellice's request to reward Buckingham with a clerkship in the Customs House. Ellice to Grey, 3 November 1831, GP, and J. R. M. Butler, *The Passing of the Great Reform Bill*, 1914, p. 151.
99. Grey to Palmerston, 15 May 1831, GP.
100. Brock, *The Great Reform Act*, pp. 95–8.
101. A. Aspinall, *Politics and the Press, 1780–1850*, 1949, p. 237.
102. Howick diary, 15 January 1838, GP; *Remarks on the Second Session of the Reformed Parliament*, anon., 1834, p. 22.
103. Bourne, *Palmerston*, p. 481. Stephen Koss, *The Rise and Fall of the Political Press in Britain: The Nineteenth Century*, 1981, puts the view that the press was generally controlled by the government before 1850. Norman Gash effectively dispels this notion in his review of Koss's book, *Journal of Modern History*, vol. 55, 1983, pp. 124–5.
104. Le Marchant to Brougham, 18 September 1834, BrP, 13500.
105. He demanded, for example, that Ellice have some of the government's independent friends like Ebrington speak out against O'Connell, who had called reporters 'wilful liars'. Ellice complied. Barnes to Ellice, 26 and 29 July 1833. EP/2, ff. 260, 264.
106. *The Times*, 23 May 1833; in Aspinall, *Three Early Nineteenth Century Diaries*, p. 341 (Le Marchant's Diary, 24 June 1833).
107. Barnes to Hobhouse, 15 April, 1833. Add. MSS 36467, f. 89.
108. A. Brundage, *The Making of the New Poor Law 1832–39*, 1978, pp. 38–9.
109. Althorp to Brougham, 11 June 1834, in *Chambers Historical News*, vol. xxviii, February 1835.
110. G. S. H. Fox-Strangways, 6th Earl of Ilchester, *Chronicles of Holland House, 1820–1900*, 1937, p. 186.
111. *The History of the Times*, 1935, vol. i, p. 236; W. N. Molesworth, *A History of England from 1830* , 1871, vol., 1, p. 317; Clarke, *The Fortunes of the Ellice Family*, p. 356; Greville, *Memoirs*, 28 March 1839, vol. iv, p. 139.
112. Lord Brougham, *The Life and Times of Henry, Lord Brougham*, 1871, vol. iii, p. 417.
113. For Parkes' attitude towards the Whigs, see Thomas, *The Philoso-*

phical Radicals, ch. 6, 'Joseph Parkes and Party'.

114. Abercromby to Ellice, 19 November 1835, EP/1A, f. 26.
115. Le Marchant to Holland, [n.d.]. Add. MSS 51591, f. 20.
116. Parkes to Stanley, 8 April 1839, PP/25.
117. Russell to Palmerston, 11 April 1839, BP GC/RU, ff. 26–7.
118. Spring Rice to Baring, [n.d.], MP, 536, f. 156.
119. Thomson to Melbourne, 9 June 1839, RA MP 15/146 and Melbourne to Russell, June 1839, RA MP 14/35.
120. R A Victoria's journal, 6 April 1839. See Thomas, *The Philosophical Radicals*, pp. 326–9, for a description of Fonblanque's increasingly Whiggish attitude.
121. J. T. Ward, (ed.), *Popular Movements 1830–1850*, 1970, p. 13.
122. Thomas, *The Philosophical Radicals*, p. 308.
123. In January 1835, Peel wrote to Taylor, the King's Secretary, to have him use his influence with the Windsor clergy in support of Walter's candidacy in the Berkshire election. 'I need say nothing as to the importance of keeping the *Times* and Mr. *Walter* in good humour', he wrote. Taylor then wrote to the Vicar of Windsor and other influential persons. Aided by the Court interest, Walter was returned unopposed. Peel to Taylor, 1 January 1835, Taylor to Peel, 2 January 1835. Add. MSS 40302, ff. 131–3.
124. In September 1839, Stanley reported to Melbourne that Carlton Club funds had been used to buy the *Courier*, a financially-troubled paper which had hitherto offered the Whigs general support. Stuart, its editor, told Stanley in 1838 that three or four thousand pounds would be necessary to purchase the majority of shares; with no means of finding that sum among the Whigs, Stanley had to let it go to the Conservatives. Stanley to Melbourne, 18 September 1839, RA MP 36/125.

3   A MINISTRY FOR REFORM

1. G. G. Lord Byron, *Don Juan, XI*, vol. lxxii, New York, 1949, p. 377.
2. Hobhouse diary, 16 November 1830, Add. MSS 56555, f. 54.
3. Grey to Howick, 10 February 1830, GP.
4. Russell to Ebrington, 20 October 1830, FP, 1262 M/FC, f. 86. Russell was thinking in terms of a moderate measure that would resemble his own earlier plans of giving representation to Manchester, Birmingham and Leeds.
5. Brougham to Russell, 5 August 1829. Add. MSS 51563, f. 94.
6. *Hansard*, 18 February 1830, vol. xxi, 678–91.
7. *Morning Chronicle*, 4 February 1830.
8. A. Aspinall (ed.), *Three Early Nineteenth Century Diaries*, 1951, p. xx.
9. N. Gash, 'Peel and the Party System, 1830–1850', *Transactions of the Royal Historical Society*, 5th series, vol. I, 1951, pp. 53–4; A. Mitchell, *The Whigs in Opposition 1815–1830*, 1967, p. 216.

10. Russell to Holland, January 1829, Add. MSS 51677, f. 66; Althorp to Holland, 8 January, 1829, Add. MSS 51724, f. 184; Mitchell, *The Whigs in Opposition*, pp. 213–4.
11. Brougham to Stanley, 18 January 1830, DP 116/1; Russell to Grey, 3 December 1829, GP.
12. Russell to Grey, 12 March 1830, GP.
13. Holland to Grey, 6 February 1830. Add. MSS 51548, f. 15.
14. Grey to Howick, 8 January 1830, GP; Grey to Lievan, 28 February 1830, G. LeStrange, (ed.), *Correspondence of Princess Lieven and Earl Grey*, 1890, vol. i, p. 459.
15. Russell to Holland, January 1829, Add. MSS 51677, f. 66; Russell to Grey, 3 and 19 December 1829, GP.
16. *Quarterly Review*, vol. xc, p. 529. J. A. Roebuck, in his *History of the Whig Ministry of 1830*, 1852, vol. i, p. 138, said that Howick and others opposed the motion not from a 'nice distinction of party interests', but from a desire to show that Brougham was not their leader. This is entirely plausible. See M. Brock, *The Great Reform Act*, 1973, pp. 73–4 for Whig fears of Brougham's behaviour.
17. Grey to Lieven, 25 February 1830, Le Strange, *Lieven-Grey Correspondence*, vol. i, p. 437; J. T. Ward, *Sir James Graham*, 1967, p. 85.
18. The three MPs were Portman, Pendarves and Lawley.
19. Sir D. Le Marchant, *Memoirs of John Charles, Viscount Althorp*, 1876, pp. 243–5; *Morning Chronicle*, 6 March 1830.
20. *Hansard*, 18 March 1830, N. S., vol. xxiii, Col. 391; Le Marchant, *Althorp*, p. 246.
21. Althorp to Grey, 6 March 1830, GP.
22. Lieven to Grey, 5 March 1830, Le Strange, *Lieven–Grey Correspondence*, vol. i, p. 464; Hobhouse diary, 14 May and 5 July 1830, Add. MSS 56554, ff. 100, 129–30.
23. Howick to Grey, 3, 11, and 23 March 1830, GP.
24. Grey to Howick, 14 March 1830, GP.
25. Grey to Holland, 4 February 1830, GP; Grey to Ellice, 17 February 1830, EP/18, f. 17 8; Grey to Lieven 29 January 1830, Le Strange, *Lieven-Grey Correspondence*, vol. i, p. 423; Brock, *The Great Reform Act*, pp. 70–1.
26. Grey to Lieven, 29 January and 12 February 1830, Le Strange, *Lieven-Grey Correspondence*, vol. i, pp. 424, 436; Grey to Ellice, 6 February 1830, EP/18, f. 309; Grey to Howick, 7 February 1830, GP.
27. Grey to Brougham, 5 February 1830, GP.
28. Grey to Howick, 16 January 1830, GP.
29. Grey to Ellice, 16 March 1830, EP/18, f. 25; Grey to Holland, 5 April 1830 and to Howick, 22 March 1830, GP.
30. Grey to Ellice, 2 March 1830, EP/18, f. 23.
31. Grey to Howick, 14 March 1830, Howick diary, 3 and 13 May, 1830, GP.
32. Brock, *The Great Reform Act*, p. 67.
33. Grey to Howick, 9, 14 and 22 March 1830, GP.
34. Howick diary, 5 and 13 May 1830, GP.

35. Grey to Lieven, 11 June 1830, Le Strange, *Lieven–Grey Correspondence*, vol. ii, p. 5.
36. *Hansard*, 30 June 1830, N. S., vol. xxv, col. 765; Grey to Lieven, 2 July 1830, Le Strange, *Lieven–Grey Correspondence*, vol. ii, p. 21.
37. *Hansard*, 30 June 1830, N. S., vol. xxv, col. 816; O'Connell to R. Barrett, 1 July 1830, W. J. Fitzpatrick (ed.), *Correspondence of Daniel O'Connell*, 1888, vol. i, p. 208.
38. Hobhouse diary, 4 July 1830, Add. MSS 56554, f. 127. Althorp to Spencer, 5 July 1830, SP; Althorp to Stanley, 5 July 1830, DP 117/3.
39. Russell to Holland, 26 July 1830, Add. MSS 51677, f. 73; Grey to Lieven, 13 August 1830, Le Strange, *Lieven-Grey Correspondence*, vol. ii, p. 49.
40. Brock, *The Great Reform Act*, p. 103. I am indebted to Brock's chapter on the 1830 election (pp. 86–118) for much of what follows.
41. *Annual Register*, July 1830, pp. 142–3; J. T. Ward, *Sir James Graham*, 1967, p. 88.
42. *The Times*, 14 July 1830; D. C. Moore, 'The Other Face of Reform', *Victorian Studies*, 5, 1961, p. 23; Brock, *The Great Reform Act*, pp. 103–4.
43. Le Marchant to Baring, 14 August 1830, T. G. Earl Northbrook (ed.), *Journals and Correspondence of F. T. Baring, Lord Northbrook*, 1905, vol. i, p. 66.
44. H. Perkin, *The Origins of Modern English Society 1780–1880*, 1969, p. 228.
45. Russell to Holland, 26 July 1830, Add. MSS 51677, f. 92.
46. Brock, *The Great Reform Act*, pp. 95–8.
47. Grey to Holland, 8 October 1830, GP; Grey to Spring Rice, 6 October 1830, MP, 11140/2; Brock, *The Great Reform Act*, p. 68.
48. *Annual Register*, 1830, p. 147.
49. C. C. F. Greville, *The Greville Memoirs*, Lytton Strachey and Roger Fulford (eds), 1938, 5 August 1830, vol. II, p. 25; *The Times*, 5 July 1830; The *Guardian*, 10 July 1830.
50. Palmerston Memorandum, July 1830, BP GMC/33. Wellington told Melbourne that he could not have made this offer earlier because George IV would not hear of taking on someone who had once resigned. Melbourne had resigned office with Canning in 1827.
51. Brock, *The Great Reform Act*, pp. 86–8.
52. Melbourne to Brougham, 19 September, BrP 43480; Palmerston to Grant, 25 September 1830, BP GMC/35; Mitchell, *The Whigs in Opposition*, p. 240.
53. For the negotiations, see Clive to Palmerston, 1 October 1830, Palmerston to Clive, 4 October 1830 and Palmerston's memorandum of his meeting with Wellington on October 30. BP GMC/36, 37 and 42.
54. Althorp to Brougham, 5 October 1830, SP; Holland to Grey, 25 September 1830, in Mitchell, *The Whigs in Opposition*, p. 240; Ellice to Grey, 28 October 1830, GP.
55. Russell to Grey, October 1830, GP.
56. Grey to Holland, 19 October 1830, GP; Hobhouse diary, 2 November 1830, Add. MSS 56555, ff. 35–6.

57. Grey to Holland, 19 September 1830, GP; Holland to Grey, 11 September and 10 October 1830, Add. MSS 51548, ff. 65, 79; Grey to Lieven, 15 September 1830, Le Strange, *Lieven–Grey Correspondence*, ii, 190; Hobhouse diary, 20 October 1830, Add. MSS 56555, f. 31.
58. Earl Russell, *Recollections and Suggestions 1813–1873*, 1875, p. 76.
59. Le Marchant, *Althorp*, p. 256; Hobhouse diary, 2 and 13 November 1830, Add. MSS 56555, ff. 36, 52; *Morning Chronicle*, 6 November 1830.
60. Cleveland to Brougham, 13 September 1830, BrP 16407; Brock, *The Great Reform Act*, pp. 126–7.
61. Graham to Brougham, 1 November 1830, BrP 14179; Hobhouse diary, 7 November 1830, Add. MSS 56555, ff. 44–5; Mitchell, *The Whigs in Opposition*, p. 247.
62. *The Times*, 20 November 1830; The *Manchester Guardian*, 20 November 1830.
63. Add MSS 27789, f. 234; Southgate, *The Passing of the Whigs*, p. 14.
64. C. Flick, 'The Fall of Wellington's Government', *Journal of Modern History*, vol. 37, 1965, pp. 63–5; J. Clive, *Thomas Babington Macaulay; The Shaping of the Historian*, 1976, p. 147.
65. G. S. H. Fox-Strangways, *Chronicles of Holland House 1820–1900*, 1937, p. 136; Melbourne to Russell, [n.d.] 1835, BP MEL/RU/135. The Whigs' attitude to Reform is discussed in the following chapter.
66. *Hansard*, 2 November 1830, vol. i, col. 65; Grey to Lieven, 7 October 1830, Le Strange, *Lieven–Grey Correspondence*, vol. ii, p. 104.
67. Russell to Holland, 18 October 1830, Add. MSS 51677, f. 82; Russell to Ebrington, 20 October 1830, FP 1262M/FC, f. 86, Hobhouse diary, 2 November 1830, Add MSS 56555, ff. 35–6.
68. On 13 August Peel was informed by the Tory agent Joseph Planta that the government's majority had increased to 100 as a result of the elections. On 28 August, the figure was revised to 134. Add. MSS 40401, ff. 127, 138. The Treasury list of November is to be found in f. 181.
69. Winchilsea's speech is quoted in Brock, *The Great Reform Act*, p. 125.
70. See Lieven to Grey, 9 November 1830, where the Princess reported a conversation with Wellington in which this view was expressed. Le Strange, *Lieven–Grey Correspondence*, vol. ii, p. 115.
71. Grey to Sir H. Taylor, 22 March 1831, Henry, Earl Grey, (ed.), *The Reform Act 1832, The Correspondence of Earl Grey with His Majesty King William IV*, 1867, vol. i, p. 186.
72. Baring to Lady Baring, 16 November 1830; Baring, *Correspondence and Journals*, vol. i, p. 71.
73. Grey to Holland, 1 August 1830, GP; Grey to Lieven, 16 November 1830, Le Strange, *Lieven–Grey Correspondence*, vol. ii, pp. 120–1.
74. L. G. Robinson (ed.), *Letters of Dorothea Lieven during her Residence in London 1812–1834*, 1902, p. 278.
75. Le Marchant, *Althorp*, p. 263; Christie, *The Transition from Aristocracy*, p. 176; Hobhouse diary, 6 November 1830, Add. MSS 56555, f. 40.
76. Grey's son-in-law Durham, Captain Barrington and Charles Wood were, respectively, Privy Seal, Lord of the Admiralty and joint Secretary of the Treasury. Brothers-in-law Ellice and Ponsonby were

Secretary of the Treasury and Commissioner to the Belgian government. His son Howick was undersecretary at the Colonial office.

77. Brock, *The Great Reform Act*, p. 132. See Southgate, *The Passing of the Whigs*, p. 10 and appendices, for the family connections.
78. Mitchell, *The Whigs in Opposition*, p. 43.
79. O. F. Christie, *The Transition from Aristocracy, 1832–1867*, 1927, p. 165; Hobhouse diary, 21 November 1830, Add. MSS 56555, f. 62; A. Aspinall, 'The Cabinet Council 1783–1835', *Proceedings of the British Academy*, 1952, p. 187.
80. Brock, *The Great Reform Act*, p. 142.
81. Russell, *Recollections and Suggestions*, p. 84.
82. *Hansard*, 5 July 1831, vol. iv, col. 776–7; Clive, *Macaulay*, p. 178.
83. Hobhouse diary, 10 December 1830, Add. MSS 56555, f. 72; Mitchell, *Holland House*, p. 78; Viscount Esher, (ed.), *The Girlhood of Queen Victoria*, 1912, vol. ii, p. 178.
84. *Parliamentary Debates*, 1 July 1819, vol. XL, col. 1496 (Russell); J. C. Hobhouse, Baron Broughton, *Recollections of a Long Life*, 1909, 4 June 1835, vol. 5, p. 38, (Melbourne); *Hansard*, 22 November 1830, vol. i, col. 613 (Grey).
85. Earl Russell, *An Essay on the History of the English Government and Constitution*, 1865, pp. 250–1.
86. *Hansard*, 3 May 1827, N. S., vol. xvii, col. 534 (Russell); Grey's speech in Brock, *The Great Reform Act*, p. 37.
87. Brock, *The Great Reform Act*, p. 37.
88. J. Hamburger, *James Mill and the Art of Revolution*, 1963, p. 34.
89. *Hansard*, 4 October 1831, vol. vii, col. 179 (Melbourne), 5 July 1831, vol. iv, cols. 773–83 (Macaulay).
90. *Hansard*, 2 March 1831, vol. ii, col. 1207 (Sandon); Melbourne to Russell, 7 September 1837, BP MEL/RU/396; Melbourne to Palmerston, 11 October 1836, BP GC/ME/133.
91. Holland to Grey, 5 November 1831, GP; Grey to the Knight of Kerry, in G. M. Trevelyan, *Lord Grey of the Reform Bill*, 1929, p. 237n.
92. *Hansard*, 22 November 1830, vol. i, col. 613.
93. *Hansard*, 20 August 1831, vol., vi, col. 339. D. C. Moore, *The Politics of Deference; A Study of the Nineteenth Century Political System*, 1976, p. 232 and 'Concession or Cure: The Sociological Premises of the First Reform Act', *Historical Journal*, vol. ix, 1966, pp. 44–5.
94. D. Cecil *Lord M*, 1954, p. 231.
95. E. P. Thompson, 'The Peculiarities of the English', *Socialist Register*, 1965, pp. 323–4. *Hansard*, 28 March 1831, 1020 (Durham). See *Hansard*, vol. ii, col. 1143 for Althorp on the same theme.
96. H. Cockburn, *Letters on the Affairs of Scotland*, 1874, p. 285. See Perkin, *Origins of Modern English Society*, p. 311 and N. Gash, *Politics in the Age of Peel*, 1953, p. 15, for a discussion of this question.
97. A. V. Dicey, *Law and Public Opinion in England during the Nineteenth Century*, 1898, 2nd edn, p. 185; J. Cannon, *Parliamentary Reform, 1640–1832*, 1973, p. 254.
98. Macaulay, 'Utilitarian Theory of Government', in Clive, *Macaulay*, pp. 125–6; Spencer to Brougham, 17 January 1841, SP.

99. Graham, *Corn and Currency*, 1826, in A. Briggs, 'Middle Class Consciousness in English Politics', *Past and Present*, 9, 1956, 69.
100. *Hansard*, 16 April 1831, vol. iii, col. 580 (Stanley), 4 October 1831, vol. vii, col. 1176 (Melbourne).
101. *Edinburgh Review*, 1832, lvi, p. 258; *Westminster Review*, 1833, vol. xviii, p. 109.
102. *Hansard*, 7 October 1831, vol. viii, col. 330 (Grey), 18 March 1831, vol. iii, col. 210 (Attwood).
103. S. Woolley, 'The Personnel of the 1833 Parliament', *English Historical Review*, 1938, pp. 259–62.
104. Hobhouse diary, 19 June 1830, Add. MSS 56554, f. 118 records Attwood's conversation with Hobhouse.
105. *Hansard*, 3 March 1830, vol. ii, col. 139; Melbourne to Anglesey (copy), 26 February 1831, DP 117/7.
106. See Holland's diary, 5 August 1832, for reference to the ministers' unanimous approval of a cabinet memorandum that represented government policy at home and abroad as 'truly *conservative*'. Add. MSS 51869, f. 559.
107. Grey to Lord Somers, 26 October 1831, GP. See Cannon, *Parliamentary Reform*, pp. 255–6 for his calculations from which these figures are taken.
108. Russell to Melbourne, 13 August 1837, PRO 30/22/2F, f.9; *Hansard*, March 1831, vol. iii, col. 1307; Althorp to Brougham, 17 January 1841, SP.
109. *Hansard*, 1 March 1831, vol. ii, cols. 1086–7.
110. As the lord did not know the waiter's Christian name, the election was declared void and a fresh election held. His name having been ascertained, the waiter was duly elected. Russell, *Recollections and Suggestions*, p. 44.
111. *Hansard*, 3 October 1831, vol. vii, col. 956.
112. Althorp to Spencer, 4 September 1832, in Le Marchant, *Althorp*, pp. 442–3. Until Euston dropped out, Althorp planned to accept an invitation to stand for Tower Hamlets free of all expense.
113. Trevelyan, *Lord Grey of the Reform Bill*, p. 245; Cannon, *Parliamentary Reform*, p. 257.

4 WHIGGERY AND THE BILL

1. Melbourne to Brougham, 13 October 1835, BrP 43538.
2. Althorp to Stanley, 15 November 1831, DP 117/3.
3. Lansdowne to Grey, 18 January 1831, GP. Bye-elections at Knaresborough and Preston were the scenes of demonstrations against the Devonshire and Derby interests. It cost £100,000 to elect Huskisson's successor in Liverpool, prompting one observer to ask 'What can call more loudly for reform?' M. Brock, *The Great Reform Act*, 1973, p. 149.
4. Howick diary, 6 November 1830, G. P. Russell said in the Commons that the measure was formed first in Grey's mind, then communicated to him. *Hansard*, 1 March 1831, vol. ii, col. 1061. Baring wrote in

his journal that 'The outline was drawn by Lord Grey'. T. G. Earl Northbrook (ed.), *Journal and Correspondence of F. T. Baring, Lord Northbrook*, 1905, vol. i, p. 83n.

5. Earl Russell, *An Essay on the History of the English Government and Constitution*, 1865, p. xxxvi; Russell to Durham, 19 October 1834, Add. MSS 38080, f. 73.

6. Grey was convinced that the price paid for the delay was the Irish tithe war. Grey to Spring Rice, 6 October 1830, MP 1140/2.

7. The instructions from cabinet are in Graham's words. See Brock, *The Great Reform Act*, p. 136. As late as 2 December, Holland suggested Russell's name as a member of the committee to Grey. Holland to Grey, 2 December 1830, GP. Letters from Durham to Grey and Grey to Lansdowne on 15 January (GP) suggest that the plan was distributed to the cabinet that day.

8. Graham to Durham, 25 January 1831, LP 1–7.

9. Hobhouse diary, 3 February 1831, Add. MSS 56555, f. 90; Grey to Durham, 24 January 1831, Henry Earl Grey (ed.), *The Reform Act 1832. The Correspondene of Earl Grey with His Majesty King William IV*, 1867, vol. i, p. 81.n. Brougham never forgave the passing over of his claim in favour of Graham. Before long, he suggested that Graham had done the government a great deal of harm in the Commons and should be sent to St. Petersburgh. Brougham to Holland, [n.d.] 1831, Add. MSS 51563, f. 147; S. J. Reid, *The Life and Letters of the First Earl of Durham*, 1906, vol. i, p. 352.

10. Lansdowne to Grey, 18 January 1831, GP.

11. Durham to Grey, 15 January 1831, GP; Durham to Brougham, 30 December 1830, BrP 10012. For the committee's deliberations and cabinet discussion of the plan, see Russell to Durham, 19 October 1834, Add MSS 38080, f. 73; Russell to Brougham, 15 November 1837, BrP 14426; Tavistock to Brougham, 7 May 1839, BrP 28103; J. Prest, *Politics in the Age of Cobden*, 1977, ch. 2 (Graham's work on the registration system); E. Halévy, *The Triumph of Reform 1830–1841*, 1961, p. 25n; Brock, *The Great Reform Act*, pp. 136–42.

12. Grey to Palmerston, 31 January 1831, BP GC/GR/1964. When Grey saw the King, the urban franchise had not yet been lowered to £10, but the King gave his approval should this change be necessary.

13. Grey to Taylor, 13 January and 4 February 1831, Grey to William IV, 8 February 1831, *Correspondence Grey–William IV*, vol. i, pp. 52, 92, 118.

14. Hume to Althorp, 11 January 1831, SP.

15. Lieven told Grey on 17 February that Wellington, Peel and Aberdeen had spoken to her in 'great moderation'; a few days later she reported a conversation at Londonderry's, where it was decided that the Tories should support ministers, provided the plan was moderate. G. Le Strange (ed.), *Correspondence of Princess Lieven and Earl Grey*, 1890, vol. ii, pp. 169–70.

16. Baring's journal for 27 February reveals the Treasury calculation. Baring, *Journals and Correspondence*, vol. i, pp. 81–2. See Brock, *The Great Reform Act*, p. 156, for the suggestion that Ellice had reason for

telling Grey less than what he might have known of the state of the Commons.

17. Lieven to Grey, 9 February 1831, Le Strange, *Lieven–Grey Correspondence*, vol. ii, pp. 159–60.
18. Hobhouse diary, 23 February 1831, Add. MSS 56555, f. 96.
19. See Chapter 7 for a discussion of Whig economic policy.
20. Baring journal, 27 February 1831, Baring, *Journals and Correspondence*, vol. i, pp. 81–2.
21. Grey to Princess Lieven, 22 January 1831, Baring, *Journals and Correspondence*, vol. i, pp. 81–2.
22. Hobhouse diary, 1 March 1831, Add. MSS 56550, f. 99.
23. Ellenborough diary, 1 March 1831, in A. Aspinall (ed.), *Three Early Nineteenth Century Diaries*, 1952, p. 62; Hobhouse diary, 1 March 1831, Add. MSS 56550, f. 99.
24. Le Marchant diary, 1 March 1831, in Aspinall, *Three Nineteenth Century Diaries*, p. 13.
25. As late as February 1, Hobhouse declined Althorp's invitation to a parliamentary dinner because he considered it a meeting of members 'notoriously' supporting the administration, 'among which members I choose not to be ranked. I am a friend but no follower, nor ought a member for Westminster to be so'. A week after Russell's motion, he told Durham that the provisions of the bill would allow him to support the administration in any manner it thought desirable. Hobhouse diary, 1 February and 7 March 1831, Add. MSS 56555, f. 100.
26. C. C. F. Greville, *The Greville Memoirs*, Lytton Strachey and Roger Fulford (eds.), 1938, 11 March 1831, vol. ii, p. 128.
27. Stanley to Anglesey, 25 and 28 February 1831, DP 167/1.
28. Grey to Palmerston, 10 April 1831, Broadlands Papers, GC/GR/1973; Grey to William IV, 19 March 1831, to Taylor, 19 March 1831, *Correspondence Grey–William IV*, vol. i, p. 154.
29. Holland to Grey, 21 April 1831, Grey Papers.
30. P. Ziegler, *King William IV*, 1973, p. 168.
31. William IV to Grey, 4 February and 21 April 1831, *Correspondence Grey–William IV*, vol. i, pp. 194, 227.
32. L. G. Robinson (ed.), *Letters of Dorothea Princess Lieven during her Residence in London 1812–1834*, 1902, p. 302; William to Grey, 17 May 1831, *Correspondence Grey–William IV*, vol. i. p. 265; Brock, *The Great Reform Act*, p. 202.
33. J. C. Hobhouse, Baron Broughton, *Recollections of a Long Life*, 1909, 22 April 1831, vol. iv, p. 209.
34. The figures are taken from Ellice's subscription list, EP/75, f. 70.
35. Lieven to Grey, 25 April 1831, *Grey–Lieven Correspondence*, vol. ii, p. 215.
36. See R. Stewart, *The Foundation of the Conservative Party 1830–1867*, 1978, pp. 77–8.
37. R. Cowherd, *The Politics of English Dissent*, 1959, p. 78.
38. Brock, *The Great Reform Act*, pp. 194–5.

39. Le Marchant, *Memoirs of John Charles Viscount Althorp*, 1876, p. 319; Greville, *Memoirs*, 29 April 1831, vol. ii. p. 25; Ellice to Grey, 27 December 1831, GP; Grey to Ellice, [n.d.], EP/18, f. 41.

40. Stewart, *The Foundation of the Conservative Party*, p. 80.

41. Baring, *Journals and Correspondence*, 8 May 1831, vol. i, p. 87.

42. Halévy, *The Triumph of Reform*, p. 39n.

43. Graham to Anglesey, 1 September 1831, GrP, MS film 130.

44. *Remarks on the Second Session of the Reformed Parliament*, (anon.) 1834, p. 33; Russell, *An Essay on the History of the English Government and Constitution*, p. cvii; Le Marchant, *Althorp*, p. 110; Grey to Althorp, 11 March 1832, SP.

45. Lord Brougham, *The Life and Times of Henry, Lord Brougham*, 1871, vol. iii, p. 74; Le Marchant, *Althorp*, p. 261.

46. Holland diary, 8 October 1831, Add. MSS 51867, f. 175.

47. Brock, *The Great Reform Act*, pp. 246–7.

48. Grey to Wharncliffe, 25 November 1831, Grey to Taylor, 25 November 1831, *Correspondence Grey–William IV*, vol. i, pp. 479, 433. The negotiations are reprinted in pp. 464–80.

49. A plan to remove 11 boroughs from Schedule B was approved by Grey, but Melbourne and Palmerston opposed the giving of additional members to the large towns which accompanied it. Grey to William IV, 3 December 1831, William IV to Grey, 4 December 1831, *Correspondence Grey–William IV*, vol. ii, pp. 9, 16.

50. Wellington to Peel, 21 May and 26 November 1831, Add. MSS 40309, ff. 247, 254; Althorp to Grey (copy), 26 November 1831, SP; Grey to Taylor, 25 November 1831, *Correspondence Grey–William IV*, vol. i, p. 443.

51. Brougham to Althorp, [n.d.] SP; Holland to Grey, 26 October 1831, GP.

52. L. C. Sanders (ed.), *Lord Melbourne's Papers*, 1889, p. 135; in Aspinall, *Three Nineteenth Century Diaries*, Littleton, 28 October 1831, pp. 152–3; Melbourne to Palmerston, 10 October 1831, BP GC/ME/12.

53. Grey, Palmerston and Richmond formed the minority. Lansdowne and Stanley would have joined them were they not absent, but their votes would have been counterbalanced by Durham and Graham's, who were also absent. Holland diary, 19 November 1831, Add. MSS 51868, f. 217. *Correspondence Grey–William IV*, i. 431.

54. Palmerston to Melbourne, 20 November 1831, RA MP 11/3; Althorp to Grey, [n.d.], SP.

55. Holland to Grey, 19 October 1831, GP.

56. Grey to Holland, 30 October 1831, GP.

57. Althorp to Grey, 20 November 1831, SP; Althorp to Parkes, 18 November 1831, PP/24.

58. Grey to Althorp, 20 November 1831, SP.

59. 'I never saw a man', wrote Littleton, 'so unvaryingly discreet and adroit in his management of differences where conciliation was an object.' Aspinall, *Three Nineteenth Century Diaries*, p. 357.

60. Grey to Holland, 30 October 1831, GP.

61. Holland diary, 6 March 1832, Add. MSS 51868, f. 389.

62. Althorp to Stanley, 15 November 1831, DP 117/3.
63. Most notably, Schedules B and D were redrawn. The 1831 census figures were used for the first time. See Brock, *The Great Reform Act*, pp.264–7, for details of the changes.
64. Palmerston and Melbourne protested at the increase in Schedule D, but were overruled. Grey to Taylor, 3 December 1831, *Correspondence Grey-William IV*, vol. ii, p.8.
65. Holland diary, 27 December 1831, Add. MSS 51868, ff.257–60.
66. Holland diary, 27 December 1831, 2 and 11 January 1832, Add. MSS 51868, ff.269, 281–8, 296; Grey to Holland, 1 January 1832, Add. MSS 51556, f.1; 'Minutes of Conversation with the King', 4 January 1832, William IV to Grey, 5 and 15 January 1832, *Correspondence Grey-William IV*, vol. ii, pp.68–9.
67. Holland diary, 15 February 1832, Add. MSS 51868, f.346; Taylor to Stanley, 15 and 27 February 1832, DP 100/2.
68. Baring, *Journals and Correspondence*, 4 February 1832, vol. i, p.92; Grey to Taylor, 14 February 1832, *Correspondence Grey-William IV*. vol. ii, p.222; Althorp to Spencer, 31 January 1832, SP.
69. Grey to Lieven, 13 February 1832, *Grey-Lieven Correspondence*, vol. ii, p.331.
70. Tavistock to Grafton, 29 February 1832, PRO 30/22/1C, f.27, in Aspinall, *Three Nineteenth Century Diaries*, p.202.
71. Althorp to Grey, 11 March 1832, Grey to Althorp, 11 March 1832, SP.
72. See D. Large, 'The Decline of "The Party of the Crown" and the Rise of parties in the House of Lords, 1783–1837', *EHR*, lxxvii, 1963, 685. Brock, *The Great Reform Act*, pp.378–9, n.19, has a full analysis of the two divisions.
73. 'Minutes of a Conversation with the King', 1 April 1832, *Correspondence Grey-William IV*, vol. ii, p.303.
74. Grey to Lieven, 10 May 1832, *Grey-Lieven Correspondence*, vol. ii, p.348; Grey to Holland, 13 and 14 May 1832, Add. MSS 51556, ff.32–4.
75. Althorp to Spencer, 14 May 1832, SP; Brougham, *Memoirs*, 9 May 1832, vol. iii, p.194.
76. Brock, *The Great Reform Act*, p.291.
77. Graham to Palmerston, 13 May 1832, BP GC/GR/19.
78. Brock, *The Great Reform Act*, pp.299, 301.
79. Holland diary, 15 and 17 May 1832, Add. MSS 51869, ff.490–8; Althorp to Spencer, 16 and 18 May 1832, SP.
80. When Taylor told Wellington, in the King's presence, that William had given a pledge in January to create peers when necessary, the Duke said at once that his opposition must be given up. Althorp to Spencer, 17 May 1832, SP.
81. See *Correspondence Grey-William IV*, vol. ii, p. 444; Baron Stockmar, *Memoirs*, 1872, vol. i, p.232 n.
82. Earl Russell, *Recollections and Suggestions 1813–1873*, 1875, pp. 458, 130.
83. N. Gash, *Politics in the Age of Peel*, 1953, p. 11; J. Cannon, *Parliamentary Reform 1640–1832*, 1973, p. 261.
84. *Hansard*, 22 November 1830, vol. i, col. 613.

85. Brock, *The Great Reform Act*, p. 146.
86. *Hansard*, 4 October 1831, vol. vii, col. 1184.
87. Russell, *Recollections and Suggestions*, pp. 121, 126.
88. Melbourne to Russell, 18 January 1839, Sanders, *Melbourne Papers*, p. 389.
89. Quoted in Russell, *Recollections and Suggestions*, p. 98.
90. Cannon, *Parliamentary Reform 1640–1832*, p. 263.

5 THE GREY MINISTRY, 1833–34

1. Le Marchant Diary, 23 June 1833 in A. Aspinall, *Thee Early Nineteenth Century Diaries*, 1952, p. 339.
2. Althorp to Spencer, 2 January 1833, SP.
3. Graham to Russell, 5 December 1832, R. Russell (ed.), *Early Correspondence of Lord John Russell 1805–1840*, 1903, vol. ii, p. 38.
4. Russell to Lady Holland, 13 September 1832, Add. MSS 51680, f. 39.
5. Sir H. Maxwell (ed.), *The Creevy Papers*, 1912, p. 594; Sir John Walsh, *Chapters on Contemporary History*, 1836, p. 43; Buckingham, *Parliamentary Review*, 1833; Durham to Ellice, 28 December 1832, f. 83; Mahon to Peel, 8 January 1833, in C. S. Parker, *Sir Robert Peel*, 1891, vol. ii, p. 204.
6. Grey to Lieven, 12 January and 9 February 1833, G. LeStrange (ed.), *Correspondence of Princess Lieven and Earl Grey*, 1890, vol. ii, pp. 428, 444; Grey to Holland, n.d. [January 1833], Add. MSS 51556, f. 104; Grey to Graham, 29 December 1832, GrP MS film 135.
7. Grey to Granville, 17 December 1832, PRO, 30/29/6-e, f. 343.
8. Wood to Grey, 31 December 1832, GP.
9. Althorp to Spencer, 8 and 10 May 1833, SP. See Chapter 6 for discussion of the slavery question.
10. *Leeds Mercury*, 2 November 1833. See Chapter 6 for discussion of the factory question.
11. See Chapter 6 for discussion of the Whig budget measures.
12. Peel to Goulburn, 3 January 1833, in Parker, *Peel*, vol. ii, pp. 212–4; N. Gash, *Sir Robert Peel*, 1972, 42–43; R. Stewart, *The Foundation of the Conservative Party, 1830–1867*, 1978, p. 95.
13. Peel to Croker, 5 March 1833, in Parker, *Peel*, vol. ii, p. 216.
14. Peel to Goulburn, 3 January 1833, in Parker, *Peel*, vol. ii, p. 212.
15. Peel to Goulburn, 25 May 1834, in Parker, *Peel*, vol. ii, pp. 243–4.
16. Gash, *Sir Robert Peel*, pp. 52–3.
17. 'I differ so much from many of our friends', he told Wellington, 'as to the prospects and as to the advantages of gaining the support of Radicals for a Government acting on really Conservative principles.' 20 July 1833, in Gash, *Sir Robert Peel*, p. 53.
18. Taylor to Brougham, 5 January 1833, BrP 39017; Lieven to Grey, 25 January 1833, *Grey-Lieven Correspondence*, vol. ii, pp. 438–9. Lieven mentioned 'my informant' and Taylor 'a very decided Tory'.

19. *Hansard*, 7 February 1833, vol. xv, col. 370; Littleton diary, 6 and 7 1833, in Aspinall, *Three Nineteenth Century Diaries*, p. 297; Hobhouse diary, 7 February 1833, Add. MSS 56557, f. 91.
20. *Hansard*, 23 April 1833, vol. xvii, cols. 506–37.
21. See Chapter 6 for this episode.
22. 'Look at the questions on which I have supported, and those on which I have opposed the Reform Government', he argued in 1835; 'compare their number, compare their relative importance, and then decide – whether I or the ultra-Reformers were the parties differing the most in views and principles from the government of Lord Grey'. *Hansard*, 24 February 1835, vol. xxvi, col. 229.
23. Stanley to Grey, 23 November 1832, GP; Russell to Lady Holland, 2 December [1832], Add. MSS 51680, f. 266.
24. See Chapter 6 for a discussion of the Irish Church question.
25. Holland to Grey, 31 December 1832, GP.
26. Ellice to Grey, (2 letters), [n.d.] and 9 January 1833, GP.
27. Le Marchant diary, 12 February 1833, in Aspinall, *Three Nineteenth Century Diaries*, p. 299.
28. Althorp to Grey, 1 January 1833, SP.
29. Ellice to Grey, 9 January 1833, GP; Grey to Ellice, 11 January 1833, EP/19, f.1.
30. Wood to Stanley, 5 January 1833, DP, 126/3; Stanley to Taylor, 25 January 1833, DP, 167/2; Althorp to Brougham, 3 February 1833, SP; Ebrington to Ellice, 1 May 1833, EP/11, f. 210.
31. Littleton diary, 21 June 1833, in Aspinall, *Three Nineteenth Century Diaries*, p. 339.
32. On Tennyson's motions to shorten the duration of parliament, 23 July 1833 and 15 May 1834, Althorp's amendment to Harvey's pension motion, 18 February 1834, and on the motion to abolish flogging in peace time, 10 April 1833.
33. *Hansard* 15 July 1833, vol. xix, col. 656.
34. Littleton diary, 12 July 1833, in Aspinall, *Three Nineteenth Century Diaries*, p.347; Holland diary, 15 July 1833, Add. MSS 51869, ff. 646–7. Holland said that Wrottesley resisted Althorp's 'earnest entreaties' to withdraw the motion. Duncannon told Grey that with the concurrence of Althorp, he wrote to everyone he knew to support the motion. Duncannon to Grey, 15 July 1833, GP.
35. Wrottesley, obviously embarrassed, offered to withdraw the motion only if none of those who supported him in the 'first part of the debate' wanted a division. When O'Connell asked for a division, it took place, and the motion was defeated by 160 to 125. Among the minority were the Whigs Abercromby, Duncannon, Ebrington, Sir George Grey, W. C. Russell, and a number of Radicals, O'Connellites and liberal ministerialists. *Hansard*, 15 July 1833, vol. xix, cols 662–3.
36. Barnes to Ellice, 16 July 1833, EP/2, f. 258.
37. Littleton diary, 12 July 1833, in Aspinall, *Three Nineteenth Century Diaries*, p.347.
38. Holland to Grey, 14 July 1833, GP. Holland must have misdated this letter, for the debate took place on the 15th.

39. On 18 February 1834, 169 ministerialists supported the Radical motion to enquire into all existing pensions. With the aid of 70 Tories, the government was able to maintain a 190 to 182 majority against Harvey. Ebrington told Holland that the government could avoid defeat on future Radical motions for quinquennial parliaments and reduced pensions by offering the compromise motion of abolishing the vacating of seats on the acceptance of certain offices. Holland to Grey, 28 March 1834, GP; Ebrington to Althorp, 8 April 1834, SP.

40. Ellice to Grey, [n.d.] GP. Richmond's influence in Chichester and Sussex (West) returned four rather conservative Whigs.

41. *The Times*, 11 April 1833; Barnes to Hobhouse, 15 April 1833, Add. MSS 36467, f. 89.

42. E. Halévy, *The Triumph of Reform*, p. 95.

43. Hobhouse resigned his cabinet post and seat rather than support the government's opposition to abolition of the house and window tax. Although he also opposed the abolition, his constituents did not. He thus stood for re-election as a supporter of these taxes. Evans polled 2027, Hobhouse, 1835 and the Conservative, Escott, 738. Hobhouse to Grey, 30 April 1833, GP; Hobhouse diary, 15 March and 27 April 1833, Add. MSS 56557, ff. 120, 137–41.

44. Tory gains were in Dover, London, Gloucester, Sunderland, Berwickshire, Dudley, Somerset, East Perthshire, Sudbury, Gloucestershire East.

45. Cf. Macaulay to Spring Rice, 11 August 1834, on the 'pretty ministry' which had turned its back on the 'centre gauche'. W. M. Torrens, *Memoirs of Rt. Hon William, 2nd Viscount Melbourne*, 1878, vol. ii, pp. 16–27.

46. Grey to Lieven, 1 July 1831, *Grey-Lieven Correspondence*, vol. ii, p. 253.

47. 'I shall take the first honourable opportunity to free myself from a situation I feel to be embarrassing & unpleasant', Russell told Holland when he heard of Stanley's promotion. 1 July 1831, Add. MSS 51977, f. 94.

48. Littleton diary, 21 July 1833, in Aspinall, *Three Nineteenth Century Diaries*, p. 350.

49. Holland diary, 1 August 1832, ADD. MSS 51869, f. 555.

50. Althorp to Grey, 6 August 1832, (copy) SP; Holland diary, 5 August 1832, Add. MSS 51869, ff. 561–2.

51. Stanley to Grey, 4 August and 6 November 1832, GP; Durham to Ellice, 28 October 1832 and 1 January 1833, EP/29, f. 70, 85; Holland diary, [n.d.], Add. MSS 51869, f. 570; Russell to Stanley, 30 December 1832, DP 130/12.

52. Stanley to Durham, 29 November 1832, Grey to Stanley, 2 December 1832, GP; Grey to Althorp, 1 December 1832, SP.

53. Grey to Holland, 6 January 1833, Add. MSS 51566, f. 96; Holland diary, 6 January 1833, Add. MSS 51869, f. 573.

54. Stanley to Grey, 4 August 1832, 6 January 1833, GP.

55. Graham to Palmerston, 12 January 1833, BP GC/GR/32; Grey to Melbourne, 9 January 1833, Melbourne to Grey, 11 and 12 January 1833, GP.
56. Stanley to Taylor, 25 January 1833, DP 167/2; Althorp to Brougham, 3 February 1833, SP; Holland diary, [n.d.], Add. MSS 51869, ff. 574–6.
57. Stanley to Brougham, 5 March 1833, BrP 16825.
58. Grey to Holland, 21 and 25 March 1833, Add. MSS 51556, f. 109–10; Holland to Grey, 25 March 1833, GP.
59. Durham's vainglorious and quarrelsome conduct had reached the point where, as Althorp told Grey in December 1832, 'there is no one of your colleagues whose opinions I know who think it possible to go on with him.' Althorp to Grey (copy), 5 December 1832, SP. His health, given as the reason for his departure, affected only the time of his resignation. See Ian D. C. Newbould, 'Lord Durham, the Whigs and Canada, 1838: the Background to Durham's Return', *Albion*, 8, 1976, 351–7.
60. Ellice went to the War Office to replace Hobhouse who succeeded Stanley as Irish Secretary on 29 March. Upon Hobhouse's resignation, Littleton became Irish Secretary on 17 May. Abercromby, Spring Rice and Bonham Carter all declined the office when Hobhouse resigned. Littleton diary, 12 May 1833, in Aspinall, *Three Nineteenth Century Diaries*, p. 328. In September, Anglesey was replaced as Lord Lieutenant by the Marquis of Wellesley.
61. Holland diary, [n.d.], Add. MSS 51869, f. 576.
62. Taylor to Stanley, 2 June 1833, DP 100/2.
63. A. D. Kriegel (ed.), *The Holland House Diaries 1831–1840*, 1977, p. 464 n. 64. The plan might have been discussed among the four the previous evening, when the King dined with the Cabinet at Holland House. Holland diary, 20 June 1833, Add. MSS 51869, f. 621.
64. On 16 and 18 June. Holland diary, Add. MSS 51869, f. 618.
65. *Hansard*, 2nd series, 4 April 1829, vol. xxi, col. 394, P. Ziegler, *King William IV*, 1973, p. 143.
66. Holland diary, 13 November 1834, Add. MSS 51870, f. 213. It was the Duke of Cumberland who first suggested to William that reforms of the Irish Church might betray his coronation oath. Taylor to Grey, 7 June and 27 July 1833, R. A. Add. 4075, 5010.
67. Taylor to Stanley, 27 January 1833, DP 100/2.
68. Taylor to Melbourne, 18 July 1834, RA MP.
69. Taylor to Col. Shawe (copy), 15 October 1834, RA MP.
70. Taylor to Stanley, 27 January 1833, DP 100/2.
71. Taylor to Stanley, 2 June 1833, DP 100/2.
72. Le Marchant diary, 3 June 1833, in Aspinall, *Three Nineteenth Century Diaries*, p. 333.
73. Holland diary, 4 June 1833, Add. MSS 51869, ff. 600–1
74. Holland diary, 4 June 1833, Add. MSS 51869, ff. 603–4; Le Marchant diary, 3 June 1833, in Aspinall, *Three Nineteenth Century Diaries*, p. 333; Ziegler, *King William IV*, p. 244.
75. *Hansard*, 27 June 1836, vol. xxxiv, col. 961. See Chapter 9.

76. Grey to Wellesley, 4 June 1843, Add. MSS 37311, ff. 79–80.
77. J. M. Sweeney, 'The House Of Lords in British Politics 1830–1841', Oxford D. Phil., 1974, pp. 288–95.
78. Lord Brougham, *The Life and Times of Henry, Lord Brougham*, 1871, vol. iii, pp. 281, 294–5.
79. Taylor to Stanley, 5 June 1833, DP 100/2.
80. Stanley to Taylor, (copy) 13 July 1833, DP 167/2.
81. Taylor to Stanley, 14 July 1833, DP 100/2.
82. Grey to Stanley, 10 December 1830, DP 117/5. The castle influence did not give an automatic entry into parliament. It cost Stanley nearly £1,500, without a contest. Stanley to Brougham, BrP 16825.
83. Stanley to Taylor, (copies), 2 and 6 December 1833, DP 170; Taylor to Stanley, 6 and 30 December 1833, DP 100/2.
84. William IV to Althorp, 4 June 1833, in Sir D. Le Marchant, *Memoirs of John Charles Viscount Althorp*, 1876, p. 471.
85. Stanley to Peel, 22 April 1832, Add. MSS 40403, f. 25; William IV to Stanley, 17 February 1832, DP 100/1.
86. Stanley to Taylor (copy), 15 July 1833, DP 167/2.
87. Taylor to Stanley, 15 and 27 July 1833, DP 100/2.
88. See for example Graham to Stanley, 3 December 1833, GrP MS film 134 and Stanley to Grey, 9 December 1833 and 10 January 1834, GP, on sub-cabinets being held at Goodwood, Richmond's estate.
89. Althorp to Littleton, 5 January 1834, Add. MSS 37306, ff. 308–9.
90. Holland diary, [n.d.] Add. MSS 51870, f. 714; Duncannon to Wellesley, 13 December 1833, Add. MSS 37306, f. 246; Littleton to Wellesley, 31 January 1834, Kriegel, *Holland Diary*, p. 468 n. 14.
91. Littleton to Wellesley, 2 May 1834, Add. MSS 37307, f.3.
92. Russell to Holland, 15 February [1834], Add. MSS 51677, f. 106.
93. Russell to Grey, 2 May 1834, Grey to Russell, 2 May 1834, Howick diary, 2 May 1834, GP; Grey to Holland, 2 May 1834, Add. MSS 51557, f. 27. The motion was defeated by 241–71. *Hansard*, 2 May 1834, vol. xxiii, cols. 429–71.
94. *Hansard*, 6 May 1834, vol. xxiii, col. 666.
95. Russell to Stanley, 28 May 1834, DP 130/12.
96. Russell to Grey, 7 May 1834, GP; Earl Russell, *Recollections and Suggestions 1813–1873*, 1875, p. 153.
97. Holland diary, [1834] Add. MSS 51870, f. 715; Howick diary, 8 May 1834, GP.
98. Littleton to Wellesley, 14 May 1834, Add. MSS 37307, f. 44; Holland to Grey, 24 May 1834, GP.
99. *Hansard*, 16 May 1834, vol. xxiii, cols. 1103–7.
100. Stanley to Spring Rice, (copy) 4 May 1835, DP 167/2; Holland to Grey, 24 May 1834, GP.
101. Stanley to Taylor (copy), 6 December 1833, DP 170; Stanley to E. B. Portman (copy), 21 June 1834, DP 167/2.
102. Stanley to Richmond (copy), 18 May 1834, DP 167/2; Stanley to Spring Rice, 4 February 1835, DP 167/2; Howick diary, 20 February 1835, GP.
103. Littleton to Wellesley, 14 May 1834, Add. MSS 37307, f. 45.

104. He opposed the government's support for O'Connell's motion to reprimand Baron Smith, a protestant Irish judge who had let his bias prejudice a jury. Grey persuaded him not to resign. Grey to Graham, 14 February 1834, GrP MS film 135; Graham to Holland, 14 February 1834, Add MSS 51542, f. 56; *Hansard*, 13 February 1834, vol. xxi, col. 283.
105. Graham to Palmerston, 22 January 1834, BP GC/GR.60.
106. Howick diary, 7 May 1834, GP; J. C. Hobhouse, Baron Broughton, *Recollections of a Long Life*, 1909, 11 May 1834, vol. iv, p. 340.
107. Littleton diary , 20 July 1833, in Aspinall, *Three Nineteenth Century Diaries*, p. 349.
108. Brougham, *Memoirs*, vol. iii, p. 376.
109. Althorp to Grey (copy), 6 August 1832, SP.
110. Grey to Goderich, 20 March 1833, Ripon to Grey, 29 January 1834, Grey to Ripon, 29 January 1834, GP; Grey to Holland, 29 March 1833, Add. MSS 51556, f. 111; W. D. Jones, *'Prosperity' Robinson, The Life of Viscount Goderich 1782–1859*, 1967, p. 236.
111. Holland diary, 2 July 1833, Add. MSS 51869, f. 633.
112. Holland diary, 1, 24 and 27 August 1833, Add. MSS 51870, ff. 669, 679–80; Littleton diary, 20 July 1833, in Aspinall, *Three Nineteenth Century Diaries*, p. 349.
113. Grey to Goderich, 17 September 1833, GP; Graham to Holland, 9 October 1833, Add. MSS 51542, f. 52; Holland to Ellice, 22 October 1833, DP/14, f. 138.
114. Holland diary, 14 and 16 January 1834, Add. MSS 51870, f. 703–6; Althorp to Spencer, 16 January 1834, SP; Grey to Ellice, 15 January 1834, EP/19, f. 17; Brougham, *Memoirs*, 111, 329.
115. Grey to Ellice, 14 February 1834, EP/19, f. 11; Howick diary, 25 April 1834, GP.
116. 'Grey has more than once observed to me', wrote Holland, that the King 'neither offered him any little favour or mark of honour nor requested him to give him his bust'. Holland diary, [July 1834], Add. MSS 51870, f. 728; Howick diary, 6 July 1834, GP; Graham to Palmerston, 16 January 1834, BP GC/GR/59.
117. Le Marchant diary, 27 May 1834, in Aspinall, *Three Nineteenth Century Diaries*, pp. 379–80; Althorp to Spencer, 28 May 1834, SP.
118. Melbourne to Wellesley, 4 May 1834, Add. MSS 37307, f. 14. Besides Littleton and Wellesley, Althorp, Grant, Abercromby, Ellice, Russell, Brougham, Holland and Melbourne were opposed to this and the courts martial clause. Holland diary, [1834], Add. MSS 51870, ff. 725–8; Howick diary, 9 July 1834, GP.
119. Brougham had induced Littleton to write a note, accompanying one from himself, to Wellesley, the Lord Lieutenant, suggesting that it would facilitate a Cabinet agreement on the point if a letter from the Lord Lieutenant to Grey should advocate such a step. Assuming from conversation with Brougham that the Cabinet would omit the clauses, Littleton further asked for, and received, permission from Althorp to apprise O'Connell of the government's views. During the ensuing conversation on 23 June, Littleton overstepped his brief by

informing O'Connell that the clause would be definitely left out. Most of the Cabinet blamed Brougham for the affair. Lord Hatherton, *Memoirs and Correspondence Relating to Political Occurrences in June and July 1834*, Henry Reeve (ed.), 1872, pp. 9–24; Holland diary, June 1834, Add. MSS 51870, ff. 724–5; Broughton, *Recollections*, vol. iv, p. 352; Howick diary, 7 and 9 July 1834, GP; Le Marchant, *Althorp*, pp. 495–6.

120. Howick diary, 7 July 1834, GP; *Hansard*, 3 July 1834, vol. xxiv, col. 1099; Le Marchant, *Althorp*, pp. 493–516.
121. Althorp to Grey, 29 June and 7 July, 1834, GP.
122. Grey to Holland, 8 July 1834, Add. MSS 51548, f. 159, and 2 November 1835, Add, MSS 51557, f. 64; Grey to Althorp, 2 December 1832 and July 1834, SP; Grey to Ellice, 11 January 1833, EP/19, f. 1.

6 REFORM GOVERNMENT, 1833–34

1. *Hansard*, 17 July 1833, vol. xix, col. 753.
2. *Hansard*, 4 February 1834, vol. xxi, cols. 1–5.
3. J. Hamburger, 'The Whig Conscience', in P. Marsh (ed.), *The Conscience of the Victorian State*, 1979, p. 18–38.
4. *Hansard*, 17 July 1833, vol. xix, col. 753.
5. Sir D. Le Marchant (ed.), *The Reform Ministry and the Reformed Parliament*, 1833, 5th edn, p. 107.
6. *Hansard*, 24 February 1835, vol. xxvi, col. 229.
7. A. Brundage, *England's 'Prussian Minister': Edwin Chadwick and the Politics of Government Growth, 1832–1854*, 1988, p. 15.
8. L. Brown, *The Board of Trade and the Free Trade Movement 1830–42*, 1958, pp. 46–7.
9. *Hansard*, 11 February 1831, vol. ii, col. 407.
10. C. C. F. Greville, *The Greville Memoirs*, Lytton Strachey and Roger Fulford (eds), 1938, 9 December 1830, vol. ii, p. 75.
11. *The Journal of Mrs Arbuthnot*, F. Bamford and the Duke of Wellington (eds), 1950, vol. ii, 345; Sir D. Le Marchant, *Memoirs of John Charles, Viscount Althorp*, 1876, pp. 238–9; Stafford Northcote, *Twenty Years of Financial Policy*, 1862, p. 26; Brown, *The Board of Trade*, pp. 10–11.
12. Le Marchant, *Althorp*, p. 284; T. G. Earl Northbrook (ed.), *Journals and Correspondence of F. T. Baring, Lord Northbrook*, 1905, 27 February 1831, vol. i, p. 81. An income tax was apparently discussed by cabinet, but rejected.
13. Althorp to Devonshire, 26 November 1830, SP.
14. Le Marchant, *Althorp*, p. 269; *Hansard*, 28 March 1831, vol. iii, col. 1078.
15. Brown, *The Board of Trade*, p. 46.
16. L. Mitchell, *Holland House*, 1980, p. 174.
17. David Roberts, *Paternalism in Early Victorian England*, 1979, p. 236; Brown, *The Board of Trade*, pp. 51–5.
18. Le Marchant diary, 4 July 1833, in A. Aspinall (ed.), *Three Early Nineteenth Century Diaries*, 1952, p. 343.

19. The deficit for 1831–32 was £1,240,000. For the calendar year 1832, it was £798,000. The improvement was so sudden that by January 1833 there was a surplus of £614,000. Althorp to Spencer, 19 January 1833, SP.
20. See A. D. Gayer, W. W. Rostow and A. J. Schwartz, *The Growth and Fluctuation of the British Economy 1790–1850*, 1953, vol. i, p. 242.
21. *Hansard*, 19 April 1833, vol. xvii, cols. 326–41.
22. Althorp to Spencer, 20 April 1833, SP.
23. *Ibid*.
24. On 21 March 1833. The division was 192 to 158.
25. Three days before Attwood's motion, Althorp wrote to Peel to verify that the course the government meant to take against the motion was not 'impolitic'. Add. MSS 40403, ff. 231–2.
26. E. Halévy, *The Triumph of Reform 1830–1841*, 1961, p. 93.
27. Gayer, Rostow and Schwartz, *The Growth and Fluctuation of the British Economy*, vol. i, p. 245.
28. The vote was 162–52. Le Marchant diary, April 1833, in Aspinall, *Three Nineteenth Century Diaries*, pp. 322–3; Le Marchant, *Althorp*, p. 461.
29. Althorp to Spencer, 27 April 1833, SP.
30. E. Myers, *Lord Althorp*, 1890, p. 147.
31. Russell to Althorp, 14 September 1833, SP.
32. Stanley to Grey, 28 April 1833, Ellice to Grey, 27 April 1833, GP.
33. Grey to Howick, 14 and 22 March 1830, GP.
34. Ellenborough diary, 1 May 1833, in Aspinall, *Three Nineteenth Century Diaries*, p.324.
35. Althorp to Peel, 28 April 1833, Add. MSS 40403, ff. 239–40, records Althorp's positive response to Peel's initiative.
36. Hume to Ellice, 27 April 1833, EP/25, f. 121.
37. *Hansard*, 29 April 1833, vol. xvii, col. 728.
38. Broughton diary, 29 April 1833, Add. MSS 56557, f. 140.'
39. *Hansard*, 3 May 1833, vol. xvii, col. 958.
40. S. Maccoby, *English Radicalism 1832–1852*, 1935, p. 84; Halévy, *The Triumph of Reform*, p. 95.
41. *Hansard*, 14 February 1834, vol. xxi, col. 365.
42. *Hansard*, 21 February 1834, vol. xxi, cols, 660, 690.
43. C. H. Phillips, *The East India Company 1784–1834*, 1961, p. 288.
44. A. Bain, *James Mill*, 1884, p. 341.
45. Phillips, *The East India Company 1784–1834*, p. 290.
46. *Hansard*, 13 June 1833, vol xviii, col. 701.
47. Ellenborough diary, 6 June 1833, in Aspinall, *Three Nineteenth Century Diaries*, p. 343.
48. Althorp told the Bank that only a legal misinterpretation of its powers had previously kept other deposit banks out of London. See J. H. Clapham, *The Bank of England 1797–1914*, 1958, vol. ii, pp. 127–9.
49. Le Marchant to Holland, [n.d.], Add. MSS 51591, f. 40.
50. *Hansard*, 3 July 1833, vol. xix, cols. 82–3; Le Marchant diary, 4 July 1833, in Aspinall, *Three Nineteenth Century Diaries*, p. 343.
51. Halévy, *The Triumph of Reform*, p. 97.

52. Earl Russell, *Recollections and Suggestions 1813–1873*, 1875, p. 140.
53. D. J. Murray, *The West Indies and the Development of Colonial Government 1801–1834*, 1965, p. 187.
54. Brown, *The Board of Trade*, p. 36.
55. *Hansard*, 15 April 1831, vol. iii, col. 1408.
56. *Hansard*, 27 June 1834, vol. iv, col. 372.
57. E. Hurwitz, *Politics and the Public Conscience*, 1973, p. 52.
58. H. W. Temperley, *British Anti-Slavery 1833–70*, 1972, pp. 12–13.
59. Quotations are from Hurwitz, *Politics and the Public Conscience*, pp. 57–9.
60. *Hansard*, 17 August 1831, vol. vi, col. 160.
61. Murray, *The West Indies and the Development of Colonial Government*, p. 191.
62. *Christian Observer*, June 1832, vol. 32, p. 368.
63. Althorp to Howick, December 1831, GP.
64. Hurwitz, *Politics and the Public Conscience*, p. 52.
65. *Hansard*, 1 June 1832, vol. xiii, col. 286; W. D. Jones, '*Prosperity Robinson*', *The Life of Viscount Goderich 1782–1859*, 1967, p. 224; Le Marchant, *Althorp*, p. 470.
66. Howick to Russell, 11 January 1833, PRO 30/22/1C, f. 111; Howick to Ellice, 9 January 1833, EP/22, f. 1; Holland to Howick, 4 January 1833, GP; Cabinet Memorandum, 4 February 1833, in Jones, *Prosperity Robinson*, p. 226.
67. Howick diary, 24 March 1833, GP.
68. *Hansard*, 14 May 1833, vol. xvii, col. 1194.
69. Temperley, *British Anti-Slavery 1833–1870*, p. 18.
70. Ellice to Grey, 4 and 9 February 1833, GP. See J. C. Clarke, *The Fortunes of the Ellice Family: from business to politics, 1760–1860*, D. Phil. thesis, Oxford, 1973, pp. 35–44 and 165–78 for the Ellice Business interests in the West Indies.
71. See Mitchell, *Holland House*, pp. 88–102. The quotation is taken from p. 92.
72. Russell to Howick, 3 December 1832, GP.
73. Howick to Russell, 11 January 1833, PRO 30/22/1C, f. 111; Howick to Ellice, 9 January 1833, EP/22, f. 1.
74. Graham to Ellice, 7 February 1833, EP/16A, f. 12; *Hansard*, 26 February 1845, vol. lxxvii, col. 1300 (Macaulay); J. Clive, *Thomas Babington Macaulay: The Shaping of the Historian*, 1976, p. 235.
75. G. T. Garrett, *Lord Brougham*, 1935, p. 243.
76. J. C. Hobhouse, Baron Broughton, *Recollections of a Long Life*, 1909, vol. iv, p. 280.
77. A. Aspinall, *Lord Brougham and the Whig Party*, 1927, p. 240; Le Marchant, *Althorp*, p. 448; R. Stewart, *Henry Brougham*, 1985, pp. 242, 286. In his article for the *Edinburgh Review*, vol. lviii, October 1833, pp. 206–7, Brougham 'deplored' the 'extravagance' of the anti-slavery party.
78. Hurwitz, *Politics and the Public Conscience*, p. 53.
79. Holland to Howick, 4 January 1833, GP.
80. Goderich to Mulgrave, 11 February 1833, MCA 0/454.

81. S. Woolley, 'The Personnel of the Parliament of 1833', *EHR*, 1938, vol. liii, p. 246.
82. George Stephens, *Anti-slavery Recollections*, H. Temperley (ed.), 1971, pp. 204–5.
83. Holland to Mulgrave, 27 May 1833, MCA M/365.
84. Holland to Grey, May 1833, GP; Ellenborough diary, 23 June 1833, in Aspinall, *Three Nineteenth Century Diaries*, pp. 340–1.
85. William IV to Goderich, 5 June 1832, in Jones, *Prosperity Robinson*, p. 222; Le Marchant diary, May 1833, in Aspinall, *Three Nineteenth Century Diaries*, p. 331; Le Marchant, *Althorp*, p. 470. There is correspondence between William IV and Stanley in the DP, Box 100, concerning this question.
86. A. D. Kriegel, 'A Convergence of Ethics: Saints and Whigs in British Antislavery', *Journal of British Studies*, 1987, vol. 26, pp. 432–50.
87. Halévy, *The Triumph of Reform*, p. 115.
88. J. Ward, *The Factory Movement 1830–1855*, 1962, p. 97.
89. C. Driver, *Tory Radical: The Life of Richard Oastler*, 1946, p. 204.
90. *Edinburgh Review*, 'Trade-Unions and Strikes', 1834, vol. lix, 342–55.
91. Ward, *The Factory Movement*, pp. 25, 30, 71, 77.
92. The quotations are found in Ward, *The Factory Movement*, pp. 414, 421, and J. T. Ward, *Popular Movements 1830–1850*, 1970, p. 55.
93. M. Thomas, *The Early Factory Legislation*, 1948, pp. 29–31; Ward, *The Factory Movement*, pp. 38–44.
94. James Grant, *The British Senate in 1838*, 1838, vol. ii, p. 199.
95. *Hansard*, 16 March 1832, vol. xi, col. 386.
96. Ward, *The Factory Movement*, pp. 87–8.
97. S. E. Finer, *The Life and Times of Sir Edwin Chadwick*, 1952, pp. 51–2.
98. Brundage, *England's Prussian Minister*, pp. 23–4.
99. *Hansard*, 17 June 1833, vol. xvii, col. 914 and 18 July 1833, vol. xix, col. 913; *Sessional Papers*, 1833 vol. xx, p. 39.
100. L. Horner, *The Factories Regulation Act Explained*, 1834, p. 21.
101. *Hansard*, 9 August 1833, vol. xx, col. 449.
102. Ward, *The Factory Movements*, p. 66.
103. *Leeds Mercury*, 2 November 1833, in Ward, *The Factory Movement*, p. 115.
104. *Hansard*, 9 February 1832, vol. x, col. 105, and 7 March 1832, vol. x, col. 1223.
105. *Hansard*, 28 February 1833, vol. xv, col. 1294.
106. Le Marchant, *The Reform Ministry and the Reformed Parliament*, p. 17.
107. Ward, *The Factory Movement*, p. 115.
108. *Annual Register*, 1837, p. 128.
109. Halévy, *The Triumph of Reform*, p. 127.
110. J. R. Poynter, *Society and Pauperism: English Ideas on the Poor Relief 1795–1834*, 1967, p. 272.
111. A. Brundage, *The Making of the New Poor Law*, 1978, pp. x, 182.
112. Russell, *Recollections and Suggestions*, pp. 141–3.
113. Brundage, *The Making of the New Poor Law*, pp. 62, 67.
114. Poynter, *Society and Pauperism*, p. 317.
115. Brundage, *The Making of the New Poor Law*, pp. 21–2.

116. A. Brundage, 'The Landed Interest and the New Poor Law: A reappraisal of the revolution in government', *EHR*, 1972, vol. lxxxvii, p. 29.

117. J. R. Poynter, *Society and Pauperism*, p. 326.

118. Ward, *The Factory Movement*, p. 121.

119. T. R. Malthus, *An Essay on Population*, 1798, pp. 84–5.

120. 'Report from His Majesty's Commissioners for inquiry into the Administration and Practical Operation of the Poor Laws', *Sessional Papers*, 1834, vol. xxvii p. 43.

121. *Hansard*, 17 April 1834, vol. xii, cols. 875–8.

122. Earl Russell, *An Essay on the History of the English Government and Constitution. From the Reign of Henry VII to the Present Time*, 2nd edn, 1823, p. 267, in W. C. Lubenow, *The Politics of Government Growth*, 1971, p. 23.

123. *Hansard*, 21 July 1834, vol. xxv, col. 235 (Brougham) and 9 June 1834, vol. xxiv, col. 334, Howick; Brundage, *The Making of the New Poor Law*, pp. 9, 62, 70.

124. Graham to Peel, 26 December 1841, Add. MSS 40446, f. 253.

125. Brundage, *The Making of the New Poor Law*, p. 69.

126. Brundage, *England's Prussian Minister*, p. 44.

127. *Hansard*, 24 February 1837, vol. xxxvi, cols. 1032–34.

128. S. & B. Webb, *English Poor Law History: The Last Hundred Years*, 1929, vol. i, p. 94; in Aspinall, *Brougham*, pp. 241–2; Le Marchant, *Althorp*, p. 483.

129. W. O. Chadwick, *The Victorian Church*, 1966, vol. i, p. 95–6.

130. Jennings, L. J. (ed.), *Croker, Correspondence and Diaries of J. W.*, 1884, vol. ii, p. 337; Lansdowne to Grey, 9 July 1834, GP.

131. See for example D. Fraser, *Urban Politics in Victorian England*, 1976, pp. 55–90; Brundage, *The Making of the New Poor Law*, ch. v and vi.

132. William IV to Althorp, 10 May 1834, SP.

133. Myers, *Althorp*, p. 176.

134. *Hansard*, 10 June 1834, vol. xxiv, col. 347, in Brundage, *The Making of the New Poor Law*, p. 63.

135. In D. Fraser, *The Evolution of the British Welfare State*, 1973, pp. 45–6.

136. Brundage, *England's Prussian Minister*, p. 45.

137. Brundage, 'The Landed Interest and the New Poor Law', p. 48.

138. S. Walpole, *Life of Lord John Russell*, 1889, vol. i, p. 367.

139. Holland to Grey, 26 October 1831, GP.

140. Gash, *Reaction and Reconstruction in English Politics 1832–1852*, 1965, p. 80n.

141. G. F. A. Best, 'The Whigs and the Church Establishment in the Age of Grey and Holland', *History*, 1960, 45, 103; R. A. Soloway, *Prelates and People*, 1969, p. 225.

142. Gash, *Reaction and Reconstruction in English Politics*, p. 82.

143. 'Surely' said Blomfield, 'the application for a Commission ought to proceed from ourselves.' In Gash, *Reaction and Reconstruction in English Politics*, p. 80.

144. Chadwick, *The Victorian Church*, vol. i, p. 41.

145. Grey to Howley, 19 October 1832, GP; *Hansard*, 7 February 1833, vol. xv, cols. 305–6.

146. Grey to Spring Rice, 6 October 1830, MP, 1140/2.

147. R. A. Victoria's journal, 13 September 1838.

148. Morpeth to Grey, 26 December 1832, in Le Marchant, *Althorp*, p. 448; Althorp to Grey, 1 January 1833, SP; Graham to Holland, 13 December 1832, Add. MSS 51542, f. 42.

149. Duke of Somerset, *Christian Theology and Modern Skepticism*, 1871, in Southgate, *The Passing of the Whigs*, p. 219.

150. R. A. Victoria's journal, 19 June 1839.

151. Chadwick, *The Victorian Church*, vol. i, p. 233.

152. Mitchell, *Holland House*, pp. 101–3; Hamburger, 'The Whig Conscience', p. 25.

153. A. D. Macintyre, *The Liberator: Daniel O'Connell and the Irish Party, 1830–1847*, 1965, p. 37.

154. Grey to Holland, 3 January 1831, GP.

155. Melbourne to Stanley, 20 December 1830, DP 117/7.

156. O'Connell to C. Fitz-Simon, 16 September 1830, *Dublin Morning Post*.

157. *Hansard*, 13 March 1832, vol. xi, cols. 176–7; Althorp to Spencer, 14 January 1831, SP; Macintyre, *O'Connell The Liberator*, pp. 20–7; Holland to Grey, 2 January 1832, GP.

158. R. McDowell, *Public Opinion and Government Policy in Ireland 1801–1846*, 1952, p. 150; Le Marchant, *Althorp*, p. 326.

159. Althorp to Holland, 6 January 1832, Add. MSS 51724, f. 202.

160. Anglesey to Graham, 12 February 1832, GrP MS film, 130.

161. Macintyre, *O'Connell The Liberator*, pp. 173–4.

162. Holland diary, 10 December 1831, Add. MSS 51868, f. 242.

163. Melbourne to Plunket, 31 May 1832, RA MP 102/47; Althorp to Grey, 26 August 1832, SP; Russell Memorandum on Ireland, 15 February 1834, DP 130/12.

164. *Hansard*, 1 March 1833, vol. xvi, col. 51.

165. *Hansard*, 20 August 1835, vol. xxx, col. 719.

166. Duncannon to Grey, 23 June 1832, GP.

167. *Hansard*, 13 July 1832, vol. xiv, col. 377.

168. Althorp to Grey, 20 October 1832, SP. Cf. Holland diary, 9 July 1832: 'It is clear that all the cabinet are not agreed on the policy to be pursued with respect to the Irish Church . . . Both [groups] may & do agree in the composition bill, but it is the ground work of a different & even of an opposite policy in the contemplation of the two parties, & there their agreement must terminate.' Add. MSS 51869, f. 543.

169. Althorp to Grey, 20 October 1832, SP; *Hansard*, 6 June 1832, vol. xxiv, cols. 252–4.

170. Grey to Althorp, 21 October 1832, SP.

171. See R. Brent, *Liberal Anglican Politics: Whiggery, Religion and Reform 1830–1841*, 1987, p. 65.

172. Russell Memorandum, 15 February 1834, DP 130/12.

173. Howick Memorandum, 1834, PRO 30/22/1C, f. 167.

174. Althorp to Grey, 20 October 1832, SP; *Hansard*, 26 April 1833, vol. xvii, cols. 675–6.
175. *Hansard*, 12 February 1833, vol. xv, col. 593.
176. Melbourne to Howick, 21 January 1837, GP.
177. Smith to Holland, November 1834, in Best, 'The Whigs and the Church Establishment in the Age of Grey and Holland', p. 116.
178. Holland diary, 9 July 1832, Add. MSS 51869, ff. 543–4; Althorp to Spencer, 12 July 1833, SP.
179. Russell Memorandum, 18 October 1833, R. Russell (ed.), *Early Correspondence of Lord John Russell 1805–1840*, 1913, vol. ii, p. 43; Russell to Stanley, 4 January 1833, DP 130/12. For Paley's doctrine, see R. Lynam, *The Complete Works of William Paley D.D.* (1825), vol. ii, vi, ch. x, pp. 388–412.
180. *Hansard*, 30 March 1835, vol. xxvii, cols. 361 and 426–8.
181. Grey to Holland, 29 October 1832, Add. MSS 51556, f. 76; Grey to Russell, 25 October 1832, Add. MSS 38080, f. 58; Russell to Grey, 20 October 1832, Add. MSS 51548, f. 131; Althorp to Grey, 21 October 1832, GP; Brougham to Grey, 4 December 1832, GP; Grey to Brougham, 4 December 1832, BrP 14143; Grey to Althorp, 4 December 1832, GP.
182. Stanley to Melbourne, 4 January 1831, DP 167/1 carries an outline of his Irish education plan; Macintyre, *O'Connell The Liberator*, pp. 28–9, describes its success; Stanley to Grey, June 1831, DP 16.
183. Stanley to the Bishop of Limerick, 3 December 1831, DP 16.
184. A. D. Kriegel, 'The Irish Policy of Lord Grey's Government', *EHR*, 1971, vol. lxxxvi, p. 29.
185. Holland diary, 12 December 1832, Add. MSS 51868, ff. 238–9.
186. Stanley to Grey, 4 August and 10 September 1832, GP.
187. Littleton diary, 12 February 1833, in Aspinall, *Three Nineteenth Century Diaries*, p. 301.
188. *Hansard*, 14 February 1832, vol. x, col. 324; Littleton diary, 16 February 1832, in Aspinall, *Three Nineteenth Century Diaries*, p. 196; Holland diary, 7 February 1832, Add, MSS 51868, f. 342; Ellice to Grey, 10 February 1832, GP; Anglesey to Graham, 12 February 1832, GrP MS film 130.
189. Wood to Stanley, 5 January 1833, DP 126/3; *Hansard*, 28 February 1833, vol. xv, col. 1362.
190. Macintyre, *O'Connell the Liberator*, p. 48.
191. Graham to Anglesey, 17 January 1833, GrP MS film 130; Lansdowne to Grey, 26 January 1833 and Grey to Lansdowne, 2 January 1833, GP.
192. Le Marchant diary, 5 March 1833, in Aspinall, *Three Nineteenth Century Diaries*, p. 313; Melbourne to Grey, 12 March 1832, GP; Sir H. L. Bulwer, *The Life of Henry John Temple, Viscount Palmerston*, 1870, vol. ii, p. 147.
193. *Hansard*, 27 February 1833, vol. xv, col. 1211; Le Marchant diary, 5 March 1833, in Aspinall, *Three Nineteenth Century Diaries*, p.312.
194. Le Marchant diary, February 1833, in Aspinall, *Three Nineteenth Century Diaries*, p. 295; Macintyre, *O'Connell The Liberator*, p. 47;

Stanley to Taylor, 25 January 1833, DP 167/2; Russell, *Recollections and Suggestions*, p. 138; *Hansard*, 28 February 1833, vol. xv, col. 1362.

195. Aspinall, *Three Nineteenth Century Diaries*, p. 295, n.4.
196. Russell suggested the creation of 16 or 17 peers, Brougham 4 or 5. Russell to Grey, 8 June 1833, GP; Lord Brougham, *The Life and Times of Henry, Lord Brougham*, 1871, vol. iii, p. 281; Grey to Brougham, 19 June 1833, in Brougham, *Memoirs*, vol. iii, pp. 294–5.
197. Holland diary, 18 June 1833, Add. MSS 51869, f. 618.
198. *Ibid.*, 619; Le Marchant diary, 21 June 1833, in Aspinall, *Three Nineteenth Century Diaries*, p. 338.
199. Holland diary, 22 June 1833, Add. MSS 51869, f. 6. See A. D. Kriegel, *The Holland House Diaries 1831–1840*, 1977, p. 464 n.64, for a discussion of the extent to which Stanley's dropping of the clause was known in the Cabinet.
200. Le Marchant diary, 21 June 1833, in Aspinall, *Three Nineteenth Century Diaries*, p. 339.
201. Holland diary, 9 and 17 July 1833, Add. MSS 51869, ff. 638–9, 648; David Large, 'The House of Lords and Ireland in the Age of Peel, 1832–50', *Irish Historical Studies*, 1955, vol. ix, 375–9.
202. *Hansard*, 18 June 1857, vol. cxiv, col. 1975, in Chadwick, *The Victorian Church*, vol. i, p. 60; Macintyre, *O'Connell The Liberator*, p. 41. Stanley's commitment to the abolition of the bishoprics might be doubted. Before the bill was through the Lords, he showed Brougham a clause he wanted inserted that would have restored the lost revenue to the bishoprics should they be reinstated in the future. Stanley to Brougham, [n.d.], BrP 46009.
203. Macintyre, *O'Connell The Liberator*, pp. 186–7.
204. Stanley to Grey, (copy) June 1831, DP 16.
205. *Hansard*, 5 July 1832, vol. xiv, cols. 95–112.
206. Holland diary, 2 June 1833, Add. MSS 51869, f. 595; *Parliamentary Papers*, 1833, vol. xxvii, pp. 491–7; Macintyre, *O'Connell The Liberator*, p. 185.
207. Graham to Hobhouse, 10 April 1833, Add. MSS 36467, f. 47; Holland diary, 2 June and 21 July 1833, Add. MSS 51869, ff. 595 and 655.
208. *Hansard*, 20 February 1834, vol. xxi, cols. 572–91. Grey had asked Melbourne in October to give the pair 'an occasional jog' on the subject. Grey to Melbourne, 11 October 1833, RA MP 5/112.
209. *Hansard*, 20 February 1834, vol. xxi, col. 596.
210. Littleton to Sir John Newport, 31 December 1833, in Macintyre, *O'Connell The Liberator*, p. 190; Littleton to Wellesley, 7 May 1834, Add. MSS 37307, f. 29.
211. Holland diary, [n.d.]., Add. MSS 51870, f. 714.
212. Althorp to Littleton, 5 May 1834, Add. MSS 37306, ff. 308–9; Lord Hatherton, *Memoirs and Correspondence relating to Political Occurrences in June and July 1834*, Henry Reeve (ed.), 1872, p. 6.
213. Grey to Wellesley, 1 March, Add. MSS 37306, f. 378; *Hansard*, 30 July 1834, vol. xxv, col. 771; Wellington to Aberdeen, 4 September 1834, in D. Large, 'The Decline of "The Party of the Crown" and the Rise of

Parties in the House of Lords, 1783–1837′, *EHR*, 1963, vol. lxxviii, p. 375.

214. T. L. Crosby, *English Farmers and the Politics of Protection 1815–1852*, 1977, pp. 14–15; W. R. Ward, 'The Tithe Question in England in the Early Nineteenth Century', *Journal of Ecclesiastical History*, 1969, vol. xvi, 67–81. See Althorp's description of the tithe as 'a check upon the improvement of agricultural property'. *Hansard*, 18 April 1833, vol. xvii, cols. 280–1. See too the *Quarterly Review*, 1830, vol. pp. 252–3.

215. Ward, 'The Tithe Question in England in the Early Nineteenth Century', pp. 69, 74, 80.

216. *Hansard*, 21 February 1834, vol. xxi, cols. 660–4 (Althorp).

217. *Hansard*, 18 April 1833, vol. xvii, cols. 273–81; 9 July 1833, vol. xix, col. 377.

218. *Hansard*, 15 April 1834, vol. xxii, cols. 818–28.

219. Chadwick, *The Victorian Church*, vol. i, pp. 62, 79–95; G.I.T. Machin, *Politics and the Churches in Great Britain 1832–1868*, 1977, pp. 39–47; Gash, *Reaction and Reconstruction in English Politics*, pp. 64–7.

220. Chadwick, *The Victorian Church*, vol. i, p. 61.

221. Grey to the Dean of Chichester, February 1834, in Best, 'The Whigs and the Church Establishment', p. 108.

222. Holland to Grey, 14 and 25 January 1834, GP. The moderate Presbyterian was Edgar Taylor.

223. *Hansard*, 25 February 1834, vol. xxi, cols. 776–9; Howick diary, 2 March 1834, GP; Le Marchant diary, 27 March 1834, in Aspinall, *Three Nineteenth Century Diaries*, p. 377.

224. Russell to Grey, April 1834, GP; Walpole, *Russell*, vol. ii, p. 468.

225. Halévy, *The Triumph of Reform*, p. 168.

226. The motion was put by Edward Divett, the Liberal Anglican MP for Exeter. *Hansard*, 8 March 1834, vol. xxii, cols. 387; 392 for Althorp's reply.

227. *Hansard*, 21 April 1834, vol. xxii, col. 1012.

228. Russell to Holland, 17 August 1834, Add. MSS 51677, f. 123.

229. *Hansard*, 21 April 1834, vol. xxii, cols. 1058–9.

230. Best, 'The Whigs and the Church Establishment', p. 108.

231. Grey to Holland, 9 March 1834, Add. MSS 51557, f. 8.

232. Le Marchant diary, 27 March 1834, in Aspinall, *Three Nineteenth Century Diaries*, p. 377.

233. anon., *Remarks on the Second Session of the Reformed Parliament*, 1834, p. 4; Greville, *Memoirs*, 24 June 1834, vol. iii, p. 49.

234. Le Marchant, *Althorp*, p. 483.

7 MELBOURNE AND OPPOSITION, 1834–35

1. H. R. Fox Bourne, *English Newspapers* 1887, vol. ii, p. 78 n.2.

2. Cf. Howick diary, 30 January 1836, GP: 'It was very amusing to hear him [Stanley] charge Melbourne, & Melbourne openly admit himself to have concurred in all the past liberal measures of late years not **from** choice but from necessity.'

3. A. Aspinall, 'The Cabinet Council', *Proceedings of the British Academy*, 1952, vol. 38, p. 193.

4. Lord Brougham, *The Life and Times of Henry, Lord Brougham*, 1871, vol. iii, p. 403. Le Marchant, Brougham's secretary, claimed that Brougham urged the King to accept Melbourne in order to avoid a Tory government that would have no room for him as Lord Chancellor. Sir D. Le Marchant, *Memoirs of John Charles, Viscount Althorp*, 1876, p. 518. See Stewart, *Henry Brougham*, 1985, pp. 303–4.

5. G. S. Fox-Strangways, 6th Earl of Ilchester, *Chronicles of Holland House, 1820–1900*, 1937, p. 170n.

6. Howick diary, 27 May 1834, GP; Althorp to Spencer, 27 May 1834, SP. Grey told Howick at Easter that the King would want a coalition with Peel to replace him. Howick diary, 25 April 1834, GP.

7. Taylor to Brougham, 10 July 1834, BrP 14392.

8. Melbourne to William IV, 10 and 11 July 1834, RA MP 110/3. Stanley told Richmond that Melbourne was right in refusing to conduct a 'sham negotiation' that could not succeed. 12 July 1834, DP 167/2.

9. C. C. F. Greville, *The Greville Memoirs*, Lytton Strachey and Roger Fulford (eds), 1938, 4 September 1834, vol. iii, p. 76. Peel had informed the King that no successful negotiations for a coalition could take place in which Melbourne had 'everything to demand and nothing to concede'. Peel to William IV, 13 July 1834, Add. MSS 40302, f. 4.

10. This was on 28 May, the day after Stanley's resignation, when he addressed a group of Bishops at his birthday levee, and spoke of the 'unhappy circumstances that have forced themselves on the observation of all'. William IV, *Address of His Majesty to the Prelates of England and Ireland on the 28th of May, 1834*, 1834; W. N. Molesworth, *The History of England from the Year 1830*, 1871, vol. l, p. 411.

11. Holland diary [July 1834], Add. MSS 51870, ff. 736–7; Melbourne to William IV, 15 July 1834, RA MP 110/3.

12. Melbourne to Brougham, 16 July 1834, BrP 43503. Duncannon succeeded Melbourne at the Home Office. Hobhouse, given Duncannon's place at the Woods and Forests, was given Carlisle's cabinet seat. Carlisle retired from politics with Grey.

13. William IV to Melbourne, 11 and 14 November 1834, RA MP; William's own memoir of the dismissal is to be found in Baron Stockmar, *Memoirs*, F. M. Mueller (ed.), 1872, vol. i, p. 333.

14. Melbourne to William IV, 14 July 1834, RA MP.

15. Melbourne to William IV, 12 November 1834, RA MP, in L. C. Sanders (ed.), *Lord Melbourne's Papers*, 1889, pp. 219–20.

16. Melbourne to William IV, 8 November 1834, Taylor to Melbourne, 8 November 1834, William IV to Melbourne, 11 November 1834, RA MP.

17. Stockmar, *Memoirs*, vol. i, p. 329.

18. It was thought that Brougham's brother James, who had died in January, had more power than any other of checking his 'extravagances', and that following his death, the Chancellor showed himself in need of such a counsellor. Holland diary, October 1834, Add. MSS

51870, ff. 751–2. When Brougham mounted a violent attack on the Duke of Wellington in 1838, and was heard to exclaim 'the Abbey yawns for him', Russell remarked, '& Bedlam for him'. Hobhouse diary, 10 July 1838, Add. MSS 56559, f. 158.

19. 'The Last Session of Parliament', *Edinburgh Review*, vol. cxxi, October 1834, pp. 249–50. See Stewart, *Brougham*, pp. 303–21. It was Russell who proposed the £20 qualification, as an antidote to Durham's ballot plan. See Grey to Ellice, 24 October 1839, EP/19, f. 29; Grey to Stanley, 23 October 1834, DP 167/2; M. Brock, *The Great Reform Act*, 1973, p. 140.
20. Holland diary, October 1834, Add. MSS 51870, f. 752; The *Examiner*, 29 September 1834.
21. Grey to Holland, 5 October 1834, GP; Taylor to Grey, 26 October 1834, RA Add, 15/18032.
22. Holland diary, 17 November 1834, Add. MSS 51870, f. 784; Stockmar, *Memoirs*, vol. i, p. 331; Melbourne to Brougham, 14 February 1835, RA MP 2/26.
23. *Morning Chronicle*, 10 November 1834; *Northern Whig*, 8 November 1834; The *Examiner*, 9 November 1834; Wellesley to Downshire, 21 January 1835, Add. MSS 37311, f. 221.
24. Holland diary, 8 November 1834, Add. MSS 51870, ff. 758–60; Sir H. Taylor to Melbourne, 8 November 1834, RA MP.
25. William IV to Melbourne, 4 November 1834; Melbourne to William IV, 4 November 1834, RA MP.
26. A series of government crises, which lasted until April 1835, led to a great deal of public debate on the function of the King in the new monarchy. A ministry led by the Duc de Bassano was appointed by Louis-Philippe on 11 November but resigned on the fourteenth, failing to get majority support in parliament. This failure was greatly regretted by the Duc d'Orléans, who regarded Bassano's liberal ministry the only one capable of restoring to the Monarchy the public favour which had been alienated by the conservative bourgeoisie. *Morning Chronicle*, 17 November 1834; Lucas–Dubreton, *The Restoration and the July Monarchy*, trans. E. F. Buckley, 1967, pp. 235–6; E. Bourgeois, *History of Modern France*, 1815–1913, 1972, 1, 173–4.
27. Melbourne to Mulgrave, 29 May 1835, MCA MM/13.
28. Duncannon to Melbourne, 12 September 1834, RA MP 3/20, 20b; Duncannon to Littleton, 2 October 1834, Add. MSS 37307, f. 182; Duncannon to Grey, n.d. [November 1834], GP.
29. William IV to Melbourne, 22 and 25 July 1834, RA MP. Reference to the pledges made by Littleton to O'Connell which preceded Grey's resignation two weeks earlier is scarcely concealed.
30. The King told Peel on 12 December that the dismissal must be mainly ascribed to his being pressed upon the very point which had caused Stanley's resignation. Add MSS 40302, f. 24.
31. Taylor to Stanley, 24 December 1834, DP 100/2.
32. Howick diary, 1 March 1835; Ellice to Grey, 20 December 1834, GP.

33. Brougham told Holland earlier that a cabal of women and princesses 'plague the King out of his life'. In one 'foul-mouthed' outburst against Adelaide, he told Holland that her method of harassing the King was to sob and cry in his bed at night, and then press her demands on his good-heartedness. Holland diary, Add. MSS 51867, f. 38–9.

34. Holland diary, 17 November 1834, Add. MSS 51870, f. 781.

35. Holland diary, 15 November 1834, Add. MSS 51870, f. 780; Holland to Grey, 15 November 1834, GP. Mary Clitherow reported that the King's children showed strong opposition to their father's actions and spoke of the Queen in an 'unpardonable' manner. *Glimpses of King William IV and Queen Adelaide in Letters of the Late Miss Clitherow*, G. C. White (ed.) 1902, p. 56; Althorp to Melbourne, 16 November 1834, RA MP 15/11.

36. 'I will not indeed conceal from you', Taylor wrote to Stanley on December 24, 'that the King had entertained sanguine expectations, amounting almost to conviction that he would . . . find in you . . . the aid and support which must be admitted to be so essential and important towards enabling Him to hold His own'. DP 100/C.

37. Stanley to Richmond, 18 November and 13 December 1834, DP 167/2.

38. William IV to Peel, 12 December 1834, Add. MSS 40302, f. 25; Taylor to Stanley, 2 January 1835, DP 100/2.

39. Grey thought that Wellington 'accroached' absolute power by assuming a number of portfolios until Peel returned from Italy, and was not sure, in fact, if he could not be impeached. Howick diary, 26 November 1834, GP.

40. *Morning Chronicle*, 20 November 1834. On the 25th, the *Chronicle* reported that a number of publicans had stopped *The Times*, which supported the new administration, rather than face a loss of custom, but the object of dislike here was Wellington rather than the King. The *Westminster Review* did, however, speak of a *coup d'état*; vol. xxii, January, 1835, p. 259.

41. Grey to Melbourne, 14 February 1835, RA MP 5/131; Grey to Holland, 24 November 1834, GP; Grey to Russell, 17 November 1834, in R. Russell (ed.), *Early Correspondence of Lord John Russell 1805–1840*, 1913, vol. ii, p. 39; Grey to Ellice, 16 November 1834, EP/19, f. 39; Grey to Melbourne, 16 November 1834, RA MP 5/126; Holland diary, 20 November 1834, Add. MSS 51870, f. 789.

42. The *Morning Chronicle*, 5 December 1834, gives a report of Melbourne's speech at Derby on December 1, in which he spoke of this sentiment. Melbourne to Grey, 14 and 18 November 1834, GP.

43. Holland diary, 12 November 1834, Add. MSS 51870, f. 772.

44. Russell to Althorp, 15 November 1834, in Le Marchant, *Althorp*, p. 525; Russell to Grey, 19 November 1834, GP; Russell to Mulgrave, 13 June 1835, MCA M/871.

45. Howick to Russell, 3 January 1835, PRO 30/22/1E, f. 35.

46. Palmerston to Melbourne, 12 July and 2 December 1834, RA MP 11/6, 12.

47. Carlisle to Melbourne, 20 November 1834, RA MP 21/68.
48. Russell to Melbourne, 28 August 1834, RA MP 13/34 and 22 September 1834, Add. MSS 38080, f. 68; Russell to Grey, 19 November 1834, GP.
49. Brougham to Melbourne, July, 1834, RA MP 1/112; *Edinburgh Review*, 1834, vol. x, p. 231.
50. Duncannon to Melbourne, 18 December 1834, RA MP 3/29; Duncannon to Wellesley, 30 January 1835, Add. MSS 37311, f. 232.
51. J. S. Mill to J. P. Nichol, 26 November 1834; J. S. Mill to A. N. Thibaudeau, 28 November 1834, in F. S. Mineka (ed.) *The Collected Works of John Stuart Mill*, 1963, vol. i, pp. 238, 240.
52. The *Morning Chronicle*, 15, 17 and 24 November 1834; *The Patriot*, 19 November 1834; The *Examiner*, 13 July 1834; E. L. Bulwer to Melbourne, [n.d.], RA MP 20/82.
53. Barnes reportedly offered Wellington the following terms of support: no mutilation of the Reform Act should occur; reform measures regarding Church and corporations already sanctioned by the Commons should be adopted; foreign policy should not be changed. Wellington agreed to these terms before Peel returned from Italy. Ilchester, *Chronicles of Holland House, 1820–1900*, p. 186.
54. Wood estimated the Whig majority at 24: Tories 302, Whigs 253, Radicals 73. Wood to Spring Rice, 24 January 1835, MP 13379.
55. Lyttleton to Melbourne, 15 December 1834, RA MP 29/154.
56. Ibid., in which Melbourne's use of this phrase in an earlier letter to Lyttleton is quoted.
57. Holland to Melbourne, 9 February 1835, Sanders, *Melbourne Papers*, p. 251; Holland to Mulgrave, 24 January 1835, MCA M/369; Howick to Grey, 23 January and 8 February, Howick diary, 21 January 1835, GP; Howick to Russell, 3 February 1835, PRO 30/22/1E, f. 25.
58. N. Gash, *Reaction and Reconstruction in English Politics 1832–1852*, 1965, pp. 170–1.
59. J. Prest, *Lord John Russell*, 1972, p. 87; A. D. Macintyre, *The Liberator: Daniel O'Connell and the Irish Party*, 1965, pp. 141–2.
60. Russell to Grey, 22 January 1835, GP.
61. 'I agree with Althorp', he told Brougham, 'that the present Gov't is an evil which ought at all events to be removed. The peace of Ireland requires it.' 18 February 1835, BrP 38142.
62. See for example Russell to Spring Rice where he asks for Rice's help to keep aloof from any 'organic changes', 18 January 1835, MP 13379; Russell to Howick, 1 February 1835 in which he states his readiness 'to oppose the radicals when they bring forward measures of organic and violent change'. Duncannon to Russell, [n.d.], in S. Walpole, *Life of Lord John Russell*, 1889, vol. ii, pp. 222–3; Russell to Howick, 1 February 1835, GP.
63. Russell to Grey, 30 January 1835, GP; Grant, *Random Recollections of the House of Commons*, 1836 p. 198; Earl Russell, *Recollections and Suggestions 1813–1873*, 1875, p. 168.
64. Sutton was accused, unjustifiably, of having influenced the King's decision to dismiss the Whigs. The best account of the charge is in *Hansard*, 19 February 1835, vol. xxvi, cols. 17–26.

65. Abercromby to Mulgrave, 22 December 1834, MCA M/3; Melbourne to Russell, 29 December 1834 and 5 January 1835, BP, MEL/RU/133 and 136.

66. Hobhouse to Melbourne, 19 January 1835, RA MP 6/78; Melbourne to Russell, 21 January 1835, BP, MEL/RU/139.

67. Abercromby to Melbourne, [n.d.], RA MP 3/149.

68. Melbourne to Grey, 6 February 1835, GP; Mulgrave to Melbourne, 7 February 1835, RA MP 10/56; Russell to Spring Rice, 7 February 1835, MP 13379; Thomson to Mulgrave, 30 January 1835, MCA 0/871.

69. Spring Rice to Spencer (copy), 18 January 1835, RA MP 9/70; Le Marchant to Lady Holland, [n.d.], Add. MSS 51591, f. 172; Russell to Howick, 1 February 1835, GP; Lansdowne to Holland, 24 January 1835, Add. MSS 51680, f. 160.

70. Spring Rice to Howick, 28 January 1835, GP.

71. Parkes to Durham, 26 and 29 January 1835, LP I–1; Warburton to O'Connell, 20 January 1835, OP 852.

72. Holland to Melbourne, 20 January 1835, RA MP 7/10; Russell to Melbourne, 11 February 1835, RA MP 13/41; Melbourne to Russell, 12 February 1835, BP, MEL/RU/143.

73. Russell to Althorp, 15 November 1834, in Le Marchant, *Althorp*, p. 525.

74. Hobhouse to Melbourne, 19 January 1835, RA MP 6/78.

75. Russell to Melbourne, 13 February 1835, BP, MEL/RU/3.

76. Howick to Grey, 18 February 1835, Howick diary, 18 February 1835, GP; Molesworth to mother, 19 February 1835, M. G. Fawcett *The Life of the Rt. Hon. Sir William Molesworth*, 1901, p. 73; Russell to Melbourne, 13 February 1835, BP, MEL/RU/3.

77. *Tait's Magazine*, MS, vol. ii, p. 215; Howick to Grey, 20 February 1835, GP.

78. *Hansard*, 19 February 1835, vol. xxvi, cols. 27–8; Spring Rice to Melbourne, 20 January 1835, RA MP 9/71; Spring Rice to Stanley, 19 January 1835, DP 117/8; Stanley to Spring Rice, 22 January 1835, DP 167/2; Howick to Grey, 19 February 1835, GP.

79. Holland diary, 12 November 1834, Add. MSS 51870, f. 774; Holland to Melbourne, 22 January 1835, RA MP 7/9; The *Morning Chronicle*, 5 December 1834 reported Melbourne's speech.

80. Melbourne to Holland, 21 January 1835, Add. MSS 51558, f. 68; Holland to Grey, 19 January 1835; Howick diary, 23 January 1835, GP; Russell to Melbourne, 11 February 1835, RA MP 13/41; Melbourne to Russell, 12 February 1835, BP, MEL/RU/143.

81. Howick to Grey, 23 January and 3 and 5 March 1835; Howick diary, 17 November and 9 December 1834, GP. Howick thought that Peel had begun to change his position by saying that he insisted on the application of the property of the Church to purposes connected with its doctrine. Peel might, Howick reasoned, use the word 'connected' as a loophole.

82. Howick to Graham, 9 March 1835; Graham to Howick, 13 March 1835; Howick to Grey, 16 March 1835, GP.

83. Spring Rice to Stanley, 30 and 31 January 1835, DP 117/8; Holland diary, 12 November 1834, Add. MSS 51870, f. 774; Russell to Spring

Rice, 23 January 1835, MP 11140(2); Lansdowne to Stanley, 23 January 1835, DP 115/2; Stanley to Graham, 30 January 1835, DP 167/2.

84. Graham to Howick, 13 March 1835, GP. Stanley's memorandum on the question of reunion was addressed to Graham, who passed it on to Howick along with his letter.

85. *Hansard*, 26 March 1834, vol. xxii, col. 704.

86. N. Gash, *Sir Robert Peel*, 1972, pp. 144–5; G. S. R. Kitson Clark, *Peel and the Conservative Party*, 1964, pp. 301–2, 323–5.

87. Stanley told one potential 'dillyite' that by good management, a party of 'no contemptable numerical strength' could be built up as a 'corps de reserve upon which, in case of accident, the King might be able to fall back'. Stanley to J. E. Denison, 20 January 1835, DP 171.

88. Stanley to Taylor, 13 April 1835, DP 167/2.

89. Stanley to Graham, 30 and 31 January 1835, DP 167/2; Howick diary, 14 December 1834, GP.

90. Wood to Spring Rice, 24 January 1835, Howick to Spring Rice, 24 January 1835, MP 13379. Wood's estimates had 253 Whigs, 73 Radicals, 235 Tories and 67 'not to be counted on'.

91. On 14 January, Duncannon predicted an opposition majority of 130. On 5 February he pared this down to 68. Duncannon to Grey, 14 January and 5 February 1835, GP; Ellice predicted a majority of 52. Ellice to Durham, [n.d.], LP XVI.

92. On 10 February, he told O'Connell that by counting on 60 Irish votes, he thought the opposition would win by 20. OP 852.

93. Russell to Grey, 29 January 1835, GP; Holland to Wellesley, 29 January 1835, Add. MSS 37311, ff. 230–1; Mulgrave to Melbourne, 5 February 1835, RA MP 10/55.

94. Russell to Melbourne, 13 February 1835, BP, MEL/RU/3; Howick diary, 14 February 1835, GP; Holland to Grey, 19 February 1835, GP; *Hansard*, 19 February 1835, vol. xxvi, Col. 56.

95. Howick to Grey, 20 January 1835, GP, reports Russell's conversation with Howick; *Chambers Historical News*, May 1835, vol. xxi.

96. Stanley to Lady Holland, 26 February 1835, Add. MSS 51556, f. 132.

97. Howick to Grey, 2 March 1835; Howick diary, 1 March 1835, GP.

98. Place memorandum on Hume's view of amendment in Add. MSS 35149, f. 18.

99. Russell to Wood, 8 March 1835, Grey to Howick, 10 March 1835, Russell to Grey, 10 March 1835, Howick to Grey, 11 March 1835, GP.

100. Howick diary, 11 and 12 March 1835, GP.

101. Mill to A. Gilbert, 19 March 1835, Mineka, *Early Letters of John Stuart Mill*, vol. i, p. 256.

102. Russell to Grey, 13 March 1835, GP.

103. *Hansard*, 17 and 20 March 1835, vol. xvi, col. 1073 and vol. xii, col. 13; Macintyre, *O'Connell The Liberator*, p. 192.

104. Ellice to Durham, 24 March 1835, LP XVI; Howick diary, 22 March 1835, GP.

105. The argument that Peel resigned *as soon as* it was clear that the majority of the Commons was against him in order to diminish the consequences of the King's rash act (Gash, *Reaction and Reconstruc-*

tion in Victorian England, p. 14) is difficult to sustain. It was clear from the opening day that a majority of the House was pledged against him, but he refused to resign until five divisions in a full House had gone against him.

106. Howick diary, 4 and 5 April 1835, GP.
107. Howick diary, 8 and 9 April 1835, GP; Holland diary, 9 April 1835, Add. MSS 51870, f. 796; Stanley to Grey, 9 April 1835, GP.
108. Taylor to Stanley, 13 April 1835, DP 167/2; Greville, *Memoirs*, 9 April 1835, vol. iii, p. 192.
109. RA Victoria's journal, 12 June 1839.
110. Greville, *Memoirs*, 11 April 1835, vol. iii, p. 195. The King's correspondence and meetings with Melbourne are described in Holland diary, Add. MSS 51870, ff. 800–8 and Howick diary, 9 April, 1835, GP. See also Sanders, *Melbourne Papers*, pp. 274–6. For Lyndhurst's role in the negotiations, see Gash, *Reactions and Reconstruction in Victorian England*, pp. 16–18.
111. Melbourne to Spring Rice, 23 December 1834, MP 13377 (8); Melbourne to Grey, 23 January 1835, GP.
112. Howick diary, 10 April 1835, GP; Walpole, *Russell*, vol. i, p. 234; Macintyre, *O'Connell The Liberator*, p. 146.
113. Howick diary, 30 May 1834, GP; Palmerston to Melbourne, 30 June 1835, RA MP 4/16.
114. William IV to Melbourne, 28 June 1835, RA MP 4/3. The story of Durham's ostracism is in J. C. Hobhouse, Baron Broughton, *Recollections of a Long Life*, 1909, 8 May 1835, v, 35; C. New, *Lord Durham*, 1929, p. 276; Ian D. C. Newbould, 'Lord Durham, the Whigs and Canada: the background to Durham's return', *Albion*, 8, 1976, 367–8.
115. Brougham to Melbourne, 15 February 1835, RA MP 2/27; Melbourne to Brougham, 14, 17 and 20 February 1835, RA MP 2/26, 28, 30; Melbourne to Mulgrave, 6 February 1835, MCA MM/9; Ilchester, *Chronicles of Holland House, 1820–1900*, p. 211.
116. Brougham to Melbourne, [n.d.], RA MP 2/21; D. Cecil, *Lord M.*, 1954, 126; Howick diary, 14 April 1835, Melbourne to Grey, 14 March 1835, GP. Justices Pepys, Shadwell and Bosanquet were made Commissioners of the Great Seal. Chief Justice Denman consented to preside over political debates in the Lords and Brougham consented to take appeals. Holland diary, 23 April 1835, Add. MSS 51870, f. 815. Pepys, as Lord Cottenham, became Chancellor in January 1836.
117. W. M. Torrens, *Memoirs of Rt. Hon. William, 2nd Viscount Melbourne*, 1878, vol. ii, pp. 107–8.
118. Holland diary, 17 and 22 April 1835, Add. MSS 51870, ff. 808, 815.
119. Melbourne *et al.* to Grey, 11 April 1835, BP, MEL/RU/147.
120. A. Aspinall, *Lord Brougham and the Whig Party*, 1927, p. 213.
121. Russell to Grey, 12 April 1835, GP. For Palmerston's insistence that he get the Foreign Office, see Melbourne to Grey, 14 April 1835, Howick diary, 14 April 1835, GP.
122. Howick diary, 12 April 1835, GP.
123. Grey to Howick, 23 and 26 January 1835, GP.
124. Grey to Howick, 11 March 1835, GP.

125. Grey to Holland, 22 February 1835, Add. MSS 51557, f. 40.
126. Grey to Melbourne, 1 February 1835, RA MP 5/128.
127. Grey to Russell, 11 March 1835, in Russell, *Early Correspondence*, p. 104.
128. Broughton, *Recollections*, 8 May 1835, vol. v, p. 36.
129. Russell to Grey, 28 February 1835, GP; Grey to Russell, 23 February 1835, in Russell, *Early Correspondence*, pp. 100–1.

8 OFFICE ONCE MORE, 1835–37

1. 23 January 1836, RA MP 40/27.
2. J. C. Hobhouse, Baron Broughton, *Recollections of a Long Life*, 1909, 8 May 1835, vol. v, p. 36.
3. Grey to Howick, 13 February 1835, GP.
4. D. H. Close, 'The Elections of 1835 and 1837 in England and Wales', Oxford D. Phil., 1977, pp. 62, 98, 154.
5. Grey to Ellice, 22 January 1835, EP/19, f. 49.
6. Palmerston to Russell, 22 January 1835, BP, GC/RU/915; K. Bourne, *Palmerston: The Early Years 1784–1841*, 1982, pp. 539–40.
7. Howick to Grey, 23 January 1835; Howick diary, 21 January 1835, GP.
8. Holland to Mulgrave, 24 January 1835, MCA M/369.
9. Howick diary, 11 April 1835, GP.
10. Ellice to Hume, 16 April 1835, EP/25, f. 126.
11. *Hansard*, 2 June 1835, vol. xxviii, col. 452. Russell failed to be re-elected in Devonshire. He was later returned at Stroud after Charles Fox resigned.
12. N. Gash, *Reaction and Reconstruction in English Politics 1832–1852*, 1965, pp. 170–71.
13. Holland diary, 18 May 1835, Add. MSS 51871, ff. 828–9.
14. Parkes to Durham, 1 June and 21 July 1835, LP I–1.
15. *Hansard*, 25 May 1835, vol. xxviii, col. 64.
16. Holland diary, 7 August 1835, Add. MSS 51871, f. 904; *Hansard*, 28 July 1835, vol. xxix, col. 1133.
17. It was during the debate on the corporation bill that they crossed the floor of the Commons. G. S. R. Kitson Clark, *Peel and the Conservative Party*, 1964, pp. 264–5.
18. Howick to Grey, 5 August 1835, GP.
19. Howick diary, 31 August and 1 September 1835, GP; W. M. Torrens, *Memoirs of Rt. Hon. William, 2nd Viscount Melbourne*, 1878, vol. ii, p. 153; *Hansard*, 31 August 1835, vol. xxx, cols. 1139–40.
20. C. C. F. Greville, *The Greville Memoirs*, Lytton Strachey and Roger Fulford (eds), 1938, 1 September 1835, vol. iii, p. 192.
21. Morpeth to Mulgrave, 1 September 1835, MCA M/482.
22. Kitson Clark, *Peel and the Conservative Party*, pp. 292–3; N. Gash, *Sir Robert Peel*, 1972, p. 139.
23. Holland diary, 7 September 1835, Add. MSS 51871, f. 907; Howick diary, 7 September 1835, GP; Torrens, *Melbourne*, vol. ii, p. 154.
24. Holland diary, November 1835, Add. MSS 51871, f. 918.

25. Place to Hume, 2 and 12 May 1835, Hume to Place, 24 April and 10 May 1835, Add. MSS 35150, f. 35–8 and 47–9.
26. Holland diary, 15 April 1835, Add. MSS 51870, f. 792.
27. Torrens, *Melbourne*, vol. ii, p. 145; Greville, *Memoirs*, 15 July 1835, vol. iii, p. 224.
28. Kitson Clark, *Peel and the Conservative Party*, pp. 265–6.
29. *The Standard*, 23 December 1835. Place had this clipping in his collection and had written in the margin that the daily talk at Grey's concerned the propriety of such a connection. Add. MSS 35150, f. 98.
30. Parkes to Durham, 3 April 1835, LP l–1.
31. Parkes to Place, 2 January 1836, Add. MSS 35150, f. 99.
32. R. E. Leader, *Life and Letters of John Arthur Roebuck*, p. 70; Parkes to Stanley, 6 September 1835, PP/25.
33. Parkes to Stanley, 11 October 1835, PP/25; W. Thomas, *The Philosophical Radicals*, 1979, pp. 286–7.
34. Parkes to Durham, 26 July 1836, LP I–1; Parkes to Stanley, 23 July 1836, PP/25; Thomas, *The Philosophical Radicals*, pp. 292–3.
35. Parkes to Durham, 29 March and 1 May, 1836, LP I–2.
36. H. Grote, *The Personal Life of George Grote*, 1873, pp. 100, 105.
37. Place to Hume, 2 May 1835, Add. MSS 35150, f. 36.
38. *Tait's Edinburgh Magazine*, February 1836, vol. iii, p. 75; Leader, *Roebuck*, pp. 76–7; J. A. Roebuck, *Pamphlets for the People*, 1835, pp. 9–10.
39. *The Examiner*, 31 July 1836.
40. Howick diary, 31 August 1835, GP; O'Connell to Thos. Lyons, 19 March 1836, Harrington Papers.
41. Holland to Mulgrave, 1 April 1836, MCA M/371; Ebrington to Tavistock, 10 October 1836, PRO 30/22/2A, f. 53.
42. Howick to Grey, 24 February 1836, GP; Stanley to Durham, 2 February 1836, LP l–9.
43. Place memorandum and Place to Hume, 12 May 1835, Add. MSS 35150, ff. 45–9.
44. Brougham to Rice, 8 May 1835, MP 13378(1).
45. Howick diary, 25 July 1985; GP; Holland to Rice, 26 July 1835 and Howick to Rice, 12 and 13 August 1835, MP 13378(1); Melbourne to Rice (copy), 13 August 1835, GP.
46. Place memorandum, Add. MSS 35150, f. 104; *Hansard*, 21 August 1835, vol. xxx, cols. 861–2; P. Hollis, *The Pauper Press: A Study in Working Class Radicalism in the 1830s*, 1970, pp. 84–5; J. H. Wiener, *The War of the Unstamped: The Movement to Repeal the British Newspaper Tax, 1830–1836*, 1969, passim.
47. *Hansard*, 21 August 1835, vol. xxx, cols. 840–50.
48. *The Examiner*, 20 March 1836; Thomas, *The Philosophical Radicals*, pp. 320–22.
49. Stanley to Durham, 18 December 1835 and 19 February 1836, LP I–9; Parkes to Brougham, 12 February 1836, BrP 5653.
50. Ellice to Parkes [n.d.], 1836, EP/41, f. 23.
51. Parkes to Durham, 9 March 1836 in J. K. Buckley, *Joseph Parkes of Birmingham*, 1926, p. 140.

52. M. G. Fawcett, *The Life of the Rt. Hon. Sir William Molesworth, Bart.*, 1901, pp. 78–9.
53. *The Examiner*, 11 September 1836.
54. Stanley to Mulgrave, 24 February 1836, MCA 0/381; Parkes to Durham, 1 March 1836, LP I–2.
55. Ward to Mulgrave, 22 January 1835, MCA 0/887.
56. N. Gash, *Politics in the Age of Peel*, 1953, p. 411.
57. *The Times*, 12 May 1835; Gash, *Sir Robert Peel*, pp. 129–30.
58. Kitson Clark, *Peel and the Conservative Party*, pp. 266–8; Greville, *Memoirs*, 1 July 1835, vol. iii, p. 218; L. C. Sanders, (ed.), *Lord Melbourne's Papers*, 1889, pp. 334–6; Gash, *Reaction and Reconstruction in English Politics*, p. 20.
59. Gash, *Sir Robert Peel*, pp. 134–6; Kitson Clark, *Peel and the Conservative Party*, p. 269.
60. Gash, *Sir Robert Peel*, p. 143; Torrens, *Melbourne*, vol. ii, p. 178.
61. Ellice to Grey, 20 May 1836, GP; Stanley to Grey, 1 March 1836, LP I–9, reports on the meeting at the Carlton Club. Le Marchant told Lady Holland that he had heard from several Tories of the reluctance of Peel's party 'as a body' to return to office, Add. MSS 51591, f. 134.
62. See for example, Rice's memorandum on 22 March. He argued that an English Church rates bill should be postponed until 'the Lords have thrown out the Irish Church Bill'. PRO 30/22/2A, f. 324.
63. Russell to Mulgrave, 2 January 1836, MCA M/817.
64. *Hansard*, 29 February 1836, vol. xxxi, col. 1052.
65. A. D. Macintyre, *The Liberator: Daniel O'Connell and the Irish Party, 1830–1847*, 1965, p. 241.
66. Melbourne to Grey, 5 June 1836, GP, makes it clear that Russell's plan had been approved by the Government well before Melbourne had argued against a creation of peers. Russell did not, as Macintyre suggests (*O'Connell the Liberator*, p. 245), offer a compromise because the alternative of a creation of peers had been disallowed. The cabinet did not rule against that possibility until the end of June. Howick diary, 28 June 1836, GP.
67. Howick to Grey, 22 August 1835 and 13 January 1837, Howick diary, 18 August 1835 and 20 May 1836, GP.
68. *Hansard*, 19 May 1836, vol. xxxiii, cols. 1087–8; Russell memorandum, 5 June 1836, PRO 30/22/2B, f. 152.
69. S. Walpole, *Life of Lord John Russell*, 1889, vol. i, p. 250; Russell to Melbourne, 9 October 1835, BP, MEL/RU/10; Russell to Holland, 26 May 1836, Add. MSS 51677, f. 162; Howick diary, 28 June 1836, GP.
70. Melbourne to Mulgrave, 13 July 1836, MCA MM/93; Melbourne to Russell, 5 June 1836, PRO 30/22/2B, f. 148.
71. Melbourne to Mulgrave, 13 July and 23 September, 1836, MCA MM/93, 103; Broughton, *Recollections*, 26 June 1836 vol. v, p. 57; *Hansard*, 27 June 1836, vol. xxxiv, col. 961.
72. *The Examiner*, 22 May, 19 June, 4 September and 9 October, 1836.
73. *Tait's Edinburgh Magazine*, October 1836, vol. iii, pp. 680, 753.
74. *The Spectator*, 2 October 1836; *The Constitutional*, 6 October 1836; Thomas, *The Philosophical Radicals*, pp. 330–32.

75. *Tait's Edinburgh Magazine*, December 1836, vol. iii, pp. 480, 553, 754.
76. *The London and Westminster Review*, January 1837, vol. iv and xxvi, pp. 291–9; Fawcett, *Molesworth*, pp. 122–5; Thomas, *The Philosophical Radicals*, pp. 234–9; Ward suggested that it was the 'extraordinary mind' of Gibbon Wakefield that furnished the mainspring of 'the Camp'. Ward to Mulgrave, 5 January 1837, MCA 0/893.
77. Stanley to Parkes, 5 September 1836, PP/25.
78. Parkes to Stanley, 9 October 1836, PP/25; Chapman to Place, 19 January 1837, Add. MSS 35150, f. 220; Parkes to Ellice, (copy) 8 January 1837, PP/25.
79. Parkes to Durham, 10 October 1836, LP I–2.
80. Melbourne to Mulgrave, 20 February 1837, MCA MM/147; Melbourne to Parkes, 22 September 1836, PP/16.
81. Parkes to Durham, 10 October 1836, LP I–2; Ellice to Parkes, (copy) 2 January 1837, EP/41, f. 27.
82. Russell to Ellice, 20 December 1836, EP/49, f. 7; Russell to Mulgrave, 8 November 1836, MCA M/845.
83. Bulwer to Melbourne, 18 October 1836, RA MP 20/99.
84. Howick memorandum, 29 November 1836, PRO 30/22/2D, ff. 83–90; Melbourne to Russell, 27 December 1836, PRO 30/22/2D, f. 260.
85. Melbourne to Mulgrave, 20 December 1836, MCA MM/124.
86. Russell to Rice, 7 March 1836, MP 13382(11).
87. Melbourne to Russell, 3 January 1837, BP, MEL/RU/284.
88. Melbourne to Mulgrave, 20 December 1836 and 2 January 1837, MCA MM/124, 127.
89. Howick diary, 10 February 1837, GP.
90. Russell to Mulgrave, 30 January 1837, MCA M/860; Russell to Grey, 27 January 1837, GP.
91. *Hansard*, 14 February 1837, vol. xxxvi, cols. 547–9.
92. *Tait's Edinburgh Magazine*, February 1837, vol. iv, pp. 129–30; Thomas, *The Philosophical Radicals*, pp. 235–6.
93. Roebuck to Place, 4 January 1837, Place memorandum and Place to Hume, 16 January 1837, Add. MSS 35150, ff. 197, 226 and 229; *The Morning Chronicle*, 24 January 1837; *The Constitutional*, 24 January 1837.
94. Parkes to Stanley, 20 January 1837, PP/25.
95. Ward to Mulgrave, 3 February 1837, MCA 0/894; J. S. Mill to Place, 10 February 1837, Add. MSS 345150, f. 239; *Hansard*, 31 January 1837, vol. xxxvi, cols. 28–47; J. Grant, *The British Senate in 1838*, 1838, vol. ii, p. 209.
96. *Hansard*, 7 February 1837, vol. xxxvi, col. 206; Holland diary, 6 June 1837, Add. MSS 51871, f. 1013; *Hansard*, 27 June 1836, vol. xxxiv, col. 961 (Melbourne).
97. *Hansard*, 8 February 1837, vol. xxxvi, cols. 404–5; Russell to Mulgrave, 8 September 1836, MCA M/838; Mulgrave to Russell, 13 September 1836, PRO 30/22/2C; Holland diary, 26 March 1837, Add. MSS 51871, f. 1000; Howick diary, 15 February 1837, GP.
98. Broughton, *Recollections*, 11 February 1837, vol. v, p. 66; Greville, *Memoirs*, 22 February 1837, vol. iii, p. 354.

99. Howick to Grey, 1 March 1837, Howick di..y, 15 and 18 February 1837, Ellice to Grey, 25 February 1837, GP.
100. Holland diary, 26 March 1837, Add. MSS 51871, ff. 994–5; *Hansard*, 11 April 1837, vol. xxxvii, cols. 1095–110 (Peel).
101. Graham to Peel, 27 March 1837, Add. MSS 40318, f. 64; Peel to Wellington, 9 April 1837 in C. S. Parker, *Sir Robert Peel*, vol. ii, p. 344; Peel memorandum, 23 April 1837, Add. MSS 40423, f. 176; Gash, *Sir Robert Peel*, pp. 158–60; Macintyre, *O'Connell the Liberator*, pp. 249–52.
102. Melbourne to Russell, 23 February and 1 April 1837, BP, MEL/RU/311, 320; Russell to Mulgrave, 6 May 1837, MCA M/867; Russell to Grey, 27 January 1837, GP.
103. Howick diary, 8, 9, 11 and 13 April 1837, GP.
104. Howick diary, 6 and 7 May 1837, GP; *Hansard*, 8 May 1837, vol. xxxviii, col. 696.
105. Wharncliffe to Peel, 13 May 1837, Add. MSS 40423, f. 227.
106. Broughton, *Recollections*, 9 July 1836, vol. v, p. 59.
107. Buckley, *Parkes*, p. 155.

9 THE QUEEN'S GOVERNMENT, 1837–39

1. P. Ziegler, *Melbourne*, 1976, p. 267.
2. RA Victoria's journal, 9 August 1837.
3. Melbourne to Russell, 18 August 1837, BP, MEL/RU/389. 'I must do her justice that since the commencement of the administration nothing has been done, with which she has not found fault nor upon which she has not given trouble.'
4. RA Victoria's journal, 8, 9 and 14 October 1837; G. S. H. Fox-Strangways, 6th Earl of Ilchester, *Chronicles of Holland House 1820–1900*, 1937, p. 216; Esher, *Victoria's Letters*, vol. i, pp. 88, 95, 103.
5. A. C. Benson and Viscount Esher (eds), *The Letters of Queen Victoria 1837–1861*, 1907, vol. i, p. 113.
6. Melbourne to Russell, 3 September 1836, BP, MEL/RU/263; Holland diary, September 1836, Add. MSS 51871, f. 973.
7. Ilchester, *Chronicles of Holland House, 1820–1900*, p. 224; Howick diary, 30 October 1837, GP; Howick to Ellice, 10 November 1837, EP/14, f. 189.
8. Russell to Melbourne, 13 August 1837, PRO 30/22/2F, f. 9.
9. Russell to Melbourne, 10 August 1837, BP, MEL/RU/37.
10. Melbourne to Russell, 30 August 1837, BP, MEL/RU/393; J. C. Hobhouse, Baron Broughton, *Recollections of a Long Life*, 1909, 10 August 1837, vol. v, p. 93; Parkes to Melbourne, 30 August 1837, RA MP 33/19; Melbourne to Howick, 22 August 1837.
11. Baring to Mallet, 16 August 1837, T. G. Earl Northbrook (ed.), *Journals and Correspondence of F. T. Baring, Lord Northbrook*, 1905, vol. i, p. 128; Wood to Howick, 16 August 1837, GP. W. Thomas, *The Philosophical Radicals*, 1979, pp. 298, 371, 419, for the Radical losses.
12. Lansdowne to Holland, 31 August 1837, Add. MSS 51868, f. 89.

13. Russell to Melbourne, 9 September 1837, PRO 30/22/2F, f. 73.
14. Russell to Melbourne, 13 September 1837, PRO 30/22/2F, f. 113. On August 15, he had told Melbourne that 'I shall never press making it an open question'. BP, MEL/RU/39. Russell to Duchess of Bedford, [1838] PRO 30/22/3C, f. 164.
15. S. Walpole, *Life of Lord John Russell*, vol. i, p. 283; *Hansard*, 20 November 1837, vol. xxxix, col. 68; Holland diary, November 1837, Add. MSS 51872, f. 1057.
16. Howick to Grey, 24 November 1837, GP; *Hansard*, 20 November 1837, vol. xxxix, col. 80.
17. Russell to Brougham, 25 November 1837, BrP 14004.
18. C. C. F. Greville, *The Greville Memoirs*, Lytton Strachey and Roger Fulford (eds), 1938, 25 August 1837, vol. iii, pp. 392–3; Russell to Melbourne, 13 August 1837, PRO 30/22/2F, f. 9.
19. Russell to Melbourne, 9 September 1837, PRO 30/22/2F, f. 73; Russell to Howick, 16 August 1837, GP.
20. Holland diary, 28 December 1837, Add. MSS 51872, ff. 1055–7.
21. Russell to Melbourne, 9 September 1837, PRO 30/22/2F, f. 73.
22. Melbourne to Victoria, 27 December 1837, Esher, *Victoria's Letters*, vol. i, p. 127.
23. Rice to Howick, 5 January 1838, Howick diary, 5 January 1838, GP.
24. *Hansard*, 22 December 1837, vol. xxxix, cols. 1428–52; Place to Baines, 4 January 1838, Add. MSS 35151, f. 47; R. E. Leader, *The Life and Letters of John Arthur Roebuck*, 1897, pp. 108–9; *Morning Chronicle*, 5 January 1839.
25. Russell to Stanley, 6 January 1838, PRO 30/22/3A, f.39; Howick diary, 11 January 1838, GP.
26. Holland diary, 28 December 1837, Add. MSS 51872, f. 1056; RA Victoria's journal, 16 January and 7 February 1838; Howick diary, 18 January 1838, GP; *Hansard*, 16 January 1837, vol. xi, cols. 7 (Wellington) and 69 (Peel).
27. Holland diary, January 1838 Add. MSS 51872, ff. 1069–70.
28. Russell memorandum, 4 January 1838, PRO 30/22/3B, f. 337; Holland diary, January 1838, Add. MSS 51872, ff. 1067–8.
29. Melbourne to Durham, 22 July 1837, LP, vol. xxii, f. 7; Durham to Ellice, January 1838, EP/22, f. 27; RA Victoria's journal, 10 January 1838.
30. RA Victoria's journal, 16 January 1838; Melbourne to Russell, 17 September 1837, BP, MEL/RU/401.
31. Melbourne to Mulgrave, 21 August 1837, MCA MM/165; Ellice to Grey, 2 February 1837, GP.
32. Melbourne to Russell, 7 July and 7 September 1837, BP, MEL/RU/367, 396; Russell to Mulgrave, 9 June 1837, MCA M/870; RA Victoria's journal, 20 August 1838; Hobhouse diary, 1 February 1838, Add. MSS 56559, f. 11.
33. *London and Westminster Review*, January 1837, vol. xxviii, p. 529; Thomas, *The Philosophical Radicals*, pp. 376–80.
34. Hume to Place, 1 January 1838; Baines to Place, 2 January 1838, Add. MSS 35151, ff. 48–51.

35. D. G. Southgate, *The Passing of the Whigs 1832–1886*, 1962, p. 72; Howick diary, 27 and 28 December 1837, GP.
36. C. S. Parker, *Sir Robert Peel*, 1891, vol. ii, p. 367.
37. Broughton, *Recollections*, 3 March 1838, vol. v, p. 122; Howick diary, 3 and 5 March 1838, GP. Melbourne to Ellice, 27 February 1838, EP/28, f. 62.
38. Morpeth to Mulgrave, 5 March 1838, MCA M/583; RA Victoria's journal, 5 March 1838; *Hansard*, 7 March 1838, vol. xli, col. 582.
39. Parker, *Peel*, vol. ii, p. 358–67.
40. Bulwer to Mulgrave, 11 March 1838, MCA 0/77.
41. C. New, *Lord Durham*, 1929, pp. 387–90.
42. Broughton, *Recollections*, 18 January 1838, vol. v, p. 116; RA Victoria's journal, 9 March 1838.
43. Hobhouse diary, 2 November 1832, Add. MSS 56557, ff. 32–3; *The Times*, 11, 12 and 19 July 1834; *Edinburgh Review*, (1834), vol. LX, p. 231; Howick diary, 13, 14 and 20 July 1834, GP; Le Marchant to Brougham, July 1834, BrP 22795.
44. Brougham to Stanley, 14 February 1838, DP 116/1.
45. Hobhouse diary, 31 March 1838, Add. MSS 56559, ff. 64–5; *Hansard*, 3 April 1838, vol. xlii, cols. 394–401.
46. *Hansard*, 30 July 1838, vol. xliv, col. 758; Melbourne to Durham, 28 July 1838, RA MP 4/44; New, *Durham*, p. 439.
47. See Ian D. C. Newbould, 'Lord Durham, The Whigs and Canada, 1838: The Background to Durham's Return', *Albion*, 8, 1976, 365–6.
48. Hobhouse diary, 8 August 1838, Add. MSS 56559, f. 186.
49. Russell to Normanby, 14 August 1838, MCA M/819; Melbourne to Victoria, 9 and 10 August 1838, RA A1, ff. 181–3; Howick to Grey, 10 August 1838, Howick diary, 9 August 1838, GP; *Hansard*, 14 August 1838, vol. xliv, col. 1211 (Russell).
50. New, *Durham*, pp. 94, 433; G. M. Trevelyan, *Lord Grey of the Reform Bill*, 1929, p. 367 n.; S. J. Reid, *The Life and Letters of the First Earl of Durham*, 1906, vol. ii, p. 205; Thomas, *The Philosophical Radicals*, pp. 391–2.
51. Roebuck to Brougham, 8 July 1838, BrP 13521; *Hansard*, 14 and 15 August 1838, vol. xliv, cols. 1242, 1307.
52. Russell to Melbourne, 6 September 1838, BP, MEL/RU/56; *Hansard*, 3 and 5 July 1838, cols. xlii, 1222, 1260.
53. *Hansard*, 27 March 1838, vol. xli, cols. 1313–9.
54. RA Victoria's journal, 10 and 11 August 1838.
55. Russell to Melbourne, 12 December 1838, R. Russell (ed.), *Early Correspondence of Lord John Russell 1805–1840*, 1913, p. 238. Lady Russell died on 1 November 1838.
56. Russell memorandum in Russell, *Early Correspondence*, p. 234; Russell to Melbourne, 18 October 1838, BP, MEL/RU/62.
57. Normanby to Melbourne, 25 November 1838, RA MP 100/100.
58. Russell to Melbourne, 26 November 1838, BP, MEL/RU/65.
59. Melbourne to Russell, 22 August 1838, RA MP 13/62.
60. Russell to Melbourne, 14 and 18 October 1838, BP, MEL/RU/61, 62; Duncannon to Melbourne, 20 October 1838, L. C. Sanders, *Lord Melbourne Papers*, 1889, p. 380.

61. Melbourne to Russell, 26 October 1838, Sanders, *Melbourne Papers*, p. 383.
62. Holland diary, November 1838, Add. MSS 51872, f. 1080; Howick to Grey, 10 November 1838, GP; O'Connell to Ebrington, 3 January 1839, FP 1262 M/Ll, f.1.
63. Howick diary, 29 January 1839, GP. The correspondence over this issue in the Grey Papers and in Melbourne's correspondence at Windsor is voluminous.
64. Russell to Melbourne, 21 January 1839, PRO 30/22/3C, f. 184; Russell to Howick, 31 January 1839, GP; RA Victoria's journal, 30 January and 1 February 1839; Holland diary, January 1839, Add. MSS 51872, ff. 1082–3; Melbourne to Glenelg, 3 February 1839, RA MP 5./77; Melbourne to Normanby, 1 February 1839, MCA MM/215.
65. Melbourne to Victoria, 25 October and 20 November 1838, and 10 February 1839, Esher, *Victoria's Letters*, vol. i, pp. 165–8, 185.
66. C. C. F. Greville, *The Greville Memoirs*, Lytton Strachey and Roger Fulford (eds), 1938, 10 February 1839, vol. iv, p. 123.
67. Melbourne to Russell, 7 September 1837, BP, MEL/RU/396.
68. *The Times*, 26 January 1839.
69. RA Victoria's Journal, 24 January 1839.
70. Russell to Melbourne, 7 January 1839, BP, MEL/RU/71.
71. Ebrington to Melbourne, 2 February 1839, RA MP 101/25.
72. Melbourne to Russell, 18–29 January 1839, Sanders, *Melbourne Papers*, pp. 389–91; Melbourne to Ebrington, 7 and 19 January 1839, FP, 1262 M/Ll, ff. 4–7.
73. On 19 February, 155 usual government supporters voted for Villiers' motion to hear evidence at the Bar of the House.
74. Thomas, *The Philosophical Radicals*, p. 334; *The Examiner*, 7, 14 and 28 April, 1839.
75. *The Examiner*, 13 and 27 January 1839.
76. Ward to Normanby, n.d. [December 1838] MCA 0/897.
77. W. Harris, *The History of the Radical Party in Parliament*, 1885, p. 287; RA Victoria's journal, 15 September 1838; Tavistock to Melbourne, 7 November 1838, RA MP 19/85.
78. *Hansard*, 5 February 1839, vol. xiv, col. 122; Tavistock to Russell, 29 December 1838, PRO 30/22/3C, f. 99; Melbourne to Russell, 5 January 1839, RA MP 13/118; Russell to Melbourne, 6 January 1839, BP, MEL/RU/70.
79. Russell to Ebrington, 11 April 1839, FP 1262 M/Ll, f. 36.
80. J. Prest, *Lord John Russell*, 1972, p. 145; Thomas, *The Philosophical Radicals*, pp. 424–5.
81. Sanders, *Melbourne Papers*, pp. 399–400.
82. Greville, *Memoirs*, 21 April 1839, vol. iv, pp. 151–2, reported his conversation with Bedford.
83. Thomas, *The Philosophical Radicals*, pp. 219, 422–3.
84. Lord J. Russell, *Letter to the Electors of Stroud on the Principles of the Reform Act*, 1838, pp. 37, 44; The *Morning Chronicle*, 8 May 1839.
85. Holland diary, March 1839, Add. MSS 51872, f. 1098; Melbourne to Queen Victoria, 22 March 1839, RA C43/1.
86. Parker, *Peel*, vol. ii, pp. 376, 384.

87. *Hansard*, 12 April 1839, vol. xivi, col. 1321.
88. Parker, *Peel*, vol. ii, pp. 358–67, 376.
89. Greville, *Memoirs*, 13 April 1839, vol. iv, p. 149, reports Peel's conversation with Graham.
90. E. Halévy, *The Triumph of Reform 1830–1841*, 1961, pp. 239–40; C. Black, *The History of Jamaica*, 1958, pp. 168–9.
91. Russell to Normanby, 24 January 1839, MCA M/928; Holland diary, January 1839, Add. MSS 51872, f. 1082; Howick diary, 28 and 30 January 1839, GP.
92. Greville, *Memoirs*, 30 April and 5 May 1839, vol. iv, pp. 156, 158; The *Morning Chronicle*, 7 May 1839.
93. Holland diary, April 1839, Add. MSS 51872, f. 1113.
94. Peel's speeches are in *Hansard*, 9 April 1838, vol. xlvi, cols. 1280–8, 22 April and 3 May 1838, vol. xlvii, cols. 460–1, 765–95.
95. P. H. Stanhope, *Notes of a Conversation with the Duke of Wellington 1831–1851*, 1888, p. 138.
96. RA Victoria's journal, 26 April 1839.
97. RA Victoria's journal, 12 May 1839.
98. Hobhouse diary, 4 and 7 May 1839, Add. MSS 56560, ff. 139, 141–2; Howick diary, 7 May 1839, GP. The motion carried 294–289.
99. *Hansard*, 7 May 1839, vol. xivii, col. 977.
100. Melbourne to Russell, 19 May 1839, RA MP 14/31; Melbourne to Victoria, 7 May 1839, RA C43/10.
101. Melbourne to Victoria, 11 and 26 April 1839, RA C43/3 and 5.
102. Greville, *Memoirs*, 5 May 1839, vol. iv, p. 159.
103. Ebrington to Melbourne, 2 May 1839, RA MP 101/29.
104. Broughton, *Recollections*, 3 April 1839, vol. v, p. 183.
105. Greville, *Memoirs*, 30 April 1839, vol. iv, p. 156, reported on a conversation with Le Marchant.
106. Ellice to Russell, 4 May 1839, PRO 30/22/3C, f. 255.
107. Spencer to Ebrington, 8 February 1839, FP 1262 M/Ll, f. 8; Leveson to Granville, 5 March 1839, PRO 30/29/6–4, f. 687.
108. Southgate, *The Passing of the Whigs*, p. 74.
109. N. Gash, *Reaction and Reconstruction in English Politics 1832–1852*, 1965, pp. 186–7.
110. Ilchester, *Chronicles of Holland House 1820–1900*, p. 251.
111. Melbourne to Victoria, 7 May 1839, RA C43/11; RA Victoria's journal, 7 May 1839.
112. RA Victoria's journal, 10 April 1839.
113. Melbourne to Victoria, 9 May 1839, RA C43/18.
114. Howick diary, 9 May 1839, GP; Gash, *Sir Robert Peel*, 1972, p. 224.
115. Melbourne to Victoria, 7 May 1839, RA C43/13; Victoria to Melbourne, 7 May 1839, RA C1/26; RA Victoria's journal, 7 May 1839.
116. Victoria to Melbourne, 9 May 1839, RA C1/27–9.
117. RA Victoria's journal, 8 and 9 May 1839.
118. Melbourne to Victoria, 10 May 1839, RA C43/27; Victoria to Peel, 10 May 1839, RA C43/28.
119. Howick diary, 9 and 15 May 1839, GP.
120. Grey to Melbourne, 10 May 1839, RA MP 5/140.

121. Howick diary (paragraph written in Lady Howick's hand), 10 May 1839, GP.
122. Cabinet memorandum, 10 May 1839, RA C43/32; Victoria to Melbourne, 10 May 1839, RA C1/33.
123. Gash, *Sir Robert Peel*, p. 227; Greville, *Memoirs*, 15 August 1839, vol. iv, pp. 194, 201.
124. RA Victoria's journal, 19 September 1839.
125. RA Victoria's journal, 12 May and 17 August 1839.
126. Rice to Melbourne, [n.d.], RA MP 10/22.
127. Melbourne to Grey, 10 May 1839, GP.
128. Ebrington to Ellice, 11 June 1839, EP/13, f. 220; Russell to Victoria, 6 June 1839, RA C6/84.
129. Elizabeth Longford, *Queen Victoria: Born to Succeed*, 1964, pp. 103–9.
130. Southgate, *The Passing of the Whigs*, p. 74.

10 THE QUEEN'S GOVERNMENT, 1839–41

1. T. G. Earl Northbrook (ed.), *Journals and Correspondence of F. T. Baring, Lord Northbrook*, 1905, vol. i, p. 147.
2. N. Gash, *Reaction and Reconstruction in English Politics 1832–1852*, 1965, p. 177.
3. Russell to Melbourne, 19 May 1839, BP, MEL/RU/88.
4. The government had not actually handed in their seals of office and therefore had not officially resigned.
5. Hume to Melbourne, 13 May 1839, RA MP 28/31; Howick diary, 12 May 1839, GP; Melbourne to Russell, 12 May 1839, RA MP 14/28; Place memorandum on meeting, 11 May 1839, Add. MSS 35151, ff. 168–71.
6. Hume to Melbourne, 25 May 1839, Melbourne to Hume, 25 May 1839, RA MP 28/32–3; Stanley to Melbourne, 13 May 1839, RA MP 35/124.
7. Russell to Melbourne, 2 May 1839, PRO 30/22/3C, f. 251; Baring to Melbourne, 13 May 1839, RA MP 76/108.
8. Byng to Russell, 7 May 1839, PRO 30/22/3C, f. 269; Melbourne to Rice, 16 and 20 May 1839, MP 13392(4); Russell to Melbourne, 19 May 1839, PRO 30/22/3C, f. 286.
9. Howick diary, 22 May 1839, GP; Hobhouse diary, 20 May 1839, Add. MSS 56560, f. 173.
10. Warburton to Place, 25 February 1840, Add. MSS 35151, ff. 217–8.
11. Howick diary, 22 May, 1839, GP; W. Thomas, *The Philosophical Radicals*, 1979, pp. 422–3.
12. D. G. Southgate, *The Passing of the Whigs 1832–1886*, 1962, p. 91.
13. Russell to Melbourne, 15 August 1837, BP, MEL/RU/39; Russell to Melbourne, 13 September 1837, PRO 30/22/2F, f. 113; Russell to Brougham, 1 August 1837, BrP 38161; Russell to Mulgrave, 5 and 17 February 1838, MCA M/896–9; RA Victoria's journal, 6 February 1838. See B. L. Kinzer, 'The unEnglishness of the Secret Ballot', *Albion*, 1978, X, 239–40, for the Whigs' opposition to ballot.
14. Western to Melbourne, 20 February 1838, RA MP 39/94.

15. Howick diary, 22 May 1839, GP; Russell memorandum, PRO 30/22/3C, f. 239.
16. Russell to Howick, 4 June 1839, GP.
17. *Hansard*, 4 June 1839, vol. xivii, cols. 1352–3; Howick diary, 28 and 29 May, 1, 2 and 4 June 1839, GP; Hobhouse diary, 28 May 1839, Add. MSS 56560, f. 173. Thomas, *The Philosophical Radicals*, p. 425, states that Russell backed down when he learned that Howick would resign, but it is clear that the cabinet knew for almost a week that Howick would resign. Howick to Russell, 2 June 1839, PRO 30/22/3C, f. 335; RA Victoria's journal, 1, 3 and 5 June 1839.
18. Normanby to Russell, 5 June 1839, RA MP 10/60.
19. RA Victoria's journal, 8 and 10 June 1839; Melbourne to Russell, 11 June 1839, RA MP 14/36; Russell to Melbourne, 12 June 1839, PRO 30/22/3C, f. 342; Hobhouse diary, 5 and 6 June 1839, Add. MSS 56561, ff. 10–16.
20. Gash, *Reaction and Reconstruction in English Politics*, pp. 174–6.
21. Howick diary, 18 June 1839, GP; *Hansard*, 18 June 1839, vol. xivii, col. 499; Tavistock to Russell, 21 June 1839, PRO 30/22/3C, f. 350.
22. See Chapter 11.
23. Howick diary, 15 May 1839, GP; Russell to Victoria, 6 June 1839, RA C6/84.
24. Howick diary, 11 August 1839, GP; Ebrington to O'Connell, 6 August 1839 and O'Connell to Ebrington, 8 August 1839, FP 1262 M/L1; Russell to Stanley, 8 August 1839, DP 130/12.
25. Russell to Victoria, 11 June and 23 July 1839, RA C6/87, 110.
26. Stanley to Ellice, 18 November 1839, EP/51, f. 140.
27. Normanby to Russell, 29 July 1839, PRO 30/22/3B, f. 230; Spencer to Melbourne, 31 July 1839, L. C. Sanders, *Lord Melbourne's Papers*, 1889, p. 401.
28. Russell to Ebrington, 4 September 1839, FP 1262 M/L1, f. 94; Holland diary, 29 August 1839, Add. MSS 51872, f. 1157; RA Victoria's journal, 17 July 1839; Howick to Grey, 14 August 1839, GP.
29. Russell to Melbourne, 19 August 1839, BP, MEL/RU/96.
30. Russell to Melbourne, 16 and 17 July 1839, BP, MEL/RU/91–2; Minto to Melbourne, 17 July 1839, RA MP 9/31.
31. RA Victoria's journal, 17 July 1839; J. Prest, *Lord John Russell*, 1972, p. 152.
32. Russell to Grey, 27 August 1839, GP.
33. Howick to Russell, 10 August 1839, RA MP 8/41; Howick to Ellice, 6 September 1839, EP/22, f. 43.
34. Howick to Melbourne, 24 and 26 August 1839, RA MP 8/45–7.
35. The holders of the Great Seal, Privy Seal and Irish Secretaryship had recently been elevated to cabinet status.
36. Howick to Grey, 27 August 1839, GP.
37. RA Victoria's journal, 20 August 1839.
38. Howick to Ellice, 6 September 1839, EP/22, f. 47; RA Victoria's journal, 24 August 1839.
39. Howick to Grey, 10 November 1838, Howick diary, 9 August 1839, GP; Howick to Russell, 10 August 1839, RA MP 8/41.

40. RA Victoria's journal, 24 September 1839.
41. Wood to Howick, 12 September 1839, GP; Monteagle to Lansdowne, 14 September 1839, MP 547, f. 126.
42. Melbourne to Russell, 29 August 1839, BP, MEL/RU/546.
43. Howick to Melbourne, 26 August 1839, RA MP 8/47.
44. Stanley to Melbourne, 30 September 1839, RA MP 36/128.
45. Holland to Melbourne, 18 September 1839, RA MP 7/23.
46. Prest, *Russell*, p. 153.
47. Russell to Melbourne, 28 August 1839, PRO 30/22/3c, f. 425; Melbourne to Ebrington, 3 September 1839, FP 1262 M/L1, f. 93.
48. Ellice to Parkes, 5 September 1839, EP/41, f. 31; Melbourne to Macaulay, 17 September 1839, RA MP 30/5.
49. Russell to Melbourne, 28 and 29 August 1839, PRO 30/22/3C, ff. 426, 441.
50. Sir H. Maxwell, (ed.), *Life and Letters of the Fourth Earl of Clarendon*, 1913, vol. i, p. 170.
51. Stanley to Ellice, 21 August 1839, EP/51, f. 131.
52. Southgate, *The Passing of the Whigs*, p. 196.
53. Howick to Melbourne, 24 August 1839, RA MP 8/45.
54. Baring, *Journals and Correspondence*, 10 August 1839, vol. i, p. 142.
55. Holland diary, 29 August 1839, Add. MSS 51872, f. 1167; Ellice to Howick, 2 September 1839, GP; Stanley to Ellice, 21 August 1839, EP/51, f. 131.
56. Russell to Melbourne, 30 October 1839, BP, MEL/RU/107; Russell to Melbourne, 31 September 1839, PRO 30/22/3C, f. 449.
57. Melbourne to Russell, 12 October 1839, RA MP 14/68.
58. Sanders, *Melbourne Papers*, p. 400.
59. Broughton, *Recollections*, 28 November 1839, vol. v, pp. 233–4.
60. N. Gash, *Sir Robert Peel*, 1972, p. 24. There is no ground for Prest's assertion (*Russell*, p. 158) that Russell's bad nature prompted the size of the offer in order to provoke Conservative wrath.
61. Elizabeth Longford, *Queen Victoria: Born to Succeed*, 1964, p. 138.
62. See Chapter 11.
63. *Hansard*, 13 February 1840, vol. lii, col. 229. The division was 182–172.
64. *Hansard*, 27 February 1840, vol. lii, col. 739; Longford, *Queen Victoria*, pp. 138–9.
65. See J. Prest, *Politics in the Age of Cobden*, 1977, pp. 51–71 for a detailed account of the problem.
66. See Russell, *Hansard*, 18 May 1840, vol. liv, col. 213.
67. Wood to Lady Holland, 4 May 1840, Add. MSS 51569, f. 226; C. C. F. Greville, *The Greville Memoirs*, Lytton Strachey and Roger Fulford (eds), 1938, 23 September 1839, vol. iv, p. 213, records Lady Holland's quip.
68. Grey to Lieven, 12 April 1840, G. Le Strange (ed.), *Correspondence of Princess Lieven and Earl Grey*, 1890, vol. iii, p. 316.
69. J. C. Hobhouse, Baron Broughton, *Recollections of a Long Life*, 1909, 13 April 1840, vol. v, p. 259.
70. Gash, *Sir Robert Peel*, pp. 240–1; *Reaction and Reconstruction in English Politics*, pp. 202–6.

71. Leveson to Granville, 24 January 1840, PRO 30/29/6–4, f. 699.
72. Prest, *Russell*, p. 164.
73. Greville, *Memoirs*, 31 December 1839 and 14 January 1840, vol. iv, pp. 222, 224.
74. G. S. R. Kitson Clark, *Peel and the Conservative Party*, 1964, pp. 449–50; Ian D. C. Newbould, 'Peel and the Conservative Party, 1832–1841: A Study in Failure?', *EHR* (1983), vol. ccclxxxviii, pp. 545–6.
75. Greville, *Memoirs*, 13 August 1840, vol. iv, pp. 268, 272.
76. Graham to Peel, 27 March 1837, in A. D. Macintyre, *The Liberator: Daniel O'Connell and the Irish Party 1830–1847*, 1965, p. 250.
77. Russell to Lady Holland, 26 December 1839, Add. MSS 51680, f. 102; Stanley to Ellice, 18 November 1839, EP/51, f. 139.
78. Melbourne to Russell, 6 August 1840, RA MP 14/141.
79. Russell to Victoria, 27 June 1840, RA C7/53.
80. Broughton, *Recollections*, 26 June 1840, vol. v, p. 275; Russell to Victoria, 27 June 1840, RA C/53.
81. Gash, *Reaction and Reconstruction in English Politics*, p. 126.
82. Parkes to Melbourne, 20 August 1840, RA MP 33/22.
83. L. Mitchell, *Holland House*, 1980, p. 295. See Mitchell, *Holland House*, pp. 292–301; Prest, *Russell*, pp. 165–70; Ziegler, *Melbourne*, pp. 318–329; K. Bourne, *Palmerston: The Early Years 1784–1841*, 1982, pp. 593–617.
84. Melbourne to Russell, 26 August 1840, RA MP 14/149; G. S. H. Fox-Strangways, 6th Earl of Ilchester, *Chronicles of Holland House, 1820–1900*, 1937, p. 284.
85. Greville, *Memoirs*, 26 September 1840, vol. iv, p. 129.
86. P. Ziegler, *Melbourne*, 1976, pp. 319, 328.
87. Greville, *Memoirs*, 30 January 1841, vol. iv, p. 351.
88. Leveson to Granville, 4 February 1841, PRO 30/29/6–4, f. 783.
89. Parkes to Stanley, 28 December 1840, PP/25; Hatherton to Melbourne, 30 December 1840, RA MP 27/99.
90. Parkes to Melbourne, 4 January 1841, RA MP 33/24; Hatherton to Melbourne, 14 January 1841, RA MP 27/101.
91. *Morning Chronicle*, 12 January 1841, Villiers to Parkes: 'Don't let the Chronicle go on attacking the League. It will do no good'. 3 January 1841, RA MP 33/23.
92. Russell to Melbourne, 24 August 1840, BP, GC/ME/412.
93. Russell memorandum, 9 February 1841, PRO 30/22/4A, f. 81.
94. Russell to Victoria, 3 February 1841, RA C7/69.
95. Russell memorandum, 9 February 1841 PRO 30/22/4A, f. 82.
96. Lansdowne to Russell, 25 April 1841, PRO 30/22/4A, f. 251; *Hansard*, 7 May 1841, vol. lviii, col. 18.
97. Hobhouse diary, 24 April 1841, Add. MSS 56564, f. 1.
98. See Chapter 12.
99. RA Victoria's journal, 24 January 1839.
100. Melbourne to Russell, 10 January 1840, RA MP 14/93.
101. Macaulay to Macvey Napier, 30 April 1841, Add. MSS 36421, f. 602; Prest, *Russell*, p. 174.

102. Hobhouse diary, 24 April 1841, Add. MSS 56564, f. 1.
103. Gash, *Sir Robert Peel*, pp. 255–7.
104. *Hansard*, 18 May 1841, vol. lviii, col. 673. Gash, *Reaction and Reconstruction in English Politics*, p. 214.
105. Ellice to Melbourne, 15 May 1841, EP/28, f. 108; Howick diary, 11 May 1841, GP; Melbourne to Victoria, 6 May 1841, RA C/21, f. 10; RA Victoria's journal, 4 and 8 May, 1841.
106. Broughton, *Recollections*, 8 May 1841, vol. vi, p. 20; Melbourne to Victoria, 8 May 1841, Esher, *Victoria's Letters*, vol. i, p. 341.
107. Melbourne to Anson, RA C21/4; Melbourne to Victoria, 28 April 1841, RA C21/1; Russell to Victoria, 4 May 1841, RA C21/7.
108. Hatherton to Granville, 28 May 1841, PRO 30/29/3, f. 478.
109. Duncannon to Melbourne, 16 May 1841, RA MP 3/103; Palmerston to Melbourne, 14 May 1841, RA MP 13/24.
110. Prest, *Russell*, p. 188; Russell to Victoria, 16 May 1841, RA C21/34.
111. Parkes to Melbourne, 5 May 1841, RA MP 33/25.
112. Victoria to Melbourne, 6 May 1841, RA C4/11; RA Victoria's journal, 15 May 1841.
113. Russell to Melbourne, 14 and 19 May 1841, PRO 30/22/4A, ff. 315, 322.
114. Duncannon to Melbourne, [n.d.], RA MP 3/99.

11 THE BUSINESS OF GOVERNMENT, 1835–41

1. D. G. Southgate, *The Passing of the Whigs 1832–1886*, 1962, p. 63.
2. Ibid.
3. W. E. Moneypenny and G. E. Buckle, *The Life of Benjamin Disraeli*, 1910, vol. i, p. 319.
4. N. Gash, *Reaction and Reconstruction in English Politics 1832–1852*, 1965, pp. 170–1.
5. A. Llewelyan, *The Decade of Reform*, 1972 p. 65.
6. See G. B. A. M. Finlayson, 'The Municipal Corporation Commission Report, 1833–35', *BIHR* (1963), vol. xxxvi, pp. 36–52, and 'The Politics of Municipal Reform, 1835', *EHR* (1966) vol. lxxxi, pp. 673–92.
7. G. B. A. M. Finlayson, *The Decade of Reform: England in the Eighteen Thirties*, 1970, p. 31.
8. O. Macdonagh, *Early Victorian Government 1830–1870*, 1977, p. 129.
9. D. Fraser, *The Evolution of the British Welfare State*, 1973, p. 74; R. Russell (ed.), *Early Correspondence of Lord John Russell 1805–1840*, 1913, vol. ii, p. 138.
10. W. O. Chadwick, *The Victorian Church*, 1966, vol. i, p. 106.
11. Melbourne to Howley, 6 May 1835, PRO 30/22/1E, f. 97; Chadwick, *The Victorian Church*, vol. i, p. 128.
12. Melbourne to Mulgrave, 5 October 1835, MCA MM/43.
13. L. C. Sanders (ed.), *Lord Melbourne's Papers*, 1889, p. 29; RA Victoria's journal, 19 June 1839.
14. Melbourne to Howley, 15 July 1840, RA MP 76/108.
15. Chadwick, *The Victorian Church*, vol. i, p. 129. The Whig members were Melbourne, Russell, Lansdowne, Cottenham and Spring Rice.

16. *Hansard*, vol. xxxii, col. 137.
17. See O. J. Brose, *Church and Parliament*, 1959, p. 136–56 for the Commission and its measures until 1840.
18. G. I. T. Machin, *Politics and the Churches in Great Britain 1832–1868*, 1977, p. 57; Chadwick, *The Victorian Church*, vol. i, p. 136.
19. Melbourne to Russell, 8 September 1835, BP, MEL/RU/172.
20. Holland diary, September 1836, Add. MSS 51871, f. 948.
21. Russell to Melbourne, 12 December 1835, Russell, *Early Correspondence*, p. 162; Howick diary, 1 February 1836, GP.
22. Chadwick, *The Victorian Church*, vol. i, p. 61.
23. G. F. A. Best, 'The Whigs and the Church Establishment in the Age of Grey and Holland', *History* 45, 1960: 108.
24. Russell to Grey, April 1834, GP. Russell to Lord Melbourne, August 17, 1834, Add. MSS 51677, f. 123; Grey to Lord Holland, 9 March 1834, Add. MSS 51557, f. 8.
25. Machin, *Politics and the Churches*, pp. 54–5.
26. *Hansard*, 3 August 1835, vol. xxix, cols, 1342–55.
27. *Hansard*, 20 March 1835, vol. xxviii, col. 76.
28. W. M. Torrens, *Memoirs of Rt. Hon. William, 2nd Viscount Melbourne*, 1878, vol. ii, p. 156.
29. Melbourne to Russell, 15 December 1835, BP, MEL/RU/281.
30. Russell to Melbourne, 17 August 1834, Add. MSS 51677, f. 123.
31. Russell memorandum, [April] 1835, PRO 30/22/1E, f. 68.
32. Lansdowne to Melbourne, April 1835, PRO 30/22/1E, f. 65; Chadwick, *The Victorian Church*, vol. i, pp. 147–8.
33. Cabinet memorandum, March 1836, PRO 30/22/2A, ff. 323–44.
34. *Hansard*, 12 February 1836, vol. xxxi, cols. 378–9.
35. Machin, *Politics and the Churches*, pp. 59–60.
36. Melbourne to Russell, 11 January 1837, BP, MEL/RU/290.
37. Ellice to Grey, 2 February 1837, GP; Spencer to Brougham, 15 March 1837, SP.
38. Melbourne to Ellice, 1 February 1837, EP/28, f. 44.
39. Memorandum to Melbourne, March 1837, PRO 30/22/2E, f. 124; Melbourne to Howley, 20 March 1837, PRO 30/22/2E, f. 132.
40. Melbourne to Rice, 16 March 1837, MP 13386(2); Melbourne to Russell, 15 March 1837, BP, MEL/RU/315.
41. Howick diary, 20 May 1837, GP.
42. C. C. F. Greville, *The Greville Memoirs*, Lytton Strachey and Roger Fulford (eds), 1938, 18 March 1837, vol. iii, p. 358.
43. Melbourne to Russell, 18 August 1837, BP, MEL/RU/389.
44. Russell to Melbourne, 11 and 28 August 1837, BP, MEL/RU/38, 42; Melbourne to Russell, 13 and 24 August 1837, BP, MEL/RU/387, 392.
45. Melbourne to Russell, 1 February 1838, BP, MEL/RU/442.
46. Although Roebuck had proposed establishing a Select Committee to enquire into the means of establishing a national system of education, Althorp in fact moved for the committee, which was allowed to enquire only into the efficacy of the 1833 Treasury grant. *Hansard*, 3 June 1834, vol. xxiv, col. 130; J. Alexander and D. G. Paz, 'The

Treasury Grants, 1833–1839', *British Journal of Education Studies*, 1973–74, vol. 22, pp. 87–8.
47. D. G. Paz, *The Politics of Working Class Education in Britain 1830–50*, 1980, pp. 62–3.
48. The five Conservative members on the committee defeated the four government supporters. R. E. Aldrich, 'Education and the Political Parties', London M. Phil., 1970, p. 193.
49. H. J. Burgess, *Enterprise in Education*, 1958, p. 68; Paz, *The Politics of Working Class Education*, p. 63; R. Johnson, 'Educating the Educators: Experts and the State 1833–9', in A. P. Donajgrodski (ed.), *Social Control in Nineteenth Century Britain*, 1977, p. 99.
50. Russell, Memorandum on Ireland, 15 February 1834, DP, 130/12.
51. S. Walpole, *Life of Lord John Russell*, 1889, vol. ii, p. 120.
52. Ibid., 486.
53. Burgess, *Enterprise in Education*, p. 70; Chadwick, *The Victorian Church*, i, 340.
54. Russell to Lord Lansdowne, 4 February, 1839, in J. Stuart Maclure, (ed.) *Educational Documents, England and Wales 1816 to the Present Day*, 1973, pp. 42–5: 'The reports of chaplains of gaols show that to a large number of unfortunate prisoners a knowledge of the fundamental truths of natural and revealed religion has never been imparted . . . by combining moral training with general instruction, the young may be saved from temptations to crime, and the whole community receive indisputable benefit.'
55. *Hansard*, 12 February 1839, vol. xiv, cols. 274, 278, 285.
56. E. Halévy, *The Triumph of Reform 1830–1841*, 1961, p. 221, n. 1.
57. Russell to Brougham, 15 and 27 August, 17 September and 2 and 20 October 1837, BrP 38162–4, 14425–6.
58. *Hansard*, 14 June 1838, vol. xliii, col. 731.
59. Johnson, 'Educating the Educators', p. 99.
60. J. C. Hobhouse, Baron Broughton, *Recollections of a Long Life*, 1909, 26 November 1838, vol. v, p. 168; Howick diary, 26 November 1838, GP; Melbourne to Russell, 27 November 1838, RA MP 13/99.
61. Rice to Melbourne, 5 September 1838, RA MP 10/1: 'Russell's present notion is to withdraw the grant altogether'.
62. Paz, *The Politics of Working Class Education*, p. 70.
63. Ibid., p. 71; Alexander and Paz, 'The Treasury Grants', pp. 83–6, 89.
64. Paz, *The Politics of Working Class Education*, p. 93.
65. Russell to Melbourne, 28 November 1838, PRO 30/22/3B, f. 376; Russell to Howick, 28 November 1838, GP.
66. R. Soloway, *Prelates and People: Ecclesiastical Social Thought in England, 1783–1852*, 1969, p. 400 estimates that 3000 hostile petitions were sent.
67. Paz, *The Politics of Working Class Education*, p. 82.
68. Machin, *Politics and the Churches*, p. 66.
69. Burgess, *Enterprise in Education*, p. 70.
70. Mulgrave to Melbourne, 10 October 1834, RA MP 10/50.
71. Holland to Grey, 13 November 1835, Add. MSS 51548, f. 215.

72. Russell to Sir Herbert Taylor, 21 October 1835, PRO 30/22/1E, f. 218.
73. R. McDowell, *Public Opinion and Government Policy in Ireland 1801–1846*, 1952, p. 190.
74. Ibid, pp. 186, 197.
75. Howick to Graham, 9 March 1835, GP.
76. Melbourne told Howick in 1837 that he preferred a Catholic establishment in Ireland as the only way to secure permanent quiet, but did not see how it could be done. Howick diary, 21 January 1837, GP.
77. *Hansard*, 30 March 1835, vol. xxvii, col. 361; Brose, *Church and Parliament*, p. 53.
78. Normanby to Russell, 10 May 1841, RA C21/23: 'If there were once again a narrower majority, could we again play the game of the appropriation clause?'.
79. Melbourne to William, 16 June 1835, Sanders, *Melbourne Papers*, p. 285; Holland diary, 18 June 1835, Add. MSS 51871, ff. 861–2.
80. Holland diary, 5 June 1835, Add. MSS 51871, f. 846; Howick diary, 15 May 1835, GP.
81. *Hansard*, 26 June 1835, vol. xxviii, col. 1344.
82. Howick diary, 25 July 1837, GP; Holland diary, 25 July 1835, Add. MSS 51871, f. 899; Melbourne to Mulgrave, 4 and 24 July 1835, MCA MM/32, 36.
83. Holland diary, 23 July 1835, Add. MSS 51871, f. 898.
84. Russell wrote to Mulgrave in Ireland that 'Nobody thinks they will pass it'; Morpeth wrote that 'the Lords [will] kick it out'. Russell to Mulgrave, 16 August 1835, Morpeth to Mulgrave, 3 July 1835, MCA M/791, 461.
85. Morpeth to Russell, 28 November 1835, PRO 30/2/1E, f. 251.
86. Lansdowne to Mulgrave, 7 January 1836, MCA 0/583.
87. 'I wish to God Ministers would make a compromise with the Conservatives', O'Connell was overheard to say at Brooks's in May. When asked how, he said 'Why, to get a good Municipal Bill, I would give up the Appropriation clause.' S. J. Reid, *The Life and Letters of the First Earl of Durham*, 1906, vol. ii, p. 106. Cf. Sir Herbert Taylor to Stanley, 3 July 1836: 'I heard some time ago that O'Connell expressed great indifference about the Appropriation clause & was quite ready to relieve the government from the obligation of supporting it provided they made a point of carrying the Municipal bill.' DP 100/2.
88. 'O'Connell said a few words at the Foreign Office yesterday volunteering entirely to throw over the appropriation clause'. Morpeth to Mulgrave, 26 April 1836, MCA M/543; Morpeth to Mulgrave, 25 June 1836, MCA M/546.
89. Mulgrave to Russell, 15 April and 16 December 1836, and 8 April 1837, PRO 30/22/2B, f. 39; 2D, f. 190; 2E, f. 160; Russell to Mulgrave, 8 September 1836, MCA M/838.
90. Morpeth to Mulgrave, 10 April 1837, MCA M/559; Russell to Melbourne, 13 September 1837, PRO 30/22/2F, f. 113; Melbourne to Russell, 11 March 1838, BP, MEL/RU/465.

91. A. D. Macintyre, *The Liberator: Daniel O'Connell and the Irish Party 1830–1847*, 1965, pp. 179–9.
92. McDowell, *Public Opinion and Government Policy in Ireland*, pp. 180–1.
93. See Macintyre, *O'Connell the Liberator*, pp. 230–5, for the commission and its report.
94. *Quarterly Review*, 1836, vol. lvii, p. 238.
95. Macintyre, *O'Connell the Liberator*, pp. 236–7.
96. Graham to Peel, 27 March 1837, Add. MSS 40318, f. 64.
97. *Hansard*, 23 and 29 May 1838, vol. xliii, cols. 132, 435; Russell to Victoria, 24 May 1838, RA C6/7.
98. Melbourne to Russell, 6 August 1840, RA MP 14/141.
99. Macintyre, *O'Connell the Liberator*, pp. 259–60.
100. Russell was critical of this estimate, thinking it far too high. *Hansard*, 1 December 1837, vol. xxxix, cols. 487–90.
101. In Macintyre, *O'Connell the Liberator*, p. 207.
102. McDowell, *Public Opinion and Government Policy in Ireland*, p. 186.
103. In Macintyre, *O'Connell the Liberator*, p. 208.
104. G. O'Brien, *An Economic History of Ireland from the Union to the Famine*, 1921, p. 171.
105. Ibid, p. 172.
106. *Hansard*, 2 May 1833, vol. xvii, cols. 848–50.
107. *Parliamentary Papers*, 1836, vol. xxx, Third Report.
108. Mulgrave to Russell, 1 February 1836, PRO 30/22/2A, f. 100.
109. Nicholls to Russell, 17 October 1836, PRO 30/22/2C, f. 273.
110. Russell to Mulgrave, 25 November 1836, MCA M/846.
111. Russell to Moore, 6 December 1836, PRO 30/22/2D, f. 113; Mulgrave to Russell, 4 December 1836, PRO 30/22/2D, f. 117.
112. Howick to Grey, 4 February 1836, GP; Rice to Russell, 20 November 1836 and 16 March 1836, PRO 30/22/2D, f. 149 and 2E, f. 128; Lansdowne to Russell, [March 1837], PRO 30/22/2E, f. 130.
113. See Stanley to Russell, 18 December 1836, PRO 30/22/2D, f. 220, for the government's prior knowledge of Conservative support.
114. Macintyre, *O'Connell the Liberator*, pp. 217–26; The *Constitutional*, 4 October 1836.
115. Rice to Wellington, 29 September 1839, in Macintyre, *O'Connell the Liberator*, p. 223.
116. McDowell, *Public Opinion and Government Policy in Ireland*, p. 208.
117. Ibid., p. 60.
118. McDowell, *Public Opinion and Government Policy in Ireland*, pp. 114–16.
119. *Hansard*, 4 and 11 August 1835, vol. xxx, cols. 58–79, 559.
120. Hume to Melbourne, 16 September 1835, RA MP 28/22.
121. Russell to Melbourne, 2 and 9 November 1835, BP, MEL/RU/17, 11; *Hansard*, 14 March 1836, vol. xxii, cols. 253–4.
122. Melbourne to Grey, 11 October 1833, GP; P. Ziegler, *Melbourne*, 1976, p. 153.
123. H. Senior, *Orangeism in Ireland and Britain 1795–1836*, 1966, pp. 270–2, suggests that the evidence, although not entirely out of the question, is problematic.

124. Russell to Melbourne, 3 October 1835, Russell, *Early Correspondence*, p. 133; Russell to Mulgrave, 3 and 6 December 1835, PRO 30/22/1E, ff. 253, 258. The second letter, undated in the PRO, is dated in the original to be found in MCA M/810.
125. Hume to Russell, 21 February 1836, PRO 30/22/2A, f. 246; *Hansard*, 22 February 1836, vol. xxxi, cols. 779, 832, 860.
126. *Hansard*, 25 February 1836, vol. xxxi, col. 946.
127. G. Broeker, *Rural Disorder and Police Reform in Ireland 1812–36*, pp. 224–5.
128. Russell to Mulgrave, 27 May 1835, MCA M/777; Howick diary, 25 July 1835, GP; Melbourne to Mulgrave, 9 and 14 October 1835, MCA MM/44, 47.2
129. Broeker, *Rural disorder and Police Reform in Ireland*, ch. XI, 'The Whigs and Ireland 1830–36', was particularly useful for this section.
130. McDowell, *Public Opinion and Government Policy in Ireland*, p. 185.
131. *Hansard*, 18 February 1836, xxxi, 543; Broeker, *Rural Disorder and Police Reform in Ireland 1812–36*, p. 223.
132. Ibid., pp. 225–6.
133. McDowell, *Public Opinion and Government Policy in Ireland*, p. 203.
134. See Chapter 8.
135. S. Walpole, *A History of England From The Conclusion Of The Great War in 1815*, 1905, vol. iv, p. 192.
136. Brown, *Board of Trade*, pp. 43–4.
137. Howick diary, 5 May 1836, GP.
138. *Hansard*, 18 May 1838, vol. xlii, col. 1372.
139. Brown, *Board of Trade*, pp. 59–60.
140. *Hansard*, 5 July 1839, vol. xiviii, col. 1354.
141. Rowland Hill, *Post Office Reform*, 1837, passim.
142. *Select Committee on Rates of Postage*, vol. xx, pp. 1837–8.
143. Place to Geo Wheatley, 21 February 1840, Add. MSS 35151, ff. 210–19; Warburton to Place, 25 February 1840, Add. MSS 35151, f. 217.
144. Hobhouse diary, 20 May 1839, Add. MSS 56560, f. 173; Spring Rice to Melbourne, September 1839, quoted in Brown, *Board of Trade*, p. 61.
145. 'The loss of consequence from ceasing to be able to frank a letter for a lady, or in travelling, for the waiter at an inn, gave great disgust to many members of both Houses, Whig as well as Tory'. Mrs Hardcastle, *Life of John, Lord Campbell*, 1881, vol. ii, p. 117.
146. From £1,649,000 to £495,000. S. Walpole. *A History of England From the Conclusion of the Great War in 1815*, 1905, vol. iv, p. 191.
147. Broughton, *Recollections*, vol v, pp. 263–4.
148. *Hansard*, 15 May 1840, vol. liv, col. 121.
149. Baring to Melbourne, 25 April 1840, RA MP 1/48.
150. Baring to Melbourne, 2 September 1840, RA MP 1/52: ' . . . revenue looks ill. Excise not quite so bad. Trade seems reviving a little. Customs very low. Everything against us – war, harvest, etc.' Melbourne to Russell, 21 August 1840, RA MP 14/147.
151. Baring to Melbourne, February 1841, RA MP 1/62.
152. T. G. Earl Northbrook (ed.), *Journals and Correspondence of F. T. Baring, Lord Northbrook*, 1905, vol. i, pp. 167–8.

153. Baring to Melbourne, 19 January and 8 February 1841, RA MP 1/61, 64.
154. Brown, *Board of Trade*, chs. 11–13.
155. RA MP 34.
156. *Hansard*, 19 April 1833, vol. xvii, cols. 343–4; 15 May 1840, vol. liv, col. 156; 2 February 1841, vol. lvi, col. 215.
157. Ebrington to Melbourne, 19 March 1841, RA MP 101/76; Southgate, *Passing of the Whigs*, 119, n.4.
158. Southgate, *Passing of the Whigs*, Chap. IV, has a good summary of the debate.
159. Brown, *Board of Trade*, p. 215; *Edinburgh Review*, 1841, vol. lxxii, p. 418.
160. Baring to Melbourne, 19 January 1841, RA MP 1/61.
161. Baring memorandum, 8 February 1841, RA MP 1/64; Russell memorandum, 9 February 1841, PRO 30/22/4A, f. 81.
162. *Hansard*, 3 May 1841, vol. lvii, col. 1376.
163. Walpole, *Russell*, vol. i, pp. 367–9, *Morning Chronicle*, 8 May 1841; Russell to Melbourne, 7 January 1839, BP, MEL/RU/71.
164. Spencer to Melbourne, 3 February 1839, Sanders, *Melbourne Papers*, p. 394; Durham to J. B. Smith, 15 January 1839, LP, vol. xxii, f. 21.
165. Howick memorandum, 9 January 1839; printed anonymous letter from 'A Hertfordshire Farmer', 18 February 1839, GP.
166. A. Bannerman to Melbourne, 3 January 1839, RA MP 19/31; Ebrington to Fortescue, 1 May 1841, FP, 1252 M/L1, f. 197.
167. Lansdowne to Russell, 25 April 1841, PRO 30/22/4A, f. 251; Melbourne to Rusell, 5 January 1839, RA MP 13/118.

12 'JUST OUT'

1. T. G. Earl Northbrook, *Journals and Correspondence of F. T. Baring, Lord Northbrook*, 1905, vol. i, p. 179.
2. See D. G. Southgate, *The Passing of Whigs 1832–1886*, 1962, pp. 428–36.
3. Hobhouse diary, 19 June 1841, Add. MSS 56564, f. 70.
4. Spencer to Brougham, 8 June 1841, SP.
5. Ellice to Normanby, July 1841, MCA 0/429.
6. Ellice to Ebrington, 29 June 1841, FP 1262 M/L1, f. 205; Spencer to Tavistock, 4 July 1841, PRO 30/22/4B, f. 9.
7. Ellice to Fortescue, *ibid.*; Russell to Queen Victoria, 14 June 1841, RA C7/87; Howick to Grey, 13 July 1841, GP; Morpeth to Melbourne, 20 July 1841, RA MP 98/129; According to *The Times*, 16 June 1841, 76 ministerialists retired, 34 Conservatives. Overall, the Conservatives fielded 131 more candidates than the combined Whigs, Liberals and Radicals.
8. *The Times*, 27 July 1841.
9. Hamilton to Melbourne, 26 June 1841, RA MP 27/42.
10. D. C. Moore, *The Politics of Deference: A Study of the Nineteenth Century Political System*, 1976, p. 58.

11. R. Stewart, *The Foundation of the Conservative Party 1830–1867*, 1978, p. 144.
12. Northbrook, *Journals and Correspondence*. vol. i, p. 87.
13. N. Gash, *Sir Robert Peel*, 1972, p. 234; J. B. Conacher, *Waterloo to the Common Market*, 1975, p. 76; G. B. A. M. Finlayson, *The Decade of Reform: England in the Eighteen Thirties*, 1970, p. 36.
14. Moore, *The Politics of Deference*, pp. 139, 283–9.
15. Stewart, *The Foundation of the Conservative Party*, pp. 143–4.
16. Spencer to Brougham, 1 August 1837, SP; Russell to Melbourne, 13 August 1837, PRO 30/22/2F, f. 9.
17. T. L. Crosby, *English Farmers and the Politics of Protection 1815–1852*, 1977, p. 104; R. J. Olney, *Lincolnshire Politics 1832–1885*, 1982, pp. 111–15.
18. Stewart, *The Foundation of the Conservative Party*, p. 172, n. 5.
19. Ibid., pp. 160, 386.
20. Hatherton to Granville, 28 May 1841, PRO 30/29/6/3, f. 478; Parkes to Russell, 7 May 1841, PRO 30/22/4A, f. 279; Earl Russell, *Recollections and Suggestions, 1813–1873*, 1875, p. 236.
21. N. McCord, *The Anti-Corn Law League 1838–1846*, 1958, p. 93; Stewart, *The Foundation of the Conservative Party*, p. 160.
22. *Canterbury Journal*, 5 June 1841.
23. *Bucks Herald*, 26 and 12 June 1841; R. Davis, *Political Change and Continuity 1760–1885*, 1972, p. 153.
24. Davis, *Political Change and Continuity*, pp. 124–6, 148, 153.
25. *Kentish Gazette*, 11 May 1841.
26. *Cambridge Chronicle*, 31 August 1839.
27. *Berkshire Chronicle*, 22 May, 19 June and 24 July 1841. See also W. S. Darten, *Reminiscences of Reading by an Octogenarian*, 1888, p. 176.
28. *Wigan Gazette*, 28 May , 11 June 1841.
29. *The Hull Rockingham*, 26 June 1841.
30. The *Hull and East Riding Times*, 6 July 1841.
31. *Blackburn Gazette*, 30 June 1841.
32. See J. A. Jowitt, 'Parliamentary Politics in Halifax, 1832–1847', *Northern History*, 1976, pp. 189–91; D. G. Wright, 'A Radical Borough: Parliamentary Politics in Bradford 1832–41', *Northern History*, 1969, pp. 146–7.
33. D. H. Close, 'The Elections of 1835 and 1837 in England and Wales', Oxford D. Phil., 1977, pp. 75, 157, 245–6, 349–50, 403–4.
34. The *Hull and East Riding Times*, 1 June 1841.
35. *Leeds Intelligencer*, 5 June 1841.
36. Ibid., 12 June 1841.
37. *Berkshire Chronicle*, 24 July 1841.
38. *Liverpool Mail*, 29 June, 1 July 1841. The Liberal *Liverpool Mercury* agreed (2 July 1841) that the protestant clergy had a great influence on the results.
39. Ashley to Bonham, 4 December 1839, in C. S. Parker, *Sir Robert Peel*, 1891, vol. ii, p. 415; Stewart, *The Foundation of the Conservative Party*, p. 158.
40. *Hampshire Advertiser*, 5 June 1841.

41. Add. MSS 56564, f. 82.
42. J. Prest, *Lord John Russell*, 1972, p. 188.
43. Parkes to Stanley, 16 December 1841, PP/25.
44. Ellice to Mulgrave, August 1841, MCA, 0/429; Ellice to Ebrington, 29 June 1841, FP 1262 M/L1, f. 205; Ellice to Parkes, 25 September 1841, PP/5.
45. Russell to Ellice, 24 July 1841, EP/49, f. 68; Ellice to Duncannon, 11 April 1846, in S. Walpole, *Life of Lord John Russell*, 1889, vol. i, p. 423 n.
46. Russell to Melbourne, 19 August 1841, BP, MEL/RU/130.
47. Spencer to Melbourne, 28 July 1841, RA MP 15/120.
48. Lefevre to Russell, 4 August 1841, PRO 30/22/4B, f. 94. It was likely the result of this decision that the ultras attempted to embarrass Peel by approaching the Whigs with a view to coalition.
49. Russell to Peel, (draft), 5 July 1841, PRO 30/22/4B, f. 13; Ellice to Russell, 30 July 1841, PRO 30.22/4B, f. 83; Melbourne to Russell, 26 August 1841, PRO 30/22/4B, f. 129.
50. Prest, *Russell*, p. 184; P. Ziegler, *Melbourne*, 1976, p. 341.
51. Queen to King Leopold, 24 August 1841, A. C. Benson and Viscount Esher (eds.), *The Letters of Queen Victoria 1837–1861*, 1907, vol. i, p. 375.

13 POSTSCRIPT

1. K. Bourne, *Palmerston: The Early Years 1784–1841*, 1982, p. 638.
2. Le Marchant Diary, 21 July 1833, in A. Aspinall (ed.), *Three Early Nineteenth Century Diaries*, 1952, p. 366.
3. Melbourne to Russell, 7 September 1837, BP MEL/RU/396.
4. J. Carswell, *The Old Cause*, 1954, p. 350.
5. *Hansard*, 4 June 1841, vol. lviii, col. 1210. Russell to Melbourne, 12 December 1838, in R. Russell, (ed.), *Early Correspondence of Lord John Russell*, 1913, vol. ii, 238; Monteagle to Wordsworth, 12 September 1839, MP, 547, f. 104.
6. L. Mitchell, *Holland House*, 1980, p. 37.
7. R. Brent, *Liberal Anglican Politics: Whiggery, Religion and Reform 1830–1841*, 1987, passim.
8. B. Hilton, *The Age of Atonement: The Influence of Evangelicalism on Social and Economic Thought, 1795–1865*, 1988, esp. chapter 6.
9. Russell to Melbourne, 9 September 1837, PRO 30/22/2F, f. 73.
10. Spring Rice to Edward Ellice, 25 August 1837, MP, 538, f. 1; W. M. Torrens, *Memoirs of Viscount Melbourne*, 1878, vol. i, p. 224; J. C. Hobhouse, Baron Broughton, *Recollections of a Long Life*, 1909, 24 December 1837, vol. v, p. 114; Howick to Grey, 24 November and 18 December 1837, GP.
11. C. C. F. Greville, *The Greville Memoirs*, Lytton Strachey and Roger Fulford (eds.), 1938, 18 February 1838.
12. Ebrington to Melbourne, 2 February 1839, RA MP 101/25.
13. See Chapter 11, p. 302.

14. Discussing Russell's dislike of Conservative support, Melbourne told the Queen: 'I don't dislike the Tories. I think they are very much like the others . . . I don't care by whom I am supported, I consider them all as one; I don't care by whom I am helped as long as I *am* helped.' R. A. Victoria's journal, 23 September 1839. See Russell to Melbourne, 9 September 1837, PRO 30/22/2F, f. 73.
15. Robert to Sydney Smith, 5 September 1841, N. C. Smith (ed.), *Selected Letters of Sydney Smith*, 1981, p. 195.

Bibliography

1 MANUSCRIPT MATERIALS

British Library: Broughton Papers   *Abbreviation*
                 Holland House Papers   Add.MSS
                 Macvey Napier Papers
                 Peel Papers
                 Place Papers
                 Ripon Papers
                 Russell Papers
                 Wellesley Papers

Broadlands Papers, Historical Manuscripts Commission BP
Brougham Papers, University College, London BrP
Derby Papers, Liverpool Record Office DP
Ellice Papers, National Library of Scotland EP
Fortescue Papers, Devon County Record Office FP
Grey Papers, University of Durham GP
Graham Papers, microfilm, Bodleian Library, Oxford GrP
Lambton Papers, Lambton Estate Office, Chester-le-Street, Co. Durham LP
Mulgrave Castle Archives, Mulgrave Castle, Whitby MCA
Monteagle Papers, National Library of Ireland, Dublin MP
O'Connell Papers, National Library of Ireland, Dublin OP
Parkes Papers, University College, London PP
Public Record Office: Russell Papers PRO
                     Granville Papers
Royal Archives, Windsor Castle: Melbourne Papers RA
                             Victorian Archives
Spencer Papers, Althorp Park, Northamptonshire SP

Other Manuscript Sources:
Drummond Papers   National Library of Ireland, Dublin
Letterbook of L. G. Jones Marylebone Public Library, London
O'Connell transcripts   Mr M. R. O'Connell, Dublin, transcripts of the
                       lowing collections:
                           Mrs M. Bennett Kilkenny, Papers
                           Fitzsimon Papers
                           Harrington Papers
                           E. G. More O'Ferral papers
                           Rathcon papers
                           Mrs. Anne Smithwick Papers.

2 NEWSPAPERS, MAGAZINES

Annual Register
Berkshire Chronicle
Blackburn Gazette
Bucks Herald
Cambridge Chronicle
Canterbury Journal
Chambers Historical News
Christian Observer
Dublin Morning Post
Edinburgh Review
Examiner
Hampshire Advertiser
Hull and East Riding Times
Kentish Gazette
Leeds Intelligencer
Leeds Mercury
Liverpool Mail
Liverpool Mercury
Morning Chronicle
Northern Whig
Parliamentary Review
Tait's Edinburgh Magazine
The Constitutional
The Guardian
The Hull Rockingham
The London and Westminster Review
The Patriot
Quarterly Review
The Spectator
The Times
Westminster Review
Wigan Gazette

3 CORRESPONDENCE, MEMOIRS, DIARIES, PAMPHLETS

anon., *Remarks on the Second Session of the Reformed Parliament*, London, 1834.

anon., *The Present and Last Parliaments*, London, 1833.

Aspinall, A. (ed.), *Three Early Nineteenth Century Diaries*, London, 1952.

Bamford, F. and the Duke of Wellington, ed., *The Journal of Mrs Arbuthnot*, 2 vols, London, 1950.

Benson, A. C. and Viscount Esher (eds), *The Letters of Queen Victoria 1837–1861*, 3 vols, London, 1907.

Brougham, Lord *The Life and Times of Henry, Lord Brougham*, 3 vols, London, 1871.

Cockburn, H. *Letters on the Affairs of Scotland*, London, 1874.

Darten, W. S. *Reminiscences of Reading by an Octogenarian*, London, 1888.
Esher, Viscount (ed.), *The Girlhood of Queen Victoria*, 2 vols, London, 1912.
Erkskine, T. L. *The Defence of the Whigs*, London, 1819.
Fitzpatrick W. J. (ed.) *Correspondence of Daniel O'Connell*, 2 vols, London, 1888.
Fox-Strangways, G. S. H., 6th Earl of Ilchester, *Chronicles of Holland House, 1820–1900*, London, 1937.
Gooch, G. P. (ed), *Later Correspondence of Lord John Russell 1840–1878*, London, 1925.
Grant, James, *Random Recollections of the House of Commons*, London, 1836.
Grant, James, *The British Senate in 1838*, London, 1838.
Greville, C. C. F., *The Greville Memoirs*, Lytton Strachey and Roger Fulford (eds), 8 vols, London, 1938.
Henry, Earl Grey (ed.), *The Reform Act 1832. The Correspondence of Earl Grey with His Majesty King William IV*, 2 vols, London, 1867.
Grote, Harriet, *The Personal Life of George Grote*, London, 1873.
Hatherton, Lord, *Memoirs and Correspondence Relating to Political Occurrences in June and July 1834*, Henry Reeve (ed.), London, 1872.
Herries, E. (ed.), *Memoirs of J. C. Herries*, 2 vols, London, 1880.
Hill, Rowland, *Post Office Reform*, London, 1837.
Hobhouse, J. C., Baron Broughton, *Recollections of a Long Life*, Lady Dorchester (ed.), 6 vols, London, 1909–11.
Holland, Lord, *Memoirs of the Whig Party*, 2 vols, London, 1852.
Horner, L., *The Factories Regulations Act Explained*, London, 1834.
Jennings, L. J. (ed.), *Croker, Correspondence and Diaries of J. W..*, 3 vols, London, 1884.
Kriegel, A. D., (ed.), *The Holland House Diaries 1831–1840*, London, 1977.
Le Marchant, Sir D., *Memoirs of John Charles, Viscount Althorp*, London, 1876.
Le Marchant, Sir D., (ed.), *The Reform Ministry and the Reformed Parliament*, 5th edn, London, 1833.
Le Strange, G. (ed.), *Correspondence of Princess Lieven and Earl Grey*, 3 vols, London, 1890.
Mallet, Bernard, *Thos. George, Earl of Northbrook, A Memoir*, London, 1906.
Malthus, T. R., *An Essay on Population*, London, 1798.
Maxwell, Sir H., (ed.), *The Creevy Papers*, London, 1912.
Maxwell, Sir H. (ed.), *Life and Letters of the Fourth Earl of Clarendon*, 2 vols, London, 1913.
Molesworth, W. N., *The History of England from the Year 1830*, London, 1871.
Northbrook, Earl T. G. (ed.), *Journals and Correspondence of F. T. Baring, Lord Northbrook*, 2 vols, London, 1905.
Northcote, Stafford, *Twenty Years of Financial Policy*, London, 1862.
Robinson, L. G. (ed.), *Letters of Dorothea Lieven during her Residence in London 1812–1834*, London, 1902.
Roebuck, J. A., *History of the Whig Ministry of 1830*, 2 vols, London, 1852.
Roebuck, J. A., *Pamphlets for the People*, London, 1835.
Russell, Earl, *An Essay on the History of the English Government and Constitution*, London, 1865.

Russell, Earl, *Recollections and Suggestions 1813–1873*, 2nd edn, London, 1875.

Russell, Lord J., *Letter to the Electors of Stroud on the Principles of the Reform Act*, London, 1838.

Russell, R. (ed.), *Early Correspondence of Lord John Russell 1805–1840*, 2 vols, London, 1913.

Sanders, L. C. (ed.), *Lord Melbourne's Papers*, London, 1889.

Smith, N. C. (ed.), *Selected Letters of Sydney Smith*, Oxford, 1981.

Stanhope, P. H., *Notes of a Conversation with the Duke of Wellington 1831–1851*, London, 1888.

Stockmar, Baron, *Memoirs*, F. M. Mueller (ed.), London, 1872.

Torrens, W. M., *Memoirs of Rt. Hon. William, 2nd Viscount Melbourne*, 2 vols, London, 1878.

Walsh, Sir John, *Chapters on Contemporary History*, London, 1836.

William IV, *Address of His Majesty to the Prelates of England and Ireland on the 28th of May, 1834*, London, 1834.

White, G. C. (ed.), *Glimpses of King William IV and Queen Adelaide in Letters of the Late Miss Clitherow*, London, 1902.

4 SECONDARY SOURCES

Aldrich, R. E., 'Education and the Political Parties', M. Phil. thesis, University of London, 1970.

Alexander, J. and D. G. Paz, 'The Treasury Grants, 1833–1839', *British Journal of Educational Studies*, vol. 22, 1973–74, pp. 83–4.

Aspinall, A., 'English Party Organization in the Nineteenth Century', *English Historical Review*, vol. xli, 1926, pp. 389–411.

Aspinall, A., *Lord Brougham and the Whig Party*, Manchester, 1927.

Aspinall, A., *Politics and the Press, 1780–1850*, London, 1949

Aspinall, A., 'The Cabinet Council 1783–1835', *Proceedings of the British Academy*, vol. 38, 1952, pp. 145–252.

Ayedelotte, W. O. 'Voting Patterns in the British House of Commons in the 1840s', *Comparative Studies in History and Society*, vol. 5, 1963, pp. 134–63.

Bain, A., *James Mill*, London, 1884.

Best, G. F. A., 'The Whigs and the Church Establishment in the Age of Grey and Holland', *History*, vol. xlv, 1960, pp. 103–18.

Black, C., *The History of Jamaica*, London, 1958.

Boswell, J., *The Journal of a Tour of the Hebrides*, L. F. Powell (ed.), London, 1958.

Boswell, J., *Life of Johnson*, London, 1969.

Bourgeois, E., *History of Modern France 1815–1913*, New York, 1972.

Bourne, H. R. Fox, *English Newspapers; chapters in the history of journalism*, 2 vols, London, 1887.

Bourne, Kenneth, *Palmerston: The Early Years 1784–1841*, London, 1982.

Brent, R., *Liberal Anglican Politics: Whiggery, Religion and Reform 1830–1841*, Oxford, 1987.

Briggs, A. 'Middle Class Consciousness in English Politics', *Past and Present*, vol. 9, 1956, pp. 65–74.

Brock, Michael, *The Great Reform Act*, London, 1973.

Broeker, G., *Rural Disorder and Police Reform in Ireland 1812–36*, London, 1970.

Brose, O. J., *Church and Parliament: The Reshaping of the Church of England 1826–1860*, London, 1959.

Brown, L., *The Board of Trade and the Free Trade Movement 1830–42*, Oxford, 1958.

Brundage, A., *England's 'Prussion Minister': Edwin Chadwick and the Politics of Government Growth, 1832–1854*, Pennsylvania, 1988.

Brundage, A., 'The Landed Interest and the New Poor Law: A reappraisal of the revolution in government', *English Historical Review*, vol. lxxxvii, 1972, pp. 27–48.

Brundage, A., *The Making of the New Poor Law 1832–39*, Rutgers, 1978.

Buckley, J. K., *Joseph Parkes of Birmingham*, London, 1926.

Bulwer, Sir H. L., *The Life of Henry John Temple, Viscount Palmerston*, London, 1870.

Burgess, H. J., *Enterprise in Education*, London 1958.

Butler, J. R. M., *The Passing of the Great Reform Bill*, London, 1914.

Butterfield, Herbert, *The Englishman and His History*, London, 1944.

Cannon, J. *Parliamentary Reform 1640–1832*, Cambridge, 1973.

Carswell, John, *The Old Cause*, London, 1954.

Cecil, D. *Lord M.*, London, 1954.

Chadwick, W. O., *The Victorian Church*, 2 vols, London, 1966.

Christie, O. F., *The Transition from Aristocracy 1832–1867*, New York, 1927.

Clapham, J. H., *The Bank of England 1797–1914*, London, 1958.

Clark, J. C. D., 'A General Theory of Party, Opposition and Government, 1688–1832', *Historical Journal*, vol. 23, 1980, pp. 295–325.

Clarke, J. C., *The fortunes of the Ellice family: from business to politics, 1760–1860*, D. Phil. thesis, Oxford, 1973.

Clive, J., *Thomas Babington Macaulay: The Shaping of the Historian*, New York, 1976.

Close, D. H., 'The formation of a two-party alignment in the house of commons between 1830 and 1841', *English Historical Review*, vol. lxxxiv, 1969, pp. 257–77.

Close, D. H., 'The Elections of 1835 and 1837 in England and Wales', D. Phil. thesis, Oxford, 1977.

Conacher, J. B., *Waterloo to the Common Market*, London, 1975.

Cowherd, R., *The Politics of English Dissent*, London, 1959.

Craig, F. W. S., *British Parliamentary Results 1832–1885*, London, 1977.

Crosby, T. L., *English Farmers and the Politics of Protection 1815–1852*, London, 1977.

Custance, R. H. D., *The political career of William Lamb, 2nd Viscount Melbourne, to 1841*, D. Phil. thesis, Oxford, 1977.

Davis, R., *Political Change and Continuity 1760–1885*, London, 1972.

Derry, J., *Charles James Fox*, London, 1972.

Dicey, A. V., *Law and Public Opinion in England during the Nineteenth Century*, 2nd edn, London, 1898.

Dod, C. R., *Electoral Facts from 1832 to 1852*, London, 1852.

Driver, C., *Tory Radical: The Life of Richard Oastler*, London, 1946.

Dunkley, Peter, 'Whigs and Paupers: The Reform of the English Poor Laws, 1830–1834', *Journal of British Studies*, vol. 20, 1981, pp. 124–49.

Fawcett, M. G., *The Life of the Rt. Hon. Sir William Molesworth, Bart.*, London, 1901.

Finer, S. E., *The Life and Times of Sir Edwin Chadwick*, London, 1952.

Finlayson, G. B. A. M., *The Decade of Reform: England in the Eighteen Thirties*, New York, 1970.

Finlayson, G. B. A. M., 'The Municipal Corporation Commission Report, 1833–35', *Bulletin of the Institute of Historical Research*, vol. xxxvi, 1963, pp. 36–52.

Finlayson, G. B. A. M., 'The Politics of Municipal Reform, 1835', *English Historical Review*, vol. lxxxi, 1966, pp. 673–92.

Flick, C., 'The Fall of Wellington's Government', *Journal of Modern History*, vol. 37, 1965, pp. 62–71.

Foord, A. S., *His Majesty's Opposition*, London, 1964.

Fraser, D., *The Evolution of the British Welfare State*, London, 1973.

Fraser, D., *Urban Politics in Victorian England*, London, 1976.

Garrett, G. T., *Lord Brougham*, London, 1935.

Gash, N., 'Peel and the Party System, 1830–1850', *Transactions of the Royal Historical Society*, 5th series, I, 1951, pp. 47–69.

Gash, N., *Reaction and Reconstruction in English Politics, 1832–52*, Oxford, 1965.

Gash, N., *Sir Robert Peel, The Life of Sir Robert Peel after 1830*, London, 1972.

Gash, N., 'The Organization of the Conservative Party 1832–1846: Part I: The Parliamentary Organization', *Parliamentary History*, vol. I, 1982, pp. 137–59.

Gash, N., *Politics in the Age of Peel: A Study in the Technique of Parliamentary Representation 1830–1850*, London, 1953.

Gayer, A. D., W. W. Rostow and A. J. Schwartz, *The Growth and Fluctuation of the British Economy 1790–1850*, 2 vols, Oxford, 1953.

Halévy, E. *The Triumph of Reform 1830–1841*, London, 1961.

Hamburger, J. *James Mill and the Art of Revolution*, Yale, 1963.

Hanham, H. J., *The 19th Century Constitution*, London, 1980.

Hardcastle, Mrs, *Life of John, Lord Campbell*, London, 1881.

Harris, W., *The History of the Radical Party in Parliament*, London, 1885.

Hill, B. W. 'Executive Monarchy and the Challenge of Parties, 1689–1832', *Historical Journal*, vol. 13, 1970, pp. 379–401.

Hilton, Boyd, *The Age of Atonement: The Influence of Evangelicalism on Social and Economic Thought, 1795–1865*, Oxford, 1988.

Hollis, P., *The Pauper Press: A Study in Working Class Radicalism in the 1830s*, Oxford, 1970.

Hurwitz, E., *Politics and the Public Conscience*, London, 1973.

Johnson, R., 'Educating the Educators: Experts and the State 1833–9', in A. P. Donajgrodski (ed.), *Social Control in Nineteenth Century Britain*, London, 1977, pp. 77–107.

Jones, W. D., 'Prosperity' Robinson. The Life of Viscount Goderich 1782–1859, London, 1967.

Jowitt, J. A., 'Parliamentary Politics in Halifax, 1832–1847, *Northern History*, 1976, 172–201.

Kinzer, B. L., 'The un-Englishness of the Secret Ballot', *Albion*, vol. 10, 1978, pp. 237–56.

Kitson, Clark, G. S. R., *Peel and the Conservative Party*, London, 1964.

Koss, Stephen, *The Rise and Fall of the Political Press in Britain: The Nineteenth Century*, Chapel Hill, 1981.

Kriegel, A. D., 'A Convergence of Ethics: Saints and Whigs in British Antislavery', *Journal of British Studies*, vol. 26, 1987, pp. 423–450.

Kriegel, A. D., 'The Irish Policy of Lord Grey's Government', *English Historical Review*, vol. lxxxvi, 1971, pp. 22–45.

Kriegel, A. D. 'Liberty and Whiggery in Early Nineteenth Century England', *Journal of Modern History*, vol. lii, 1980, pp. 253–78.

Large, D., 'The Decline of "The Party of the Crown" and the Rise of parties in the House of Lords, 1783–1837', *English Historical Review*, vol. lxxviii, 1963.

Large, D., 'The House of Lords and Ireland in the Age of Peel, 1832–50', *Irish Historical Studies*, vol. IX, 1955, pp. 367–90.

Leader, R. E., *Life and Letters of John Arthur Roebuck*, London, 1897.

Llewelyan, A., *The Decade of Reform*, London, 1972.

Longford, Elizabeth, *Queen Victoria: Born to Succeed*, London, 1964.

Lubenow, W. C., *The Politics of Government Growth*, Hampden Connecticut, 1971.

Lucas-Dubreton, J., *The Restoration and the July Monarchy*, trans. E. F. Buckley, New York, 1967.

Lynam, R., *The Complete Works of William Paley D. D.*, London, 1825.

Machin, G. I. T., *Politics and the Churches in Great Britain 1832–1868*, Oxford, 1977.

Macintyre, A. D., *The Liberator: Daniel O'Connell and the Irish Party 1830–1847*, London, 1965.

Maccoby, S., *English Radicalism 1832–1852*, London, 1935.

Macdonagh, O., *Early Victorian Government 1830–1870*, London, 1977.

Maclure, J. Stuart (ed.), *Educational Documents, England and Wales 1816 to the Present Day*, London, 1973.

Mandler, Peter, 'The Making of the New Poor Law "Redivivus" ', *Past and Present*, vol. 117, 1987, pp. 131–57.

Marsh, P. (ed.), *The Conscience of the Victorian State*, London, 1979.

McCord, N., *The Ani-Corn Law League 1838–1846*, London, 1958.

McDowell, R., *Public Opinion and Government Policy in Ireland 1801–1846*, London, 1952.

Mineka, F. S. (ed.), *The Collected Works of John Stuart Mill*, Toronto, 1963.

Mitchell, Austin, *The Whigs in Opposition, 1815–1830*, Oxford, 1967.

Mitchell, L., *Charles James Fox and the Distintegration of the Whig Party*, London, 1971.

Mitchell, L., *Holland House*, London, 1980.

Moneypenny, W. E. and Buckle, G. E., *The Life of Benjamin Disraeli*, 6 vols, London, 1910–20.

Moore, D. C. 'The Other Face of Reform', *Victorian Studies*, vol. 5, 1961, pp. 7–34.

Moore, D. C., *The Politics of Deference: A Study of the Nineteenth Century Political System*, Sussex, 1976.

Moore, D. C., 'Concession or Cure: The Sociological Premises of the First Reform Act', *Historical Journal*, vol. ix, 1966, pp. 39–50.

Murray, D. J., *The West Indies and the Development of Colonial Government 1801–1834*, London, 1965.

Myers, E., *Lord Althorp*, London, 1890.

Namier, Sir Lewis, *Monarchy and the Party System*, Oxford, 1952.

New, C., *Lord Durham*, Oxford, 1929.

Newbould, Ian D. C., 'The Emergence of a Two-Party System in England from 1830 to 1841: Roll Call and Reconsideration', *Parliaments, Estates and Representation*, vol. 5, 1985, pp. 25–31.

Newbould, Ian D. C., 'Lord Durham, the Whigs and Canada, 1838: the Background to Durham's Return', *Albion*, vol. 8, 1976, pp. 351–74.

Newbould, Ian D. C., 'Sir Robert Peel and the Conservative Party, 1832–1841: A Study in Failure?', *English Historical Review*, vol. xcviii, 1983, pp. 529–57.

Newbould, Ian D. C., 'Whiggery and the Dilemma of Reform: Liberals, Radicals and the Melbourne Administration, 1835–9', *Bulletin of the Institute of Historical Research*, vol. LIII, 1980, pp. 229–41.

Newbould, Ian D. C., 'Whiggery and the Growth of Party 1830–1841: Organization and the Challenge of Reform', *Parliamentary History*, vol. 4, 1985, pp. 137–56.

Newbould, Ian D. C., 'William IV and the Dismissal of the Whigs, 1834', *Canadian Journal of History*, vol. xi, 1976, pp. 311–30.

O'Brien, G., *An Economic History of Ireland from the Union to the Famine*, London, 1921.

O'Gorman, Frank, *The Emergence of the British Two-Party System 1760–1832*, London, 1982.

O'Gorman, F., *The Whig Party and the French Revolution*, London, 1967.

Olney, R. J., *Lincolnshire Politics 1832–1885*, London, 1982.

Parker, C. S., *Sir Robert Peel*, 2 vols., London, 1891.

Paz, D. G., *The Politics of Working Class Education in Britain 1830–50*, Manchester, 1980.

Perkin, H., *The Origins of Modern English Society 1780–1880*, London, 1969.

Phillips, C. H., *The East India Company 1784–1834*, London, 1961.

Poynter, J. R., *Society and Pauperism: English Ideas on Poor Relief 1795–1834*, London, 1967.

Prest, J., *Lord John Russell*, London, 1972.

Prest, J., *Politics in the Age of Cobden*, London, 1977.

Reid, S. J., *The Life and Letters of the First Earl of Durham*, 2 vols, London, 1906.

Roberts, David, *Paternalism in Early Victorian England*, Rutgers, 1979.

Robson, R. (ed.), *Ideas and Institutions of Victorian Britain*, London, 1967.

Senior, H., *Orangeism in Ireland and Britain 1795–1836*, London, 1966.

Smith, E., *Whig Principles and Party Politics*, London, 1976.

Soloway, R. A., *Prelates and People: Ecclesiastical Social Thought in England, 1783–1852*, London, 1969.

Southgate, D. G., *The Passing of the Whigs 1832–1886*, London, 1962.

Stephens, George, *Anti-Slavery Recollections*, H. Temperley (ed.), London, 1971.

Stewart, R., *The Foundation of the Conservative Party 1830–1867*, London, 1978.

Stewart, R., *Henry Brougham*, London, 1985.

Sweeney, J. Morgan, 'The House of Lords in British Politics 1830–1841', D. Phil. thesis, Oxford, 1974.

Temperley, H. W., *British Anti-Slavery 1833–70*, London, 1972.

Thomas, M., *The Early Factory Legislation*, London, 1948.

Thomas, W., *The Philosophical Radicals. Nine Studies in Theory and Practice, 1817–1841*, Oxford, 1979.

Thompson, E. P., 'The Peculiarities of the English', *Socialist Register*, London, 1965.

Trevelyan, G. M., *Lord Grey of the Reform Bill*, London, 1929.

Walpole, S., *Life of Lord John Russell*, 2 vols, London, 1889.

Walpole, S., *A History of England From The Conclusion Of The Great War in 1815*, London, 1905.

Ward, J. T. (ed.), *Popular Movements 1830–1850*, London, 1970.

Ward, J. T., *Sir James Graham*, London, 1967.

Ward, J. T., *The Factory Movement 1830–1855*, London, 1962.

Ward, W. R., 'The Tithe Question in England in the Early Nineteenth Century', *Journal of Ecclesiastical History*, vol. xvi, 1969, pp. 67–81.

Webb, S. and B., *English Poor Law History: The Last Hundred Years*, London, 1929.

Wiener, J. H., *The War of the Unstamped: The Movement to Repeal the British Newspaper Tax, 1830–1836*, Ithaca, 1969.

Willman, R., 'The Origins of "Whig" and "Tory" in English Political Language', *The Historical Journal*, vol. XVII, 1974, pp. 247–64.

Woolley, S. F., 'The Personnel of the 1833 Parliament', *English Historical Review*, vol. liii, 1938, pp. 240–62.

Wright, D. G., 'A Radical Borough: Parliamentary Politics in Bradford 1832–41', *Northern History*, 1969, pp. 132–66.

Zegger, Robert, E., *John Cam Hobhouse*, Columbia, 1973.

Ziegler, P., *Melbourne*, London, 1976.

Ziegler, P., *King William IV*, London, 1973.

Index

261–4, 302–4; dismissal 1834, 8–9, 36, 152, 154–9; and Dissenters, 147–50, 272–77; economic policy, 102–12, 119, 126, 298–303; and education plan 1839, 138, 246, 277–82; electoral organisation, 29–34; factory reform, 83, 119–4; government formed 1830, 71; government formed 1835, 175–80; historical principles, 1–8; on House of Lords, 94, 103, 144, 199; and Ireland, 134–46, 283–97; and Irish Church, 85–7, 90–9, 134–47, 157, 168, 283–8; municipal corporations, England, 184–5, 191, 268, 273; municipal corporations, Ireland, 170, 198, 288–9; parliamentary management, 24–9, 38–9; parliamentary reform, 8–10, 39, 48–9, 52, 55–80; party, 13–15; on patronage, 5; penny post, 244; poor laws, England, 124–9; poor laws, Ireland, 291–3; and Radicals, 7–10, 31–4, 38–9, 81, 86–9, 152, 160–5, 183–96, 200–5, 212–19, 228–30, 235, 243–5, 257, 285;

reform of Irish administration, 293–8; and Queen Victoria, 210, 236–41; on reunion with Stanley and Graham, 167–70; resignation 1839, 37–8, 234–5; stamp duties, 193–4, 298; on Wellington's government, 42–53; *see also* Budgets, Elections, Bye–elections

Wilkes, John, 274

William IV, 26, 36, 46–7, 93, 102, 109, 118, 129, 153, 160, 170, 174, 188, 197–200, 208–9, 240, 286, 294–5; attitude to Whigs, 68, 92–100, 144, 189, 211; dismissal of Whigs, 152, 154–9; formation of Whig government 1835, 175–80; and parliamentary reform, 63–77; and Stanley, 92–100

Wood, Charles, 26, 30, 49, 75, 82, 87, 109, 123–4, 142, 172–3, 183, 212, 251, 254, 256

Wrottesley, Sir John, 88, 182

Wynn, Charles, 143

Wyse, Thomas S., 234, 281

Young, Thomas, 26, 36, 153